ROUTLEDGE LIBRARY EDITIONS: FINANCIAL MARKETS

Volume 1

BOND DURATION AND IMMUNIZATION

BOND DURATION AND IMMUNIZATION

Early Developments and Recent Contributions

edited by
GABRIEL A. HAWAWINI

Routledge
Taylor & Francis Group

LONDON AND NEW YORK

First published in 1982 by Garland Publishing, Inc.

This edition first published in 2018
by Routledge
2 Park Square, Milton Park, Abingdon, Oxon OX14 4RN

and by Routledge
711 Third Avenue, New York, NY 10017

Routledge is an imprint of the Taylor & Francis Group, an informa business

British Library Cataloguing in Publication Data
A catalogue record for this book is available from the British Library

ISBN: 978-1-138-56537-1 (Set)
ISBN: 978-0-203-70248-2 (Set) (ebk)
ISBN: 978-1-138-50435-6 (Volume 1) (hbk)
ISBN: 978-1-138-50436-3 (Volume 1) (pbk)
ISBN: 978-1-315-14597-6 (Volume 1) (ebk)

Publisher's Note
The publisher has gone to great lengths to ensure the quality of this reprint but points out that some imperfections in the original copies may be apparent.

Disclaimer
The publisher has made every effort to trace copyright holders and would welcome correspondence from those they have been unable to trace.

Bond Duration and Immunization:
Early Developments and Recent Contributions

edited by
Gabriel A. Hawawini

Garland Publishing, Inc.
New York & London   1982

ACKNOWLEDGMENTS

The excerpt from Frederick Macaulay's book has been reprinted by permission of the National Bureau of Economic Research, Inc. The excerpt from John Hicks's book has been reprinted by permission of Oxford University Press. The article from the *American Economic Review* has been reprinted by permission of the Review and the authors. Articles from the *Journal of Finance* have been reprinted by permission of the Journal and the authors. Articles from the *Journal of Financial and Quantitative Analysis* have been reprinted by permission of the Journal and the authors. Articles from the *Journal of the Institute of Actuaries* and the *Journal of the Institute of Actuaries Students' Societies* have been reprinted by permission of the Institute of Actuaries. Articles from the *Journal of Business* have been reprinted by permission of the University of Chicago Press and the authors. The article from *Transactions of the Faculty of Actuaries* has been reprinted by permission of the Faculty of Actuaries. Copyright, however, rests with the Faculty.

Library of Congress Cataloging in Publication Data

Main entry under title:

Bond duration and immunization.

(Accountancy in transition)
1. Bonds—Addresses, essays, lectures.   I. Hawawini,
Gabriel A.   II. Series.
HG4651.B66   1982   322.63'23   82-82490
ISBN 0-8240-5338-9

The volumes in this series are printed on acid-free, 250-year-life paper.

Printed in the United States of America

Preface

The purpose of this collection of works on bond duration and immunization is twofold. First, we wanted to reprint a number of seminal papers and excerpts from books which are often not available in business libraries. These include passages from Frederick Macaulay's book, John Hicks's book as well as the often cited article by Redington which appeared in a British insurance journal in 1952. We have also reprinted several articles which were published in British actuarial journals not often found in libraries in the United States and abroad. Our second purpose was to reprint some recent articles which made significant contributions in the area of bond duration and immunization.

No anthology can be truly comprehensive. Because of space limitation several important papers on the subject of bond duration and immunization could not be reprinted in this collection. The reader who wishes to go beyond the pieces reprinted here will find in the introductory chapter an alphabetical reference list which covers practically all the literature on bond duration and immunization. To aid the reader in his search for specific references, we have also compiled a bibliographical index in which relevant references are listed by topics.

Gabriel Hawawini
Marlton, New Jersey
May 1982

Contents

Bond Duration and Immunization: An Introduction and a
Bibliographical Index, Gabriel A. Hawawini

Part I • Bond Duration

Some Theoretical Problems Suggested by the Movement of Interest
Rates, Bond Yield, and Stock Prices in the United States Since
1856, New York: Columbia University Press (1938) pp. 44–53,
Frederick R. Macaulay

On the Mathematics of Macaulay's Duration, Gabriel A. Hawawini

Value and Capital, Oxford: Clarendon Press (1939) pp. 185–188,
John R. Hicks

Bond Price Volatility and the Term to Maturity: A Generalized
Respecification, *American Economic Review*, September 1973,
Michael H. Hopewell and George G. Kaufman.

A 'Duration' Fallacy, *Journal of Finance*, March 1977, Miles
Livingston and John Caks

Duration Forty Years Later, *Journal of Financial and Quantitative
Analysis*, November 1978, Jonathan E. Ingersoll, Jeffrey Skelton
and Roman L. Weil

Duration and Risk Assessment for Bonds and Common Stocks: A
Note, *Journal of Finance*, December 1975, John A. Boquist,
George A. Racette and Gary S. Schlarbaum

Part II • Immunization

Review of the Principles of Life-Office Valuations, *Journal of the
Institute of Actuaries*, Volume 78, 1952, F. M. Redington

Immunization, *Journal of the Institute of Actuaries Students'
Societies*, Volume 15, 1960, G. E. Wallas

Coping with the Risk of Interest-Rate Fluctuations: Returns to Bondholders from Naive and Optimal Strategies, *Journal of Business*, July 1977, Lawrence Fisher and Roman L. Weil

Coping with the Risk of Interest-Rate Fluctuations: A Note, *Journal of Business*, July 1977, G. O. Bierwag and George F. Kaufman

Immunization, Duration, and the Term Structure of Interest Rates, *Journal of Financial and Quantitative Analysis*, December 1977, G. O. Bierwag

A Practical Approach to Applying Immunization Theory, *Transactions of the Faculty of Actuaries*, Volume 35, 1977, A. D. Shedden

Immunization Under Stochastic Models of the Term Structure, *Journal of the Institute of Actuaries*, Volume 108, 1978, P. P. Boyle

BOND DURATION AND IMMUNIZATION:

AN INTRODUCTION AND A BIBLIOGRAPHICAL INDEX

Gabriel A. Hawawini

INTRODUCTION

Consider the following two default-free bonds. Bond A has a 10 percent annual coupon rate and a 2-year maturity. Bond B is a zero-coupon bond with the same maturity as Bond A. Both bonds are priced to yield 10 percent if held to maturity. Bond A is currently worth $100 and will pay a $10 coupon income at the end of the first year and $110 at maturity.

Clearly, there is a difference in the time-pattern of the two bonds' cash inflows. Bond B produces no intermediate income and pays $121 at maturity whereas the holder of Bond A will receive $10 of coupon income at the end of year one followed by $110 at maturity. The two bonds have the same present value ($100), the same yield to maturity (10 percent) and the same term to maturity (2 years) but they are not identical. Bond A has a shorter "payback period" than Bond B since a holder of Bond A will recover a fraction of that bond's current price after one year whereas Bond B offers no early fractional recovery.

EARLY DEVELOPMENTS OF THE CONCEPT OF DURATION

The preceding example serves to illustrate the fact that
bonds with identical maturities but different coupon rates
can be viewed as having different "effective maturities". In
other words, the term to maturity does not adequately reflect
the time dimension of a bond. It is this observation that
led Frederick Macaulay [79] in 1938 to suggest an alternative
measure of a bond's "longness" which would capture the effect
of the size and frequency of that bond's coupon payments.
Macaulay proposed a measure which he called "duration" and
considered it to be "the essence of the time element of a loan."
(p. 44). Macaulay's duration (D) is calculated using the following formula:

$$D = \frac{1}{P} \left\{ \sum_{t=1}^{n} t \cdot C \cdot DF_t + n \cdot F \cdot DF_n \right\} \tag{1}$$

where P is the bond's price, C its periodic coupon payment, F
its face value and n its term to maturity. DF is the discount
factor at the prevailing yield to maturity. Macaulay's duration is simply the weighted average number of years until the
bond's cash flows occur, where the weights used are the present
values of each payment relative to the bond's price.

A zero-coupon bond has a duration equal to its maturity and coupon-bearing bonds have durations shorter than maturities. Returning to our introductory example and applying Macaulay's duration formula we find that Bond A has a duration of 1.91 years and that Bond B has a duration of 2 years. For a further examination of the properties of Macaulay's duration the reader is referred to selection 1 in the text which is a reprint of the relevant pages of Macaulay's text [79] dealing with duration, and selection 2, Hawawini [54].

The development of the concept of duration is also attributed to Sir John Hicks [57] and Paul Samuelson [85] who, independently of Macaulay, suggested the same basic measure as that given in equation (1). In chapter 14 of his 1939 book "Value and Capital" Hicks [57] presents a formula analogous to that of Macaulay which he called the "average period" of a stream of payments. The relevant pages of Hick's chapter are reproduced as selection 3. In 1945, Paul Samuelson, apparently unaware of the work of Macaulay and Hicks, derived a measure of a financial asset's duration similar to that given in equation (1) which he called the "weighted average time period" of that asset's stream of payments.

Students of bond duration and related issues seem to agree that the development of the concept of duration should be attributed to Macaulay (1938) and Hicks (1939). In an unpublished note, Brief [25] argues that the foundation of the duration concept may have been actually laid down as far back as 1895 by George J. Lidstone [74], a British actuary. Lidstone's objective was to develop an approximation to the rate of interest for an increasing annuity (the present value of an increasing annuity as defined by Lidstone is given by the terms within the curly brackets of equation (1)). If B is the present value of a straight annuity at the rate of interest i, Lidstone [74] showed that the present value of an increasing annuity (IB) at the same rate of interest i is equal to:

$$IB = -(1+i)\frac{dB}{di} \qquad (2)$$

The above relationship can be rewritten as:

$$\frac{dB}{B} = -\frac{IBdi}{B(1+i)} \equiv -D\frac{di}{(1+i)} \qquad (3)$$

Equation (3) is obtained by noting that Macaulay's duration is simply the ratio of the present value of an increasing annuity (IB) to the present value of a straight annuity (B).

We will see later that equation (3) has been rediscovered by several authors seeking to link a bond's duration to its interest elasticity. Brief [25] suggests that Hick's discussion of "average period" and "interest elasticity" could have been motivated by Lidstone's paper since one might conjecture that Hick's saw the possible economic implications of Lidstone's equation which was reproduced in the standard actuarial text-book of the time [Ralph Todhunter, Institute of Actuaries' Textbook, Part I (Interest), First edition published in 1915 by Charles and Edwin Layton, London]

BOND PRICE VOLATILITY AND DURATION

In the introductory example we compared a 2-year, 10 per-cent coupon-bearing bond (Bond A) to a 2-year zero-coupon bond (Bond B). We established that Bond A has a shorter duration than Bond B. Another difference between these two bonds is their price volatility. It can be shown numerically that the percentage change in the price of Bond A resulting from a given percentage change in the level of the interest rate is smaller (in absolute value) than the percentage change in the price of Bond B. In other words, Bond A is less in-terest-sensitive than Bond B. The reason is quite simple. Bond A has a shorter "effective maturity" (duration) than Bond

B. It is duration rather than maturity which determines a bond's price volatility.

Macaulay devised his measure of duration in order to throw "a flood of light on the fluctuations of bond yields on the actual market." (p. 50). So did Hicks, who wanted to obtain a measure of the elasticity of capital value with respect to the one-period discount factor (which Hicks calls the discount ratio $i/(1+i)$). As pointed out in the previous section, a simple manipulation of Lidstone's equation (2) will yield the elasticity measure derived by Hicks (p. 186). Note that the elasticity of capital value with respect to the discount ratio is simply $(dB/B)/(di/1+i)$ which, according to equation (3), is the asset's duration multiplied by negative one since elasticity is a negative number. Hence, the shorter a bond's duration the smaller the absolute value of its interest-elasticity coefficient. This argument is presented formally by Hopewell and Kaufman [58] in selection 4.

THE TERM STRUCTURE OF INTEREST RATES AND DURATION

Having shown that the time dimension of a bond is best measured by its duration one may be tempted to conclude that observed yields to maturity on bonds should be related to their durations and not to their maturities. One may think that yield curves should be drawn using duration as the time dimension instead of the term to maturity. This is indeed what Macaulay [79] suggested when he stated that "yields could (at least theoretically) be corrected by a statistically-derived equation relating yield to duration." (p. 68). Also, Hopewell and Kaufman [58] in selection 4 suggest that "it may be more useful to derive yield curves with respect to duration than to maturity." (p. 752).

In selection 5, Livingston and Caks [75] argue that the above reasoning is incorrect. They prove that "although duration is a function of the yield curve, the yield curve is not a function of duration. Thus one cannot 'correct the yield curve for duration' because bonds with identical durations do not necessarily have identical yields." (p. 186).

It should be emphasized that the shape of the yield curve, which reflects the term structure of interest rates, is an important factor in calculating a bond's duration. We have pointed out earlier that Macaulay's duration is computed using the bond's yield to maturity. Hence, each one of the future payments a bond is expected to produce is discounted at the same rate, the yield to maturity. But this is only a special case. Macaulay's duration given in equation (1) implicitly assumes a horizontal yield curve as well as unexpected changes in interest rates that shift the yield curve only in a parallel fashion. In general, discounting should be carried out with different periodic rates reflecting the shape of the yield curve. Doing so will produce duration measures that differ from that of Macaulay. Alternative measures of duration and the impact of the yield curve on duration are examined by Ingersoll et al. [60] in selection 6. Additional references are given in the bibliographical index at the end of this introduction. In particular see the work of Bierwag [6]. We will return to the problem of how the term structure of interest rates affects duration when we discuss immunization strategies.

SYSTEMATIC RISK AND DURATION

The systematic risk of a common stock, also known as its beta coefficient, measure the sensitivity of the stock's returns to the movements in the returns of a market index. Since duration is related to a bond's price volatility through equation (3) it should also be related to that bond's systematic risk. This relationship was first established by Boquist et al. [22] in selection 7. The relationship was also extended to the case of financial assets other than straight default-free bonds by Boquist et al. [22], Livingston [76] and Jarrow [61].

Livingston [76] shows that the beta coefficient of bond i at time t (β_{it}) is given by:

$$\beta_{it} = \left[\frac{D_{it}}{D_{mt}}\right] \cdot \left[\frac{\text{Cov}(dr_{it}, \ dr_{mt})}{\text{var}(dr_{mt})}\right] \qquad (4)$$

where D_{it} and D_{mt} are the bond's duration and a market index's duration, respectively. According to equation (6) the systematic risk of a bond is equal to the ratio of its duration to the duration of the market multiplied by the ratio of the anticipated covariance between the changes in the yield to maturity of the bond (dr_{it}) and those in the required return on the market (dr_{mt}) to the anticipated variance of the changes in the required return on a market index. Clearly, a bond's beta is not stable since duration shortens as the bond approaches maturity. A relationship similar to that in equation (4) can be established for the case of a common stock with constant perpetual growth. Additional work relating beta to duration, some of which is empirical, can be found in the bibliographical index at the end of the paper.

BOND RISK-RETURN ANALYSIS AND DURATION

The expected return on a common stock has been shown, both theoretically and empirically, to be linearly related to the risk of that stock as measured by its beta coefficient. Drawing a parallel between common stocks and bonds and noting that the duration of a bond portfolio (like the systematic risk of an equity portfolio) is equal to the weighted average of the durations of the component bonds, Wagner - Tito [93], [94] and others have suggested that a similar linear relationship may also hold between the return on a bond portfolio and its duration. In the same vein, the concept of duration has raised early hopes that it might provide a useful tool for bond portfolio management and the evaluation of bond portfolio performance. Unfortunately, Dietz, et al. [33] and others have shown empirically that duration is not linearly related to a bond's return. Recently, Yawitz and Marshall [102] have argued convincingly that duration is not an adequate risk measure for a bond. For further discussions on duration, bond risk-return analysis and bond portfolio management, the reader is referred to the bibliographical index which lists several papers on the subject.

IMMUNIZED INVESTMENT AND DURATION

Let us return to our early example in which we compared two default-free bonds. Bond A is a 2-year, 10 percent coupon-bearing bond selling at $100 and Bond B is a 2-year zero-coupon bond also selling at $100. Both bonds are priced to yield 10 percent to maturity. What is the interest-rate risk of these bonds for an investor with a 2-year holding period? Since both bonds are held to maturity they have no price risk, that is, the probability of selling either bond at a loss is zero. Bond A, however, carries some reinvestment risk; that is, there is a risk of having to reinvest $10 of coupon income for an additional year at an unknown rate. Bond B being a zero-coupon bond has no reinvestment risk. To summarize: if the holding period is equal to the maturity of a coupon-bearing bond, the holder bears only a reinvestment risk but no price risk. If the holding period is equal to the maturity of a zero-coupon bond, the holder bears no interest-rate risk (both price and reinvestment risks are zero). Note that the risk borne is not only a function of the bond's characteristics but also a function of the investor's holding period.

Is it possible to eliminate the reinvestment risk attached to a coupon-bearing bond such as Bond A? The answer is yes.

An investor can eliminate the reinvestment risk of a coupon-
bearing bond by holding it over a period equal to the bond's
duration. In other words, by matching the bond's duration
with his holding period an investor can, in principle, eliminate that bond's interest-rate risk. This result is achieved
simply because price risk and reinvestment risk cancel each
other out over a period of time equal to the bond's duration.
To illustrate, suppose that the interest rate rises unexpec-
tedly from 10 to 11 percent immediately after Bond A is
purchased. As a result, the price of Bond A drops producing
a capital loss (price risk) but the $10 coupon income can now
be reinvested at a higher rate (reinvestment risk) to exactly
offset the loss of capital if Bond A is held for 1.91 years
(Bond A's duration). Bond A is said to be immunized against
interest-rate changes. Its holder can realize a riskless
return of 10 percent assuming the bond is default-free. Note
that Bond B, the zero-coupon bond, is immunized over a 2-year
holding period since in this case duration is equal to maturity.
In other words, matching maturity with holding period will
only immunize zero-coupon bonds.

Our example assumes a flat yield curve at 10 percent and
a single small change in the level of the interest rate occurring

immediately after the bond is purchased. The horizontal
yield curve shifts upward in a parallel fashion when the
level of the interest rate rises to 11 percent. This is a
very restrictive situation. Fisher and Weil [40] have
demonstrated in selection 10, theoretically and empirically,
that a similar immunization strategy can be carried out in
the more general case where the yield curve is not horizontal.
Of course, their measure of duration will differ from that
given in equation (1).

The discovery of the technique described above is
usually attributed to the British actuary F. M. Redington
[82] who actually coined the term "immunization." In a
seminal paper published in 1952 and reproduced in the text as
selection 8, Redington derived a measure of duration similar
to that given in equation (1). He called it "mean term" and
proved that "the existing business is immune to a general
change in the rate of interest" when the mean term of the
firm's assets is set equal to the mean term of the firm's
liabilities. (p. 10). However, Samuelson [85] in a paper
published in 1947 had already established the same result.
Bierwag et al. [14] note that "it is ironic that Redington's
article, published in an actuarial journal not widely read by

non actuarials, has received wider recognition than Samuelson's similar and earlier article in the American Economic Review." (p. 3). The early developments of the immunization concept and its practical implementation are discussed by Wallas [92] in selection 9. Additional references can be found in the bibliographical index.

IMMUNIZATION AND THE TERM STRUCTURE OF INTEREST RATES

We have seen that immunization strategies such as those discussed in the previous section are based on a certain number of restrictive assumptions. The strategy devised and tested by Fisher and Weil [40] in their classical paper assumes that: (1) there is only a one-time change in interest rates of equal magnitude for all maturities, that is, the yield curve shifts in a parallel fashion, (2) there are no taxes, (3) there are no trasaction costs, and (4) returns are compounded continously. As pointed out earlier, Fisher and Weil do not assume a flat yield curve. In their measures of duration, discount rates are equal to the forward rates prevailing over each future period "t".

Following Fisher and Weil, several researchers, for example Bierwag and Kaufman [7] (selection 11), Bierwag [4] (Selection 12), Ingersoll et al. [60] (selection 6), Shedden [87] (selection 13), Boyle [23] (selection 14) and others have shown that it is possible to devise immunization strategies for default-free coupon-bearing bonds under less restrictive assumptions than those made originally by Fisher and Weil. Specifically, one can immunize a bond portfolio under the following conditions: (1) there exist more than one unexpected change in interest rates over the holding period (see [60]), (2) the unexpected change in interest rates need not be of equal magnitude for all maturities; for example, unexpected interest rate changes may affect short-term maturities more than long-term maturities or affect long-term maturities more than short-term maturities. In other words, the yield curve may shift in a non parallel fashion (see [12], [65]), (3) there exist multiple planning periods (see [10]), (4) the planning period is uncertain (see [56]), (5) there are taxes (see [55]), and (6) discrete compounding is used (see [4]).

The implementation of more general immunization strategies based on multiple unexpected changes in interest rates with different effects across maturities will require that the investor specifies correctly the random process generating the changes in interest rates. Consequently, the definition of duration which will achieve immunization will depend on the nature of the random process generating the changes in interest rates after the purchase of the bond portfolio. In other words, the optimal selection of an immunized bond portfolio is related to the term structure of interest rates. (see Bierwag [4], selection 12; and Boyle [23], selection 14).

A final note. An immunized strategy is a technique which allows investors to reduce or eliminate the interest-rate risk of their bond portfolios. An alternative hedging technique is provided by the financial futures markets. The reader interested in this alternative hedging technique and its relationship to immunization strategies is referred to the papers listed in the bibliographical index under the heading "Immunization Strategies Using Interest Rate Futures."

CONCLUDING REMARKS

The purpose of this introductory chapter was to present, in a limited fashion, the basic ideas behind the concept of duration and to show how it relates to the technique of immunized investment. Also we wanted to introduce the content of the various articles that make up this volume. For further information, the reader is once more referred to the bibliographical index that appears in the following pages.

A BIBLIOGRAPHICAL INDEX ON

BOND DURATION AND IMMUNIZATION

An asterisk indicates that the
article is reprinted in this book.

PART I: DURATION

HISTORY OF DURATION
    Brief, Richard [25]
  * Ingersoll, Jonathan E., Jeffrey Skelton and Roman L. Weil [60]
    Weil, Roman L. [95]

GENERAL INTRODUCTION AND USES OF DURATION
    Diller, Stanley [32]
    Leibowitz, Martin L., editor [70]
    Reilly, Frank K. and Rupindu S. Sidhu [83]

OVERVIEWS AND REVIEWS
    Bierwag, G. O., George G. Kaufman and Chulsoon Khang [9]
  * Ingersoll, Jonathan E., Jeffrey Skelton and Roman L. Weil [60]

CONCEPT AND MEASUREMENT OF DURATION
    Bierwag, G. O. [6]
    Cox, John C., Jonathan E. Ingersoll and Stephen A. Ross [31]
  * Hawawini, Gabriel A. [54]
  * Hicks, John R. [57]
  * Ingersoll, Jonathan E., Jeffrey Skelton and Roman L. Weil [60]
    Lidstone, George J. [74]
  * Macaulay, Frederick R. [79]

DURATION OF ASSETS OTHER THAN BONDS
    Durand, David [34]
    Haugen, Robert A. and Dean W. Wichern [52]
    Vanderhoof, Irwin T. [90]

DURATION AND BOND PRICE VOLATILITY
    Fisher, Lawrence [38]
  * Hopewell, Michael H. and George G. Kaufman [58]
    Whittaker, John [97]
    Yawitz, Jess [100]

DURATION AND THE TERM STRUCTURE OF INTEREST RATES
    Babbel, David [1]
    Bierwag, G. O. [4]
    Caks, John [26]
    Carr, J. L., P. J. Halpern and J. S. McCallum [27]
    Carr, J. L., P. J. Halpern and J. S. McCallum [28]
    Cooper, Ian A. [30]
    Cox, John C., Jonathan E. Ingersoll and Stephen A. Ross [31]
  * Ingersoll, Jonathan E., Jeffrey Skelton and Roman L. Weil [60]
  * Livingston, Miles and John Caks [75]

DURATION AND THE ELASTICITY OF FINANCIAL ASSETS
    Haugen, Robert A. and Dean W. Wichern [52]
    Haugen, Robert A. and Dean W. Wichern [53]
  * Hopewell, Michael H. and George G. Kaufman [58]

DURATION AND SYSTEMATIC RISK
    Bildersee, John S. and Gordon J. Roberts [19]
  * Boquist, John A., George A. Racette and Gary G. Schlarbaum [22]
    Einhorn, Madeline [36]
    Gordon, Alexander J. [48]
    Jarrow, Robert A. [61]
    Lanstein, Ronald and William F. Sharpe [69]
    Livingston, Miles [76]
    Rao, Ramesh K. S. [81]
    Weinstein, Mark [96]

DURATION AND BOND RISK-RETURN ANALYSIS
    Bierwag, G. O., George G. Kaufman and Alden Toevs, Editors [13]
    Bierwag, G. O., George G. Kaufman and Alden Toevs [14]
    Bierwag, G. O., George G. Kaufman, Robert Schweitzer, and Alden
      Toevs [16]
    Bildersee, John S. [20]
    Carr, J. L., P. J. Halpern and J. S. McCallum [27]
    Dietz, P. O., H. R. Fogler and A. U. Rivers [33]
    Kaufman, George G. [63]
    Kaufman, George G., Thomas A. Loeffler and Robert L. Schweitzer [64]
    Smidt, Seymour [88]
    Tito, Dennis A. and Wayne H. Wagner [89]
    Wagner, Wayne H. and Dennis A. Tito [93]
    Wagner, Wayne H. and Dennis A. Tito [94]
    Yawitz, Jess B. [100]
    Yawitz, Jess B., George H. Hempel and William J. Marshall [101]
    Yawitz, Jess B. and William J. Marshall [102]

DURATION AND BOND PORTFOLIO MANAGEMENT
    Bierwag, G. O. and George G. Kaufman [8]
    Bierwag, G. O., George G. Kaufman, Robert L. Schweitzer and
        Alden Toevs [17]
    Brennan, Michael and Eduardo Schwartz [24]
    Tito, Dennis A. and Wayne H. Wagner [89]
    Vanderhoof, Irwin T. [91]
    Wagner, Wayne H. and Dennis A. Tito [93]
    Wagner, Wayne H. and Dennis A. Tito [94]

DURATION AND CAPITAL BUDGETING
    Blocher, Edward and Clyde Stickney [21]
    Durand, David [35]
    Whittaker, John [98]

DURATION AND THE CAPITAL ASSET PRICING MODEL
    Casabona, Patrick and Ashok Vora [29]
    Kaufman, George G. [62]

DURATION AND TAXATION
    Hessel, Christopher A. and Lucy Huffman [55]

DURATION AND BOND IMMUNIZATION STRATEGIES
    See references listed in Part II.

PART II: IMMUNIZATION

THE CONCEPT AND TECHNIQUES OF IMMUNIZATION
    Babcock, Guilford C. [2]
    Bayley, G. V. and Wilfred Perks [3]
    Bierwag, G. O. and Chulsoon Khang [18]
    Bierwag, G. O. and George G. Kaufman [7]
    Bierwag, G. O., George G. Kaufman and Alden Toevs, editors [13]
    Ezra, Don D. [37]
    Grove, Myron A. [49]
    Grove, Myron A. [50]
    Koopmans, Mjalling C. [68]
    Leibowtiz, Martin L., editor [70]
    McEnally, Richard W. [77]
    McEnally, Richard W. [78]
  * Redington, F. M. [82]
    Robertson, D. J. and I. L. B. Sturrock [84]
    Samuelson, Paul A. [85]
    Vanderhoof, Irwin T. [90]
  * Wallas, G. E. [92]

IMPLEMENTATION OF IMMUNIZATION STRATEGIES
    Bierwag, G. O., George G. Kaufman and Alden Toevs [15]
    Fisher, Lawrence and Martin Leibowitz [39]
    Foglers, Russell H. [41]
    Foglers, Russell H. [42]
    Fong, Gifford H. and Oldrich A. Vasicek [43]
    Fong, Gifford H. and Oldrich A. Vasicek [44]
    Gushee, Charles H. [51]
    Leibowitz, Martin L. [70]
    Leibowitz, Martin L. [71]
    Leibowitz, Martin L. and Alfred Weinberger [72]
    Leibowitz, Martin L. and Alfred Weinberger [73]
    Marshall, William J. and Yawitz, Jess B. [80]
  * Shedden, A. D. [87]
    Wissner, Len [99]
    Yawitz, Jess B. and William J. Marshall [103]

BOND IMMUNIZATION STRATEGIES: THE EVIDENCE
  * Bierwag, G. O. and George G. Kaufman [7]
    Bierwag, G. O., George G. Kaufman, Robert L. Schweitzer and
        Alden Toevs [16]
  * Fisher, Lawrence and Roman L. Weil [40]
    Ingersoll, Jonathan E. [59]

IMMUNIZATION AND THE TERM STRUCTURE OF INTEREST RATES
* Bierwag, G. O. [4]
  Bierwag, G. O. [5]
  Bierwag, G. O., George G. Kaufman and Alden Toevs [11]
  Bierwag, G. O., George G. Kaufman and Alden Toevs [12]
  Bierwag, G. O., George G. Kaufman, Robert Schweitzer and Alden
      Toevs [15]
* Boyle, P. P. [23]
  Cox, John C., Jonathan E. Ingersoll and Stephen A. Ross [31]
  Khang, Chulsoon [65]
  Schaefer, Stephen [86]

IMMUNIZATION STRATEGIES USING INTEREST RATE FUTURES
  Gay, Gerald D., Robert W. Kolb and Raymond Chiang [45]
  Gay, Gerald D. and Robert W. Kolb [46]
  Gay, Gerald D. and Robert W. Kolb [47]
  Kolb, Robert W. and Raymond Chiang [66]
  Kolb, Robert W. and Raymond Chiang [67]

FISCAL ASPECTS OF IMMUNIZATION STRATEGIES
  Hessel, Christopher A. and Lucy Huffman [55]

IMMUNIZATION AND THE PLANNING PERIOD
  Bierwag, G. O. George G. Kaufman and Alden Toevs [10]
  Hessel, Christopher A. and Lucy Huffman [56]

REFERENCES

[1] Babbel, David, "Duration and the Term Structure of Interest Rate Volatility," Reprinted in [13].

[2] Babcock, Guilford C., "A Modified Measure of Duration," presented at the 11-th Annual Conference of the Western Finance Association, June, 1976.

[3] Bayley, G. V. and Wilfred Perks, "A Consistent System of Investment and Bonus Distribution For the Life Office," Journal of the Institute of Actuaries, Volume 79, (1953), pp. 15-73.

[4] Bierwag, G. O., "Immunization, Duration and the Term Structure of Interest Rates," Journal of Financial and Quantitative Analysis, December 1977, pp. 725-741.

[5] Bierwag, G. O., "Dynamic Immunization and Portfolio Policy," Journal of Banking and Finance, April 1979, pp. 23-42.

[6] Bierwag, G. O., "Measures of Duration," Economic Inquiry, October 1978, pp. 497-507.

[7] Bierwag, G. O. and George G. Kaufman, "Coping With the Risk of Interest-Rate Fluctuation: A Note," Journal of Business, July 1977, pp. 364-370.

[8] Bierwag, G. O. and George G. Kaufman, "Bond Portfolio Strategy Simulations: Critique," Journal of Financial and Quantitative Analysis, September 1978, pp. 519-526.

[9] Bierwag, G. O., George G. Kaufman and Chulsoon Khang, "Duration and Bond Portfolio Analysis: An Overview," Journal of Financial and Quantitative Analysis, November 1978, pp. 671-679.

[10] Bierwag, G. O., George G. Kaufman and Alden Toevs, "Immunization for Multiple Planning Periods," Working Paper, University of Oregon, June 1980.

[11] Bierwag, G. O., George G. Kaufman and Alden Toevs, "The Sensitivity of Immunization to Correctly and Incorrectly Identified Stochastic Processes," Working Paper, University of Oregon, August 1980.

[12] Bierwag, G. O., George G. Kaufman and Alden Toevs, "Bond Portfolio Immunization and Stochastic Process Risk," Journal of Bank Research, forthcoming.

[13] Bierwag, G. O., George G. Kaufman and Alden Toevs, editors,
      Innovations in Bond Portfolio Management: Duration Analysis
      and Immunization, JAI Press, forthcoming.

[14] Bierwag, G. O., George G. Kaufman and Alden Toevs, "Single Factor
      Duration Models in a General Equilibrium Framework," presented at
      the Annual Meeting of the American Finance Association, Washington,
      D.C., December 1981.

[15] Bierwag, G. O., George G. Kaufman and Alden Toevs," Recent
      Developments in and Portfolio Immunization Strategies," Reprinted
      in [13].

[16] Bierwag, G. O., George G. Kaufman, Robert L. Schweitzer and Alden
      Toevs, "The Art of Risk Management in Bond Portfolios," Journal of
      Portfolio Management, Spring 1981, pp. 27-36.

[17] Bierwag, G. O., George G. Kaufman, Robert L. Schweitzer and Alden
      Toevs, "Risk and Return for Active and Passive and Portfolio
      Management: Theory and Evidence," Working Paper, University of Oregon,
      October 1979.

[18] Bierwag, G. O. and Chulsoon Khang, "An Immunization Strategy is a
      minimax Strategy," Journal of Finance, May 1979, pp. 389-399.

[19] Bildersee, John S. and Gordon S. Roberts, "Beta Instability When
      Interest Level Change," Journal of Financial and Quantitative
      Analysis, September 1981, pp. 375-380.

[20] Bildersee, John S., "Discussion," Journal of Finance, May 1975,
      pp. 334-336.

[21] Blocher, Edward and Clyde Stickney, "Duration and Risk Assessment in
      Capital Budgeting," Accounting Review, January 1979, pp. 180-188.

[22] Boquist, John A., George A. Racette and G. Schlarbaum, "Duration and
      Risk Assessment for Bonds and Common Stocks," Journal of Finance,
      December 1975, pp. 1360-1365.

[23] Boyle, P. P., "Immunization and Stochastic Models of the Term
      Structure," Journal of the Institute of Actuaries, Volume 108, (1978),
      pp. 177-187.

[24] Brennan, Michael and Eduardo Schwartz, "Duration, Bond Pricing, and
      Portfolio Management," Reprinted in [13].

[25] Brief, Richard, "A Note on Interest Rates Approximations," Working Paper, New York University, 1978.

[26] Caks, John, "The Coupon Effect on Yield to Maturity," Journal of Finance, March 1977, pp. 103-116.

[27] Carr, J. L., P. J. Halpern and J. S. McCallum, "Correcting the Yield Curve: A re-interpretation of the Duration Problem," Journal of Finance, September 1974, pp. 1287-1294.

[28] Carr, J. L., P. J. Halpern and J. S. McCallum, "Comments on Single-Valued Duration Measures," Journal of Finance, September 1978, pp. 1241-1248.

[29] Casabona, Patrick and Ashok Vora, "The Bias of Conventional Risk Premium in Empirical Tests of the Capital Asset Pricing Model," Financial Management, Summer 1982.

[30] Cooper, Ian A., "Asset Values, Interest Rate-Changes and Duration," Journal of Financial and Quantitative Analysis, December 1977, pp. 701-723.

[31] Cox, John, Jonathan E. Ingersoll and Stephen A. Ross, "Duration and Measurement of Basis Risk," Journal of Business, January 1979, pp. 57-61.

[32] Diller, Stanley, "A Three Part Series on the Use of Duration in Bond Analysis and Portfolio Management," Money Manager, January 29, 1979 and February 13, 1979.

[33] Dietz, Peter O., H. Russell Foglers and Anthony U. Rivers, "Duration, Nonlinearity, and Bond Portfolio Performance," Journal of Portfolio Management, Spring 1981, pp. 37-41.

[34] Durand, David, "Growth Stocks and the Petersburg Paradox," Journal of Finance, September 1957, pp. 348-363.

[35] Durand, David, "Payout Period, Time Spread and Duration: Aids to Judgement in Capital Budgeting," Journal of Bank Research, Spring 1974, pp. 20-34.

[36] Einhorn, Madeline, "Breaking Tradition in Bond Portfolio Investment," Journal of Portfolio Management, Spring 1975, pp. 38-43.

[37] Ezra, Don D., "Immunization: A New Look for Financial Liabilities," Journal of Portfolio Management, Winter 1976, pp. 50-53.

[38] Fisher, Lawrence, "An Algorithm for Finding Rates of Return," Journal of Business, January 1966, pp. 111-118.

[39] Fisher, Lawrence and Martin Leibowitz, "Target Returns on Immunized Portfolios, Effects of Interactions among Term Structures of Interest Rates," Reprinted in [13].

[40] Fisher, Lawrence and Roman L. Weil, "Coping With the Risk of Market-Rate Fluctuations: Returns to Bondholders from Naive and Optimal Strategies," Journal of Business, October 1971, pp. 408-431.

[41] Foglers, Russell H., "Irving Fisher's Equation, Bonds, and Portfolio Immunization: A Generalization," Working Paper funded by the S. S. Huebner Foundation, University of Pennsylvania, 1979.

[42] Foglers, Russell H., "Life Insurance Liabilities, Three Types of Risk, and Bond Portfolio Immunization," Working Paper funded by the S. S. Huebner Foundation, University of Pennsylvania, 1979.

[43] Fong, Gifford H. and Oldrich A. Vasicek, "Return Maximization for Immunized Portfolios," Reprinted in [13].

[44] Fong, Gifford H. and Oldrich A. Vasicek, "A Risk Minimizing Strategy for Multiple Liability Immunization," Unpublished Manuscript, revised February 1982.

[45] Gay, Gerald D., Robert W. Kolb and Raymond Chiang, "Interest Rate Hedging: An Empirical Test of Alternative Strategies," Working Paper, 1981.

[46] Gay, Gerald D., and Robert W. Kolb, "Hedge Models and the Management of Interest Rate," Journal of Portfolio Management, forthcoming.

[47] Gay, Gerald D., and Robert W. Kolb, "Interest Rate Futures: A New Perspective on Immunization," Journal of Portfolio Management, forthcoming.

[48] Gordon, Alexander J., "Applying the Market Model to Long-Term Corporate Bonds," Journal of Financial and Quantitative Analysis, December 1980, pp. 1063-1080.

[49] Grove, Myron A., "A Model of Maturity Profile of the Balance Sheet," Metroeconomics, April 1966, pp. 40-55.

[50] Grove, Myron A., "On 'Duration' and the Optimal Maturity Structure of the Balance Sheet," The Bell Journal of Economics, Autumn 1974, pp. 698-709.

[51] Gushee, Charles H., "How to Hedge A Bond Investment," Financial Analysts Journal, March-April 1981, pp. 44-51.

[52] Haugan, Robert A., and Dean W. Wichern, "The Elasticity of Financial Assets," Journal of Finance, September 1974, pp. 1229-1240.

[53] Haugan, Robert A., and Dean W. Wichern, "The Intricate Relationship Between Financial Leverage and the Stability of Stock Prices," Journal of Finance, December 1975, pp. 1283-1292.

[54] Hawawini, Gabriel A., "On the Mathematics of Macaulay's Duration: A Note" Working Paper, Baruch College of the City University of New York, November 1981.

[55] Hessel, Christopher A. and Lucy Huffman, "The Effects of Taxation on Immunization Rules and Duration Estimation," Journal of Finance, December 1981, pp. 1127-1142.

[56] Hessel, Christopher A. and Lucy Huffman, "Immunization and the Problem of the Unknown Time Horizon," Working Paper, Baruch College of the City University of New York, 1980.

[57] Hicks, John R., "Value and Capital" Oxford: Claredon Press (1939), pp. 185-188.

[58] Hopewell, Michael H. and George G. Kaufman, "Bond Price Volatility and Term to Maturity: A Generalized Respecification," American Economic Review, September 1973, pp. 749-753.

[59] Ingersoll, Jonathan E., "Is Immunization Feasible: Evidence from the CRSP Data," Reprinted in [13].

[60] Ingersoll, Jonathan E., Jeffrey Skelton and Roman L. Weil, "Duration Forty Years Later," Journal of Financial and Quantitative Analysis, November 1978, pp. 621-650.

[61] Jarrow, Robert A., "The Relationship Between Yield, Risk and Return of Corporate Bonds," Journal of Finance, September 1978, pp. 1235-1240.

[62] Kaufman, George G., "Duration, Planning Period, and Tests of the Capital Asset Pricing Model," Journal of Financial Research, Spring 1980, pp. 1-9.

[63] Kaufman, George G., "Measuring Risk and Return for Bonds: A New Approach," Journal of Bank Research, Summer 1978, pp. 82-90.

[64] Kaufman, George G., Thomas A. Loeffler and Robert L. Schweitzer, "Measuring Risk and Return for Portfolios of Coupon Bonds," Paper presented at the Annual Meeting of Financial Management Association, Minneapolis, October 1978.

[65] Khang, Chulsoon, "Bond Immunization When Short Term Interest Rates Fluctuate More than Long Term Rates," Journal of Financial and Quantitative Analysis, December 1979, pp. 1085-1090.

[66] Kolb, Robert W. and Raymond Chiang, "Improving Hedging Performance Using Interest Rate Futures," Financial Management, Autumn 1981, pp. 72-79.

[67] Kolb, Robert W. and Raymond Chiang, "Duration, Immunization, and Hedging with Interest Rate Futures," Journal of Financial Research, forthcoming.

[68] Koopmans, Tjalling C., "The Risk of Interest Fluctuations in Life Insurance Companies," Philadelphia: Penn Mutual Life Insurance 1942.

[69] Lanstein, Ronald and William F. Sharpe, "Duration and Systematic Risk," Journal of Financial and Quantitative Analysis, November 1978, pp. 653-668.

[70] Leibowitz, Martin L., editor, Pros and Cons of Immunization, Salomon Brothers, New York: 1980.

[71] Leibowitz, Martin L., "Bond Immunization: A Procedure for Realizing Target Levels of Returns," Memoranda, October 10, 1979, November 27, 1979 and December 12, 1979, Salomon Brothers, Reprinted in [13].

[72] Leibowitz, Martin L. and Alfred Weinberger, "The Uses of Contingent Immunization," Journal of Portfolio Management, Fall 1981, pp. 51-55.

[73] Leibowitz, Martin L. and Alfred Weinberger, "Contingent Immunization," Salomon Brothers, New York: January 1981.

[74] Lidstone, George J., "On the Approximate Calculation of the Values of Increasing Annuities and Assurances," Journal of the Institute of Actuaries, Volume 31, (1895), pp. 398-402.

[75] Livingston , Miles and John Caks, "A 'Duration' Fallacy," Journal of Finance, March 1977, pp. 185-188.

[76] Livingston , Miles, "Duration and Risk Assessment for Bonds and Common Stocks: A Note," Journal of Finance, March 1978, pp. 293-295.

[77] McEnally, Richard W., "Duration as a Practical Tool in Bond Management," Journal of Portfolio Management, Summer 1977, pp. 53-57.

[78] McEnally, Richard W., "How to Neutralize Reinvestment Rate Risk," Journal of Portfolio Management, Spring 1980, pp. 59-63.

[79] Macaulay, Frederick, R., "Some Theoretical Problems Suggested by the Movement of Interest Rates, Bonds, Yields, and Stock Prices in the United States since 1856," New York, Columbia University Press (1938), pp. 44-53.

[80] Marshall, William J. and Yawitz, Jess J., "Lower Bounds on Portfolio Performance: An Extension of the Immunization Strategy," Working Paper, Washington University, January 1979.

[81] Rao, Ramesh K. S., "The Impact of Yield Changes on the Systematic Risk of Bonds," Journal of Financial and Quantitative Analysis, March 1982, pp. 115-127.

[82] Redington, F. M., "Review of the Principle of Life-Office Valuations," Journal of the Institute of Actuaries, Volume 78, (1952), pp. 286-340.

[83] Reilly, Frank K. and Rupinder S. Sidha, "The Many Uses of Bond Duration," Financial Analysts Journal, July-August 1980, pp. 58-72.

[84] Robertson, D. J. and I. L. B. Sturrock, "Active Investment Policy Related to the Holding of Matched Assets," Transactions of the Faculty of Actuaries, Volume 22, (1964), pp. 36-97.

[85] Samuelson, Paul A., "The Effects of Interest Rates Increases on The Banking System," American Economic Review, March 1945, pp. 16-27.

[86] Schaefer, Stephen and Jeffrey Nelson, "Dynamics of the Term Structure and Alternative Portfolio Immunization Strategies," Reprinted in [13].

[87] Shedden, A. D., "A Practical Approach to Applying Immunization Theory," Transactions of the Faculty of Actuaries, Volume 35, (1977), pp. 313-364.

[88] Smidt, Seymour, "Investment Horizons and Performance Measurements, Journal of Portfolio Management, Winter 1978, pp. 18-22.

[89] Tito, Dennis A. and Wayne H. Wagner, "Definitive New Measures of Bond Performance and Risk," Wilshire Associates, 1977.

[90] Vanderhoof, Irwin T., "The Interest Rate Assumption and the Maturity Structure of Assets of a Life Insurance Company," Transactions of the Society of Actuaries, Volume 24, (1972), pp. 157-192.

[91] Vanderhoof, Irwin T., "The Use of Duration in the Dynamic Programming of Investments," Reprinted in [13].

[92] Wallas, F. E., "Immunization," Journal of the Institute of Actuaries Students' Society, Volume 15, (1960), pp. 345-357.

[93] Wagner, Wayne H. and Dennis A. Tito, "Definitive New Measures of Bond Performance and Risk," Pension World, May 1977, pp. 10-12.

[94] Wagner, Wayne H. and Dennis A. Tito, "Is Your Bond Manager Skillful? - Definitive New Measures of Bond Performance and Risk," Pension World, June 1977, pp. 9-13.

[95] Weil, Roman L., "Macaulay's Duration: An Appreciation," Journal of Business, October 1973, pp. 589-592.

[96] Weinstein, Mark, "The Systematic Risk of Corporate Bonds," Journal of Financial and Quantitative Analysis, September 1981, pp. 257-278.

[97] Whittaker, John, "Minimizing the Burden of the Dollar Premium," Investment Analyst, October 1969, pp. 26-33.

[98] Whittaker, John, "The Relevance of Duration," Journal of Business Finance, Spring 1970, pp. 34-41.

[99] Wissner, Len, Editor, "Immunization and Duration: State of the Art," Proceedings of the Smith Barney Seminar, Tarrytown, New York, October 1978.

[100] Yawitz, Jess B., "The Relative Importance of Duration and Yield Volatility on Bond Price Volatility," Journal of Money, Credit and Banking, February 1977, pp. 97-102.

[101] Yawitz, Jess B., George H. Hempel and William J. Marshall, "The Use of Average Maturity and a Risk Proxy in Investment Portfolios," Journal of Finance, May 1975, pp. 325-333.

[102] Yawitz, Jess B. and William J. Marshall, "The Shortcomings of
       Duration as a Risk Measure for Bonds," _Journal of Financial_
       Research, Summer 1981, pp. 91-101.

[103] Yawitz, Jess B. and William J. Marshall, "The Investor's Holding
       Period and the Need to Rebalance an Immunized Portfolio," Working
       Paper 81-3, Washington University, 1981.

PART I

BOND DURATION

FROM 'SOME THEORETICAL PROBLEMS SUGGESTED BY THE MOVEMENTS OF INTEREST RATES, BOND YIELD, AND STOCK PRICES IN THE UNITED STATES SINCE 1856'

Frederick R. Macaulay

We have, so far in this chapter, been discussing the subject of long time interest rates without asking the question: how much longer term is one loan than another? For a study of the relations between long and short time interest rates, it would seem highly desirable to have some adequate measure of 'longness'. Let us use the word 'duration' to signify the essence of the time element in a loan. If one loan is essentially a longer term loan than another we shall speak of it as having greater 'duration'.

Now the promise contained in a loan is either a promise to make one and only one future payment or a promise to make more than one future payment. If two loans are made at the same rate of interest, and if each loan involves a promise to make one future payment only, the loan whose future payment is to be made earlier is clearly a shorter term loan than the other. For example, if $100 be lent for one year at 5 per cent per annum, the only payment to be $105 at the end of the year, and if another $100 be lent for two years at 5 per cent per annum, the only payment to be $110.25 at the end of the two years, the first loan is clearly a shorter term loan than the second. If, on the other hand, either or both loans involve a promise to make more than one future payment, or if the rates of interest ascribed to the two loans are not the same, it may be extremely difficult to decide which is essentially the longer term loan.

It is clear that 'number of years to maturity' is a most inadequate measure of 'duration'. We must remember that the 'maturity' of a loan is the date of the last and final payment only. It tells us nothing about the sizes of any other payments or the dates on which they are to be made. It is clearly only one of the factors determining 'duration'. Sometimes, as in the case of a low coupon, short term bond, it may be overwhelmingly the most important factor. At other times, as in the case of a long term, diminishing annuity, its importance may be so small as to be almost negligible. Because of its nature, length of time to maturity is not an accurate or even a good measure of 'duration'. 'Duration' is a reality of which 'maturity' is only one factor.

Whether one bond represents an essentially shorter or an essentially longer term loan than another bond depends not only upon the respective 'maturities' of the two bonds but also upon their respective 'coupon rates'—and, under certain circumstances, on their respective 'yields'. Only if maturities, coupon rates and yields are identical can we say, without calculation, that the 'durations' of two bonds are the same.

If two bonds have the same maturity and the same yield but one has a higher coupon rate than the other, the one having the higher coupon rate represents an essentially shorter term loan than the other. For example, if each bond is selling on a 5 per cent basis, a 6 per cent bond maturing in 25 years necessarily represents an essentially shorter term loan than a 4 per cent bond maturing in 25 years. This may easily be seen by comparing a $400 face value 6 per cent bond maturing in 25 years with a $500 face value 4 per cent bond maturing in 25 years. On both bonds the total of all future payments, both principal and interest, is $1,000. But on the 6 per cent bond the payments are $12 each six months for $24\frac{1}{2}$ years, and then a final payment of $412, while on the 4 per cent bond the payments are $10 each six months for $24\frac{1}{2}$ years, and then a final payment of $510. It is plain that the $1,000 is being paid earlier on the 6 than on the 4 per cent bond. Though both have the same 'maturity', the 6 per cent bond represents a loan of shorter 'duration' than the 4 per cent bond.

The difference in 'duration' of the two bonds is manifest in their prices. As the payments are made earlier on the 6 per cent bond, its price (if the 'yields' of the two bonds are the same) is necessarily higher. For example, as each bond 'yields' 5 per cent, the price of the $400 face value 6 per cent bond will be $456.72, while the price of the $500 face value 4 per cent bond will be only $429.10.

We see, then, that if two bonds have the same yield and the same maturity but different coupon rates, the bond having the higher coupon rate represents the loan of shorter 'duration'. Instead of examining in a similar manner the case in which the two bonds have the same coupon rate and the same maturity but different yields, and the case in which they have the same coupon rate and the same yield but different maturities, we shall now consider directly the general problem of how to measure 'duration'. Let us approach this problem by considering the maturity of a bond as a function of the maturities of the separate loans of which it may be said to consist.

It would seem almost natural to assume that the 'duration' of any loan involving more than one future payment should be some sort of a weighted average of the maturities of the individual loans that correspond to each future payment. Two sets of weights immediately present themselves—the *present* and the *future* values of the various individual loans.

Future value weighting seems clearly inadmissible. It gives absurdly long 'durations'. If $2,000 be lent at 5 per cent per annum in the form of two loans, one of $1,000 at 5 per cent per annum [19] payable in one lump sum of $1,050 at the end of one year, and one of $1,000 at 5 per cent per annum payable in one lump sum of $131,501.26 at the end of 100 years, the 'average maturity' or 'duration' of the two loans, if calculated by taking an arithmetic average of the two maturities, using the *present* values as weights, is 50½ years. If the *future* values ($1,050 and $131,501.26) be used as weights, the 'average maturity' is found to be more than 99 years.

In this illustration, the *present* values (or amounts lent) were equal. Let us examine a case in which the *future* values are equal. If $959.98 be lent at 5 per cent per annum in the form of two loans, one of $952.38 at 5 per cent per annum payable in one lump sum of $1,000 at the end of one year, and one of $7.60 at 5 per cent per annum payable in one lump sum of $1,000 at the end of 100 years, the 'average maturity' or 'duration' of the two loans, if calculated by taking an arithmetic average of the two maturities, using the *present* values ($952.38 and $7.60) as weights, is about 21½ *months*. If the *future* values be used as weights, the average maturity is 50½ years.

How absurd it seems to think of a loan of $2,000 made up of two loans each of $1,000, one maturing in one year and one in 100 years, as having a 'duration' of over 99 years. And how absurd to think of a loan of $1,000 made up of two loans, one of $952.38 maturing in one year and the other of $7.60—less than 1 per cent of the larger loan—maturing in 100 years, as having a 'duration' of 50½ years. [20]

[19] In the present discussions, we have not followed the 'semi-annual compounding' convention. For simplicity of treatment, we have assumed throughout that payments are made *annually* and compounding is done *annually*.

[20] If one billion dollars were to be lent as a single payment loan at 5 per cent per annum for one year, and one cent as a single payment loan at 5 per cent per annum

But are not the results obtained by using *present* values as weights also open to criticism? If the 'durations' obtained by using *future* value weighting seem unmistakably too long, does not at least one of the 'durations' obtained from *present* value weighting seem very short?

Moreover, if the average maturity of two equal *future* payments be assumed to be the arithmetic average of the two maturities with the *present* values of the future payments as weights, some seemingly paradoxical results may appear. For example, if the yield be 5 per cent and if the two future payments be $1 at the end of one year and $1 at the end of 10 years, the average maturity will be about $4\frac{1}{2}$ years. If the dates of payment be one year and 27 years, the average maturity will be about 6.7 years. But if they be one year and 50 years the average maturity will be only 5.1 years, and if the dates of payment be one year and 100 years the average maturity will be appreciably less than 2 years! In this particular illustration, the average maturity has a maximum when the second payment is made in about 27 years! However, these results do not seem so ridiculous if we remember that, as the date of payment of the second $1 becomes arithmetically more and more distant, *its present value, or the amount actually lent*, becomes geometrically smaller and smaller. In the limiting case, in which the second $1 is paid at infinity, the 'average maturity' is one year, but the amount of the loan for which the second dollar is to be paid is zero. The argument for present value weighting seems strong.[21]

(Footnote 20 concluded)
for 520 years, *future* value weighting would give the composite loan a duration of about 260 years.

[21] The actuaries have proposed and solved a problem that must not be confounded with ours. It is termed the problem "of finding the *equated time* for a number of sums due at different times, or, in other words, the average date at which, on the basis of an agreed rate of interest, all the sums might be paid without theoretical advantage or disadvantage to either party" (British) *Institute of Actuaries Text-Book, Part I*, pp. 24 and 25.

The answer is a date such that, if the *sum* of all the *present* values of the different future payments was compounded to that date at the rate of interest used to obtain those individual present values, it would amount to the sum of all the future payments. This is a neat and symmetrical answer to the problem proposed, and it gives better results in practice than the common method of 'equating time', which is based on *future* weighting, but it seems an unreal answer to an unreal question. It is quite logical in assuming that the present value of the single future payment must equal the present value of the sum of the individual future payments, but it seems to beg the question when it also assumes that the *future* value of the single payment at the date of its payment must equal the sum of the individual

Now, if present value weighting be used, the 'duration' of a bond is an average of the durations of the separate single payment loans into which the bond may be broken up. To calculate this average the duration of each individual single payment loan must be weighted in proportion to the size of the individual loan; in other words, by the ratio of the present value of the individual future payment to the sum of all the present values, which is, of course, the price paid for the bond.[22]

Let $F =$ the 'face' value of the bond in dollars, i.e. the 'principal' sum in dollars;

$I =$ the number of dollars paid semi-annually, i.e. the number of dollars called for by one 'coupon';

$P =$ the number of dollars paid for the bond, i.e. the 'price' in dollars;

$n =$ the number of half years the bond has to run, i.e. the number of half years to 'maturity';

$R =$ the semi-annual *rate* of the 'yield', e.g. if the bond is selling to yield 4 per cent per annum, $R = 1.02$ (under the semi-annual convention of the bond tables);

$Q =$ the ratio of the face value of the bond to a coupon payment, i.e., $Q = \dfrac{F}{I}$;

$D =$ the 'duration' of the bond—in half years;

Then

$$D = \frac{\dfrac{I}{R} + \dfrac{2I}{R^2} + \dfrac{3I}{R^3} + \ldots + \dfrac{nI}{R^n} + \dfrac{nF}{R^n}}{\dfrac{I}{R} + \dfrac{I}{R^2} + \dfrac{I}{R^3} + \ldots + \dfrac{I}{R^n} + \dfrac{F}{R^n}}.$$

(Footnote [21] concluded)
future payments each taken at its particular date of payment. This assumption overweights the time importance of distant payments.

[22] In terms of the symbols of the next paragraph,

$$P = \frac{I}{R} + \frac{I}{R^2} + \frac{I}{R^3} + \ldots + \frac{I}{R^n} + \frac{F}{R^n} = \frac{I}{R-1} - \frac{\dfrac{I}{R-1} - F}{R^n}$$

Summing the terms in the numerator, and in the denominator, of this fraction and substituting QI for F, we find that

$$D = \frac{R}{R-1} - \frac{QR + n(1+Q-QR)}{R^n - 1 - Q + QR}.$$

An examination of this expression for the value of D shows that the larger the value of Q the greater the duration; in other words, the smaller the 'coupon' payments are relatively to the face value of the bond the greater is the duration of the bond. Furthermore, the larger the value of R the smaller the duration. D increases with n, though, if R be greater than $1 + \frac{1}{Q}$, in other words if the bond be selling below par, D reaches a maximum before n reaches infinity, declining gradually thereafter to $\frac{R}{R-1}$, the value reached when n equals infinity.

When $Q = 0$, in other words, when the series of future payments constitutes a mere annuity without any 'principal' payment whatever, $D = \frac{R}{R-1} - \frac{n}{R^n - 1}$. When Q equals infinity, in other words, if the loan is single payment, $D = n$.

If $R = 1$, in other words if the 'yield' of the bond be zero,

$$D = \frac{\frac{n^2+n}{2} + nQ \text{ (note 23)}}{n + Q}.$$ Unity is the limiting value of D as R approaches infinity.

23    $\frac{R}{R-1} - \frac{QR + n(1+Q-QR)}{R^n-1-Q+QR}$

$= \frac{R(R^n-1-Q+QR) - (R-1)[QR + n(1+Q-QR)]}{(R-1)(R^n-1-Q+QR)}$

which, when 1 is substituted for R, takes the indeterminate form of $\frac{0}{0}$. However, the fraction may easily be evaluated by the ordinary methods of the calculus. The first derivative of the numerator divided by the first derivative of the denominator is, if $R = 1$, still indeterminate. However, taking second derivatives, we get

$$\frac{n(n+1) R^{n-1} + 2nQ}{n(n+1) R^{n-1} + 2Q - n(n-1) R^{n-2}}.$$

Letting $R = 1$ in this expression we obtain the value for D given in the text.

When $n = 1$, $D = 1$. When n equals infinity, as when a bond (such as Canadian Pacific debenture 4's) has no maturity date, $D = \dfrac{R}{R-1}$.

But, if R be greater than $1 + \dfrac{1}{Q}$, in other words if the bond be selling below par, D will attain a maximum value before n reaches infinity.[24] However, unless R be very large, the value of n making D a maximum will be large and the maximum value of D will be very little greater than the value associated with an infinite value for n.[25]

A short table presenting the relations between time to maturity and duration, for a 4, a 5, and a 6 per cent bond each selling at par, will illustrate the ordinary characteristics of the duration concept (p. 51).

The concept of 'duration' throws a flood of light on the fluctuations of bond yields in the actual market. Not merely do the yields of long term bonds tend to fluctuate much less violently than the yields of short term bonds or the rates on short term loans, such as are represented by commercial paper, but the relation between maturity and violence of fluctuation in yield is much as we would expect to find it from our analysis of the nature of 'duration'. While there is a great difference between the amplitude of the fluctuations in yield of bonds of

[24] The explanation of seeming paradoxes of this type has already been discussed.

[25] Equating to zero the derivative of D with respect to n leads to an insoluble equation; but an approximate solution is that, for other than extremely large values of R, D will reach a maximum when n is a shade greater than $\dfrac{R}{R-1} + \dfrac{QR}{QR-Q-1}$. For example, if a 4 per cent bond be selling on a 6 per cent basis (3 per cent per half year on the semi-annual compounding convention), $\dfrac{R}{R-1} + \dfrac{QR}{QR-Q-1}$ will equal $134\frac{1}{3}$, and this is approximately the value of n (in half years) that will, in fact, make D a maximum. But this maximum value of D, when n equals $134\frac{1}{3}$, is less than $34\frac{2}{3}$ half years and when n equals infinity D equals $34\frac{1}{3}$ half years, a decline of less than two months in its value.

A higher yield will, of course, give a maximum value for D with a smaller value for n and the difference between the maximum value of D and its value when n equals infinity will be increased. For example, if the 4 per cent bond be selling on an 8 per cent basis, $\dfrac{R}{R-1} + \dfrac{QR}{QR-Q-1}$ will equal 78. When D is actually a maximum, n lies between 78 and 79 half years. The maximum value of D is then slightly less than $27\frac{1}{8}$ half years but the value of D when n equals infinity is only 26 half years, a difference of a little more than half a year.

DURATION IN YEARS [26]

YEARS TO MATURITY	4 PER CENT BOND	5 PER CENT BOND	6 PER CENT BOND
1	.990	.987	.985
3	2.857	2.823	2.790
6	5.393	5.257	5.126
10	8.339	7.989	7.662
15	11.422	10.727	10.094
25	16.026	14.536	13.254
50	21.970	18.765	16.273
100	25.014	20.353	17.120
Infinity	25.5	20.5	17.167

extremely short maturity and of those having ten years or so to run, and an appreciable difference between the fluctuations in yield of the latter and of bonds having forty-five or fifty years to run, there is virtually no discernible difference between the action of these last bonds and the action of those having a hundred years or more to run.

The concept is, of course, full of theoretical difficulties. It is easy to think of the 'duration' of a bond as increasing while the time to maturity is decreasing, if 'long term interest rates' are declining during the period. It would seem only logical, for the purposes of our problem, to think of time not in terms of years or months but in terms of its relation to the growth of capital. But in all our illustrations we have, for purposes of computation, used as 'yield' the yield of *the individual bond* whose 'duration' we were discussing. This amounts to assuming that 'duration' is lengthened by mere increase of security as well as by a true decrease in the 'preference for present over (assured) future money'.

But this assumption leads us into one of the quagmires of 'pure' interest. Are the promised future payments of a low grade bond really

[26] If the interest were payable and compounded annually, instead of semi-annually, the durations would be slightly greater than those given above, the difference increasing with increases in the time to maturity. For infinite maturities they would be one-half year greater, that is 26, 21 and 17⅔ years instead of 25½, 20½ and 17 1/6 years.

If the ordinary concept of 'equated time' (see note 21) were used to calculate duration, no maximum values would appear. A bond with an infinite maturity like British Consols or Canadian Pacific debenture 4's would have an infinite duration. A 6 per cent bond selling at par and maturing in 10 years would have a duration of 7.95 years (instead of 7.66 as in the text table), if it matured in 25 years its duration would be 15.50 years (instead of 13.25), for 50 years its duration would be 23.45 (instead of 16.27), for 100 years 32.92 (instead of 17.12), and if it matured in 200 years its duration would be 43.39 years instead of less than 17 1/6 years as in the text table.

discounted at higher rates than the promised future payments of a high grade bond, or is the difference in 'yield' traceable not to any difference in rates of discount but to a difference in what is discounted, this being, in the case of an ultra high grade bond, the actually promised payments, but, in the case of a low grade bond, the mathematical 'expectations' that result from multiplying each promised payment by the assumed probability that it will be met? [27]

Another difficulty connected with the problem will be merely mentioned. We have made the assumption that the rate of interest for each future six month period is the rate corresponding to the 'yield' of the bond. Now the reader realizes that this assumption may easily be contrary to fact. However, we drew attention, earlier in this chapter, to the insuperable difficulties connected with any attempt to discover the real rates of discount for each half-yearly period in the future. If we knew these future discount rates we might then be able to state that two bonds which, *at different dates*, each had the same number of years to run, the same coupon rate and the same 'yield' had quite different durations.

If, for example, the 'yield' of the earlier bond involved a set of relatively high discount rates for the years of the immediate future and low discount rates for the succeeding years to maturity, while this condition was reversed for the later bond, the earlier bond would have a longer duration than the later bond. Because the coupon rates, yields and maturities are identical, the prices of the two bonds will be the same. In other words, the sum of the present values of the future payments will be the same. Hence that bond in which the earlier payments are relatively heavily discounted, and therefore the 'weights' applicable to the shorter constituent maturities are relatively light, will have a longer duration.

The difficulties connected with the problem of arriving at a completely satisfactory concept of 'duration' are, indeed, extremely great. Any proposed solution almost necessarily involves some paradoxes. We have tried to open the reader's eyes to the existence of the problem. The logical atmosphere in which the analysis has had to be carried on may seem to have been somewhat rarefied at times; but we believe that, if the reader has followed the arguments carefully, he will at least not

[27] But see Ch. III, note 8.

accuse the writer of being like the good Puritan knight who, in religious controversy,

> ". . . could raise scruples dark and nice,
> And after solve 'em in a trice
> As if Divinity had catch'd
> The itch, on purpose to be scratch'd."

ON THE MATHEMATICS OF
MACAULAY'S DURATION

Gabriel A. Hawawini

THE MATHEMATICS OF MACAULAY'S DURATION

Gabriel Hawawini

I. Introduction

A bond's duration was defined by Macaulay as the weighted average number of years until the bond's cash flows occur, where the weights used are the present values of each payment relative to the bond's price. We can express Macaulay's definition of a bond's duration as:

$$D(n,io,i) = \frac{\sum_{1}^{n} i_o tv^t + nv^n}{P/F} = \frac{i_o \sum_{1}^{n} tv^t + nv^n}{i_o \sum_{1}^{n} v^t + v^n} \tag{1}$$

where D = bond's duration

   P = bond's price

   F = bond's par-value or principal

   i_o = bond's coupon-rate

   n = bond's term to maturity

   i = bond's yield to maturity or market yield

   $v = (1+i)^{-1}$ = one period discount factor at rate i

In the next section we modify the standard duration expression in (1) into a more tractable form. This alternative expression will then allow us to examine in Section III the maturity-behavior of duration, that is, the response of duration (D) to changes in maturity (n) with the coupon-rate (i_o) and the yield (i) remaining the same. In section IV and V we investigate the coupon-behavior and the yield-behavior of duration, respectively. The last section contains concluding remarks.

II. Duration: A More Tractable Expression

In this secton we derive an alternative expression for a bond's duration which will facilitate the examination of both the maturity-behavior and the coupon-behavior of duration. We will see, however, that the examination of the yield-behavior of duration can be carried out more easily using the original definitional expression of duration given in (1).

The partial derivative, with respect to yield, of the bond's price given in the denominator of (1) is:

$$\frac{\partial P/F}{\partial i} = - v(i_o \sum_1^n tv^t + nv^n) \tag{2}$$

Using (2), the duration given in (1) can be rewritten as:

$$D = - (F/P) \left(\frac{\partial P/F}{\partial i}\right) v^{-1} \tag{3}$$

Alternatively the bond's price can be expressed as[1]

$$P/F = (i_o + (i-i_o)v^n)i^{-1} \tag{4}$$

and hence:

$$\frac{\partial P/F}{\partial i} = - [(i_o + (i-i_o)v^n)i^{-1} + ((i-i_o)v^n - v^n)]i^{-1} \tag{5}$$

$$= -[i_o a + n(i-i_o)v^{n+1}]i^{-1}$$

where "a" is the present value of an n-period one-dollar annuity at a rate i such as $a = (1 + v^n)i^{-1}$.

Substituting (5) and (4) in (3) we get:

$$D(n,i_o,i) = \frac{(1+i)a\,i_o + n(i-i_o)v^n}{i_o + (i-i_o)v^n} \qquad (6)$$

which is an expression of a bond's duration that is easier to analyze than the definitional expression in (1), particularly when we examine the maturity-behavior and the coupon-behavior of duration. The advantages of expression (6) over expression (1) are: (i) the summation signs have been eliminated which greatly simplifies the examination of the maturity-behavior of duraton, (ii) the term $(i-i_o)$ appears in (6) which allows us to explicitly examine the differential effects of changes in maturity on the duration of bonds selling above par $(i_o<i)$ or below par $(i_o>i)$, (iii) the numerator of (6) is its demoninator in which the first term is multiplied by $(1+i)a$ and the second term multiplied by n.

We will also find it convenient to rearrange (6) in the following manner:

$$\frac{D}{n} = \frac{\alpha i_o + (i-i_o)v^n}{i_o + (i-i_o)v^n} \quad, \text{ where } \alpha = (1+i)a/n \qquad (7)$$

According to (7) the ratio of a bond's duration to its maturity is such as the numerator is the denominator with its first term multiplied by $\alpha = (1+i)a/n$.

III. The Maturity-Behavior of Macaulay's Duration

Theorem 1 "A bond's duration is equal to its maturity if and only if it is a zero-coupon bond (pure discount issue) or a one-period-coupon bearing bond."

Proof: According to (7), D/n is equal to one if and only if $i_o = 0$ or $\alpha = 1$. The former case is that of a zero-coupon bond. The latter case implies

$(1+i_o)a=n$ which is satisfied only if $n=1$, that is, if the bond is a one-period coupon-bearing issue. Q.E.D.

> Theorem 2: "The duration of a coupon-bearing bond with a finite maturity of more than one period $(1<n<\infty)$ has a duration which is shorter than its term to maturity."

Proof: For a coupon-bearing bond with $1<n<\infty$ we have[2] $\alpha<1$ and therefore the numerator of D/n in smaller than its denominator. Hence D/n <1 : maturity exceeds duration. Q.E.D.

> Theorem 3: "The duration of a perpetual bond $(n=\infty)$ is equal to $(1+i^{-1})$ irrespective of its coupon rate."

Proof: As n goes to infinity both nv^n and v^n approach zero and "a" approaches i^{-1}. Referring to (6) we can see that the limiting value of D becomes $(1+i^{-1})$ as the term to maturity goes to infinity."

> Corollary: "The duration of a coupon-bearing bond approaches the limit $(1+i^{-1})$ as the bond's maturing is lengthened to infinity"

> Theorem 4: "The duration of a coupon-bearing bond selling at par (io=i) or above par (io>i) increases monotonically with its term to maturity and approaches $(1+i^{-1})$ as the term to maturity goes to inifinity."

Proof: This theorem can be proved by examining the sign of the partial derivative of D(n) with respect to n. This exercise in somewhat more difficult than proving the preceding three theorems because the sign of $\partial D/\partial n$ is not readily determined. We want to prove that $\partial D/\partial n > 0$ if $i_o \geq i$. Taking the derivative of (6) with respect to n we get:

$$\frac{\partial D}{\partial n} = \frac{v^n[io(1+i)\log(1+i) + io(i-io)+(i-io)^2 v^n - nio(i-io)\log(1+i)]}{[io + (i-io)v^n]^2} \qquad (8)$$

The second and third terms in the numerator of (8) can be rearranged such as:

$$io(i-io) + (i-io)^2 v^n = (i-io)iv^n + io(i-io)ia$$

and hence the terms between brackets in the numerator of (8) can be rewritten as:

$$i_o(1+i)\log(1+i) + (i-i_o)iv^n - i_o(i-i_o)(n\log(1+i) - ia) \qquad (9)$$

We will now prove that the sum of the first and second terms in (9) is always positive. To prove this, note that $\log(1+i)$ is larger than $i/(1+i)^3$ and hence we have:

$$(1+i)\log(1+i) = i+e \quad \text{with} \quad e>0$$

Consequently the first and the second terms in (9) can be expressed as:

$$i_o(i+e) + i^2v^n - i_oiv^n = i_oi(1-v^n) + i_oe + i^2v^n > 0.$$

If a bond sells at par ($i_o=i$) then the third term in the numerator of (8) in zero and $\partial D/\partial n>0$.

We now prove that the sign of the last term in (9) is that of (i_o-i). Consequently if the bond sells above par ($i_o>i$) the last term in the numerator of (8) is positive and, again, $\partial D/\partial n>0$. We can write:

$$n\log(1+i) - ia = n\log(1+i) + (1+i)a.i/(1+i)$$

and since $n>(1+i)a$ and $\log(1+i)>i/(1+i)$ it follows that ($n\log(1+i)-ia$) is positive and that the third term in (9) has the sign of (i_o-i). Q.E.D.

> **Theorem 5** "The duration of a coupon-bearing bond selling below par ($i_o<i$) reaches a maximum before maturity reaches infinity and then recedes toward the limit ($1+i^{-1}$)."

Proof: When the bond sells below par ($i_o<i$) the last term in (9) is negative and $\partial D/\partial n$ may be zero or negative. Consequently $D(n)$ may have one or more extrema. First let us show that there exists a value of n for which

$\partial D / \partial n \lessgtr 0$. The sum of the terms between brackets in the numerator of (8) is zero or negative if:[4]

$$n \geqq \frac{i_o(1+i) \log(1+i) + (i-i_o)(i_o+(i-i_o)v^n)}{i_o(i-i_o)\log(1+i)} \qquad (10)$$

Since $[(1+i)/(i-i_o)]>1$ it follows that the RHS of (10) is larger than one and hence D/n can be zero or negative. When $\partial D/\partial n=0$ we have:

$$\frac{\partial^2 D}{\partial n^2} = \frac{(i-i_o)v^n\log(1+i)}{i_o + (i-i_o)v^n} < 0$$

It follows that $D(n)$ has a **maximum** when the bond sells below par ($i_o<i$). We now have to establish that the maximum value of duration, D_{max}, exceeds the limiting value of duration $D_{lim} = (1+i^{-1})$. The values of n which $D(n) \geqq D_{lim}$ is satisfied are:

$$n \geqq \frac{1+i}{i-i_o}$$

Consequently when a bond sells below par ($i_o<i$) there exist values of n for which duration exceeds its limiting value $D_{lim} = (1+i^{-1})$. Note that if the bond sells either at par ($i_o=i$) or above ($i_o>i$) there are no finite value of n for which $D(n) \geqq D_{lim}$. Q.E.D.

> Theorem 6 "The duration of a coupon-bearing bond selling below par reaches its maximum at a maturity directly related to the bond's coupon rate and inversely related to the market yield."

Proof: We have shown that the value of n for which D(n) intersects D_{lim} is $n*=(1+i)/(i-i_o)$. We have:

$$\frac{\partial n*}{\partial io} = \frac{1+i}{(i-io)^2} > 0 \quad \text{and} \quad \frac{\partial n*}{\partial i} = - \frac{1+i}{(i-io)^2} < o$$

and therefore D_{max} is directly related to i_o and inversely related to i. Q.E.D.

Theorem 7 "The longer a bond's term to maturity, the greater the difference between its term and its duration."

Proof: Note that:

$$\frac{\partial(n-D)}{\partial n} = 1 - \frac{\partial D}{\partial n} > 0 \quad \text{since} \quad \frac{\partial D}{\partial n} < 1$$

$\partial D/\partial n$ is smaller than one because for $0<n<\infty$ we have $0<D/n<1$. Q.E.D.

IV. The Coupon-Behavior of Macaulay's Bond Duration

Theorem 8 "A bond's duration varies inversely with its coupon rate (except for one period and perpetual bonds)."

Proof: Simply take the partial derivative of (6) with respect to i_o:

$$\frac{\partial D}{\partial io} = \frac{i[(1+i)a - n]v^n}{[io + (i-io)v^n]^2} < 0$$

The above derivative is negative since for $1<n<\infty$ we have $(1+i)a<n$. Q.E.D.

V. The Yield-Behavior of Macaulay's Bond Duration

Theorem 9 "The duration of a coupon-bearing bond is inversely related to its yield to maturity."

Proof: This theorem can be proved be determining the sign of $\partial D/\partial i$. This sign can be more easily determined if we take the derivative of D(i) as expressed in (1) rather than (6). We have:

$$\frac{\partial D(i)}{\partial i} = \frac{- i_o v \; \Delta(n) + n i_o v^{n+1} \; \sum_1^n (n-t) v^t + i_o v^n \; \sum_1^n (n-t) t v^{t+1}}{[i_o + (i-i_o) v^n]^2} < 0$$

with $\Delta(n) = \sum_1^n t^2 v^t \; \sum_1^n v^t - \sum_1^n t v^t \; \sum_1^n t v^t > 0$

$\Delta(n)$ is positive since it is the difference between two positive terms, the first being larger than the second. The second and third terms in the numerator of $\partial D/\partial i$ are also positive and hence $\partial D/\partial i < 0$. Q.E.D.

> Theorem 10   "The duration of a "zero-yield" bond is equal to
> $(1/2(n^2+n)i_o + 1)/(ni_o + 1)$."

Proof: We have, using (1):

$$\lim_{i \to 0} D(i) = \frac{i_o \sum_1^n t + 1}{i_o n + 1} = \frac{1/2(n^2+n)i_o + 1}{ni_o + 1} \quad . \quad Q.E.D.$$

> Theorem 11   "A bond's duration approaches unity as the bond's yield
> approaches infinity."

Proof: The limit of $(1+i)a$ as $i \to \infty$ is one. The limit of $(i-i_o)v^n$ as $i \to \infty$ is zero. It follows from the expression of duration in (6) that the limit of $D(i)$ as $i \to \infty$ is equal to $(i_o/i_o) = 1$. Q.E.D.

VI.   Concluding Remarks

The purpose of this note was to examine mathematically the relationships between a bond's duration and its term, coupon and yield. A review of published work on the subject has revealed that these relationships have been generally examined in the past via numerical evaluation, computer simulation or casual analytical observation. The mathematical approach adopted in this note has been carried out with the help of a modified expression of a bond's duration which is more amenable to mathematical manipulations than Macaulay's original definitional expression for a bond's duration.

Footnotes

1. Note that $P/F = i_o(1-v^n)/i + v^n$ from which (4) is easily derived.

2. Note that $(1+i)a = \sum_1^n (1+i)^{-t+1} < n$ and hence $\alpha = (1+i)a/n < 1$.

3. This can be easily shown by expanding $\log(1+i)$ by Taylor's series.

4. Note that (10) implies that for a discount bond, duration achieves its maximum where:

$$n = \frac{1}{\log(1+i)} + \frac{1+i}{i-i_o} + \frac{i - i_o}{i_o(1+i)^n \log(1+i)}$$

The above expression differs slightly from the one suggested by Bierwag. See Hopewell and Kaufman "Bond Price Volatility and the Term to Maturity : A Generalized Respecification," American Economic Review, September 1973, footnote 4, p.750.

FROM 'VALUE AND CAPITAL'

John R. Hicks

2. Any stream of values whatsoever has a capitalized value, which may now be regarded as a function of the rate of interest; this function may then be drawn out in the form of a curve. As it turns out, it proves most convenient to draw this curve in a slightly different form from that which would seem most natural at first sight. We shall measure the capitalized values along the horizontal axis,[1] but along the vertical we shall measure, not the rate of interest, but what may be called the *discount ratio*—the proportion in which a sum of money has to be reduced in order to discount it for one week. (If the rate of interest per week is i, then β, the discount ratio, equals $1/(1+i)$.)

Corresponding to the given expected stream of receipts, we have a capital-value curve RR, which will slope upwards because a rise in the discount ratio (a fall in the rate of interest) raises capitalized value. Corresponding to any particular level of income, we have a capital-value curve (dotted in the diagram) which shows the present value of the standard stream corresponding to that particular level of income (according to the definition of income we are using) at various discount ratios. Such a curve can be drawn for any level of income. If the discount ratio is OH, the present value of the prospective receipts is HA, and the level of income is that represented by the dotted curve SS, which passes through A.

---

[1] Adopting the convention, usual in economics, of putting the dependent variable on the horizontal axis.

If the discount ratio rises, *A* will move to the right along *RR*; and it will be evident from the diagram that this means moving on to a dotted curve representing a higher income, if, as we have drawn them, *SS* is more steeply inclined than *RR*—or, what comes to the same thing, *SS* is less elastic than *RR*. Everything thus depends upon the relative elasticities of the *RR* and *SS* curves.

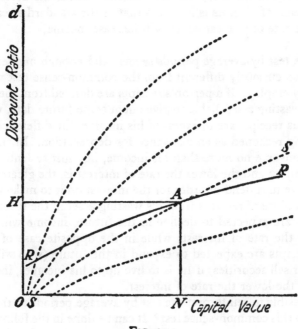

FIG. 23.

The capital value of a stream of payments $(x_0, x_1, x_2, ..., x_\nu)$ is $x_0 + \beta x_1 + \beta^2 x_2 + ... + \beta^\nu x_\nu$. The elasticity of this capital value with respect to the discount ratio β is

$$\frac{\beta x_1 + 2\beta^2 x_2 + 3\beta^3 x_3 + ... + \nu \beta^\nu x_\nu}{x_0 + \beta x_1 + \beta^2 x_2 + \beta^3 x_3 + ... + \beta^\nu x_\nu}$$

(for the elasticity of a sum is the *average* of the elasticities of its parts). Now when we look at the form of this elasticity we see that it may be very properly described as the *Average Period* of the stream; for it is the *average length of time for which the various payments are deferred from the present, when the times of deferment are weighted by the discounted values of the payments*. (The reader may perhaps be angry with me for appropriating the term 'Average Period' to this quantity, since he may have in his head what appears to be a very different meaning of the term. I hope to show at a later stage, however, that the meaning I am giving it is a fair extension of the traditional meaning.)[1]

It follows at once from all this that if the average period of the stream of receipts is greater than the average period of the standard stream with which we are comparing it, a fall in the rate of interest will raise the capital value of the receipts stream more than that of the standard stream, and will therefore increase income. But if the average period of the stream of receipts is less than that of the standard stream, it is a rise in the rate of interest which will increase income.

3. This test by average periods seems valid enough mathematically; but it looks curiously different from the common-sense test we should commonly employ. If a person's receipts are derived from the exploitation of a wasting asset, liable to give out at some future date, we should say that his receipts are in excess of his income, the difference between them being reckoned as an allowance for depreciation. In this case, if he is to consume no more than his income, he must re-lend some part of his receipts; and the lower the rate of interest is, the greater the sum he will have to re-lend in order for the interest on it to make up for the expected failure of receipts from his wasting asset in the future. Thus, if receipts are expected to decline in the future, income will be lower the lower the rate of interest; while in the opposite case of a person whose receipts are expected to expand in the future (who will have to borrow, or sell securities, if he is to live up to his income), income will be higher the lower the rate of interest.

Is it possible to reinterpret the test by average periods so that it shall agree with this common-sense test? It can be done in the following way.

Let us confine attention to the case where neither interest rates nor prices are expected to change, so that all three 'approximations' to the concept of income coincide, and the standard stream corresponding to any of them is a standard stream constant in money terms from week to week.

Remembering that the prospective stream of receipts and the standard stream from which income is calculated must have the same capitalized value, it follows that if the average period of receipts is greater than the standard average period, then the prospective stream must tend to be *below standard* in the near future, while somewhere in the more distant future it must compensate by being *above standard*. Looked at as a whole, it must have a rising tendency; as we may say, a *crescendo*. The

---

[1] See below, Chapter XVII. The reader may also find it rather surprising that an elasticity, usually supposed to be a pure number, independent of units, turns out to be equal to a length of time. This is a consequence of compound interest. The rate of interest for two years is not double that for one; so that time cannot be eliminated by considering proportional changes.

average period turns out to be nothing else but an exact method of measuring the *crescendo* (or *diminuendo*) of a stream of values.

What is in fact the average period of a stream of constant size and indefinite length, discounted throughout at the same rate of interest? It can easily be shown that it is equal to the reciprocal of the rate of interest, i.e. to the number of 'years' purchase'.[1] If the rate of interest is 5 per cent. per annum, the average period of a standard stream is 20 years. If the average period of any other stream comes out at more than 20 years, this means nothing else than that the stream has a *crescendo*; if it comes out at less than 20 years, the stream has a *diminuendo*. That is all the average period means.[2]

This way of measuring the trend of a stream of values can be used for any stream whatsoever; it seems to have more significance than any other from the point of view of economic theory. We shall come back to it again when we consider the effects of interest changes on the organization of production.

[1] For
$$\frac{\beta+2\beta^2+3\beta^3+\dots}{1+\beta+\beta^2+\beta^3+\dots} = \frac{\beta}{(1-\beta)^2}\Big/\frac{1}{1-\beta} = \frac{\beta}{1-\beta} = \frac{1}{i}.$$

[2] The best numerical definition for the *crescendo* of a stream of values is the rate of expansion of a stream, continuously expanding by the same proportion in every period, which has the same average period as the original stream. This rate of expansion is related to the average period by a simple formula. If P is the average period of a stream, i the rate of interest, and c the *crescendo*, so defined, then
$$c = i - \frac{1}{P}.$$

BOND PRICE VOLATITLITY AND THE TERM TO
MATURITY: A GENERALIZED RESPECIFICATION

Michael H. Hopewell
George G. Kaufman

Bond Price Volatility and Term to Maturity: A Generalized Respecification

By Michael H. Hopewell and George G. Kaufman*

One of the more common and accepted generalizations in the mathematics of bond prices is that " . . . for a given change in yields, the fluctuations in market price will be greater the longer the term to maturity" (W. C. Freund, p. 51). Similar statements may be found in almost every book discussing the mechanics of bond prices.[1] This paper demonstrates that this proposition does not hold in all cases, and we derive the general relationship.

In his important book on the term structure, Burton Malkiel specifies the above relationship between bond prices and maturity as the second of his five general theorems:

> For a given change in yield from the nominal yield, changes in bond prices are greater, the longer the term to maturity. [p. 54]

However, shortly afterwards he notes:

> This theorem is not generally true when yield changes are measured from a base other than the nominal yield. In particular, when bonds are selling at a discount . . . it is possible to find cases where longer-term securities are actually less sensitive to a given change in market interest rates than are shorter issues. [p. 55]

Malkiel does not consider this point to have much "practical importance" and does not explore the reasons for its existence. Moreover, it does not prevent him from proceeding to this third theorem:

> The percentage price changes described in Theorem 2 increase at a di-

minishing rate as N (maturity) increases. [p. 55]

However, the high market rates of interest in recent years have given greater practical importance to the inverse relationship between term to maturity and change in bond price. In a recent book directed at portfolio managers, Sidney Homer and Martin Leibowitz demonstrate this phenomenon numerically for hypothetical bonds. They show that when market interest yields are reduced by 25 percent from 9.5 percent to 7.1 percent, " . . . 20-year 1's, 2's, 3's, and 4's (coupons) are more volatile than 30-year 9's" (p. 52). The authors find no easy answer for the "puzzling" behavior and conclude that " . . . the volatility of any conventional high-grade bond results from the interaction of three factors: maturity, coupon, and the starting level of yields" (p. 51).

The apparent inability of analysts to explain this unusual bond price pattern reflects an incomplete understanding of the mathematics of bond prices. While price volatility is related to the time structure of a bond, it is not mathematically related to term to maturity in any simple way. Rather, it is proportionately related to the duration of the bond.[2] The general theorem may be stated:

For a given basis point change in market yield, percentage changes in bond prices vary proportionately with duration and are greater, the greater the duration of the bond.

The validity of this statement for all bonds

---

* University of Oregon. We are indebted to our colleague, G. O. Bierwag, for helpful comments throughout the development of this paper.

[1] For example, Sergei Dobrovolsky, p. 309; Reuben Kessel, p. 45; Henry Latané and Donald Tuttle, p. 472; Harry Sauvain, pp. 169–73; James Van Horne, p. 76; G. Walter Woodworth, p. 191.

[2] This relationship is implicit in Macaulay's analysis of short- and long-term interest rates but is not rigorously developed. The theorem also lurks in the background in a number of other discussions of bond prices, but, to our best knowledge, has never been stated explicitly. For example, the three elements comprising the definition of duration are all identified by Homer and Leibowitz as affecting bond price volatility but are not put together. Macaulay, pp. 50–51, 61–62; Homer and Leibowitz, pp. 50–53.

is demonstrated below. It will also be demonstrated that this proposition underlies Malkiel's third theorem and that this theorem, like his second theorem, represents a special case that applies only to coupon bonds that sell at or above their par value, and to zero coupon bonds.

Duration is a concept first introduced by Frederick Macaulay to provide more complete summary information about the time structure of a bond than term to maturity.[3] Maturity provides information only about the date of final payment. However, nonzero coupon bonds generate regularly scheduled payments before maturity. Thus, maturity provides an incomplete description of the time pattern of all the payments of a bond. The longer the term to maturity, the higher the coupon rate, or the higher the market yield, the more important are the coupon payments relative to the maturity payment. Duration views a conventional nonzero coupon bond as a zero coupon serial bond with consecutive maturity payments equal to the coupon payments plus a larger payment at final maturity. It thus considers all payments generated by a bond. Duration is defined as:

$$(1) \quad D = \frac{\displaystyle\sum_{t=1}^{n} \frac{(C_t)t}{(1+r_t)^t} + \frac{An}{(1+r_n)^n}}{\displaystyle\sum_{t=1}^{n} \frac{C_t}{(1+r_t)^t} + \frac{A}{(1+r_n)^n}}$$

where

$D =$ Duration
$C =$ Dollar value of coupon payment
$A =$ Dollar value of maturity payment
$t =$ Period in which payment is made
$r =$ Interest rate applicable for period t
$n =$ Maturity period

This formulation is seen to be an ordinary weighted average of the time periods in which payments are to be made. Each period

[3] Macaulay, pp. 45–53. A brief history of duration is traced by Fisher and Weil, pp. 415–16. Although not cited by these authors, J. R. Hicks independently of Macaulay appears to have developed the concept of duration, which he refers to as "average period" (p. 186).

is weighted by the present value of the corresponding payment or price of the maturing serial bond. That is, duration identifies the length of time from the present at which the bond generates the average present value dollar. This period may be considered the average life of the bond. It is equal to the maturity of a single payment zero coupon bond selling at the same market price as the coupon bond, generating the same yield, and having a par value equal to the sum of the total payments generated by the bond when all coupons are reinvested to maturity.

For zero coupon bonds, duration is equal to maturity. For all other bonds, duration is shorter than maturity. However, the relationship between duration and maturity is non-linear and complex. For bonds priced at or above par, duration increases monotonically with maturity but at a decreasing rate. This explains both the much publicized direct relation between price volatility and term to maturity cited earlier and Malkiel's Theorem 3. For discount bonds, the relationship is more complex. Duration increases with maturity to a point before perpetuity, peaks at that point, and subsequently declines.[4] For all bonds, differences between duration and maturity are small for short maturities but increase as maturity increases. Lawrence Fisher and Roman Weil note that for all bonds duration is bounded at perpetuity by $(r+p)/rp$, where r is the yield to maturity and p is the number of times per year inter-

[4] For discount bonds, duration achieves its maximum when

$$n = \frac{1}{r} + \frac{1}{r-c} + \frac{r}{r-c} + \frac{r-c}{cr(1+r)^n}$$

where $r =$ interest yield to maturity, $c =$ coupon rate, $n =$ term to maturity, and declines when term to maturity is larger than the value of the right side of the expression. The first three terms of this equation are equivalent to the expression developed by Macaulay as an approximation of the term to maturity at which duration is at a maximum and no longer increases with increases in term to maturity. The complete expression was derived by G. O. Bierwag and may be obtained from the authors on request. As n approaches infinity, the final term approaches zero and Macaulay's approximation is obtained. See Macaulay, p. 50n. The possibility that the duration of discount bonds can be inversely related to maturity appears to have been overlooked by Malkiel, p. 57.

TABLE 1—DURATION OF SELECTED BONDS
AT MARKET YIELD OF 6 PERCENT

Years to Maturity	Coupon Rate[a]			
	.02	.04	.06	.08
	Years			
1	0.995	0.990	0.985	0.981
5	4.756	4.558	4.393	4.254
10	8.891	8.169	7.662	7.286
20	14.981	12.980	11.904	11.232
50	19.452	17.129	16.273	15.829
100	17.567	17.232	17.120	17.064
∞	17.167	17.167	17.167	17.167

[a] Coupon payments and compounding semi-annually.
Source: Fisher and Weil, p. 418.

est is paid and compounded (p. 418). For par and premium bonds, this boundary value represents maximum duration; for discount bonds it is less than maximum duration. Examples of the relationship between duration, maturity, market yield, and coupon rate are shown in Table 1 developed by Fisher and Weil. Long-term bonds are seen not to be as long as they may appear.

Duration varies inversely with the coupon interest rate. A 50-year 8 percent coupon bond yielding 6 percent is seen from Table 1 to have approximately the same duration as a 20-year 2 percent coupon bond yielding 6 percent. Fisher and Weil proceed to demonstrate the usefulness of duration in optimizing bond portfolio strategy.

The unique role of duration in relating changes in bond price to changes in interest yields may be derived by computing the differential of bond price with respect to interest rate.[5] The price of a bond (P) is equal to the sum of the present values of the stream of coupon payments and of the final payment at maturity.

$$(2) \quad P = \sum_{t=1}^{n} \frac{C_t}{(1+r)^t} + \frac{A}{(1+r)^n}$$

Taking the differential:

$$(3) \quad dP = \left[\sum_{t=1}^{n} \frac{-(C_t)t}{(1+r)^{t+1}} - \frac{An}{(1+r)^{n+1}} \right] dr$$

[5] Other properties of duration are described by William Brock and Roman Weil, and Myron Grove.

Factoring $-1/(1+r)$ from both terms in the bracket:

$$(4) \quad dP = - \left[\sum_{t=1}^{n} \frac{(C_t)t}{(1+r)^t} + \frac{An}{(1+r)^n} \right] \frac{dr}{(1+r)}$$

If all coupon payments are discounted by the yield to maturity, the term in brackets is equivalent to the numerator in the definition of duration specified in equation (1). The denominator of equation (1) is equivalent to the definition of bond price specified in equation (2). Substituting from equations (2) and (4) into equation (1) yields:

$$(5) \quad D = - \frac{dP}{P} \left[\frac{(1+r)}{dr} \right]$$

and solving for dP/P.

$$(6) \quad \frac{dP}{P} = - D \frac{dr}{(1+r)}$$

For continuous discounting, r approaches 0 and equation (6) reduces to:[6]

$$(7) \quad \frac{dP}{P} = - D \, dr$$

Equations (6) and (7) confirm the general theorem stated earlier. For a given change in interest rates, percentage changes in bond prices vary proportionately with duration. The maximum change in price occurs when the duration is at a maximum. It follows that the relationship between changes in bond prices and term to maturity depends on the relationship between duration and maturity. If, as maturity increases, duration also increases, the magnitude of the price change increases although at a declining rate. If, as maturity increases, duration decreases, the magnitude of price changes also declines.[7]

[6] These solutions were derived in a different context by Fisher, pp. 113–14.

[7] For example, in his appendix to ch. 3, Malkiel considers a series of hypothetical 2 percent coupon bonds with maturities ranging from one year to perpetuity. He observes that when the market yield is increased from 5.40 to 5.50 percent, the maximum percentage decline in price occurs for a bond with 50 years to maturity. From equation (1), this is also computed to be the approximate maturity of the bond possessing the maximum duration. Both duration and the magnitude

As the relationship between maturity and duration is complex, the relationship between maturity and bond price volatility is also complex.

The linear mathematical dependency of bond prices on duration and not on maturity has a number of important practical implications for the analysis of interest rate behavior. For example, it may be more useful to derive yield curves with respect to duration than to maturity.[8] In recent years, this would show longer maturity Treasury securities to have approximately similar average lives but greatly different before-or after-tax yields. Likewise, it may be necessary to reconsider the contents of the information obtained from forward rates conventionally calculated from yield curves derived from observed coupon securities. It is unlikely that a rate computed for two coupon bonds of different maturities but similar durations indicates the rate an investor would pay now for a forward security commencing at the maturity of the shorter security and maturing at the maturity of the longer security. This may help to explain the limited success of empirical tests in differentiating among competing theories of the term structure.

Lastly, the use of maturity rather than of duration to compare securities may affect the empirical measurements of both liquidity and default risk premiums. The higher interest rates are, the shorter is duration. Thus, the absolute difference in duration between a given pair of short- and long-term bonds will be greater when interest rates are low than when rates are high. As a result, the finding that in a symmetrical cycle yields on long-term securities exceed yields on short-term securities when yields are low by more than short-term yields exceed long-term yields when yields are high may in part or in total reflect the failure to maintain constant the difference in duration.[9] This measurement

error may also help explain the inverse relationship between liquidity premiums and the level of interest rates reported by some investigators.[10]

The inverse relationship between duration and coupon makes a higher coupon bond a shorter term bond than a lower coupon bond of the same maturity. To the extent bonds possessing higher risks of default carry higher coupons than default free bonds, a comparison of the rates on these two bonds of equal maturity will underestimate the magnitude of the default risk premium in periods of upward sloping yield curves and overestimate the premium in periods of downward sloping yield curves.[11]

REFERENCES

W. Brock and R. L. Weil, *The Axiomatics of Macaulay's Duration*, Univ. of Chicago, May 1971.

S. P. Dobrovolsky, *The Economics of Corporation Finance*, New York 1971.

L. Fisher, "An Algorithm for Finding Exact Rates of Return," *J. Bus. Univ. Chicago*, Jan. 1966, *39*, 111–18.

———, "Determinants of Risk Premiums on Corporate Bonds," *J. Polit. Econ.*, June 1959, *67*, 217–37.

——— and R. L. Weil, "Coping With the Risk of Interest Rate Fluctuations: Returns to Bondholders From Naive and Optional Strategies," *J. Bus. Univ. Chicago*, Oct. 1971, *44*, 408–31.

W. C. Freund, *Investment Fundamentals*, Washington 1970.

M. A. Grove, "A Model of the Maturity Profile of the Balance Sheet," *Metroecon.*, Jan.-Apr. 1966, *18*, 40–55.

J. R. Hicks, *Value and Capital*, Oxford 1939.

S. Homer and M. Leibowitz, *Inside the Yield Book*, Englewood Cliffs 1971.

R. A. Kessel, *The Cyclical Behavior of the*

---

of the price decline diminish as the maturity of the discount bonds increase beyond this point. See Malkiel, p. 80.

[8] This is suggested by Macaulay, pp. 44, 50–51, 51–62, 68.

[9] See Kessel, pp. 81–90. To the extent liquidity premiums are a linear function of the price riskiness of bonds and price risk is a linear function of duration,

liquidity premiums are also a linear function of duration. As, in turn, duration increases with term to maturity but at a decreasing rate, this explains the hypothesis that liquidity premiums increase with term to maturity at a decreasing rate. See Malkiel, pp. 24–28.

[10] See Kessel, pp. 25–28; Van Horne, pp. 347–50.

[11] See Fisher, pp. 217–37.

Term Structure of Interest Rates, New York 1965.

H. A. Latané and D. L. Tuttle, *Security Analysis and Portfolio Management*, New York 1970.

F. R. Macaulay, *Some Theoretical Problems Suggested by the Movements of Interest Rates, Bond Yields and Stock Prices in the U.S. Since 1856*, New York 1938.

B. G. Malkiel, *The Term Structure of Interest Rates*, Princeton 1966.

H. Sauvain, *Investment Management*, Englewood Cliffs 1967.

J. C. Van Horne, *Function and Analysis of Capital Market Rates*, Englewood Cliffs 1970.

———, "Interest-Rate Risk and the Term Structure of Interest Rates," *J. Polit. Econ.*, Aug. 1965, *73*, 344–51.

G. W. Woodworth, *The Money Market and Monetary Management*, 2d ed., New York 1972.

A 'DURATION' FALLACY

Miles Livingston
John Caks

THE JOURNAL OF FINANCE · VOL. XXXII, NO. 1 · MARCH 1977

A "DURATION" FALLACY

MILES LIVINGSTON* AND JOHN CAKS**

I.

FREDERICK MACAULAY DEFINED "duration" to be "…the essence of the time element in a loan."[1] After rejecting several possible measures, he defined the duration of a bond to be

$$D = \left[\sum_{t=1}^{N} \frac{tC}{(1+y)^t} + \frac{NF}{(1+y)^N} \right] \bigg/ \left[\sum_{t=1}^{N} \frac{C}{(1+y)^t} + \frac{F}{(1+y)^N} \right] \tag{1}$$

where D = "duration"
N = periods to maturity
C = coupon paid at the end of each of the next N periods
F = face payment paid N periods hence
y = "yield to maturity" discount rate

Bonds with identical durations presumably have identical "true lengths," identical "effective maturities," etc.

Many authors have recognized that the coupon level of a bond affects its yield to maturity. One explanation that has been proposed is that the observed yields of bonds are related to their durations and not to their maturities; i.e., an N-period bond with duration D is somehow equivalent to a D-period zero-coupon bond and both "should" be discounted by the same rate. Thus Hopewell and Kaufman suggest that "…it may be more useful to derive yield curves with respect to duration than to maturity."[2] This is also suggested by Macaulay.[3] The notion that the yield curve is a function of duration has been often mentioned in the literature.[4]

Another approach to the "coupon effect" problem is based on the following representation of bond price:

$$P = \sum_{t=1}^{N} \frac{C}{(1+R_t)^t} + \frac{F}{(1+R_N)^N} \tag{2}$$

* Concordia University.

** Harris Trust and Savings Bank, Chicago, Illinois. The authors thank the referees, George Kaufman and Roman Weil, for their helpful comments.

1. Macaulay [6], p. 44.

2. Hopewell and Kaufman [5], p. 752.

3. Macaulay [6], p. 68, states "And, of course, yields could (at least theoretically) be corrected by a statistically-derived equation relating yield to duration."

4. Cf. Buse [1] for references to some of the erroneous statements in the literature. Other uses of duration are surveyed in Weil [8].

where $(1 + R_t)^t = \prod_{i=1}^{t}(1 + r_i)$ and r_i is the ith forward rate. The technique for calculating forward rates from market data was described by John Burr Williams [10] and other authors.[5] Having determined the forward rates, it is easy to specify the correct zero-coupon yield curve. It is not apparent how the observed yield curve is related to duration. In fact, Buse [1] and Grant [4] have asserted that there is no relationship. Yet the intuitive appeal of using duration to correct the observed yield curve lingers on.

An interesting example is the recent Note by Carr, Halpern, and McCallum [2]. The authors recount their rediscovery of the method described above. But the interpretation they give of their analysis is that it corrects the yield curve for duration. For example, they state that "the 'true' term to maturity..."[6] of bonds is their duration and that "Fisher and Weil estimated the duration of a 6% 10-year coupon bond to be 7.45 years. The market will price this as a 7.45 year bond..."[7] They conclude that "In other words, the yield curve should be a function of duration and not term to maturity."[8]

We will prove that although duration is a function of the yield curve, the yield curve is not a function of duration. Thus one cannot "correct the yield curve for duration" because bonds with identical durations do not necessarily have identical yields.

II.

Let us assume that bonds with identical durations must have identical yields to maturity. We now demonstrate that the first N forward rates, $N > 2$, determine what the $(N + 1)$th forward rate must be. Given $r_1, r_2, \ldots, r_N$, we know that the yield to maturity of an N-period zero-coupon bond is

$$y = \left[\prod_{i=1}^{N}(1 + r_i) \right]^{1/N} - 1 \qquad (3)$$

A zero-coupon N-period bond has a duration of N. To determine the coupon necessary for an $(N + 1)$-period bond to have duration N and (presumably) a yield to maturity of y, we solve the following equation for C:

$$N = \left[\sum_{t=1}^{N+1} \frac{tC}{(1+y)^t} + \frac{(N+1)F}{(1+y)^{N+1}} \right] \Big/ \left[\sum_{t=1}^{N+1} \frac{C}{(1+y)^t} + \frac{F}{(1+y)^{N+1}} \right] \qquad (4)$$

Defining $Z = \sum_{t=1}^{N+1}(N-t)/(1+y)^t$, it is clear that $0 < Z < \infty$ for $N > 2$ and $0 < y < \infty$. Then equation 4 implies

$$C = \frac{1}{Z} \frac{F}{(1+y)^{N+1}} \qquad (5)$$

5. Similar approaches are taken by Weingartner [9], Fisher and Weil [3], and Buse [1].

6. Carr et al. [2], p. 1288.

7. *ibid.*, p. 1292.

8. *ibid.*, p. 1288.

Given y and N and having derived the appropriate C, we can determine the price, P_{N+1}, of an $(N+1)$-period C-coupon bond that has duration N by use of the standard formula. But it is also true that

$$P_{N+1} = \sum_{i=1}^{N} \frac{C}{(1+R_i)^i} + \frac{C}{(1+R_N)^N(1+r_{n+1})} + \frac{F}{(1+R_N)^N(1+r_{n+1})} \qquad (6)$$

This implies

$$r_{N+1} = \frac{C+F}{\left[P_{N+1} - \sum_{i=1}^{N} \frac{C}{(1+R_i)^i}\right](1+R_N)^N} - 1 \qquad (7)$$

Equation 7 shows that r_{N+1} is exactly determined by the first N forward rates. By making the appropriate substitutions into (7), one can obtain a complicated formula for r_{N+1} in terms of N, F, and $r_1, r_2, \ldots, r_N$.

The analysis given above proves[9] that if bonds with identical durations always have identical yields to maturity, then the entire term structure of interest rates is determined by the first two rates; given r_1 and r_2, we can calculate r_3 and then (recursively) all subsequent forward rates. This result contradicts experience and the theoretical work done on term structure.

Thus, we have demonstrated that the yield curve is not a function of duration and that "correcting the yield curve for duration" is a mistaken concept.

REFERENCES

1. A. Buse. "Expectations, Prices, Coupons, and Yields," *Journal of Finance*, Vol. XXV (September, 1970), pp. 809–818.
2. J. L. Carr, P. J. Halpern, J. S. McCallum. "Correcting the Yield Curve: A Re-Interpretation of the Duration Problem," *Journal of Finance*, Vol. XXIX (September, 1974), pp. 1287–1294.
3. L. Fisher and R. Weil. "Coping with the Risk of Interest Rate Fluctuations: Returns to Bondholders from Naive and Optimal Strategies," *Journal of Business*, Vol. 44 (October, 1971), pp. 408–432.
4. J. A. Grant. "Reply," *Economica*, Vol. 33 (November 1964), pp. 419–422.
5. M. H. Hopewell and G. C. Kaufman. "Bond Price Volatility and Term to Maturity: A Generalized Respecification," *American Economic Review*, Vol LXII (September, 1973), pp. 749–753.
6. F. R. Macaulay. *Some Theoretical Problems Suggested by the Movements of Interest Rates, Bond Yields and Stock Prices in the United States since 1856*, National Bureau of Economic Research, New York, 1938.
7. B. G. Malkiel. "Expectations, Bond Prices, and the Term Structure of Interest Rates," *Quarterly Journal of Economics*, Vol. LXXVI (May, 1962), pp. 197–218.
8. R. Weil. "Macaulay's Duration: An Appreciation," *Journal of Business*, Vol. 46 (October, 1973), pp. 589–592.
9. H. Weingartner. "The Generalized Rate of Return," *Journal of Financial and Quantitative Analysis*, Vol. 1 (September, 1966), pp. 1–29.
10. J. B. Williams. *The Theory of Investment Value*. Cambridge: Harvard University Press, 1938.

9. Our analysis used duration as defined by Macaulay. Weil [8] gives a slightly different definition of duration; using his definition requires only minor changes in the argument. Copies of this proof are available to interested readers from the authors.

DURATION FORTY YEARS LATER

Jonathan E. Ingersoll
Jeffrey Skelton
Roman Weil

JOURNAL OF FINANCIAL AND QUANTITATIVE ANALYSIS
Proceedings Issue - November 1978

DURATION FORTY YEARS LATER

Jonathan E. Ingersoll, Jr., Jeffrey Skelton, and Roman L. Weil*

I. Introduction

The risk inherent in the price fluctuations of bonds has many dimensions. These
include default risk, inflation risk, and call risk. The most important single source of
risk, particularly for government and high-grade corporate bonds, is basis-risk price
fluctuations caused by shifts in interest rates. For a given shift in the yield curve,
and holding other factors unchanged, longer term-to-maturity bonds generally suffer
greater price changes than shorter maturity bonds. This characterization is not exact
because high coupon bonds are less volatile than low coupon bonds. Intuition says that
this is to be expected because, other things being equal, high coupon bonds have a greater
percentage of their value due to the interim coupons and, hence, have a shorter "effective" maturity. Duration may be interpreted as an attempt to quantify this qualitative
statement through the use of a single, numerical measure intended to be used in place of
maturity.

Macaulay [26] originally defined duration as the mean length of time that would pass
before the present value would be returned by a stream of known fixed payments. For a
set of certain payments $X(t)$ and $P(t)$ the present value function giving the present value
of one dollar to be received at time t, duration is given by

$$D \equiv \Sigma\ tX(t)P(t)/\Sigma\ X(t)P(t)$$

or more commonly by

$$D' \equiv \Sigma\ tX(t)e^{-yt}/\Sigma\ X(t)e^{-yt}$$

where y is the continuously compounded yield to maturity for the payment stream $X(t)$.

II. Literature Review

Before examining the theory and use of duration, we review some of the recent literature on the subject. Much of the work on duration written before 1973 was reviewed by
Weil [32]. We do not here reproduce that review, but concentrate on the large body of
literature produced since 1973. Furthermore, the papers mentioned here are not the entire
duration literature, but only represent the directions that the study of the meaning and
uses of duration has taken.

*All, University of Chicago. The research reported on here was partially supported
by the National Science Foundation under grant APR-7614968. The authors thank George G.
Kaufman for the invitation to do this review. Weil acknowledges that the contribution of
his two co-authors is more than proportional.*

Alternative Measures of Duration

Fisher and Weil [16] showed that, under certain restrictive assumptions (of additivity) about how shifts in the yield curve occur, Macaulay's duration could be used to construct an "immunized" bond portfolio; that is, a portfolio with a return guaranteed to be at least as large as that implied by the forward rates of interest. This is accomplished by choosing a bond portfolio with duration equal to the investor's time horizon. Since 1971, several new papers have addressed the problem of immunization using measures of duration different from Macaulay's.

For example, Bierwag and Kaufman [4] approached immunization assuming that changes in the term structure of interest rates occur in a multiplicative fashion rather than additively. That is, if i(t) denotes the function that gives the forward instantaneous rate of interest for future time t, then any shift Δ in i(t) that occurs can be characterized as

$$i(t) = i(t)(1 + \Delta)$$

rather than

$$i(t) = i(t) + \Delta$$

as had been assumed by Fisher and Weil. In order to address this problem, Bierwag and Kaufman defined a duration measure somewhat different from that of Macaulay. The resulting measure of duration was compared with the two versions of Macaulay's measure for bonds of various coupons and maturities, but little difference was found for maturities less than 20 years.

In two other papers Bierwag ([2], [1]) derived continuous coupon versions of duration for one-time additive, multiplicative, and mixed additive-multiplicative shifts in the yield curve:

$$i(t) = i(t)(1 + \Delta_1) + \Delta_2$$

where Δ_1 is the multiplicative component and Δ_2 is the additive component. Bierwag [2] generalized his previous work to account for multiple rather than one-time shifts in the term structure. Khang [23] derived a measure of duration for changes in the yield curve given by

$$i(t) = i(t) + \Delta/(1 + t),$$

one special case in which yields on shorter maturity bonds change by more than those on longer maturity bonds.

Cox, Ingersoll, and Ross [10] demonstrated a general method for determining an alternative measure of duration with its own immunizing procedure that allows consideration of multiple shocks that can change the shape as well as the location of the yield curve. The Cox, Ingersoll, Ross method was derived from a general model of the term structure based on the assumption that the shortest, or spot, rate of interest follows a Gauss-Markov process. They computed this duration measure for a class of specific mean-reverting interest rate processes and established that it differed substantially from Macaulay's duration. Boyle [8] used this duration measure and one derived from a similar model of the term structure proposed by Vasicek [31] to treat the problem of immunization for insurance companies.

Duration Used as a Risk Proxy

Hicks [20] was the first to demonstrate the risky-proxying property of duration. He showed that for a given (infinitesimal) change in yield, the percentage change in an asset's value is proportional to its duration. Since 1972 a number of authors have expanded on Hicks' result.

Hopewell and Kaufman [21], for example, documented a positive relationship between the maturity and interest rate sensitivity of bonds but noted that this relationship does not always hold for coupon bonds selling at a discount. This apparent contradiction disappeared when duration was substituted for maturity as the time measure of the bonds. For coupon bonds selling at par or at a premium, duration and interest rate risk were shown to increase at a decreasing rate with maturity. For discount coupon bonds, both duration and interest rate risk increase and then fall as maturity increases.

The success of duration as a measure of the interest rate sensitivity of a bond prompted Hopewell and Kaufman to suggest that "it may be more useful to derive yield curves with respect to duration rather than maturity." Carr, Halpern, and McCallum [9] expressed the same notion in a slightly different way. Livingston and Caks [25], however, showed that for the yield curve to be a function of duration alone requires forward rates of interest to be uniquely determined by the rates preceding them.

Haugen and Wichern [19] in a more general study of the interest rate sensitivity of financial assets, mathematically restated the results of Hopewell and Kaufman. Boquist, Racette, and Schlarbaum [7] integrated duration concepts and the systematic (beta) risk of bonds and stocks.

Despite the evidence supporting some duration measure as being a proxy for interest rate sensitivity and the usefulness in immunizing bond portfolios, a large body of work dealing with bond portfolio strategies seems to have ignored duration. As Bierwag and Kaufman [5] noted, recently published studies of alternative bond portfolio strategies have produced mixed results in the attempt to find a maturity mix which is optimal in terms of interest rate risk and return because these works compared portfolios which were constructed with no attention to duration. In fact they showed that popular competing strategies such as the "dumbbell" (one long bond, one short bond) and the "ladder" (evenly spaced maturities) may be indistinguishable since both can be constructed to produce identical durations and hence identical interest rate risk.

Other Uses of Duration

A number of recent papers have used duration measures outside the pure immunization framework. Durand [13] suggested integrating time concepts such as duration with the usual profitability analysis of capital budgeting. Grove [18] used duration in a formal treatment of risk and the relative changes in the values of asset and liability streams. Following Durand and Grove, Blocher and Stickney [6] examined the effect of changes in the firm's required rate of return on the duration of its projects and suggested project selection rules appropriate for the manager's risk tolerance. Bierwag and, Khang [1978] showed that a duration-derived immunization strategy is optimal given that an investor's preferences are adequately described by Fishburn's [15] measure of "downside" risk. Tito and Wagner [30] suggested evaluating pension fund managers on the basis of portfolio return for a given duration, and Keintz and Stickney [22] considered the problems and advisability of using duration concepts to immunize pension funds from interest rate changes.

Evaluation of Prior Work

The preceding review makes clear that the duration literature has taken new directions since we last looked at it in 1973. A number of different measures of duration derived from alternative assumptions about how the yield curve changes have been proposed and further claims on the usefulness of Macaulay's duration as a measure of interest rate risk have been presented. Several new uses have also been suggested. Largely missing, however, are any equilibrium considerations in modeling the stochastic process governing the yield structure. This issue is discussed in the next section of this paper. Also lacking for a meaningful evaluation are empirical comparisons of competing duration measures.

The original Fisher and Weil paper was the first to use actual bond data to determine the efficacy of an immunization strategy. Since then, a number of theoretical papers have expanded on their methods. We are unable, however, to find any work that goes beyond either simulations or appeals to experience for empirical verification.

Fisher and Weil and other authors assumed additive shifts in the term structure that cannot occur in equilibrium in a competitive market. Nevertheless, Fisher and Weil tested the implications of their theorem with real data to show that the implied immunization strategy, while not perfect, could yield a substantial reduction in risk over the 30 years examined.

Many of those who assumed other types of changes in the yield curve also did so without considering whether such shifts can occur in equilibrium or do occur in fact. In addition these theoretical results are unsupported by any empirical tests to determine if bond portfolios can actually be immunized. Furthermore, in light of the recent work by Boyle [8] and Cox, Ingersoll, and Ross [10] suggesting that traditional duration measures give, at times, grossly misleading measurements of risk, we are justified in concluding only that we have made but one small step in risk reduction along the road to immunization.

III. Duration Is Not a General Risk Proxy

Most of the literature surveyed above uses duration as a proxy for interest rate risk. In the next two sections we show that duration cannot be a risk proxy for markets in competitive equilibrium except under very restrictive conditions. The steps are as follows:

(A) Some writers have corrupted Macaulay's definition in a way that uses yield to maturity in the present value calculations, rather than forward interest rates. We show that the resulting definition of duration cannot serve as a risk proxy unless the term structure is flat.

(B) It is acceptable to use Macaulay's (Bierwag's) definition of duration for risk measurement when the yield curve is not flat only so long as all changes in the yield curve are infinitesimal and of uniform constant (proportional) magnitude.

(C) Except for the singular cases discussed in the Appendix, the occurrence of non-infinitesimal, uniform changes in the yield curve implies arbitrage opportunities.

Thus, noninfinitesimal uniform changes in interest rates assumed by many authors cannot occur in a competitive equilibrium.

Using Yield to Maturity for Discounting Causes Problems

For a set of certain payments, $X(t)$, and the present value function giving the present value of one dollar at time t, $P(t)$, duration was defined by Macaulay as

$$(1) \qquad D \equiv \Sigma\, tX(t)P(t)/\Sigma\, X(t)P(t).$$

In practice this measure has been generally corrupted (even by its originator) to

$$(2) \qquad D' \equiv \Sigma\, tX(t)e^{-yt}/\Sigma\, X(t)e^{-yt}$$

or the discrete period discounted equivalent. In (2) y is the continuously-compounded yield-to-maturity for the payment stream $X(t)$.[1] These definitions of duration are equivalent if and only if the discount rate implicit in the present value function is the constant y. We prove below (Theorem 2) that when the two measures differ, it is only the original (1) which is appropriate for risk measurement. Nevertheless, the second rendering is much more commonly used in practice presumably because of the relative difficulty of determining the present value function $P(t)$.

Hicks [20] independently derived an elasticity measure, which he called "average period," equivalent to the second definition above and was the first to point out its risk-proxying properties. If $V \equiv \Sigma\, X(t)P(t) \equiv \Sigma\, X(t)e^{-yt}$ is the value of the payment stream, then from (2)

$$(3) \qquad \frac{dV}{V} = -D'dy\,.$$

Thus, for a given infinitesimal change in yield, the percentage change in an asset's value is proportional to its duration. This theorem has been rediscovered by Samuelson [29], Redington [28], Fisher [17],[2] Hopewell and Kaufman [21], and perhaps others. This relationship would appear to justify the use of the second duration measure (2) to quantify relative basis risk *as long as the yields on assets of different durations always changed by the same amount*. In general, however, this cannot occur. All yields to maturity cannot change identically for an arbitrary set of assets with fixed payments unless the yield curve is flat.

Theorem 1: Yields to maturity on all assets with known fixed payments can change by the same amount if and only if the yield curve is flat (Yields to maturity on pure discount bonds of all maturities are the same) and makes a parallel shift.

------

[1]If the payment stream has negative cash flows, then multiple yield-to-maturity solutions are possible. In this case, the second duration definition may not give a unique value. Typically duration is used for bonds for which this will not be a problem.

[2]Fisher [17] was the first to use continuous discounting in Hicks' theorem. Earlier authors had all derived the result $dV/V = -D'dy/(1 + y)$ or the equivalent.

Proof: Let $R(t)$ denote the yield to maturity on a pure discount bond of maturity t, i.e., $P(t) = \exp[-R(t)t]$. Now if the yield curve is flat, $R(t) \equiv r$, then all yields to maturity equal r before the shift and $r + dr$ after the shift, and sufficiency is trivially proved. We prove necessity by contradiction. Assume that all yields do make an identical change for a sloped yield curve. Consider two maturities, t_1 and t_2, with different yields. Without loss of generality we may take $R(t_2) > R(t_1)$. Consider an asset with positive payments at times t_1 and t_2 and no other payments. Its yield, the solution y, to

$$(4) \qquad V = \sum_{i=1}^{2} X(t_i)\exp[-R(t_i)t_i] = \sum_{i=1}^{2} X(t_i)e^{-yt_i},$$

satisfies $R(t_1) < y < R(t_2)$ since the exponential function is monotonic. If an infinitesimal shift of the assumed type occurs, then $dy = dR(t_1) = dR(t_2)$. This interest rate shift causes a value change of

$$(5) \qquad dV = -\sum_{i=1}^{2} X(t_i)t_i \exp[-R(t_i)t_i]dR(t_i) = -\sum_{i=1}^{2} X(t_i)t_i e^{-yt_i}dy.$$

Now multiplying V in (4) by t_1 and adding dV/dy from (5)

$$(6) \qquad t_1 V - \frac{dV}{dy} = (t_1 - t_2)X(t_2)e^{-R(t_2)t_2} = (t_1 - t_2)X(t_2)e^{-yt_2}.$$

But this can be true only if $R(t_2) = y$ resulting in a contradiction. Thus, yields to maturity cannot make identifiable shifts on all of an arbitrary set of assets if the yield curve is not flat.

$$Q.E.D.$$

We have just demonstrated the unsuitability of the second duration measure (2) as a general risk proxy. Under some circumstances we can go further and establish the sign of the relative bias. With a rising term structure, the change in yields to maturity for bonds of the same maturity caused by a uniform displacement of the yield curve is smaller the higher the coupon rate of the bond. Thus, duration as given in (2) would tend to overstate the basis risk of high coupon bonds relative to low coupon bonds. For a falling term structure, the opposite is true. The relative risk of low coupon bonds is overstated.

Thus, Hicks' result is not a dynamic relationship which can be used in risk measurement; rather it must be considered only as a comparative statics result for a one time change in the level of a flat yield curve.

Macaulay's Definition Will Serve as a Risk Proxy under Restrictive Conditions

Despite the shortcomings of the duration measure generally used, we should point out that it is not theoretically inconsistent to use the original definition of duration (1) for risk measurement even if the yield curve is not flat, so long as it makes only constant uniform infinitesimal shifts. Apparently, this result has not been reported previously although Fisher and Weil [16] proved a similar theorem discussed below. To justify the use of the original duration definition in risk measurement for this special case we prove the following theorem.

Theorem 2: For infinitesimal shifts in the yield curve, the percentage change in value of any asset with fixed payments is proportional to Macaulay's duration measure as defined in (1) if and only if the entire yield curve (the continuously-compounded yields-to-maturity R(t) on pure discount bonds) undergoes a uniform additive displacement, $dR(t) = dR$ for all t.

Proof: An asset's value is $V = \Sigma\, X(t)e^{-R(t)t}$, thus

(7a)
$$\frac{dV}{V} = \frac{-\Sigma\, tX(t)e^{-R(t)t}dR(t)}{V} = -DdR$$

if $dR(t) \equiv dR$. This proves sufficiency. To prove necessity, recall that the duration of a pure discount bond is its maturity. For two pure discount bonds of maturities t_1 and t_2

(7b)
$$\frac{dP(t_1)/P(t_1)}{dP(t_2)/P(t_2)} = \frac{-t_1 dR(t_1)}{-t_2 dR(t_2)} .$$

which equals t_1/t_2 only if $dR(t_1) = dR(t_2)$.

For discrete period-by-period discounting Theorem 2 may be restated as follows:

Corollary: If all (per-period) discount factors (the effective per-period discount rate plus unity) undergo the same *proportional* change, the percentage changes in asset values are proportional to Macaulay's duration.

Proof: Define the discount factor for maturity t to be p(t), then $[p(t)]^{-t} \equiv \exp[-R(t)t]$. Differentiating

(8)
$$-t[p(t)]^{-t-1}dp(t) = -te^{-R(t)t}dR(t)$$

$$\frac{dp(t)}{p(t)} = dR(t) .$$

Thus, if $dp(t)/p(t)$ is the same for all t, then so is $dR(t)$ and by the previous theorem percentage asset value changes are proportional to Macaulay's duration.

$Q.E.D.$

For *infinitesimal* multiplicative shifts in the yield curve a similar result can be proved for Bierwag's [3] measure of duration

(9)
$$D_B \equiv \frac{\Sigma\, tR(t)P(t)X(t)}{\Sigma\, P(t)X(t)} .$$

Theorem 3: For infinitesimal shifts in the yield curve, the percentage change in the value of any asset with positive payments is proportional to Bierwag's duration measure (9) if and only if the entire yield curve undergoes a uniform multiplicative displacement, $dR(t) = R(t)dr/r$ for all t.

Corollary: For infinitesimal shifts in the yield curve, the percentage change in the value of any asset with positive payments is proportional to a weighted combination of Bierwag's and Macaulay's duration measures $aD_B/r + (1 - a)D$ if and only if the entire yield curve undergoes a uniform displacement, linear in R(t), $dR(t) = [aR(t)/r + (1 - a)]dr$.

Proofs: The proofs are exactly like that of Theorem 2 above.

Noninfinitesimal Uniform Shifts in the Yield Curve Imply Arbitrage

Thus far we have examined only infinitesimal changes in interest rates. Fisher and Weil [16], Bierwag [3], and Bierwag and Kaufman [5] explicitly considered large interest rate changes in proving theorems apparently more general than those above. Fisher and Weil (Bierwag) demonstrated that if all forward rates of interest change by the same amount (proportionally), then a portfolio of positive payments is *immunized* with respect to a holding period of length T if its Macaulay (Bierwag) duration is T ($R(T)T$). An asset is said to be immunized against a shift in interest rates if its postshift holding period return is at least as great as the holding period return would have been in the absence of the shift.[3]

Since holding period returns can only be measured at the end of the period in a stochastic environment, these results apply only in the context of a one-time shift in the yield curve. However, by modifying the theorems slightly we can obtain similar dynamic results. Specifically we show that if it is possible to construct a duration matching portfolio of positive payments for the desired holding period, then any uniform shift in the yield curve will result in a greater profit being realized on the portfolio than on an equal investment in a pure discount bond whose maturity matches the holding period. By continually updating this portfolio strategy, immunization can be achieved over any holding period even if multiple interest rate shifts are possible.

Theorem 4. A portfolio of positive payments with duration T and current value V equal to the present value of one dollar in T years (i.e., $V = \exp[-R(T)T]$, will, after a noninfinitesimal shift of size δ in the entire yield curve $R(t)$,[4] be worth more than the new present value of one dollar in T years (i.e., $V' > \exp[-R(T)T - \delta T]$).

Proof: To prove this theorem we first consider only portfolios of two separate payments at times t_1 and t_2 with $t_1 < T < t_2$. The general case follows immediately by induction. Consider two pure discount unit bonds of maturities t_1 and t_2. The prices of these bonds before and after the interest rate shift are denoted by $V_i = \exp[-R(t_i)t_i]$ and $V'_i = \exp[-R'(t_i)t_i]$ where $R'(t)t = R(t) + \delta$. Consider a portfolio holding n_1, $n_2 > 0$ of these bonds with current value V and duration T, i.e.,

(10a)
$$n_1 V_1 + n_2 V_2 = V \equiv e^{-R(T)T}$$

(10b)
$$\frac{n_1 V_1}{V} t_1 + \frac{n_2 V_2}{V} t_2 = T$$

---

[3]Redington [28] was the first to use the term immunization in this context.

[4]A constant "parallel" shift in the forward rate function $i(t)$ which Fisher and Weil assume is equivalent to the same constant "parallel" shift in the yield curve $R(t)$ assumed here. $R(t) \equiv -\ln[P(t)]/t$ and $P(t) \equiv \exp[-\int_0^t i(s)ds]$. Thus,

$$R(t) = \frac{1}{t} \int_0^t i(s)ds$$
$$i(t) = -\frac{\partial}{\partial t} \ln[P(t)] = R(t) + t\frac{\partial R(t)}{\partial t}$$

and a constant shape-preserving shift of δ in either curve must result in the identical shift in the other curve.

or

$$n_i V_i = V(t_j - T)/(t_j - t_i).$$

Now since

$$V'_i = V_i e^{\delta t_i},$$

the post-shift value of the portfolio is

$$(11) \qquad V' = n_1 V'_1 + n_2 V'_2 = n_1 V_1 e^{-\delta t_1} + n_2 V_2 e^{-\delta t_2}$$

$$= \frac{V}{t_2 - t_1} [(t_2 - T)e^{-\delta t_1} + (T - t_1)e^{-\delta t_2}]$$

after substituting for $n_i V_i$. The post shift ratio of the value of this portfolio to
that of the pure discount bond of maturity T is

$$Q \equiv V'/\exp[-R'(T)T] = V'e^{\delta T}/V.$$

Evaluating this expression using (10) gives

$$(12) \qquad Q = \frac{(t_2 - T)e^{\delta(T - t_1)} + (T - t_1)e^{\delta(T - t_2)}}{t_2 - t_1},$$

with

$$(13) \qquad \frac{dQ}{d\delta} = \frac{(t_2 - T)(T - t_1)}{t_2 - t_1} [e^{\delta(T - t_1)} - e^{\delta(T - t_2)}] \gtrless 0 \text{ as } \delta \gtrless 0.$$

$$\frac{d^2Q}{d\delta^2} = \frac{(t_2 - T)(T - t_1)}{t_2 - t_1} [(T - t_1)e^{\delta(T - t_1)} + (t_2 - T)e^{\delta(T - t_2)}] > 0.$$

From (13) we see that this ratio reaches a unique minimum at a zero shift where it has
the value one. For any nonzero shift, the portfolio value will be greater than that of
the pure discount bond. This proof can be trivially extended to portfolios of three or
more payments by showing that a portfolio of payments at t_1, t_2, and t_3 is more valuable
after the shift than two pure discount bonds of maturities T and t_3 which, in turn, is
more valuable than a pure discount bond of maturity T' equal to the duration of the three
payments.   Q.E.D.

Theorem 4 includes Theorem 2 as a special case. For a constant infinitesimal shift
in the yield curve, a portfolio of final payments will suffer a percentage change in
value exactly equal to that of a pure discount bond whose maturity matches the duration
of the portfolio. For a noninfinitesimal increase (decrease) in interest rates, the portfolio value will decrease by less (increase by more) in percentage terms than the discount bond.

While this result is a straightforward extension of the previous theorem, it is in
fact "too good." If it were known that the yield curve could change only by a constant

noninfinitesimal shift, then it is apparent that arbitrage[5] profits could be earned by buying two discount bonds and shorting a third with an intermediate maturity equal to the duration of the long position. Obviously in such a world the only bonds anyone would hold would be those with the shortest and longest durations--in the limit, instantaneous shorts and perpetual discounts. Clearly this is an absurd conclusion, which in any case would lead to an undefined yield curve. The only way to avoid this dilemma is to reject the premise of the theorem. A constant noninfinitesimal shift in the yield curve cannot be the *only* possible type of change.[6] But if it is not, then duration cannot be a complete measure of risk. To get a better understanding of this statement, consider the following example.

Example. Suppose that the state of the world is to be revealed one instance hence. The yield curve at that time will be either $R_1(t)$ or $R_2(t) = R_1(t) + \delta$, for $\delta > 0$, with probabilities $p > 0$ and $1 - p > 0$ respectively. Obviously δ must be a constant for, if we wish to have a chance that the yield curve will only make "parallel" shifts, we must begin with "parallel" outcomes. If investors are neutral towards this risk, then the pre-shift prices of discount bonds will be

$$(14) \qquad P_0(t) = pe^{-R_1(t)t} + (1 - p)e^{-[R_1(t) + \delta]t}$$

The yield curve will be

$$(15) \qquad R_0(t) = -\log[P_0(t)]/t = R_1(t) - \log[p + (1 - p)e^{-\delta t}]/t.$$

Only for $\delta = 0$ or $p = 0, 1$ will the second term be a constant. Except for these singular cases, with only one final yield curve, the initial yield curve will not be a simple translation of the final possibilities. Rather it will be less steeply sloped (or more downward sloping) starting between the two at $R_0(0) = R_1(0) + (1 - p)\delta$ and approaching the lower curve $R_1(t)$ asymptotically. Thus, yields will not all change identically; yields on longer bonds will change by more (less) than shorter yields if there is a general increase (decrease) in interest rates.

Not surprisingly a similar result can be demonstrated as well for the remaining types of shifts in the yield curve proposed by other authors writing on duration. Whenever it can be shown that some "duration-matching" strategy will create a portfolio which leaves an investor better off than holding a pure discount under some conditions and no worse off under all conditions, then it can only be concluded that arbitrage possibilities would prevent the yield curve from behaving in the assumed manner. Thus the assumptions of constant, proportional, linear, and decreasing in term noninfinitesimal shifts in the yield curve by Fisher and Weil [16], Bierwag and Kaufman [4], Bierwag [3], and Khang [23]

---

[5]"Arbitrage" is used here in the qualified sense that it is known with certainty that only constant shifts in the yield curve will occur.

[6]As the example below indicates, changes in the yield curve can consist solely of constant noninfinitesimal shifts if they occur at any instant with vanishingly small probability. However, in this case duration is not the proper risk measure. This issue is addressed in the appendix.

are all impossible under equilibrium. Of course, under certain conditions the corresponding infinitesimal shifts may occur. This is examined in the next section.

IV. Interest Rate Dynamics Required for Duration
Measures to be Proper Risk Proxies

Generally, as we have seen, duration measures will not serve as a proper proxy for risk. Under certain restrictive conditions, however, it will. The only questions remaining are what type of equilibrium conditions could give rise to such behavior and are these conditions a reasonably accurate description of the world.

In answering these questions we shall examine the case when the spot rate of interest is the single state variable of importance conveying all relevant information about the default-free bond market to investors.[7] This is the logical place to start for with more than one stochastic state variable it is not obvious what, exactly, is meant by the term "basis risk."[8] In the previous section we saw that duration could be a proper risk proxy only if the yield curve does not make discontinuous shifts; therefore, the interest rate must have a continuous sample path. Furthermore, since it is a complete description of the bond market, it must be a Markov random variable with evolution governed by the Ito differential equation

(16) $$dr = b(r)dt + a(r)dz$$

where b is the expected drift in the spot rate, a^2 is the instantaneous variance of change, and dz is a Gauss-Wiener process.[9]

The value V of an asset with a default-free payment stream $X(t)$ will possess the dynamics

(17) $$dV = [\alpha(r,t)V - X(t)]dt + \omega(r,t)Vdz$$

where α is the continuously-compounded expected rate of return and ω^2 is the variance of return. Using Ito's lemma the following relationships can be derived

(18a) $$\alpha(r,t)V = \frac{1}{2} a^2(r)V_{rr} + b(r)V_r + V_t + X(t)$$

---

[7] Results for multiple state variables have similar qualitative properties but can be obtained only through significantly greater manipulations.

[8] We could permit additional nonstochastic state variables and still have a meaningful interpretation of basis risk as we do in section V. In general with n sources of uncertainty there would be n types of basis risk.

[9] For any interesting results we must obviously use a continuous time model since if the yield curve only changes infinitesimally at fixed discrete points of time, we have for all practical purposes a static model. See Cox, Ingersoll, and Ross [11] for a complete development of diffusion-process term structure models. If a and b are functions of time, the analysis is unchanged. We suppress consideration of nonstationary Markov processes for expositional convenience.

(18b)
$$\omega(r,t) = V_r \, a(r)/V$$

where subscripts on V denote partial differentiation. From (17) and (18b) the percentage
change in the value of the asset attributable to an unexpected shift in the interest rate
is proportion to $V_r \, a(r)/V$. Since $a(r)$ is common to all assets, V_r/V is a proper metric
of basis risk. This is a formal verification of the perhaps heuristic use of this measure in the previous section.

Since (17) holds for all assets with fixed payments whose values are dependent solely
upon the spot rate and time, the returns on all of these assets must be instantaneously
perfectly correlated. Consequently we have the no-arbitrage condition[10] for two assets
i and j

(19)
$$\frac{\alpha_i(r,t) - r}{\omega_i(r,t)} = \frac{\alpha_j(r,t) - r}{\omega_j(r,t)} = \lambda(r).$$

In (17) and (18a) α may have an induced dependency upon time if the asset matures or ex-
pires or the fixed payments are otherwise time-dependent. There is, however, no direct
time dependence, because the stochastic interest rate process was assumed to be stationary. Because all the time dependency of α is asset-specific, the market price of basis
risk, λ, must be time independent as indicated in (19).

Substituting (19) and (18b) into (18a) we derive the general valuation equation

(20)
$$\frac{1}{2} a^2(r) \, V_{rr} + [b(r) - \lambda(r) \, a(r)]V_r - rV + V_t + X(t) = 0.$$

Equation (20) together with appropriate boundary conditions can be used to value any
interest rate dependent security. In particular a pure discount bond maturing with unit
value at time t_i must satisfy (20) subject to $V(r,t_i) = 1$. Denoting a discount bond with
time until maturity T by $P(r,T)$ as before then, since $dt = -dT$, we have

(21)
$$\frac{1}{2} a^2(r)P_{rr} + b^*(r)P_r - rP - P_T = 0.$$

From Theorem 2 Macaulay duration will be a valid measure of basis risk only if the
entire yield curve shifts by a constant. Since changes in r are the only source of uncertainty, this requires that the yield curve, $R(r,T) \equiv -\log[P(r,T)]/T$, be given by

(22)
$$R(r,T) = f(r) + h(T).$$

Furthermore, $R(r, 0) \equiv r$ so $f(r) = r$ and $h(0) = 0$. The dynamics of a constant maturity
yield are thus $dR(r, T) = dr$ independent of T as required. Substituting (22) for
$f(r) = r$ into (21) we obtain

---

(23)
$$[\frac{1}{2} a^2(r)T^2 - b^*(r)T + h'(T)T + h(T)]P(r,T) = 0$$

and since $P(r,T) > 0$

(24)
$$b^*(r) - \frac{1}{2} a^2(r)T = h'(T) + h(T)/T.$$

The right hand side of (24) is independent of r; therefore, the left hand side must be as well. But since b^* does not depend upon T while $\frac{1}{2} a^2(r)T$ obviously does, the left hand side of (24) will be independent of r for all T only if both a and b^* are constants.

In this case investors value bonds *as if* changes in the interest rate were normally distributed (with mean b^* and variance a^2 independent of the current level) and the expected rate of return on all bonds were the spot interest rate.[11] While such a characterization might be reasonably accurate over short intervals of a year, as the evidence of Fama [14] would suggest, it could not describe investors' long-term beliefs. The solution to the pricing equation (21) for a and b^* constants has been given by Merton [27] as

(25)
$$P(r,T) = \exp[-rT - \frac{1}{2} b^*T^2 + \frac{1}{6} a^2 T^3].$$

For $T > (b^* + \sqrt{b^{*2} + 2ra^2})/a^2$, this pricing function is increasing with maturity. Furthermore, it has a limiting value of infinity rather than zero. Thus, we must conclude that this justification for the use of duration as a measure of basis risk is flawed at least for long holding periods, the range of primary concern.

From Theorem 3 Bierwag duration will be a valid measure of basis risk only if the yield curve always makes proportional shifts. For the continuous time model here this requires that

(26)
$$R(r, T) = h(T)f(r) = H(T)f(r)/T.$$

The definition $R(r, 0) = r$ requires that $f(r) = r$, $h(0) = 1$, giving $\partial R = R\partial r/r$. Substituting (26) into (21) we obtain

(27)
$$\frac{a^2(r)}{2r} H^2(T) - \frac{b^*(r)}{r} H(T) - 1 + H'(T) = 0.$$

This equation can be satisfied in general only if $a^2(r)$ and $b^*(r)$ are proportional to r; that is, the stochastic evolution of the interest rate is according to

(28)
$$dr = krdt + \sigma\sqrt{r}dz$$

This is a special case of the process examined by Cox, Ingersoll, and Ross [11]. While

---

[11]The true distribution of interest rate changes need not be a level-independent. For example we could have the mean reverting Orstein-Uhlenbeck process with $b(r) = \beta(\mu - r)$ if $\lambda(r) = -\beta r$ giving $b = \beta\mu$ a constant.

this process does preclude the possibility of negative interest rates unlike the Gaussian model above, it does possess a similar undesirable property. With probability one the interest rate will eventually be "trapped" at zero. Consequently for any value of k no matter how large, the yield curve will be downward sloping and approach zero in the limit for long maturities.

The assumptions of linear and decreasing-in-term shifts made by Bierwag [3] and Khang [23] require yield curves of the form

(29)
$$R(r, T) = r + H(T)A(r)$$

$$R(r, T) = \frac{r}{1 + T} + H(T)$$

respectively, with $H(0) = 0$ in each case. Neither of these forms can be obtained as a solution to equation (21).

In the last two sections we have discussed and dismissed the possible theoretical arguments for the use of duration as a measure of basis risk. Nevertheless, the two cases examined above may provide a practical justification for Macaulay or Bierwag duration provided that the "true" interest rate process is "sufficiently close" to one of the two models for reasonably long periods of time. This is a question requiring empirical verification which we shall not address here. In the next section, however, we develop an alternate measure for basis risk for a general class of interest rate processes and compare it to duration. This analysis provides a method for determining a metric to measure the basis risk similarity of two different stochastic processes.

V. A Measure of Risk for General Interest Rate Shifts

In the previous section we concluded that the conditions under which Macaulay duration would be a proper measure for basis risk were, at best, unrealistic. In this section we derive basis risk measures for more realistic assumptions about changes in the yield curve and examine the error inherent in the traditional duration measure. To obtain such a measure we first require a consistent theory of the term structure and its relationship to the stochastic dynamics of the spot rate, i.e., to basis risk.

To allow for many possible interest rate effects we postulate the following general stochastic evolution of the spot rate

(29a)
$$dr = [v + k(\mu - r)]dt + \sigma dz$$

(29b)
$$dv = -\beta v dt + \eta [dr - E(dr)]$$

$$= -\beta v dt + \eta \sigma dz .$$

The expected drift of the interest rate has two components, a regression back towards its mean level of μ and an extrapolative "velocity" v. In the regressive term, k measures the speed of adjustment and $1/k$ may be interpreted as a measure of mean reversion time. This autoregressive model (with $v = \beta = \eta = 0$) is consistent with the Keynesian hypothesis of "normal backwardation" and has been examined by Vasicek [30]. Extrapolative interest rate models were originally proposed by Duesenberry [12]. From (29b), if the interest rate changes by more (less) than expected, then v is increased (decreased) proportionately, and at the same time the extrapolative component of past changes is damped at the rate β. Thus any unexpected change in the spot rate is perpetuated into the future with ever decreasing magnitude.

An alternate interpretation of this model may be given as follows. Define $\bar{r} \equiv (r - v/\eta - k\mu/\delta)\delta/(\delta - k)$, $\delta \equiv \beta + \eta$, $\hat{\eta} \equiv \eta(1 - k/\delta)$, and $\hat{k} \equiv k(1 - \eta/\delta)$; then from (29)

$$dr = [\hat{\eta}(r - \bar{r}) + \hat{k}(\mu - r)]dt + \sigma dz$$

(30)

$$d\bar{r} = \delta(r - \bar{r})dt.$$

$\bar{r}$ is then an exponential weighted average of past rates with mean lag $1/\delta$

(31)
$$\bar{r}(t) = \delta \int_0^\infty e^{-\delta s} r(t - s)ds$$

and the drift of r is regressive towards its long-run constant mean μ and extrapolative away from the average of recent values $\bar{r}$.

For the model postulated, the price of a unit discount bond will satisfy the equation[12]

(32) $\quad \frac{1}{2} \sigma^2 P_{rr} + \frac{1}{2} \eta^2 \sigma^2 P_{vv} + \eta\sigma^2 P_{rv} + [v + k(\mu - r)]P_r - \beta v P_v - rP - P_T = 0.$

The solution to (32) is

$$P(r, v, T) = \exp[A(T)r + B(T)v + C(T)]$$

where

$$A(T) = -(1 - e^{-kT})/k$$

(33)

$$B(T) = -[\beta(1 - e^{-kT}) - k(1 - e^{-\beta T})]/k\beta(\beta - k)$$

and $C(T)$ is a maturity dependent function not affecting risk.

The dynamics of the bond price are

(34) $\quad dP/P = rdt - [A(T) + \eta B(T)]\sigma dz.$

Thus the quantity $\phi \equiv A(T) + \eta B(T)$ measures relative basis risk. If ϕ increases linearly

---

[12]See Cox, Ingersoll, and Ross [11] or Vasicek [31] for a general derivation of the term structure equation. In (32) it is assumed that the expected rate of return on all bonds equals the current spot rate. As shown in (19), (20), and (21) any risk premium can be incorporated in to the drift terms.

with maturity, then Macaulay duration is a correct measure of basis risk. On the other hand if ϕ increases with T at an increasing (decreasing) rate, then duration will overstate the relative risk of short (long) maturity bonds. The following properties of ϕ will be useful in our discussion to follow:

(35a)
$$\phi(T) - T + (\eta - k)T^2/2 \qquad\qquad T \to 0$$

(35b)
$$\phi(\infty) = [1 + \eta/\beta]/k$$

(35c)
$$\frac{\partial \phi}{\partial T} = e^{-kT} + \frac{\eta}{k - \beta}(e^{-\beta T} - e^{-kT}) > 0$$

(35d)
$$\frac{\partial^2 \phi}{\partial T^2} = -ke^{-kT} - \frac{\eta}{k - \beta}(\beta e^{-\beta T} - ke^{-kT}) \gtrless 0 .$$

Now if $\eta = k = 0$, then there is no mean reversion or extrapolation, and this model reduces to the random walk model of the previous section. If $\eta = k$, then the extrapolative and regressive forces are equal; if in addition $\beta = 0$, then the extrapolation is not damped out, and the extrapolative and regressive forces balance for all time. In either case from (35a, c) $\phi = T$, and Macaulay duration will be a valid measure of risk. If $k > \eta$, the regressive term dominates; then $\partial^2 \phi / \partial T^2 < 0$ and duration overstates the risk of long-term-to-maturity bonds. If $\eta > k$, then in the short term, extrapolation dominates; however, it is damped out so (if $\beta \neq 0$) regression dominates in the long-term end of the yield curve. In this case the relative risk of intermediate term-to-maturity ($T \overset{\sim}{\gtrless} T*$)

(36)
$$T* \equiv \frac{1}{k} - \beta \log \left[\frac{k(\beta - k + \eta)}{\eta\beta}\right]$$

is understated by duration relative to both shorter and longer bonds.

Table 1 displays this risk measure for various parameter values. The qualitative properties mentioned earlier are clear in this table; however, the table further demonstrates how severe an error can be made by using duration to proxy risk.

RELATIVE BASIS RISK MEASURE φ FOR PURE DISCOUNT BONDS OF VARIOUS MATURITIES UNDER A REGRESSIVE-EXTRAPOLATIVE INTEREST RATE MODEL:

$$dr = [n(r - \bar{r}) + \hat{k}(\mu - r)]dt + \sigma dz$$

$$\bar{r}(t) = \delta \int_0^\infty e^{-\delta s} r(t - s)ds$$

Panel A
δ = .5 (Mean lag in r̄ = 2 years)

T =	k = .0 n = .0	.01	.1	.5	k = .01 n = .0	.01	.1	.5
1	1.00	1.00	1.04	1.25	1.00	1.00	1.04	1.24
3	3.00	3.03	3.31	5.25	2.96	2.98	3.27	5.18
5	5.00	5.06	5.71	11.25	4.88	4.94	5.57	11.03
7	7.00	7.10	8.16	19.25	6.76	6.86	7.89	18.73
10	10.00	10.16	11.89	35.00	9.52	9.67	11.33	33.70
25	25.00	25.47	30.63	181.25	22.12	22.53	27.15	166.12
50	50.00	50.98	61.88	625.00	39.35	40.12	48.79	572.00

T =	k = .1 n = .0	.01	.1	.5	k = .5 n = .0	.01	.1	.5
1	0.95	0.96	0.99	1.19	0.77	0.79	0.82	1.00
3	2.59	2.62	2.87	4.63	1.55	1.57	1.75	3.00
5	3.93	3.99	4.53	9.26	1.84	1.86	2.16	5.00
7	5.03	5.11	5.93	14.86	1.94	1.97	2.35	7.00
10	6.32	6.43	7.61	24.72	1.98	2.03	2.45	10.00
25	9.18	9.36	11.41	88.28	2.00	2.04	2.50	25.00
50	9.93	10.14	12.41	210.27	2.00	2.04	2.50	50.00

Panel B
δ = 1 (Mean lag in r̄ = 1 year)

T =	k = .0 n = .0	.01	.1	.5	k = .01 n = .0	.01	.1	.5
1	1.00	1.00	1.04	1.21	1.00	1.00	1.03	1.21
3	3.00	3.02	3.22	4.44	2.96	2.98	3.17	4.39
5	5.00	5.04	5.43	8.16	4.88	4.92	5.30	7.98
7	7.00	7.06	7.65	12.06	6.76	6.82	7.40	11.68
10	10.00	10.09	10.99	18.01	9.52	9.60	10.46	17.20
25	25.00	25.24	27.65	48.00	22.12	22.34	24.48	42.65
50	50.00	50.49	55.43	98.00	39.35	39.74	43.64	77.46

T =	k = .1 n = .0	.01	.1	.5	k = .5 n = .0	.01	.1	.5
1	0.95	0.96	0.99	1.16	0.77	0.79	0.82	0.97
3	2.59	2.61	2.77	3.89	1.55	1.57	1.68	2.44
5	3.93	3.97	4.29	6.56	1.84	1.85	2.02	3.26
7	5.03	5.08	5.52	8.90	1.94	1.96	2.15	3.67
10	6.32	6.38	6.97	11.74	1.99	2.01	2.21	3.91
25	9.18	9.27	10.19	18.15	2.00	2.02	2.22	4.00
50	9.93	10.03	11.04	19.85	2.00	2.02	2.22	4.00

TABLE 1--Continued

Panel C

δ = 2 (Mean lag in r̄ = .5 year)

T =	k = .0				k = .01			
	n = .0	.01	.1	.5	n = .0	.01	.1	.5
1	1.00	1.00	1.03	1.16	1.00	1.00	1.02	1.16
3	3.00	3.01	3.13	3.78	2.96	2.97	3.08	3.73
5	5.00	5.02	5.24	6.44	4.88	4.90	5.10	6.29
10	10.00	10.04	10.50	13.11	9.52	9.56	9.99	12.49
25	25.00	25.12	26.29	33.11	22.12	22.23	23.26	29.32
50	50.00	50.25	52.60	66.44	39.35	39.54	41.40	52.33

T =	k = .1				k = .5			
	n = .0	.01	.1	.5	n = .0	.01	.1	.5
1	0.95	0.95	0.98	1.11	0.77	0.79	0.81	0.92
3	2.59	2.60	2.71	3.28	1.55	1.56	1.63	2.00
5	3.93	3.95	4.12	5.10	1.84	1.84	1.93	2.42
7	5.03	5.06	5.28	6.59	1.94	1.95	2.04	2.58
10	6.32	6.35	6.64	8.34	1.99	2.00	2.09	2.65
25	9.18	9.23	9.66	12.22	2.00	2.01	2.11	2.67
50	9.93	9.98	10.46	13.24	2.00	2.01	2.11	2.67

Panel D

δ = 4 (Mean lag in r̄ = .25 year)

T =	k = .0				k = .01			
	n = .0	.01	.1	.5	n = .0	.01	.1	.5
1	1.00	1.00	1.02	1.10	1.00	1.00	1.01	1.10
3	3.00	3.01	3.07	3.38	2.96	2.96	3.02	3.02
5	5.00	5.01	5.12	5.67	4.88	4.89	5.00	5.53
10	10.00	10.02	10.25	11.39	9.52	9.54	9.75	10.84
25	25.00	25.06	25.63	28.53	22.12	22.17	22.68	25.25
50	50.00	50.12	51.28	57.10	39.35	39.45	40.35	44.94

T =	k = .1				k = .5			
	n = .0	.01	.1	.5	n = .0	.01	.1	.5
1	0.95	0.95	0.97	1.05	0.79	0.79	0.80	0.87
3	2.59	2.60	2.65	2.93	1.55	1.56	1.59	1.77
5	3.93	3.94	4.03	4.47	1.84	1.84	1.88	2.09
7	5.03	5.05	5.16	5.57	1.94	1.94	1.99	2.22
10	6.32	6.34	6.48	7.21	1.99	1.99	2.04	2.27
25	9.18	9.20	9.41	10.49	2.00	2.00	2.05	2.29
50	9.93	9.96	10.19	11.35	2.00	2.00	2.05	2.29

APPENDIX

A PROPER MEASURE OF RISK FOR NONINFINITESIMAL UNIFORM
SHIFTS IN THE YIELD CURVE

In Section III it was demonstrated that a noninfinitesimal uniform shift in the yield curve would lead to arbitrage possibilities unless such a shift could occur at any moment only with vanishingly small probability. In this appendix we examine a model permitting such changes and derive the proper measure of risk.

Suppose the spot rate of interest is subjected to random shocks each of which causes an increase of magnitude $\bar{\delta}$. If these shocks are Poisson events (intervals between events have exponential distribution with mean $1/\lambda$), then we may write the spot rate dynamics as

(A1) $$dr = \mu(r)dt + \bar{\delta}(r)d\phi$$

where ϕ is a continuous-time Poisson process

$$\text{Prob } [\phi(t + dt) - \phi(t) = 1] = \lambda dt + o(dt)$$
$$\text{Prob } [\phi(t + dt) - \phi(t) = 0] = 1 - \lambda dt + o(dt)$$
$$\text{Prob } [\phi(t + dt) - \phi(t) > 1] = o(dt)$$

where $o(s)$ is the asymptotic order symbol with the property $\lim\limits_{s \to 0} [o(s)/s] = 0$. The price dynamics of discount bonds will be[13]

(A3) $$dP(r,T) = [\mu P_r - P_T]dt + [P(r + \bar{\delta},T) - P(r,T)]d\phi.$$

Suppose for simplicity that bonds of all maturities are priced so that their expected rates of return equal the prevailing spot rate. Then, since $E[d\phi] = \lambda dt$

(A4) $$rPdt = E[dP] = (\mu P_r - P_T + \lambda E[P(r + \bar{\delta},T) - P(r,T)]dt.$$

If all yields are to change equally, then the solution to (A4) must have the property $R(r,T) = r + h(T)$ as in (22) or

(A5) $$P(r,T) = e^{-rT + H(T)}.$$

Substituting (A5) into (A4) yields an equation of the form

(A6) $$0 = -T\mu(r) - H'(T) + \lambda(r)[1 - E(e^{-\bar{\delta}(r)T})].$$

For (A6) to be satisfied for all T, we must have μ, λ and $\bar{\delta}$ constants independent of r. If $\bar{\delta}$ is a positive[14] constant, then the easily verified solution to (A4) is

---

[13] The first two terms in (A3) are derived through the chain rule. An intuitive interpretation of the last term is obvious; for a rigorous development of the mathematics of continuous time Poisson processes see Kushner [24].

[14] If $\delta < 0$, then (A7) is still the correct solution. However, since the interest rate can become arbitrarily negative, the pricing equation possesses the unreasonable property that $P(r, \infty) = \infty$.

(A7)
$$P(r,T) = \exp[-(r + \lambda)T + \lambda(1 - e^{-\delta T})/\delta]$$

with yield curve

(A8)
$$R(r,T) \equiv -\frac{1}{T}\log P = r + \lambda - \frac{\lambda}{\delta T}(1 - e^{-\delta T}).$$

From (A7) whenever a Poisson event occurs, bond prices will change discontinuously to

(A9)
$$P(r \dot{+} \delta, T) = e^{-\delta T}P(r,T)$$

and all yields will increase by δ. Whenever a Poisson event does not occur, bond prices will change at the rate

(A10)
$$\frac{\partial P(r,T)/\partial T}{P(r,T)} = [r + \lambda(1 - e^{-\delta T})].$$

This verifies that the dynamic behavior of the yield curve may consist entirely of non-infinitesimal uniform shifts if they occur with vanishingly small probability at any point of time. Nevertheless, Macaulay's duration will not be a proper measure of basis risk in the model just developed. Moreover, duration matching will not provide immunization, as is demonstrated below.

Suppose we wish to form a portfolio to immunize a liability of one dollar due in T years with a present value of V. Consider first the duration matching portfolio of Theorem 4 composed of $n_1 P(r,t_1) = V(t_2 - T)/(t_2 - t_1)$ and $n_2 P(r,t_2) = V(T - t_1)/(t_2 - t_1)$ dollars of discount bonds of maturities t_1 and t_2. If the interest rate jumps, then from (A9) we will receive a windfall of

(A11)
$$n_1 P(r,t_1)(e^{-\delta t_1} - 1) + n_2 P(r,t_2)(e^{-\delta t_2} - 1) - V(e^{-\delta T} - 1)$$
$$= V\left[\frac{(t_2 - T)e^{-\delta t_1} + (T - t_1)e^{-\delta t_2}}{t_2 - t_1} - e^{-\delta T}\right] > 0$$

which is positive by (12) and (13) in Theorem 4. However, this windfall profit will accrue only once every $1/\lambda$ units of time on average. The remainder of the time, the portfolio will suffer a continuous decrease in value at the rate

(A12)
$$-\left[n_1 \frac{\partial P(r,t_1)}{\partial t_1} + n_2 \frac{\partial P(r,t_2)}{\partial t_2} - \frac{\partial P(r,T)}{\partial T}\right]dt$$
$$= -\lambda[n_1 P(r,t_1)(e^{-\delta t_1} - 1) + n_2 P(r,t_2)(e^{-\delta t_2} - 1) - V(e^{-\delta T} -)] \, dt < 0 \text{[15]}$$

---

[15]The quantity given in (A12) is the negative of the first line in (A11); hence from (12) and (13) it is negative in value.

which is λdt times the windfall gain in (A11). Since λdt is also the probability of receiving the gain at any point of time, the portfolio will not be immunized since we cannot know in advance the number of Poisson events that will occur.

Instead of duration matching, consider the portfolio strategy of matching the present value and the Poisson shock response of the assets to that of the liability by choosing n_1' and n_2' such that $n_1'P(r, t_1) + n_2'P(r, t_2) = V$ and

(A13) $$n_1'P(r,t_1)(e^{-\delta t_1} - 1) + n_2'P(r,t_2)(e^{-\delta t_2} - 1) = V(e^{-\delta T} - 1).$$

The proper investment in each bond to achieve this end is

(A14)
$$n_1'P(r,t_1) = V\frac{e^{-\delta t_2} - e^{-\delta T}}{e^{-\delta t_2} - e^{-\delta t_1}} \left. \right\}$$
$$n_2'P(r,t_2) = V\frac{e^{-\delta T} - e^{-\delta t_1}}{e^{-\delta t_2} - e^{-\delta t_1}}.$$

By construction, this portfolio will not change in value when a shock occurs. In the absence of a shock, the portfolio will grow in value at the continuous rate of

(A15)
$$-\left[n_1'\frac{\partial P(r,t_1)}{\partial t_1} + n_2'\frac{\partial P(r,t_2)}{\partial t_2} - \frac{\partial P(r,T)}{\partial T}\right]dt$$
$$= \lambda V\left[\frac{e^{-\delta t_2} - e^{-\delta T}}{e^{-\delta t_2} - e^{-\delta t_1}}e^{-\delta t_1} + \frac{e^{-\delta T} - e^{-\delta t_1}}{e^{-\delta t_2} - e^{-\delta t_1}}e^{-\delta t_2} - e^{-\delta T}\right] = 0$$

where the second line follows by the introduction of (A10) and (A14) and the zero investment condition $n_1'P(r, t_1) + n_2'P(r, t_2) = V$. Thus, we have formed a combination of assets which always matches the value of the liability and hence is the immunizing strategy sought. Furthermore, we have achieved immunization, not through duration, but by matching the shock response of assets to that of the liability.

In the context of the model just developed, it is obvious that the basis risk of a pure discount bond is proportional not to its maturity, T, but rather the quantity $1 - \exp(-\delta T)$ and the proper measure of basis risk for a stream of cash payments is thus

(A16) $$\Sigma(1 - e^{-\delta t})P(r,t)X(t)/\Sigma P(r,t)X(t).$$

This definition gives a measure very similar to duration (1). Both are weighted averages of the risks of the component cash flows, and in each case the weights are the proportionate contribution of the cash flow to the asset's value. The primary differences are: (a) risk increases with maturity of the cash flow at less than a linear rate, and (b) the measure has no dimension, rather than having units of time.

An intuitive explanation for (a) is that over a long interval of time the average number of shocks per period will be more tightly distributed about the expected number than over a shorter interval. Since the expected number of shocks is proportional to the interval, the uncertainty must be less than proportionate. Difference (b) can be removed if a measure with time units is desired by defining the "stochastic duration," D* of an asset to be the maturity of a pure discount bond with the same risk, i.e., for the model above[16]

(A17) $$D^* = -\frac{1}{\delta}\log[1 - \Sigma(1 - e^{-\delta t})P(t)X(t)/\Sigma P(t)X(t)].$$

If in place of taking μ, λ, and $\tilde{\delta}$ as constants, we choose $\mu = 0$, $\lambda(r) = \lambda r$, and $\tilde{\delta}$ a constant, then the solution to (A4) is

(A18) $$P(r, T) = \left[\frac{1 + \lambda}{\lambda + e^{\delta(1+\lambda)T}}\right]^{r/\delta} \equiv [A(T)]^{r/\delta}$$

with the yield curve

(A19) $$R(r, T) = -\frac{1}{\delta T}\ln[A(T)]r.$$

So all yields are in constant proportion and change multiplicatively at a Poisson event. The proper measure of basis risk for multiple payment assets is in this case

(A20) $$\frac{\Sigma A(T)X(T)P(T)}{\Sigma X(T)P(T)} - 1$$

rather than Bierwag's duration measure

(A21) $$D_B = \frac{\Sigma R(T)TP(T)X(T)}{\Sigma X(T)P(T)} = -\frac{r}{\delta}\frac{\Sigma \ln[A(T)]X(T)P(T)}{\Sigma X(T)P(T)}.$$

---

[16]We set $1 - \exp[-\delta D^*]$ equal to the expression in (A16) and solve for D^*.

REFERENCES

[1] Bierwag, G. O. "Measures of Duration." University of Oregon Working Paper (1976) (forthcoming in *Economic Inquiry*).

[2] _____. "Dynamic Portfolio Immunization Policies." University of Oregon Working Paper (1977).

[3] _____. "Immunization, Duration and the Term Structure of Interest Rates." *Journal of Financial and Quantitative Analysis* (December 1977).

[4] Bierwag, G. O., and George Kaufman. "Coping with the Risk of Interest Rate Fluctuations: A Note." *Journal of Business* (July 1977).

[5] _____. "Bond Portfolio Strategy Simulations: A Critique." University of Oregon Working Paper (1978) (forthcoming in *Journal of Financial and Quantitative Analysis*).

[6] Blocher, E., and Clyde Stickney. "Duration and Risk Assessments in Capital Budgeting." University of North Carolina Working Paper (1975) (forthcoming in *The Accounting Review*) (1978).

[7] Boquist, J. A.; G. A. Racette; and Schlarbaum. "Duration and Risk Assessment for Bonds and Common Stocks." *Journal of Finance* (1975).

[8] Boyle, P. P. "Immunization under Stochastic Models of the Term Structure" (forthcoming in the *Journal of the Institute of Actuaries* (UK), University of British Columbia Working Paper (1977).

[9] Carr, J. L.; P. J. Halpern; and J. S. McCallum. "Correcting the Yield Curve: A Re-interpretation of the Duration Problem." *Journal of Finance* (1974).

[10] Cox, John C.; Jonathan Ingersoll; and Stephen Ross. "Duration and the Measurement of Basis Risk." Stanford/Chicago/Yale Working Paper (1977) (forthcoming in *Journal of Business*).

[11] _____. "A Theory of the Term Structure of Interest Rates." University of Chicago Working Paper (1978).

[12] Duesenberry, J. S. *Business Cycles and Economic Growth*. New York: McGraw-Hill (1958).

[13] Durand, David. "Payout Period, Time Spread, and Duration: Aids to Judgment in Capital Budgeting." *Journal of Bank Research* (Spring 1974).

[14] Fama, E. "Forward Rates as Predictors of Future Spot Rates." *Journal of Financial Economics* (October 1976).

[15] Fishburn, Peter C. "Mean-Risk Analysis with Risk Associated with Below-Target Returns." *American Economic Review* (March 1977).

[16] Fisher, Lawrence, and Roman L. Weil. "Coping with the Risk of Interest Rate Fluctuations: Returns to Bondholders from Naive and Optimal Strategies." *Journal of Business* (October 1971).

[17] Fisher, Lawrence. "An Algorithm for Finding Exact Rates of Return." *Journal of Business* (January 1966).

[18] Grove, Myron A. "On Duration and the Optimal Maturity Structure of the Balance Sheet." *The Bell Journal of Economics and Management Science* (Autumn 1975).

[19] Haugen, Robert A., and Dean W. Wichern. "The Elasticity of Financial Assets." *Journal of Finance* (September 1974).

[20] Hicks, J. R. *Value and Capital*. Oxford: Clarendon Press (1939).

[21] Hopewell, Michael, and George Kaufman. "Bond Price Volatility and Term to Maturity: A Generalized Respecification." *The American Economic Review* (September 1973).

[22] Keintz, Richard, and Clyde Stickney. "Immunization of Pension Funds from Interest Rate Changes." Dartmouth College Working Paper (1977).

[23] Khang, Chulson. "Bond Immunization When Short-Term Interest Rates Fluctuate More Than Long-Term Rates." University of Oregon Working Paper (1977).

[24] Kushner, H. *Stochastic Stability and Control.* New York: Academic Press (1967).

[25] Livingston, Miles, and John Caks. "A Duration Fallacy." *Journal of Finance* (March 1977).

[26] Macaulay, Frederick. R. *Some Theoretical Problems Suggested by the Movements of Interest Rates, Bond Yields, and Stock Prices in the United States since 1856.* New York: Columbia University Press (1938).

[27] Merton, R. "A Dynamic General Equilibrium Model of the Asset Market and Its Application to the Pricing of the Capital Structure of the Firm." Sloan School of Management Working Paper, MIT (1970).

[28] Redington, F. M. "Review of the Principles of Life-Office Valuations." *Journal of the Institute of Actuaries,* Vol. 18 (1952).

[29] Samuelson, Paul A. "The Effects of Interest Rate Increases on the Banking System." *American Economic Review* (March 1945).

[30] Tito, D., and W. Wagner. "Definitive New Measures of Bond Performance and Risk." Wilshire Associates (1977).

[31] Vasicek, O. A. "An Equilibrium Characterization of the Term Structure." *Journal of Financial Economics* (November 1977).

[32] Weil, Roman L. "Macaulay's Duration: An Appreciation." *Journal of Business* (October 1973).

DURATION AND RISK ASSESSMENT FOR
BONDS AND COMMON STOCKS: A NOTE

John A. Boquist
George A. Racette
Gary S. Schlarbaum

DURATION AND RISK ASSESSMENT FOR BONDS AND COMMON STOCKS

JOHN A. BOQUIST, GEORGE A. RACETTE, GARY G. SCHLARBAUM*

THIS PAPER IDENTIFIES a specific time-risk relationship using a measure of time known as duration and develops some important implications of the relationship. Although a duration-risk link has been alleged in the literature [4, 6, 9, 10, 13, 15, 20, 21], previous investigators have stopped short of the formal analysis which we hope to supply.

The beta coefficient is the most widely recognized measure of the risk of an asset. Here we relate beta and duration first in the limited context of a default-free, finite-lived security represented by a government bond, then in the more general context of an asset with perpetual, but uncertain, cash flows represented by a common stock.

In the course of analysis, several conclusions become apparent: 1) Duration is a critical link in a dynamic relationship between risk and return. 2) Through duration, risk and its associated equilibrium return are dependent upon the *time pattern* of cash flows anticipated by the market. 3) Estimation of *ex ante* risk from a distribution of *ex post* time series return relatives may be unwarranted since individual relatives are likely to be single observations from different distributions at each point in time. 4) The latter problem is likely to be particularly acute for finite lived securities but cannot be ruled out for assets such as common stocks with anticipated perpetual lives. Suggestions for empirical research are offered in our concluding section.

I. DURATION AND RISK

In his study of bond yields Macaulay [15] defined and used duration as the measure of the length of a loan. Unlike maturity, which looks only at the last payment, duration gives some weight to the time at which *each* cash payment occurs. The weight assigned to each period is the present value of the cash flow for that period divided by the current price of the security.

Following Fisher and Weil [10], duration measured at time t_0 can be expressed as

$$D_{t_0} = \left[\sum_{j=1}^{N} (t_j - t_0) A_{t_j} \right] \Big/ \sum_{j=1}^{N} A_{t_j} = \left[\sum_{j=1}^{N} t_j A_{t_j} \Big/ \sum_{j=1}^{N} A_{t_j} \right] - t_0 \qquad (1)$$

* Indiana University, University of Oregon and Purdue University respectively. The authors would like to thank Professor Mike Hopewell for thoughtful suggestions regarding both the duration literature and the content of the paper. Also, suggestions from Roman L. Weil were helpful. Any errors are ours.

where A_{t_j} is the present value measured at time t_o of certain cash flows to be received in period t. Any investment which provides cash payments before maturity necessarily has duration less than maturity. Also, for a given current bond price, the larger the periodic coupon payments or the discount rate, the smaller the duration.[1]

The link between the bond price volatility and duration is developed by Fisher [9] and extended in a recent paper by Hopewell and Kaufman [13]. Assuming continuous compounding at the yield to maturity it is shown that for small yield changes

$$\frac{dP_{it}}{P_{it}} = -D_{it} \, dr_{it} \qquad (2)$$

where dP_{it} and P_{it} are the price change and initial bond price respectively; D_{it} is the duration of the bond at time t and dr_{it} is the change in yield to maturity.[2] Duration is a constant of proportionality relating percentage bond price changes to changes in yield. Since the time to maturity, N, has a weight, $A_{t_n}\big/\sum_{j=1}^{N} A_{t_j}$, it will have some impact upon the duration. However, the size of that impact will depend upon the size of interim coupon payments, the yield to maturity, the time of maturity and the size of the principal payment. Clearly, two default-free bonds could have the same maturity but quite different durations; there need be no formal relationship between maturity and volatility.

The question of how equation (2) can be incorporated into a risk measure for bonds remains to be considered. We begin by briefly reviewing the linear market model.

The linear market model asserts that the one-period return of any capital asset, $\tilde{R}_{it}$, is a linear function of a market factor common to all assets, $\tilde{M}_t$, and independent factors unique to asset i, $\tilde{\epsilon}_{it}$.[3] The relationship is expressed as

$$\tilde{R}_{it} = \alpha_{it} + \beta_{it}\tilde{M}_t + \tilde{\epsilon}_{it} \qquad (3)$$

where α_{it} and β_{it} are parameters and the expected value of $\tilde{\epsilon}_{it}$ is equal to zero. The independence assumption implies that $\mathrm{Cov}(\tilde{\epsilon}_{it},\tilde{M}_t)$ is zero and the $\mathrm{Cov}(\tilde{\epsilon}_{it},\tilde{\epsilon}_{jt})$, $j \neq i$, are equal to zero.[4]

If, as is the accepted practice, we assume that the market factor can be adequately approximated by the return relative on the market portfolio, the beta coefficient may be expressed as

1. For other complete discussions of duration see [3, 4, 6, 10, 11, 12, 13, 14, 15, 20, 21].

2. In the discrete case (3) becomes $dP/P = Ddr/(1 + r)$. See Hopewell and Kaufman [13], equations (6) and (7).

3. See Blume [1].

4. The available empirical evidence [2, 8] suggests that the unique factors, ϵ_{it}, correspond more closely to non-normal stable variates than to normal ones. This conclusion implies that the variance and covariances of the unique factors do not exist. Nonetheless, it has been shown that the beta coefficient, β_{it}, can still be interpreted as a measure of risk under the assumption that ϵ_{it}'s are non-normal stable variates with identical characteristic exponents greater than 1. For purposes of exposition, the existence of variances and covariances is assumed in our subsequent discussion. See Fama and Miller [8] pp. 313-319.

$$\beta_{it} = \frac{\text{Cov}(\tilde{R}_{it}, \tilde{R}_{mt})}{\sigma^2(\tilde{R}_{mt})} = \frac{\rho(\tilde{R}_{it}, \tilde{R}_{mt})\sigma(\tilde{R}_{it})}{\sigma(\tilde{R}_{mt})} \tag{4}$$

where $\rho(\tilde{R}_{it}, \tilde{R}_{mt})$ is the correlation coefficient between the market factor and the security return, $\sigma(\tilde{R}_{it})$ is the standard deviation of returns for security i, $\sigma(\tilde{R}_{mt})$ is the standard deviation of the market factor and $\sigma^2(\tilde{R}_{mt})$ is the variance of that factor. Given (4) an explicit relationship between risk and duration of a default-free bond is easily specified.

A. *Securities With Risk-Free Cash Flows and Finite Lives*

Over a short time interval, the return relative for a default-free bond is defined as

$$\tilde{R}_{it} = \frac{P_{it} + C_{it} + \tilde{dP}_{it}}{P_{it}} \tag{5}$$

where

P_{it} = initial price of the bond

C_{it} = coupons paid to bondholders

$\tilde{dP}_{it}$ = the bond price change, a random variable

Substituting the expression for dP_{it} from (2) into (5) and the resultant expression for $\tilde{R}_{it}$ into (4) gives an equation for the risk of a default-free bond.

$$\beta_{it} = \frac{-D_{it}\text{Cov}(\tilde{dr}_{it}, \tilde{R}_{mt})}{\sigma^2(\tilde{R}_{mt})} = \frac{-D_{it}\rho(\tilde{dr}_{it}, \tilde{R}_{mt})\ \sigma(\tilde{dr}_{it})}{\sigma(\tilde{R}_{mt})} \tag{6}$$

This formulation suggests several points of empirical significance. First, the sign of β_{it} is opposite that of the correlation coefficient.[5] Second, the risk of a bond is critically dependent upon duration which is measured in units of time. With all other factors held constant, a change in risk is directly related to a change in duration. Third, duration and $\sigma(\tilde{dr}_{it})$ capture the dispersion of relative prices for bond i. Given the evidence that short-term rates tend to fluctuate more than long-term rates, the risk effect implied by shorter duration may be partially offset by an associated increase in $\sigma(\tilde{dr}_{it})$.[6] Fourth, any attempt to estimate risk of a bond from historical time series data involves a trade-off between the benefits associated with many observations and the cost of non-stationarity.

---

5. The measured correlation between $\tilde{dr}_{it}$ and R_{mt} could be positive, negative or zero. If we are working with default-free bonds, $\tilde{dr}_{it}$ reflects changes in the "required" return on these bonds. These changes are likely to alter the discount rate for all securities in the same direction. Since movements in the discount rate are inversely related to security price movements, the correlation coefficient is expected to be negative.

6. Such evidence appears in Van Horne [18]. If there exists a stable inverse relationship between duration and $\sigma(\tilde{dr}_{it})$ then it may be possible to substitute this relationship into (5) thus eliminating a direct estimate of $\sigma(\tilde{dr}_{it})$ from the equation.

B. *Securities With Risky Cash Flows and Perpetual Lives*[7]

The specification of risk in equation (6) is more than a mathematical curiosity unique to the bond valuation problem. Rather it is a special part of a more general valuation model that isolates two components of risk—that stemming from changes in the yield structure and that stemming from changes in cash flow expectations. Since bond coupon payments were assumed certain in the previous analysis, this latter risk component was not identified. As will be shown below, the concept of duration is also critical to the valuation of common stock, which possesses both risk components.

Consider the expression for the duration of a common share with anticipated constant perpetual growth in dividends at the rate g_i and with the dividend in period t, d_{it}, equal to $d_{io}(1 + g_i)^t$. The expression for duration is

$$D_i = \frac{d_{io}\sum_{t=1}^{\infty} t(1 + g_i)^t/(1 + k_i)^t}{d_{io}\sum_{t=1}^{\infty} (1 + g_i)^t/(1 + k_i)^t} = \frac{\sum_{t=1}^{\infty} t(1 + g_i)^t/(1 + k_i)^t}{\sum_{t=1}^{\infty} (1 + g_i)^t/(1 + k_i)^t}. \tag{7}$$

As long as $g < k$, both the numerator and denominator are convergent. They can be shown equal to $\dfrac{(1 + g_i)(1 + k_i)}{(k_i - g_i)^2}$ and $\dfrac{(1 + g_i)}{k_i - g_i}$ respectively. Therefore, (7) becomes[8]

$$D_i = \frac{1 + k_i}{k_i - g_i}. \tag{8}$$

If, for example, a share's dividends are expected to grow at the rate of 8% annually and investors require a 10% annual return on the shares, the duration of the stream of payments from the share would be 55 years. An increase of k to 12% lowers duration to 28 years whereas an increase in g to 9% raises the duration to 100 years, *ceteris paribus*. Thus it is clear that $\dfrac{\alpha D}{\alpha k} < 0$ and $\dfrac{\alpha D}{\alpha g} < 0$.[9]

---

7. We have purposely ignored the case of finite lived securities with uncertain cash flows, such as corporate bonds, because such a discussion would simply duplicate much of the discussion in this and the previous section. The interested reader can easily derive an expression for risk in this case given some simplifying assumptions.

8. The precise expression for Di does, of course, depend upon both the form of discounting (continuous vs discrete) and the timing of the flows. The expression above stems from Durand [4], who followed Macaulay's convention of discrete discounting from t = 1. Hicks, on the other hand, finds that using discrete compounding from t = 0, $D_i = 1 + g_i/(k_i - g_i)$ [1, p. 245] while with continuous compounding $D_i = 1/(k_i - g_i)$ [12, p. 329]. The latter two formulations are interesting in that $P_i = d_{io}D_i$ and duration is simply the inverse of the dividend yield. The latter was pointed out by Lintner [14]. For both simplicity and continuity we will use the continuous discounting form in our following analyses.

9. Specifically:

$$\frac{\alpha D_i}{\alpha k_i} = \frac{-(1 + g_i)}{(k_i - g_i)^2} \text{ and } \frac{\alpha D_i}{\alpha g_i} = \frac{(1 + k_i)}{(k_i - g_i)^2}$$

for discrete compounding intervals with t = 1, . . . , ∞.

An expression for common stock duration can be incorporated into the risk measure of the linear market model in a manner similar to that developed for bonds.[10] First consider the price of a common stock in the constant perpetual growth case with continuous discounting:[11]

$$P_i = \frac{d_{io}}{(k_i - g_i)} \tag{9}$$

The link between stock price volatility and duration is established by the total differential of (9)

$$dP_i = \frac{\partial P_i}{\partial g_i} dg_i + \frac{\partial P_i}{\partial k_i} dk_i = \left[\frac{d_{io}}{(K_i - g_i)^2}\right] dg_i - \left[\frac{d_{io}}{(K_i - g_i)^2}\right] dk_i \tag{10}$$

which after simplification becomes

$$dP_i = P_i D_i \, dg_i - P_i D_i \, dk_i \tag{11}$$

and

$$\frac{dP_i}{P_i} = D_i(dg_i - dk_i). \tag{12}$$

Defining the return relative for a common stock as $\bar{R}_i$ and following the same procedure used in the previous section, the appropriate risk measure for a common stock is[12]

$$\beta_i = \frac{D_i[Cov(\bar{d}g_i, \bar{R}m) - Cov(\bar{d}k_i, \bar{R}m)]}{Var(\bar{R}m)}. \tag{13}$$

A more general risk measure must therefore incorporate the relationships between each component of stock price volatility and the market return. More important, however, equation (13) emphasizes the vital role of duration in the risk assessment of assets characterized by uncertain cash flow expectations. Any change in expected payments is likely to alter duration and therefore beta. In addition, any exogenous change in the structure of equilibrium rates of return will also be accompanied by a new covariance relation that serves to mitigate the necessary alteration of beta. Nonetheless, the prospect for a constant beta in the fact of such changes is unlikely.

II. Implications for Empirical Research

From an empirical viewpoint, equation (6) rather than (13) is the most interesting. While (13) confirms the theoretical role of duration in determining the risk of a common stock and provides a rationale for non-stationarity of beta's, the two covariance terms do not appear to be empirically viable. But (6) may prove useful to investigate the behavior

10. Pettit and Westerfield [17] employ a similar procedure.

11. This is a very restrictive case. However, it does serve to highlight the role of duration in common stock valuation which is not specific to this model.

12. The market return, Rm, could also be broken into gm and km components. However, such a division would add little to an understanding of the components of β_i. Also no assumptions concerning the resultant cross-product terms are necessary in the framework used here.

of the components of risk of fixed-income, default-free securities such as government bonds. Duration can be computed at any point in time, correlation coefficients and standard deviation can be approximated for short time intervals with daily or weekly data. Using this summary data, several questions might be addressed. They include 1) to what extent are changes in duration offset by changes in $\sigma(d\bar{r}_{lt})$ over the life of a bond; and 2) can the risk of the bond segment of a diversified portfolio be more effectively estimated and controlled using historical estimates of $\rho(d\bar{r}_{lt},$ $\bar{R}_{mt})$ and $\rho(d\bar{r}_{lt})$ in conjunction with *current* duration rather than simple extrapolation of an historical beta? Given our lack of knowledge regarding the behavior of bond risk, tentative answers to such questions could provide the necessary foundation for further empirical research.

REFERENCES

1. Marshall E. Blume. "On the Assessment of Risk," *Journal of Finance* XXVI (March, 1971), 1-10.
2. ————. "Portfolio Theory: A Step Toward Its Practical Applications," *Journal of Business*, XVII (April, 1970), 152-173.
3. John A. Boquist. "A Duration-Based Bond Valuation Model," unpublished Ph.D. Dissertation, Purdue University, 1973.
4. David Durand. "Growth Stocks and the Petersburg Paradox," *Journal of Finance*, XII (September, 1957), 348-363.
5. ————. "Indices of Profitability: Aids to Judgment in Capital Budgeting," *Journal of Bank Research*, III (Winter, 1973), 200-219.
6. ————. "Payout Period, Time Spread and Duration: Aids to Judgment in Capital Budgeting," *Journal of Bank Research*, IV (Spring, 1974), 20-34.
7. Eugene F. Fama. "The Behavior of Stock Market Prices," *Journal of Business*, 38 (January, 1965), 34-105.
8. Eugene F. Fama and Merton H. Miller. *The Theory of Finance* (New York: Holt, Rinehart and Winston, Inc., 1972).
9. Lawrence Fisher. "An Algorithm for Finding Exact Rates of Return," *Journal of Business*, XXXIX (January, 1966), 111-118.
10. Lawrence Fisher and Roman L. Weil. "Coping with the Risk of Interest Rate Fluctuations: Returns of Bondholders From Naive and Optimal Strategies," *Journal of Business*, XLIV (October, 1971).
11. John R. Hicks. *Value and Capital* (Oxford: Clarendon Press, 1939. 2nd Ed. 1946).
12. ————. *Value and Growth* (New York and Oxford: Oxford University Press, 1965).
13. Michael H. Hopewell and George G. Kaufman. "Bond Price Volatility and Term to Maturity: A Generalized Respectification," *American Economic Review*, LXII (September, 1973), 749-753.
14. John Lintner. "Corporate Growth Under Uncertainty," *The Corporate Economy*, Robin Morris, Ed. (London: MacMillan, 1971).
15. Frederic R. Macaulay. *Some Theoretical Problems Suggested by the Movements of Interest Rates, Bond Yields, and Stock Prices Since 1856* (New York: National Bureau of Economic Research, 1938).
16. Merton H. Miller and Franco Modigliani. "Dividend Policy, Growth, and the Valuation of Shares," *Journal of Business*, XXXIV (October, 1961), 411-433.
17. R. Richardson Pettit and Randolph Westerfield. "A Model of Capital Asset Risk," *Journal of Financial and Quantitative Analysis*, VII (March, 1972), 1649-1672.
18. James C. Van Horne. *The Function and Analysis of Capital Market Rates* (Englewood Cliffs: Prentice-Hall, Inc. 1970).
19. Roman L. Weil. "Macaulay's Duration: An Appreciation," *Journal of Business*, XLVI (October, 1973), 589-592.
20. John Whittacker. "Minimizing the Burden of the Dollar Premium," *Investment Analyst*, 24 (October, 1969), 26-31.
21. ————. "The Relevance of Duration," *Journal of Business Finance*, I, No. 3 (1970), 34-41.

PART II

IMMUNIZATION

REVIEW OF THE PRINCIPLES OF

LIFE-OFFICE VALUATIONS

F. M. Redington

REVIEW OF THE PRINCIPLES OF LIFE-OFFICE VALUATIONS

By F. M. REDINGTON, M.A., F.I.A.
Actuary, Prudential Assurance Company Ltd.

[Submitted to the Institute, 28 April 1952]

Our most convinced answers are only questions,....
CHRISTOPHER FRY

THE original purpose of this paper—undertaken at request but not un-willingly—was to review the principles and practice of life-office valuations in the light of modern conditions. It was difficult, however, to deal satis-factorily with the principles of valuation *in vacuo* without reference to more fundamental principles. As a consequence the paper has become more ambitious in its scope than originally intended—and has threatened to run away with itself. The reader will perhaps be less disappointed if he is warned in advance that he is to be taken on a ramble through the actuarial countryside and that any interest lies in the journey rather than the destination.

In the enlargement of its scope the paper has become a more intimate expression of a personal point of view, and more controversial. For this reason it is desirable to emphasize that the views expressed must not be taken as necessarily representing the views of my colleagues.

For the same reason I have felt it best to make occasional use of the first person singular. It would be less than fair to give an air of finality to views which are personal and which indeed are still developing.

1. NATURE OF OUR ESTIMATES

The foundations of actuarial practice were laid before the 1914 war. Since then there has been a considerable change in general outlook, the magnitude of which time may prove to have been greater than we now realize. Before 1914 there was the promise of uninterrupted stability in economics, and social affairs, and there was apparently much justification for faith in the unlimited progress of science and the ultimate conquest of all our problems. To-day, what then seemed most certain has in many ways proved to be most un-certain, and in science the rigid and somewhat arid era of physical deter-minism has given way to a more flexible philosophy with probability and statistics as the prominent factors.

In our own sphere this growth in uncertainty has been emphasized by the different financial consequences of two world wars, the first of which was accompanied by a rise in the long-term gilt-edged rates of interest from 3% to 6% and the second by a fall from $3\frac{1}{2}$% to less than $2\frac{1}{2}$%. In our early literature it was mortality only that demanded treatment by the methods of probability. Now, mortality is perhaps the least of the actuary's uncer-tainties; interest, taxation and expense, though not susceptible to formal treatment by the methods of probability, are nevertheless factors about which probability must decide the shape of our thinking. We are less concerned about the technique of valuing at $2\frac{1}{2}$% than at the significance and the consequences of the $2\frac{1}{2}$% itself.

To begin at the beginning, therefore, what is the nature of our thoughts if we assume—and we have to make some assumption—that the gross rate of interest earned on our funds in 1970 will be 4%? We shall not lose dignity by admitting that we do not know what the rate will be, and we should be unwise perhaps even to use the word forecast.

Behind the assumption is a vague feeling of a continuous series of probability distributions which would express our expectation of the rate of interest at successive points of future time. In the immediate future the distribution would be compact—the margin of uncertainty being small. The uncertainty grows rapidly, however, so that for a point of time, say, five years hence the distribution is more widely dispersed. But the process of widening slows down. Our states of mind concerning the rate of interest ten and thirty years hence are not very different.

Thus we may say that there is an expanding funnel of doubt. The contours of the funnel vary with each one of us, for the concept is personal. Nevertheless, they must inevitably have much in common, since they all start from a common point now.

If we could give numerical values to our uncertainties we could construct a probability dispersion table. For example, we might say that the probability that in 1960 the rate of interest will lie between $3\frac{3}{4}\%$ and $4\frac{1}{4}\%$ is ·15. We cannot, of course, do this in practice. Yet the expanding funnel of doubt is in the background of our thoughts not only in regard to interest but also in regard to the other factors: mortality, expenses, taxation.

2. PREMIUM CALCULATIONS

Whatever may be the convenient working formula finally adopted for the practical calculation of life-office premiums, the original structure may be analysed as follows:

(*a*) the premium for the basic contract, using the best estimate we can make of the future rates of mortality, interest, expense and taxation, without any margins whatsoever and designed to produce neither profit nor loss;

(*b*) a loading for bonus in the form dictated by the requirements of equity and general policy;

(*c*) a loading for contingencies and for variations from the rates involved in (*a*);

(*d*) a loading for options.

In my opinion it does not lead to clarity of thought to make arbitrary exchanges between these groups. It may be convenient for calculation to adopt a simplified working formula, but such a proceeding should never obscure the proper analysis of the rate-structure.

It is not the purpose here to expand on the question of premiums other than is necessary to set the stage for the discussion on valuation. A few brief comments must therefore suffice.

Gross interest. The meaning behind the words 'rate of interest' is discussed later. The only question at this stage is the risk content in the interest on high-yielding securities, e.g. equities. This risk content is a form of insurance premium, and a strong case can be made that it should be deducted from interest and reserved to meet the exigencies for which it was obtained. This comment is made without prejudice to the particular system of accounting to be adopted. It is assumed in all that follows that the risk-premium has been so deducted from interest and put to reserve.

Taxation. The future rate is a matter of opinion, but so long as the basis remains as at present it seems essential to deduct full tax separately from interest and expenses—at least in the Ordinary branch. To deduct from interest alone the net rate of tax payable on interest less expenses is not only unrealistic and inequitable but dangerous, since, in these days of inflated new business, expenses are high and the net rate of tax is low. The possibility that the basis will be altered must be relegated to the list of miscellaneous contingencies.

Bonus loadings. The rate of reversionary bonus to be allowed for is not dealt with in this paper, although the later sections discuss much that is relevant to the decision.

Options. The concealed danger of options, both in assets and liabilities, is a recurring note in this paper. In theory, options should be charged for, and the option premiums received should be accumulated in a fund to provide the cost of meeting the options when they are selected.

Contingencies. In principle, contingencies are of two main forms, although the separation cannot always be made in practice: chance variations about the mean rate, and variations in the mean rate itself.

If the probability dispersion table were taken as a model a strict theory could be constructed, but in practice our thoughts must be largely intuitive, since the table is itself no more than a vague background. Furthermore, there are many other factors to be considered. For example, the matching of investments and liabilities can reduce the need for contingency loadings. The main features are, however, that contingency loadings should be related to the risks of serious loss, bearing in mind the size of the office's reserves, and that on receipt they should be reserved against the contingencies for which they were charged. The normal process would be a steady accumulation of contingency loadings into contingency funds and a withdrawal therefrom to meet emergencies as they arise.

A subsidiary question is that the contingency loadings for individual policies should be related to the degree of doubt expressed in the dispersion schedule. It would be academic to pursue this in detail, but the general principle emerges that with the 'expanding funnel of doubt' there is more risk attached to long-term than to short-term policies. I am inclined to think that in general we tend to undercharge long-term non-profit contracts and overcharge short-term policies.

The question whether with-profit policies require contingency loadings or contingency funds is embedded in the principles and methods of valuation and bonus distribution. Contingency funds may be required for with-profit business as for non-profit, though perhaps not equally; but it is rather academic to discuss whether it is better, for example, to load for 35s. % bonus or to load for 30s. % bonus with a 3s. % addition to the premiums for contingencies.

3. MATCHING OF INVESTMENTS—IMMUNIZATION

The word 'matching' implies the distribution of assets to make them, as far as possible, equally as vulnerable as the liabilities to those influences which affect both. In its widest sense this principle includes such important aspects as the matching of assets and liabilities in currencies.

In the narrower sense to which the remainder of this section applies, 'matching' implies the distribution of the term of the assets in relation to the term of the liabilities in such a way as to reduce the possibility of loss arising from a change in interest rates. This aspect of life assurance is of the greatest importance. It is one of the three main factors within our control which can endanger the solvency of an office (the other two being the covering of war risks and the granting of guaranteed option values, particularly surrender and settlement options). 'Matching' fundamentally affects and should be affected by the bonus policy of the office. The day-to-day investment of a life fund brings many practical problems, but it is important that in the exigencies of the work the general goal should not be overlooked.

The subject has recently been profitably discussed by Suttie, Whyte, and Coe and Ogborn (in the text-book shortly to be published). It is fair to say, however, that there is a considerable variety of view within the profession, and that there is nowhere in our literature a precise and accepted statement of principle. I find it desirable therefore to submit a theoretical basis as a springboard for discussion.

The word 'matching' has such a wide and general connotation that it is necessary to adopt a new label with a more precise significance. For this purpose I use the word 'immunization' to signify the investment of the assets in such a way that the existing business is immune to a general change in the rate of interest. The definition is not exact, but it should not mislead. On the basis of this definition immunization is to be regarded as a particular form of matching.

Adopting certain convenient simplifications of the practical problem, it will be assumed that, at a given moment of time, securities can be obtained to yield a uniform rate of interest whatever the term, and that all the funds are invested in fixed-interest securities which are either irredeemable or redeemable at a fixed date. For the moment it will be convenient to treat bonuses as guaranteed and included in the benefits.

Symbolically, the problem presents no difficulties.

Let L_t be the expected net outgo of the existing business in calendar year t, viz. claims and expenses less premiums (described hereafter as liability-outgo).* L_t can be positive or negative. For a growing company it will usually be negative in the near future and positive later.

Let A_t be the expected proceeds from the existing assets in year t, viz. interest plus maturing investments (described hereafter as asset-proceeds). It will be seen later that these definitions are crucial to a simple solution of the problem—and particularly the inclusion of interest in asset-proceeds. It is sounder to treat interest as part of the asset-proceeds rather than as a deduction from liability-outgo. In this way the liability-outgo is a fixed element in the investigation independent of investment policy. To deduct interest from the liability-outgo is to confuse the dependent and independent variables. Indeed, these definitions point the way directly to the main part of the solution; in the broadest sense, it is apparent without mathematical proof that if the liability-outgo and asset-proceeds are to be equally sensitive to changes in the rate of interest they must have roughly the same mean

* (1) The incidence of tax is assumed to be appropriately allowed for, e.g. tax is deducted separately from expenses and interest in the U.K. (2) Surrenders are ignored, the assumption being that the values granted are kept within the amounts available.

terms. This intuitive solution is not quite sufficient, as will be seen later, but is mentioned here to give the reader a common-sense foundation to his appreciation of the mathematical passages which follow.

Let V_L be the present value of the liability-outgo at the ruling rate of interest (force δ), so that $V_L = \Sigma v^t L_t$. Let V_A be the present value of the asset-proceeds at the same rate of interest so that $V_A = \Sigma v^t A_t$. Let it be further assumed that at the present moment $V_A = V_L$, any excess assets being 'free' funds to be separately invested.

Now suppose that the force of interest changes from δ to $(\delta + \epsilon)$ with a consequent change of V_A and V_L to V'_A and V'_L. Then the position after the change of interest is given by Taylor's theorem:

$$V'_A - V'_L = (V_A - V_L) + \epsilon \frac{d(V_A - V_L)}{d\delta} + \frac{\epsilon^2}{2!} \frac{d^2(V_A - V_L)}{d\delta^2} + \dots.$$

The first term in the expansion vanishes since $V_A = V_L$. It is clear that if there is to be no profit or loss whatever from the change in the force of interest then all the successive derivatives must vanish. In practice the first derivative is the most important for small changes of the rate of interest, and I shall therefore define a fund as immunized if the assets are so invested that $\frac{d(V_A - V_L)}{d\delta}$ is zero.

If the second derivative is positive, then, since the coefficient $\epsilon^2/2!$ is positive whether ϵ is positive or negative, any change in the force of interest will result in a profit to the fund so long as the change is not so large that the higher terms in the expansion begin to take effect. It is desirable, therefore, although the illustrations given later show that the point is not of great importance, that $\frac{d^2(V_A - V_L)}{d\delta^2}$ should be positive.[*]

A satisfactory immunization policy can, therefore, be expressed symbolically in the two equations

$$\frac{d(V_A - V_L)}{d\delta} = 0, \tag{1}$$

$$\frac{d^2(V_A - V_L)}{d\delta^2} > 0. \tag{2}$$

These expressions can be given verbal interpretation by expanding as follows:

$$V_A = \Sigma v^t A_t,$$

$$\frac{dV_A}{d\delta} = -\Sigma t v^t A_t,$$

$$\frac{d^2V_A}{d\delta^2} = \Sigma t^2 v^t A_t,$$

and similarly for V_L.

Thus equation (1) can be expressed as

$$\Sigma t v^t A_t = \Sigma t v^t L_t, \tag{3}$$

or, verbally,

the mean term of the value of the asset-proceeds must equal the mean term of the value of the liability-outgo.

---

[*] By analogy with equilibrium in statics we could describe a fund as immunized if the first derivative is zero, and the immunization as stable or unstable according as the second derivative is positive or negative.

Equation (2) can be expressed as

$$\Sigma t^2 v^t A_t > \Sigma t^2 v^t L_t, \tag{4}$$

or, in broad terms,

> the spread of the value of the asset-proceeds about the mean term should be greater than the spread of the value of the liability-outgo.

The simplicity of these formulae is due to the inclusion of interest in the asset-proceeds, but a further step has to be taken before the principles can be translated into a form which produces asset-maturity dates.

To illustrate the argument, consider the simple case where the liability-outgo consists of a single payment of one unit in 10 years' time. If the rate of interest is $2\frac{1}{2}\%$ net, the present value of the liability, $V_L = v^{10} = \cdot 78120$. This is also the present value of the asset we have to invest. There are an infinite number of ways of investing this asset to satisfy equation (3). If we could find an asset with no running yield (e.g. a savings certificate) maturing in 10 years time then we could immunize the liability by such an asset without further complication. But if, as is generally the case, we have to employ interest-bearing assets the term of the asset must be longer than 10 years, so that the mean term of the maturing investment plus the interest income equals 10 years. If we take the simplest case of investing in a single security yielding $2\frac{1}{2}\%$ net we find that the term of that asset must be $11\cdot485$ years. The mean term of the value of the total asset-proceeds (viz. interest of $\cdot01953$ for $11\cdot485$ years plus the redeemed asset of $\cdot78120$) is 10 years—the same as the mean term of the value of the liability-outgo. This illustration establishes an important theoretical and practical point that the term of the asset-maturity dates will be appreciably longer than the term of the value of the asset-proceeds and of the liability-outgo—but see (c) below. As a rough guide, for a given investment maturing in N years, if the interest-income gives a running yield at the same rate as the rate, i, at which the calculations are being made, then the mean term of the value of the asset-proceeds from that investment is $\bar{a}_{\overline{N}|}$. Put the other way round, if we have a particular liability due in T years' time, it can be immunized by an investment maturing in N years time where $\bar{a}_{\overline{N}|} = T$. For example, if $i = \cdot025$ and $T = 20$ then N is about 28 years. This example illustrates the lengthening of the asset-maturity compared with the asset-proceeds term. Another feature is disclosed by this illustration: There is a maximum value for T, viz. $1/\delta$, at which $\bar{a}_{\overline{N}|}$ is a perpetuity and N is infinity. If T is greater than this then there is no real solution for N. It is to be noted that in this paragraph the assets have been assumed to be invested in securities with the same running yield as the rate at which the calculations are made. If there were no running yield (e.g. savings certificates) the asset-maturity date would coincide with the mean term of the value of the asset-proceeds because the mean term of the proceeds of an asset with no running yield is the same as the term to maturity.

Examples of immunization and comments thereon are given in Appendix 1.

In regard to the basic equations (3) and (4), a few general observations can be made.

(a) There are usually an infinite number of solutions to the two equations, although, as has been seen, there may be no real solution for the asset-maturity dates.

(b) The interest-income included in the asset-proceeds represents no particular rate of interest. It is merely the income from the investments included in the fund, whether they were bought above or below par, or even bought in the distant past when quite different yields were obtainable.

(c) The equations define the position at a moment of time. Their solutions change continuously. For a fixed block of business followed through its history the difference between the term of asset-maturities and that of liability-outgo diminishes with the passage of time until, when the final liability payment falls due, it has become zero.

(d) The solution of the equations is dependent upon the current rate of interest.

(e) Changes in the constitution of the business inevitably affect the solution of the equations. For this reason, and also for the reasons given in (c) and (d), continual changes will be required in the investment portfolio. This does not invalidate the theoretical answer, since the necessary changes can be made without impairing the basic equation $V_A = V_L$.

(f) For a fund which without further new business would decline there is a particular theoretical solution to the equations when the asset-proceeds are arranged to coincide absolutely with the liability-outgo. This solution makes all the terms in the Taylor expansion zero and is therefore absolutely immune to all changes in interest however violent. This special case of immunization can be described as 'absolute' matching.

A sceptical reader may ask how it is possible to immunize existing business when, even if no new business is written, the funds will continue to grow for some years and require the investment of that growth at unknown rates of interest. The verbal answer to this question is that, if the rate of interest falls, there will be a shortfall in the yield on the future investments which have to be made, but there will be an exactly balancing excess in the appreciation of existing investments which have been invested for longer terms than the liabilities they have to meet. And similarly *mutatis mutandis* for a rise in the rate of interest.

This section may be fittingly concluded with a summary. The essence of the immunization theory is contained in two definitions, two rules and a rider. The definitions are 'liability-outgo' and 'asset-proceeds' and need not be repeated. (It is assumed that the present values of the two are equal.)

Rule 1. The mean term of the value of the asset-proceeds must equal the mean term of the value of the liability-outgo.

Rule 2. The spread about the mean of the value of the asset-proceeds should be greater than the spread of the value of the liability-outgo.

Rider. The mean term of the asset-maturity dates is considerably greater than that of the value of the asset-proceeds.

To these rules there should be added a clear warning that the whole examination is theoretical. Not only are there many and serious difficulties in giving practical effect to the theory (amounting in many circumstances to impossibility), but the extent to which it would be wise in practice to adopt the theory is a matter for consideration. It has to be remembered that apart from the minor second-derivative profits the immunization is against profit as well as loss.

4. CONSEQUENCES OF IMMUNIZATION

Let us consider a fund immunized at a rate of interest of $2\frac{1}{2}\%$ and assume that for the time being the rate of interest remains unchanged. The term of the maturities of the investments will usually be very long for a young fund. As the fund ages, this term shortens. If the fund becomes younger by heavy influx of business the term lengthens again. But so long as the fund does not become so very young that the term reaches infinity, the whole of the business, including any new business, can theoretically be immediately immunized at the $2\frac{1}{2}\%$ rate of interest. For a fund kept stationary by the influx of new business the theory entails a steady process of selling shorts and buying longs in order to maintain the same mean term.

Let us consider what happens when there is a change in the rate of interest. Any existing non-profit business has fixed benefits and premiums and is assumed to have been immunized at the $2\frac{1}{2}\%$ rate of interest. For with-profit business we can regard the bonus as guaranteed for this purpose, and it will have been immunized at the rate of bonus supported by a $2\frac{1}{2}\%$ rate of interest. If the interest changes to $3\frac{1}{2}\%$ the mean term of the value of the liability-outgo will change slightly, and a small rearrangement of the portfolio will be required which will give rise to a small 'second-derivative' profit or loss, although substantially the existing business will be unaffected. The benefits and premiums and the old guaranteed rate of bonus remain unchanged. When this rearrangement has been made the whole fund is immunized on a $3\frac{1}{2}\%$ basis, and the fact that it was once on a $2\frac{1}{2}\%$ basis can be forgotten except for the one fact that it is still the rate of bonus on the basis of $2\frac{1}{2}\%$ interest which has been immunized.

Now let us consider theoretically what happens when new business enters immediately after the rate of interest has changed. Considering non-profit business first, it is easier to see what happens if it is assumed that the rates of premium are changed from a $2\frac{1}{2}$ to $3\frac{1}{2}\%$ level, so that for this new business at the new rates of premium and the new rate of interest the premiums exactly match the benefits. If the investments for the whole fund continue to be made so as to fit the immunization equation, this new business will be completely immunized at a $3\frac{1}{2}\%$ level. For with-profit business we can reduce the premiums so as to produce the same bonus as the existing business. If we do this, the whole business, old and new, is immunized at the old rate of bonus. Or we can keep the old rate of premium which will now support a higher rate of bonus (say 45s. compared with the previous 30s.) and the new business will then be immunized at a 45s. rate of bonus.

The mathematical consequences of following this immunization procedure would be far-reaching. For well-established funds the theory brings these conclusions:

(*a*) That even though assurance contracts run for long periods into the future they could generally be immunized at the rate of interest ruling *at the date of issue* by immunizing the whole fund, including existing business and new business. (It is to be remembered, however, that it is the presence of the existing business which makes the immunization of new business possible.)

(*b*) That for non-profit business it is mathematically appropriate to change the rates of premium immediately upon a change in the general level of interest.

(*c*) That if a uniform rate of bonus is to be maintained it is also theoretically reasonable to change the with-profit premium rates immediately upon a change in the rate of interest. The theoretical alternative would be, while maintaining the same rates of premium, to differentiate the bonus according to the date of issue of the policies.

These mathematical results may be surprising and their appropriateness in practice may be questioned. As has been explained, the purpose of the section on immunization is not to advocate a system of investment, and it is perhaps desirable having proceeded so far to mention some of the practical complications:

(*a*) There is difficulty in relating varied yields on assets to some particular rate of interest for valuing liabilities. Yields are not uniform for all terms of assets, and the differentials are not stable in time. Nor are the differentials between classes of assets stable.

(*b*) The theory is considerably disturbed by the wide range of redemption dates contained in many Government securities. Options, whether in the assets or the liabilities, can be serious danger points.

(*c*) The theory would be difficult to interpret in practice because of the existence of such assets as equity shares, properties, mortgages on an open basis, and so on. Either the income, or the term, or both, of many assets are indeterminate.

(*d*) Offices would be reluctant, and properly so, to invest heavily in long-term securities in a period of very low interest rates.

(*e*) Investment policy must be flexible to take advantage of special opportunities.

(*f*) Offices have considerable surplus funds, which can be regarded as falling outside the immunization theory.

It may well be concluded that the immunization theory should not dictate investment policies, although it is enlightening about the consequences and points to a norm.

In addition to the difficulties of implementing the theory there are problems of the public presentation of results. These problems are discussed in the later sections on the valuation of assets and liabilities. There are some aspects, however, which can best be dealt with here.

Immunization implies that a fall in the value of assets would be matched by a fall in the value of liabilities, but in published results this will be realized only if the system of valuing the liabilities follows the logic of the theory, that is to say, if it is a gross premium valuation of the anticipated actual income and outgo. If some other system of valuation is used then the correspondence between the fall in assets and liabilities will not necessarily be apparent. For example, net premium valuations are far less responsive to changes in interest rates than gross premium valuations. It is true that by investing relatively short the sensitiveness of assets to a change in the rate of interest could be made to correspond to the comparative insensitiveness of liabilities valued on a net premium basis. But this is not genuine immunization. A particular valuation basis may be desirable for many reasons but it must be a servant of realities for it cannot be their master.

There is a point to notice, however, in connexion with practical valuations. If the rate of interest rises, a valuation of liabilities at this higher rate may produce negative values. The immunization theory implies that these negative values are real, whereas policy-holders may exercise their option to lapse.

This is a particular example of the general option problem. There is no theoretical solution, but it might be reasonable for the younger funds, where negative values may be substantial, to invest somewhat short of the theoretical asset-maturity dates.

5. VALUATION PRELIMINARIES

The following comments, amounting almost to definitions, will simplify later sections.

Gross rate of interest

The gross rate of interest apparent from a life assurance revenue account may, of course, be misleading. The interest shown in the account may include interest on capital and contingency funds which are themselves not included in the 'life assurance fund'. A more realistic rate would be obtained by dividing the total interest by the total assets shown in the balance sheet. But this is still misleading, since the balance-sheet value of the assets may differ from the market value—if, indeed, market value is itself a final denominator. Further to confuse the issue, as the value of the assets changes under changing conditions so should the amount of interest. For example, the value of a debenture yielding 4%, redeemable in 10 years and standing at par, may rise to 108 upon a general fall in interest rates to 3% and still give an apparent yield of £3. 14s.; but this yield is misleading, since the interest receipts include part of the extra capital which will be written off over the term to maturity. Finally, there is normally a considerable range between the interest yields on long-term and short-term investments and between the various categories of security. In these confused circumstances, what do we mean by 'the' rate of interest?

It is a tempering thought that, at the very foundation of the subject, the main factor should be so elusive. There is, I believe, no easy remedy. When the actuary values the liabilities at a gross rate of interest of, say, 4%, his meaning is clear enough, but it will need internal investigation to verify that this rate has a reasonable prospect of being maintained.

The principle that for redeemable assets the amount of interest should change as the value of assets changes is fundamental and forms an undercurrent to the whole valuation problem. Our thoughts on the subject would be more efficient if we had a more precise set of verbal tools. We should adopt some such phrase as 'income from investments' to cover the current income which appears in our revenue accounts as 'Interest, Dividends and Rents'. The word 'Interest' is dangerous, and a broader title would make it clearer that this income has no specific relationship to any valid 'rate of interest'. In the example given above the only true figure at that moment of time for a rate of accumulation is 3%, and there are obvious dangers in allowing thoughts of 4% (if the book value is kept at 100) or of £3. 14s. 0d.% (if the book value is written up to 108) to enter our calculations. We must always distinguish between g and i.

Income tax

In order to make proper allowance for tax on 'interest less expenses' I believe that the full rate of taxation (now 7s. 6d. in the £) should be deducted from both items and that this should be done not only in premium calculations but also in valuation. This has been disputed, but it is doubtful if a certificate of solvency should be given to a fund which would not stand a test on this basis. To do less is to rely on a subsidy from future new business. (For industrial business the practical basis of taxation is often 'proprietors' profits', and the existence of the alternatives raises a complex technical issue which cannot be discussed here.)

Estate

A life office may, and usually will, have some margins or reserves in three places:

(a) within the valuation of liabilities, either explicit or implied in a stringent valuation basis,

(b) in asset-margins, and

(c) in central reserve or contingency funds or capital.

It is convenient to give a title to all these reserves combined, and the word 'estate' has a useful connotation.

It is illuminating to examine the distributed surplus for a valuation period under the following three headings—without too close examination of the words at this stage.

			£
	(i)	True surplus earned by existing business	......
plus	(ii)	Interest contribution from the existing estate	......
less	(iii)	Contribution from surplus to the estate	......
		Total (= distributed surplus)	

These three items alone form an interesting commentary on the inner history of a life assurance fund and go a long way to rectify any confusion arising from conventional presentations.

New business expenses in valuation

It has become conventional in this country to allow, directly or indirectly, for future expenses at the over-all level experienced by a continuing fund and to ignore the fact that, new business expenses having already been incurred, future expenses on the existing business will be renewal expenses only. The consequence is usually (depending upon the precise method of valuation) that new business causes a heavy strain, and that the resulting surplus is considerably distorted.

There is no question but that the distortion may obscure the truth of events, even for the actuary himself, unless correction is made. For internal purposes I think it is essential therefore to use a modified valuation basis which eliminates this distortion as far as possible.

For a net premium valuation the phrase 'unmodified net premium valuation' will be used to denote a valuation employing the unloaded net premium P_x, and the phrase 'modified net premium valuation' to denote a valuation employing net premiums adjusted for new business expenses ($P'_x = P_x + K/d$, where K represents the additional new business expenses per unit sum assured, net of tax, which it is felt can be appropriately spread over the future).

It is well known that (where premiums are payable throughout the full duration)

$$V_z' = V_z - K(S - V_z),$$

and, in the usual way, $K(S - V_z)$ is referred to as the Zillmer deduction, and V_z' as modified or Zillmerized reserves, etc.

Although it is well appreciated that new business strain can arise under an unmodified net premium valuation, it is not equally appreciated that it can also arise under a gross premium valuation. Discussion has taken place in the past as to whether under a gross premium valuation future expenses should be allowed for at the over-all level or the renewal level. The best answer is probably neither, because if the fund were closed to new business the rate of renewal expense would rise. Subject to this qualification, however, the rate of expense employed in a realistic valuation should approximate to the renewal level rather than the over-all level.

The phrases 'unmodified' and 'modified' will be applied to gross premium valuations with the same significance as for net premium valuations. Where no specific reference is made it is to be understood that modified valuations are being considered.

There may be the soundest reasons for holding additional reserves and the use of the over-all level of future expense may be an excellent way of holding such reserves, but for internal purposes, in trying to arrive at the true trend of events, renewal expenses only must be debited against business on the books. The acceptance of new business strain may be a pleasant luxury or even a near-necessity, but it is better to regard it as an adjustment made after the surplus has been examined and not before.

Changes of basis

It is a commonplace that the basis of valuation does not directly affect the present value of the surplus which will ultimately accrue but merely the incidence of the emergence of surplus. In Appendix II this is illustrated by the separate histories of a given block of business controlled by different valuation bases. Theoretically, a strong valuation basis dams up the surplus and provides a deeper reservoir.

It is important, however, to consider what happens when the valuation basis is changed—for example, when it is weakened by an increase in the rate of interest employed. The theoretical result is a large release of surplus in the year in question associated with smaller surpluses in all future years. In practice, however, the outcome depends on the use which is made of the large release in the year in question; if, in fact, it is reserved and not distributed it will continue to earn interest and to contribute to surplus. The ultimate effect will depend on the future history of the office. If the business declines, the office may ultimately prove to be stronger by reason of having weakened its valuation basis and having put the release to reserve than if it had maintained a stronger valuation basis and distributed the resulting higher surplus as bonus.

This train of thought has to be borne in mind throughout the rest of the paper. Under changing conditions there is a continual interchange between current liabilities and the estate, just as there is between capital and interest in the revenue account.

6. VALUATION PRINCIPLES

The preceding sections of the paper have been in the nature of a preliminary to a consideration of the problems of valuation proper. They have dealt primarily with the underlying realities, whereas valuation is to a considerable extent a problem of presentation.

A valuation has two main purposes, and the fundamental difficulty is that these two purposes are in conflict. The first and primary purpose is to ensure that the office is solvent. The second is to allow the surplus to emerge in an equitable way suited to the bonus system. The solvency criterion leads to a changing valuation basis, influenced solely by prospective considerations and probably uniform for all policies. On the other hand, the pursuit of equity of emergence of surplus tends to lead to stable valuation bases, influenced mainly by retrospective considerations and possibly differentiated according to the terms at issue. We are thus faced at the beginning with that most fruitful source of controversy, the attempt to reply to two different questions in a single answer.

A third main purpose of valuation should perhaps be added: the presentation of results in a proper manner for public scrutiny. This duty may be troublesome when so much of the problem is complex and technical; but it is probably, in the long run, in the best interests of the offices.

There is a further fundamental conflict: the valuation of assets and the valuation of liabilities have a different rationale. Assets and liabilities are different in nature, the value of the former being more speculative, but this difference is not sufficient to justify the odd position into which history has led us. The customary test applied to the valuation of assets is a test appropriate to a solvency valuation, namely, 'Are the assets of the value stated?' On the other hand, the valuation of liabilities has, in the course of time, acquired most of the attributes of an equity valuation. It is an interesting train of thought to consider what the valuation process would be if we adopted a similar basis for both assets and liabilities.

Fig. 1 shows the same problem in a different light. This diagram illustrates for a hypothetical office the value of assets and liabilities at different rates of interest. The heavy lines A and L show the position if there were no options. The dotted lines show the effect of various options.

A' is typical of the effect on the value of assets if the fixed-interest securities have a wide range of redemption dates at the option of the borrower.

L' shows the effect of options to take cash, e.g. guaranteed cash surrender values, or options with a smaller interest content than the basic contract.

L'' shows the effect of options with a larger interest content than the basic contract, e.g. annuity options at maturity.

The office shown in Fig. 1 is, as the result of holding properly matched investments, basically sound because the assets exceed the liabilities at all rates of interest, but the dotted lines show how the effect of options can whittle away the surplus, especially in the extreme conditions of high and low interest rates.

Figs. 2 and 3 illustrate the effect, in two offices with the same liabilities, first of investing short, and second of investing long. Both these diagrams show a similar substantial surplus if the gross rate of interest is 4% but show that insolvency would result if the rate of interest falls low enough for the first example, or rises high enough for the second.

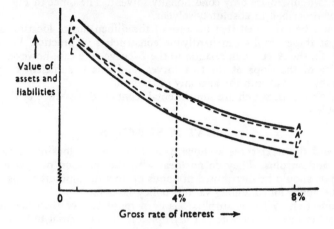

Fig. 1

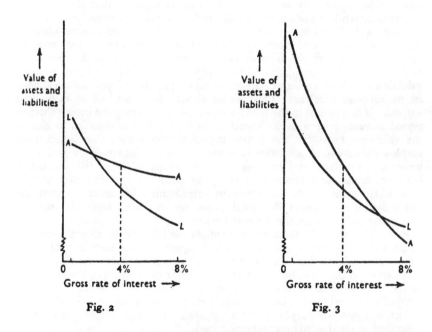

Fig. 2   Fig. 3

Fig. 1. Illustration of the variations in the values of assets (*A*) and liabilities (*L*) with the rate of interest when the fund is immunized, and of the effect of options.

Fig. 2. Illustration of the variations in the values of assets (*A*) and liabilities (*L*) with the rate of interest when the fund is invested short.

Fig. 3. Illustration of the variations in the values of assets (*A*) and liabilities (*L*) with the rate of interest when the fund is invested long.

These two offices are only conditionally solvent. The office in Fig. 1 could almost be described as absolutely solvent.

It should be explained that because of the difficulties of locating the rate of interest these graphs can hardly be constructed in practice. We cannot precisely fix the A-curve in relation to the L-curve. We can, however, obtain a fair idea of the slope of the two curves, and this is sufficient to give us considerable insight into the anatomy of the fund.

These diagrams, which are fundamental, contain the essence of the valuation problem.

7. WHAT IS SURPLUS?

This and the next three sections deal with the interlocking of valuation practice and surplus. They do not deal with the question of how much of the surplus should be distributed in bonus or how the amount so distributed should be apportioned among various policy-holders.

The question 'What is surplus?' is even more elusive than the question 'What is the rate of interest?' In my opinion, it is essential to keep a clear distinction between two aspects of surplus which for convenience I shall call 'revenue surplus' and 'capitalized surplus'. An explanation of these terms is best given by an illustration. Let us suppose that the mortality experience, while showing the usual random variations from year to year, discloses a declining trend over a long period. A time may come when we decide that the basis of mortality employed in valuation in the past must be lightened. Although the facts move gradually and certainly, the decision is both sudden and speculative. The change to a lighter mortality basis in valuation will have an immediate effect on surplus in the year in question— let us suppose a release. This release should be described as capitalized surplus. It is due, not to the favourable experience during the inter-valuation period as compared with the valuation basis, but to the decision to change the valuation basis for the future expected experience, thus anticipating surplus which would otherwise have accrued in the future. This distinction between capitalized and revenue surplus has parallels in the distinction between capital and revenue in company accounts and indeed embraces some of the same points, since revenue surplus for a life assurance company can only be ascertained if capital items are excluded from the revenue account as well as from the valuation results.

It would perhaps be tendentious to apply the label 'true' to any particular figure for the surplus, but there is one figure for the surplus which can legitimately claim the title of 'natural', namely, surplus resulting from a valuation on the same bases as were used in the calculation of the premiums and based on revenue accounts from which all capital items have been scrupulously excluded. Surplus calculated by this system can be described as 'natural revenue surplus', and a valuation on the premium basis can be described as on the 'natural valuation basis'.*

* It may be that with-profit premium rates are left unchanged for many years, and that the nominal formula employed becomes obsolete and out of step with current experience. It is desirable, however, to re-express the premium rates actually charged in the light of the actuary's assessment of the future experience at the time of issue. The re-cast formula expresses the plan or intention at the time a policy is issued, and it is a valuation on the basis of this original plan which earns the title of a 'natural valuation'.

The concept of 'natural revenue surplus' is fundamental to the appreciation of the following sections. Some comments may point the issue. There may be—indeed, there often are—good reasons why an office should capitalize future losses even perhaps at a time when their occurrence is still only problematical. It nevertheless remains desirable for clarity of thought that we should distinguish between such capitalized losses and the natural revenue surplus. Here again we note the conflict between a solvency valuation and an equity valuation. 'Natural revenue surplus' corresponds essentially to an equity valuation, whereas our instinct to capitalize future losses is a reflexion of our proper desire also to conduct a solvency valuation. A valuation on the premium basis has no direct connexion with solvency and could in exceptional circumstances leave the office insolvent.

A final illustration may help. Let us consider the position of an office which has not matched its assets to its liabilities and has, for example, invested short. On a change in the rate of interest, the failure to match will result in large profits or losses if any attempt is made to capitalize the situation as it appears at the moment of valuation. These profits or losses may in fact never materialize if the rate of interest reverts to its original level. The surplus under such conditions would fluctuate, and what we think of as profit at one moment may ultimately prove to be a loss. If, however, for that same office the valuation of liabilities is conducted on the natural valuation basis and the valuation of assets is unchanged, the consequences of the failure to immunize affect the surplus as and when they materialize—namely, when the over-short investments having matured and fresh investments having been made, a higher or lower rate of interest than originally anticipated is physically received. This illustration shows that whatever qualifications may need to be attached to the natural revenue surplus as a practical instrument it is at any rate a clear conception, whereas any other estimate of the surplus is not.

8. VALUATION UNDER STABLE CONDITIONS

For with-profit premiums which include a bonus loading, a valuation on the natural or premium basis would normally be described as a bonus reserve valuation. The phrase 'bonus reserve valuation' usually implies a gross premium valuation, but it is of course possible to have net premium bonus reserve valuations. A valuation on the same basis as that employed in the premiums can equally well be described as a gross premium bonus reserve valuation or as a net premium bonus reserve valuation, since the two are identical.

It is well known that the conventional net premium valuation basis adopted by most British offices can be made to approximate closely to a bonus reserve valuation on the premium basis by employing a Zillmer factor and by an artificial reduction in the rate of interest. The table in Appendix II shows the emergence of surplus for a given block of new business on various valuation bases, and it is seen that the emergence of surplus under basis *b* (iii) is very similar to that on the strict premium basis.

If these were the only considerations the bonus reserve method of valuation would appear to have the advantage over the net premium method; the bonus reserve valuation is direct and self-explanatory, whereas the net premium valuation is artificial. Further, a gross premium bonus reserve valuation, not requiring a net premium constant, is simpler.

There is, however, an aspect of the problem which does not appear in a theoretical examination but greatly affects the practice of valuation. Premium bases are delicate instruments which can and do include refinements to allow for all the many factors influencing the actuary's judgment in fixing his premium scales. They can, for example, allow for a different rate of interest for different terms of policy, for different mortality adjustments at different ages and so on. It is not practicable to carry these refinements into a valuation. Expediency demands that a simple valuation basis be adopted which applies generally to policies issued in the past under quite different premium bases. The difficulty of a bonus reserve valuation is that it immediately capitalizes any difference between the premium basis and the valuation basis; it inevitably introduces a capitalized element into the revenue surplus. If, for example, we consider the simple case of a block of new business, it is not possible to value each policy on its individual premium basis; an aggregate basis has to be used, and this aggregate basis may produce a substantial and immediate new business strain. It is not easy to identify this new business strain, and it can produce a substantial distortion of surplus. The modified net premium valuation has an advantage in this respect, since the emergence of surplus thereunder is not seriously distorted even if the valuation basis does differ slightly from the premium basis.

The great justification for the net premium valuation is that it gives an approximation to the premium basis of valuation and therefore to the natural revenue surplus. As such it is relatively fool-proof and cannot easily be abused. It cannot be used, for example, to capitalize future profits and thereby to bolster a position where expenses are running at an untenable level. When we consider that the life assurance fund of a well-established company contains the history of many years of changing events, there is great virtue in a net premium valuation which can be made to approximate to all the various premium bases which have been employed.

The view is sometimes held that in some way a bonus reserve valuation is scientifically accurate, whereas the net premium valuation is no more than a convenient façade. It is odd that those holding such an opinion do not ask themselves the simple question whether it is in fact right to assume a *uniform* future bonus. The answer is clearly negative; changes in the experience and in the constitution of the business should have a direct influence upon surplus. Any claims to some peculiar virtue in a bonus reserve valuation in my opinion arise from a misunderstanding. The bonus reserve valuation is an instrument, like the net premium valuation, with its own uses and its own limitations.

These remarks are not to be interpreted as an attack on the bonus reserve method of valuation. As will be seen later there are circumstances in which the net premium valuation fails us, and when this happens there is much to be said for a bonus reserve valuation. But in stable conditions my personal preference is for a net premium valuation, and I base this preference not upon expediency but upon the personal insight to be gained into the anatomy of a life assurance fund. Three main documents are required to investigate the position of a life assurance fund:

(*a*) An analysis of surplus on a modified net premium valuation basis uniform throughout the period examined. The picture gains in vividness if each item of surplus is expressed as a rate of bonus.

(*b*) Comments on the trend in each of the items in the analysis. The main items of information missing from the analysis are the future trends of the loading surplus and interest income resulting from the past history of premium changes and investment practice. With this knowledge it is comparatively simple to estimate the way the fund will unfold in the future if conditions remain unchanged.

(*c*) Some statement of the position of the office regarding the matching of investments against liabilities.

If the valuation has been conducted on a bonus reserve basis, the assessment of the situation is in some ways more difficult; the capitalized surplus or loss which has inevitably crept in has to be excluded. This may not be easy. The future rate of bonus reserved for in the valuation cannot necessarily be regarded as a forecast of future events. It is highly sensitive among other things to the rate of interest employed in the valuation. Similarly, the rate of bonus depends on an estimate of all the valuation factors, including rates of withdrawal. There is a further danger to which all valuation methods are liable, but perhaps particularly the bonus reserve method: if care is not taken to distinguish the estate from the other funds, a valuation which aims to be realistic may disclose excessively high bonus prospects by implying the release of the whole or a large part of the office's estate throughout the lifetime of the present policy-holders.

Some of these difficulties can be avoided by the following internal analysis of a bonus reserve valuation.

On the basis of the best possible estimate of all valuation factors, including provision for withdrawal and bringing in the full market value of assets, let it be supposed that

(*a*) the rate of bonus supportable by existing business using all the existing assets is, say, 52*s*.%,

(*b*) the rate of bonus supportable by current new business is, say, 35*s*.%.

Let it be further supposed that the amount of the reserves released on existing business if the future rate of bonus were 35*s*. instead of 52*s*., is £X. This figure of £X can be treated as the estate, so that a fair summary of the position of the office is that the rate of bonus supportable in the future is 35*s*., and that to this there can be added such bonus, not necessarily uniform, as the interest on the estate, less any contributions which it is planned to make to the estate, will provide.

This is a clear enough picture, but it has to be admitted that it is laborious to obtain; that it is precarious, since it is highly sensitive to the valuation factors adopted; and that it brings one, uncertainly, to a result which can be readily seen from a net premium valuation. However, I do not wish to exaggerate the difficulties of a bonus reserve valuation. A competent actuary can interpret the results of either a net premium or a gross premium valuation and use them to estimate future trends. The ease and reliability with which he does so will depend more on the scrupulousness of the analysis of surplus than on the method of valuation employed.

9. ACTIVE OR PASSIVE VALUATION POLICY

External conditions are continually changing. Should effect be given to these changes in the valuation?

A preliminary question is 'Can effect be given to them?' and the answer is 'Only very roughly.' A valuation is a crude instrument which cannot

reflect in detail the variety and complexity of events. There has been a considerable increase in the rate of interest during 1951. But exactly how much?
The longs and shorts, gilt-edged, debentures, equities have each undergone
a different experience. If we attempt to adopt an active valuation policy and
give effect to the year's events by altering both our liability and asset valuations, how are we to ensure that the alteration we make to the one corresponds
with the alteration to the other? An error of $\frac{1}{8}\%$ in the rate of interest in
a gross premium valuation will entirely distort the surplus.

It must be concluded that an active valuation policy has to be ruled out
as a satisfactory means of estimating or controlling the real emergence of
surplus. Surplus can be estimated only by a passive valuation policy which
leaves the valuation basis both of assets and liabilities unchanged, however
much the answer so produced may need qualification in practice. Yet when
we turn to the question of solvency there is no word to be said in favour of
a passive policy; it is only an active policy, paying full regard to existing (and
estimated future) experience, which has any significance. It is this conflict
between the solvency demand for an active policy and the equity demand
for a passive policy which is the core of our problem.

In practice, the event which brings the problem most forcibly to our
attention is a swing in the general rate of interest associated with a swing in
the market value of securities. An attempt is sometimes made to side-step
the issue by using notional values for certain securities so that in the event
of a sharp depression in market values at some 31 December the assets can
in total be stated in the balance sheet at a value higher than their market
value—the higher value probably being obtained by including redeemable
securities at their present value on a lower rate of interest than that ruling at
the time. So long as this lower rate of interest is not lower than the rate
employed in the valuation then the argument for notional values can be
appreciated and in times of sudden crisis their use may have value. · In my
opinion, however, the use of notional values as a general practice is dubious,
and the public instinct to take account of market values of securities has
justification. The indiscriminate use of notional values can conceal real
insolvency arising from badly matched assets; if the investments are excessively long-dated, the fall in value of the assets will be greater than the
fall in the value of liabilities and the loss may prove to be permanent.

One can imagine an intelligent member of the public speaking to this
effect: 'I know that any solvency test can only be conditional. It can only
say that the fund is solvent in certain specified conditions. But the best I can
do is to ask you to certify solvency at the end of each valuation period in the
conditions then ruling. It is true that those conditions may not be permanent,
but then they may be. If you continue to certify solvency on the basis of the
market values ruling at the time of valuation, I shall be satisfied that your
successive certificates of conditional solvency amount to a certificate of
absolute solvency. If, however, I grant you a dispensation every time you
are embarrassed by depreciation I shall always be in doubt. Further, though
you may not like doing what I ask it will be good for you too because it will
keep you face-to-face with realities.'

The practice which has gradually developed in this country for over-
coming the basic difficulty has been to build up reserves to cushion the impact
of events. As indicated earlier, such reserves can be held in three places:
in the liabilities, either explicitly or implicitly in a strong valuation basis;

in the assets, by way of margin between book and market values; and in central reserve or contingency funds. When market values fall the asset-margin takes the first blow, and if this is insufficient the central reserves are used to write down assets or to support a balance-sheet certificate which is qualified to the effect that 'the market value of the assets plus reserve funds is greater than the book value'. In such circumstances the liability-cushion cannot be used except by changing the valuation basis and releasing funds from the liabilities to assist the assets. When the wind blows from the opposite quarter, the rate of interest has dropped and market values are high. In this event it is normally only the liability-margin which is immediately available to enable the actuary to sign his report with a clear conscience. It is to be noted, however, that the actuary's certificate as to liabilities is of a less rigorous nature than the market-value test customarily applied to the balance-sheet value of assets; it is a certificate not of fact but of opinion, and while the actuary has the duty not only to satisfy himself but also to give sufficient evidence to make his certificate acceptable to the public, it is also legitimate for him to bear in mind the existence of the other cushions, and if necessary to draw attention to them.

In the earlier days of our profession it was no doubt often the case that the only cushion the actuary could establish—and that with difficulty—was the liability-cushion. It may be that nowadays we are in danger of going too far the other way. There is a great deal to be said for this three-cushion system but it is achieved at the expense of past generations of policy-holders and can be carried to the point of luxury. In these days of rapid inflation even the most mature companies are feeling the strain of new growth, and we have to ask ourselves how far we should ask the present generation to contribute to the estate.

The three-cushion system is wasteful of resources in that the liability-margin and asset-margin are not easily available to meet a difficulty on the other side of the balance sheet. In this respect the central reserve has a great advantage. It can be used to support a qualified balance-sheet certificate, and I would put it to the profession that it could properly be used to support a qualified certificate by the actuary. For example, the actuary could value the liabilities at $2\frac{1}{2}\%$ and add a rider that the reserve funds would enable him to value at 2%. Of course the reserve funds could not be used simultaneously to support both a qualified balance-sheet certificate and a qualified certificate by the actuary. But that is not our problem. As L. Brown recently put it in cogent terms, 'the rate of interest cannot both rise and fall at the same time'.

If at a particular moment of time an office possesses a liability-margin of $\pounds X$ which is sufficient to withstand a drop of $x\%$ in the rate of interest and an asset-margin of $\pounds Y$ sufficient to withstand a rise of $y\%$ in the rate of interest, then—assuming assets and liabilities to be well matched—it can, by placing the two margins in a central reserve fund of $\pounds(X+Y)$, put itself in the position that it can withstand either a rise or a fall of approximately $(x+y)\%$ in the rate of interest. The central reserve fund has a flexibility which the asset and liability-margins do not possess and is an economy which, in the interests of the present generation of policy-holders, we ought not to overlook.

A major item in the liability-margin is the new business strain locked up by the use of unmodified reserves. The use of unmodified reserves is to be respected, and their adoption as a standard of strength by British offices has undoubtedly contributed greatly to sound progress. But the reserves so locked up, being largely inaccessible, have not relieved offices from the desire to build up asset-margins and central reserves. We have to ask ourselves at what pace is it reasonable to augment our margins and where is the most service-able place to hold them. I venture to suggest that unmodified reserves have been an excellent servant but should not be our master, and that circumstances may arise in which justice requires us to depart from them. Would not the equivalent amount held in a central reserve fund be an even better servant?

The broad picture which emerges from these considerations is that a passive valuation policy is desirable in the interests of equity, and that the main-tenance of central reserve funds at a reasonable level is an economical way of holding the additional reserves which may be required to demonstrate solvency in changing conditions.

10. MINOR VARIATIONS IN CONDITIONS

The preceding sections have made a case for a passive valuation policy on the natural valuation basis, and have defended the use of the net premium method in practice on the grounds that it is an approximation thereto. It is, however, only an approximation. The time came, for example, when O^M mortality had to be abandoned in favour of A1924–29. On the theory of the natural valuation basis this time arrived, not immediately when the mortality experience confirmed itself at the lower level (whenever that was), but when the bulk of the business had premiums based on A1924–29. In other words, the philosophy of the net premium basis does not call for hurry in giving effect to changes in experience, whether they be in interest, mortality or expense.

This leisurely process in making valuation changes does, however, ignore the demands for a solvency test. It implies that the valuation basis is always likely to be more or less obsolete. In truth it has to be admitted that it is sometimes not immediately apparent from the published returns of a British life office that it could in fact satisfy a rigid solvency test, because strength in one direction, e.g. more than adequate expense margins, has to be offset against weakness in, say, the interest basis. It has to be quickly added, however, that it seldom needs serious examination to discover that the office is indeed handsomely solvent.

In fact, the offices have reached a typically British compromise. In the main they adopt a passive valuation policy allowing the surplus to emerge in what is probably a reasonable approximation to the natural emergence. They do, however, recognize the need for a solvency test by making such occasional modifications in the valuation basis as will serve to satisfy the public that a solvency test could be passed without difficulty. Moreover, it is clear that in the main the cost of these capital changes is—as I think, properly—met out of the company's 'estate' and not out of immediate revenue surplus.

There is a great deal of experience behind the valuation practice of British offices, and while a superficial theoretical examination of that practice might be critical, a more profound examination would conclude that the current practice in this country is at least as satisfactory as the more elaborate attempts at theoretical accuracy which are adopted (or enforced) in some other countries.

The preceding paragraphs in this section have been written with the thought of a net premium valuation uppermost in mind. The position as regards a gross premium bonus reserve valuation is not so clear. The phrase bonus reserve valuation tends to imply an active valuation policy. It is apparent, however, that in practice it is used, if not entirely, at least to a considerable extent as another method of passive valuation. Minor changes are customary, but, generally speaking, there is little attempt to give full recognition to the current and estimated future experience at the moment of valuation. With one notable exception, offices using a bonus reserve valuation do not bring in their assets at market value, which may be regarded as the hall-mark of a truly active policy. In short the offices using a bonus reserve valuation are adopting a similar type of compromise to those using a net premium valuation. Their instrument is in many ways more flexible: while they may find it harder to decide what the 'true and fair' surplus for the year should be, they probably find it a good deal easier to present their results in such a way that the right surplus emerges and that at the same time the company's solvency can be demonstrated.

The view is sometimes expressed that a net premium valuation is a convenient form of presentation of results, but that to find the truth an internal bonus reserve valuation should be made. Paradoxically, perhaps, I believe the exact reverse to be the case: given a thorough analysis of surplus on a reasonable net premium basis, the anatomy of a life fund is clear enough and a bonus reserve valuation, if it gives a different answer (which it frequently does), calls for further investigation. But as a means of presentation of results a gross premium valuation has undisputed advantages and, as will be seen in the next section, may in certain circumstances be imperative.

11. EXTREME VARIATIONS IN CONDITIONS

It remains to consider what is to be done when the swing in the rate of interest is so large that the available buffers are insufficient. It is clear that the basis of valuation of liabilities may have to be changed, but this raises a number of subsidiary problems.

Let us consider a sharp rise in the rate of interest and a fall in market values. If the office has adopted a sound matching policy and has not been careless in granting options, its fundamental position should not be greatly affected. But funds have to be found out of the fall in the value of liabilities to support the assets.

In the first place, it is to be noted that, theoretically, such support for the assets from the liabilities should be a loan and not a gift. This can be seen from consideration of either the liabilities or the assets. If the support is used to write down redeemable assets below their par value, the time will come, as securities approach maturity, when the support is no longer needed and has become asset-surplus.

In the second place the net premium valuation may fail to meet the situation. As has already been mentioned, a net premium valuation is only partially sensitive to a change in the rate of interest because the change in the rate is accompanied by a change in the net premiums—a technical idiosyncrasy which has no counterpart in the facts. In general, a net premium valuation can be described as about one-third or one-half sensitive to interest changes. If, therefore, the rate of interest rises sufficiently high, the associated fall in the value of assets may be so great that the partial relief from changing the net premium valuation rate of interest will be inadequate. Further relief may be found by using modified reserves and releasing the Zillmer deduction or by bringing in contingency funds. Taking the extreme case, however, when. although the office is basically sound, there is still a shortfall in the assets let us consider the mechanics of what happens. Suppose that before the rise in interest the company was earning $2\frac{1}{2}\%$ net, at which rate its existing and new business could each support a 30s. simple reversionary bonus, that by valuing its with-profit business on a 2% modified net premium basis, the surplus was emerging at the rate required to grant such a bonus, and that the business had been approximately immunized on this basis. Now let us suppose that the net rate of interest rises suddenly to $3\frac{1}{2}\%$, that the premium rates are unchanged and for new business will support 45s. bonus at the new rate of interest. For new business a net premium valuation of with-profit business at about $2\frac{3}{4}\%$ would allow the new 45s. rate of bonus to emerge. However, this same basis cannot be achieved for existing business, since it would, equally as it does for new business, set up reserves sufficient to support a 45s. bonus in the future, and there are only enough assets to support 30s. bonus.

But a gross premium valuation is not without similar difficulties. A bonus reserve valuation with 30s. future bonus and using $3\frac{1}{2}\%$ interest will give approximately the right answer for the existing business and will release sufficient reserves to meet the fall in assets. But the same basis, if employed for new business, will capitalize into surplus the whole of the 15s. additional future bonus which the higher rate of interest will support.

There is no simple answer, as this illustration shows. If the change in the rate of interest were permanent and were immediately known to be permanent. it would be possible, and perhaps right, to close the fund for old business and to start a new fund for future business; but it is a principle of this paper that we cannot know that such changes are permanent.

It is perhaps desirable to admit to ourselves that if there is a sufficiently large break in the rate of interest there is no single valuation basis which will adequately answer the two basic questions: 'is the company solvent?' and 'is surplus emerging satisfactorily?' In such circumstances it becomes necessary to divorce the two questions and to concentrate, in the public presentation of results, on an adequate answer to the solvency question, dealing separately with the question of emergence of surplus by internal investigation.

12. BONUS POLICY

A passive system of valuation strictly on the premium bases would allow the surplus to emerge naturally and equitably. This would, of course, entail innumerable subdivisions of the business in valuation according to premium basis at the date of issue. In practice, however, any reasonable net premium basis will be a fair substitute.

How is this surplus to be apportioned among the various policy-holders? If the office has strictly adopted the immunization theory the mathematical consequences to bonus policy of following the theory through would be both uncompromising and uncomfortable. The implications following from the fact that contracts can be immunized at the rate of interest ruling at the date of issue are entirely foreign to the habits of life assurance in this country. Followed to a logical conclusion they would lead either to day-to-day variations in with-profit premium rates, or to complete fragmentation of the business for bonus purposes.

However, while matching in a general sense is desirable there are many practical reasons for departing from strict immunization. The sharp edges of the mathematical theory are blurred in practice, and it has to be remembered that the immunization of new business is only possible by reason of the existence of the large fund of existing business.

There is much to be said in equity for extending the insurance principle not only to cover variations within groups of policy-holders but also to cover variations between successive groups.

More important, however, than these considerations is the relationship between office and policy-holder. There is an unwritten understanding with the policy-holder that the bonus declaration should be simple and such as to commend itself to him. Justice must not only be done but must be seen to be done, and there is no doubt that a policy of differentiating bonuses according to the rate of interest ruling at issue would never be understood.

Few British actuaries would differ from the conclusion that the wider grounds for uniformity in bonus declarations override the mathematical grounds for differentiation.

If we decide in favour of uniform bonus (simple or compound), the final question is 'at what rate?' This is a deep question, but the following breakdown of the situation clarifies the picture. (The figures are purely hypothetical and explanations follow.)

Source of surplus	Rate of bonus		
	Now	10 years time	20 years time
A. Bonus emerging under existing business (excluding interest on the estate)	18s.	21s.	20s.
B. Bonus earned by new business at current rates of premiums	23s.	24s.	25s.
C. Estimated effect of amalgamating A and B	18s.	22s.	23s.
D. Interest on the estate then existing, spread as a rate of bonus over the estimated business in force	7s.	5s.	4s.
E. Total bonus coming under review = C + D	25s.	27s.	27s.
F. Contributions from current surplus to estate as planned	4s.	4s.	3s.
G. Declarable bonus = E − F	21s.	23s.	24s.

Notes.

(1) The figures are based on anticipated future experience. They are, of course, highly speculative in the future, but one must do one's best.

(2) The hypothetical variations in A may be due for example to anticipated mortality improvement or to past changes in premium rates.

(3) Item C is based on estimated quantities of future new business.

(4) Item F assumes that the office has some plan for controlling its estate. If it adopts an unmodified net premium basis of valuation there may be a substantial automatic contribution to the estate each year from the net new business strain.

The analysis is illustrative of a technique and the figures are not to be interpreted as a suggested code of conduct.

13. CONCLUSION

It is fitting perhaps that this lengthy ramble through several aspects of current actuarial problems should terminate on an inconclusive note. It is perhaps the strength of our profession that it is both art and science, and the later stages of this paper have entered those fields where the synthesis of wide judgment is a better guide than the analysis of narrow mathematics (and where the natural desire of an author to be comprehensive may lead him to over-simplify). It is well, however, that we should occasionally pause in the exigencies of our practical routines to consider fundamentals, and that has been the main purpose of this paper.

It remains only to express my acknowledgments. In the main they must go to the profession as a whole, and to the office for which I work, both of which have a corporate mind to which any of their members is a profound debtor. Much of what is contained in this paper has been said before in our proceedings; in particular, I must mention Elderton and Perks (1948, *J.I.A.* LXXIV, 203) and hesitate to do so only because the mention of these names leaves an uncomfortable sense of the names which are omitted. The immunization theory contained in the paper is, I believe, original, and it is important therefore to state that, though they used different approaches, at least two members of the office for which I work reached independently similar general conclusions before the writing of this paper forced my own thoughts into precision, namely, W. E. H. Hickox and P. E. Moody. I should also mention that comments by A. T. Haynes (1945, *J.I.A.* LXXIII, 63) and by Haynes and Kirton (1944, *T.F.A.* XVII, 165–6) while general in form are clearly directed to the same objective as immunization.

Finally, I must thank R. S. Skerman for constant companionship in the work of this paper, and many colleagues—too many to mention individually—for helpful comments.

APPENDIX I

EXAMPLES OF IMMUNIZATION

Table 1 on p. 311 gives a few thumb-nail sketches of typical funds. Some comments on these examples will underline the main points.

(i) In all the examples Rule 1 has been observed, viz. the mean terms of the values of the liability-outgo and of the asset-proceeds have been made the same. The smallness of the profits or losses ensuing on a change in the rate of interest demonstrates the efficacy of this rule as a protection against interest changes.

(ii) Since the liability in example A1 is a single payment, the asset-proceeds are necessarily more widely spread and a small profit is shown, as Rule 2 implies, whether the interest rises or falls. The amount is, however, very slight. In A2 the liability is the same but the assets are more widely spread still and the profit is larger.

The only case to show a loss is B1, where the spread of liabilities is greater than the assets. The loss is very small but could be larger for a real fund with liabilities for all terms.

(iii) The C and D examples are more typical of active life-assurance funds, since the liability-outgo is negative in the early years. The effect of this in

Table 1. Examples of immunization

Example	Pattern of liability-outgo (1)	Present value at 2½% of liability-outgo (2)	Mean term of the value of the liability-outgo (and of asset-proceeds) in years (3)	Typical immunized asset-maturity pattern using 2½% interest (4)	Profit (per cent. of present value of liabilities) from change in interest rate of	
					+⅛% (5) %	−⅛% (6) %
A1	£100 after 10 years	£ 78·120	10	£78·120 after 11·485 years	·012	·012
A2	Ditto	78·120	10	{£39·060 after 5 years, £39·060 after 19·210 years}	·054	·059
B1	£50 after 5 years, £50 after 10 years	83·253	7·346	£83·253 after 8·106 years	−·005	−·006
B2	£100 after 7·346 years	83·253	7·346	£83·253 after 8·106 years	·005	·005
C1	−£100 after 5 years, £200 after 10 years	67·854	16·513	£67·854 after 21·214 years	·137	·155
C2	Ditto	67·854	16·513	{£33·927 after 5 years, £33·927 after 48·672 years}	·396	·485
D1	−£30 after 5 years, £60 after 15 years, £50 after 25 years, £20 after 35 years	50·309	28·982	£50·309 after 50·926 years	·485	·626
D2	Ditto	50·309	28·982	{£25·155 after 40 years, £25·155 after 65·937 years}	·529	·696
D3	Ditto	50·309	28·982	{£25·155 after 22·856 years, £25·155 after ∞ years}	1·022	1·780

Note. Investments are for convenience assumed to be made in stock purchased and redeemable at par under which interest at 2½% per annum is payable continuously, but the principles are the same if stock is purchased at different prices and with different running yields; investments could be made in savings certificates (with no income) or in annuities (with no final capital payments).

lengthening the mean term for the value of the liability-outgo is noteworthy In particular, the D examples, which can be taken as representative of the funds of most British offices at the present time, show a long mean term for the value of the liability-outgo and consequently a very long mean asset-maturity term (50 years).

(iv) The negative liabilities in the C and D examples not only greatly lengthen the mean term but they are equivalent to narrowing the spread of the liabilities. Indeed, investigation shows that for both these examples the variance, if such a term is permissible in this context, is negative and the standard deviation imaginary. Consequently the second derivative of A substantially exceeds that of L and Rule 2 is obeyed.

(v) The present values in the examples are calculated on $2\frac{1}{2}\%$ interest. If the rate changes, the equations will be slightly different and the weighted mean terms will alter, but not greatly. For example, in D1 the mean term of the revised value of the liability-outgo at 3% interest is 29·666 years.

In moving from col. (3) to col. (4) however the asset-maturity dates are more sensitive to the proportion of income to capital. In D1 (keeping to the example with present values calculated at $2\frac{1}{2}\%$ interest as shown in the schedule) the liability-outgo could be immunized,

(a) by £43·885 nominal of 3% stock redeemable at par in 54·997 years, or
(b) by £58·163 nominal of 2% stock redeemable at par in 46·388 years.

Both these stocks have the required market value at $2\frac{1}{2}\%$ interest of £50·309 and a mean term for the $2\frac{1}{2}\%$ value of the proceeds of 28·982 years.

Another interesting illustration is to follow a single block of policies through their career. The salient points are shown in Tables 2 and 3 on p. 313, illustrating whole-life and endowment assurances respectively.

It is found that there is no real solution for the asset-maturity dates in the early durations of the block. It is obvious that no investment of the first premium in an interest-bearing asset can protect the fund against future changes in the rate of interest. In general, it is found that for a block of new business considered in isolation it cannot be immunized for about the first quarter of the term for endowment assurances or for about a third of the expectation of life for whole-life assurances. At these turning-points immunization requires that the whole of the assets be irredeemable. As the duration of the block of business advances the mean term reduces until finally the assets would all be invested for redemption at maturity.

Table 2. Working of immunization over the duration of £100 non-profit whole-life assurance with continuous premiums effected at age 25

Duration in force in years t (1)	Present value of liabilities before change $100_t \bar{V}(\bar{A}_{25})$ at A 1924–29 ult. 2½% (2)	Mean term (from t) of the value of the liability-outgo (and of asset-income) in years (3)	Immunized asset-maturity term in years (from t) if all assets mature on same date (4)	Profit (per cent. of present value of liabilities) from change in interest rate of	
				+½% (5)	−½% (6)
	£			%	%
10	12·325	71·807	No real solution	—	—
20	27·298	34·938	80·417	·784	1·136
30	44·469	20·222	28·017	·036	·040
40	61·920	11·747	13·874	−·034	−·039
50	76·602	6·582	7·183	−·023	−·025
60	86·381	3·679	3·857	−·009	−·009
70	92·044	2·118	2·176	−·001	−·003

Table 3. Working of immunization over the duration of £100 non-profit 20-year endowment assurance with continuous premiums effected at age 25

Duration in force in years t (1)	Present value of liabilities before change $100_t \bar{V}(\bar{A}_{25:\overline{20}|})$ at A 1924–29 ult. 2½% (2)	Mean term (from t) of the value of the liability-outgo (and of asset-income) in years (3)	Immunized asset-maturity term in years (from t) if all assets mature on same date (4)	Profit (per cent. of present value of liabilities) from change in interest rate of	
				+½% (5)	−½% (6)
	£			%	%
3	11·834	56·420	No real solution	—	—
5	20·271	33·151	69·130	1·135	1·500
10	43·411	13·873	16·985	·076	·088
15	69·778	5·616	6·045	·004	·006

Note. In Tables 2 and 3, investments are assumed to be made in stock purchased and redeemable at par under which interest at 2½% per annum is payable continuously.

APPENDIX II

EMERGENCE OF BONUS ON DIFFERENT VALUATION BASES

The table on p. 315 illustrates the effect on bonus earnings of differences between the premium basis and the valuation basis. It must be stressed that these examples are purely illustrative of the consequences of such differences and are not intended to imply that the valuation bases given would be appropriate for practical use. A group of policies issued simultaneously has been examined throughout its lifetime.

Data. The contracts examined are 25-year with-profit endowment assurances effected at exact age 35 subject to an annual premium calculated on the following basis:

Mortality: A1924–29 ultimate.

Income tax: 7s. 6d. in £ deducted from both interest and expenses separately.

Interest: £3. 12s. 0d.% gross (2¼% net).

Expense loadings: New business 3·25% (2·03125% net) of sum assured.
4% (2·5% net) of premium.

Renewal ·25% (·15625% net) of sum assured.
4% (2·5% net) of premium.

Bonus loading: Provision for 20s.% simple reversionary bonuses vesting at the end of each policy year.

Contingency loading: Nil.

The premium rate is ·04343092 per unit sum assured.

Assumptions

(1) That the experience as regards mortality, tax, interest and expenses, is that assumed in the premium basis.

(2) That claims are paid at the end of the year of death or on survival to maturity and that no withdrawals occur.

(3) That the whole of the surplus emerging in any year (whether positive or negative) is immediately distributed as bonus.

(4) That the valuation basis is always based on A1924–29 ultimate mortality.

Table 4. Rate of bonus per cent. which emerges in the assumed
conditions according to various bases of valuation

Example	Valuation basis	Rate of bonus per £100 emerging in year						
		1	2	5	10	15	20	25
(a) Unmodified net premium	(i) 2¼% interest	−32s. 4d.	37s. 3d.	32s. 3d.	25s. 6d.	19s. 6d.	14s. 1d.	9s. 2d.
	(ii) 2¼% interest	−34s. 11d.	27s. 11d.	26s. 2d.	23s. 8d.	21s. 5d.	19s. 4d.	17s. 7d.
	(iii) 2% interest	−36s. 0d.	23s. 8d.	23s. 4d.	22s. 9d.	22s. 4d.	21s. 11d.	21s. 8d.
(b) Modified net premium	(i) 2¼% interest	34s. 6d.	33s. 1d.	28s. 10d.	22s. 3d.	16s. 6d.	11s. 7d.	7s. 0d.
	(ii) 2¼% interest	24s. 11d.	24s. 5d.	23s. 0d.	20s. 11d.	18s. 10d.	17s. 0d.	15s. 5d.
	(iii) 2% interest	20s. 8d.	20s. 7d.	20s. 4d.	20s. 1d.	19s. 10d.	19s. 8d.	19s. 7d.
(c) Unmodified bonus reserve	2¼% interest 20s.% future bonus}	−63s. 7d.	24s. 9d.	24s. 6d.	24s. 1d.	23s. 8d.	23s. 3d.	23s. 0d.
(d) Modified bonus reserve	(i) 2¼% interest 20s.% future bonus}	16s. 2d.	20s. 3d.	20s. 2d.	20s. 2d.	20s. 2d.	20s. 2d.	20s. 2d.
	(ii) 3% interest 20s.% future bonus}	25s. 8d.	18s. 6d.	15s. 7d.	11s. 3d.	7s. 5d.	4s. 3d.	1s. 9d.
	(iii) 3% interest 30s.% future bonus}	34s. 10d.	28s. 6d.	25s. 6d.	21s. 3d.	17s. 4d.	14s. 1d.	11s. 6d.

Notes. (1) In (*b*) a Zillmer rate was used corresponding to the additional new business expenses in the premium basis (i.e. 3 % gross = 1·875 % net).

(2) The expense ratios used in (*c*) and (*d*) were 15 % gross (9·375 % net) over-all and 10 % gross (6·25 % net) renewal respectively, and as such are crude practical approximations to the premium basis.

ABSTRACT OF THE DISCUSSION

Mr F. M. Redington, in introducing his paper, referred to the paper by Messrs Haynes and Kirton which had been submitted to the Faculty in the previous month and which he hoped members of the Institute would read. Both they and he had, at a late stage, become aware that they were writing papers on similar subjects, but they had deliberately avoided discussion, which would have been embarrassing to both, during the preparation of the papers. Their paper, he thought it fair to say, dealt primarily with matching, valuation being a by-product; his own paper dealt primarily with valuation, matching being a by-product. It was remarkable how closely they agreed in their fundamental conclusions.

He wished to remove any misunderstanding that might have been left by his reference to a bonus reserve valuation. In his opinion the bonus reserve valuation was an exceedingly useful practical instrument. In certain extreme conditions of high or low interest rates offices might be compelled to depart from the net premium valuation and to adopt a bonus reserve valuation. Speaking for himself he would be quite happy to do so. His objections arose when the bonus reserve valuation was put forward as the proper method of valuation. He could not accept such a view, if only for the simple and, it seemed to him, obvious reason that there was no basic principle by which a uniform future bonus should be expected. The assumption of uniformity evaded the whole theoretical issue.

Mr G. V. Bayley, in opening the discussion, said that the author had, in his own words, taken the reader on a ramble through the actuarial countryside. The journey fell naturally into two parts, the first being concerned with the theory of matching assets and liabilities. Immunization was defined on p. 289 as

the investment of the assets in such a way that the existing business is immune to a general change in the rate of interest.

It was perfectly general, and as it stood it did not attempt to provide for a marching forward of events. It was concerned only with the position on a certain date. That was simply illustrated by the numerical example on p. 291, where a single payment at the end of ten years was matched by a $2\frac{1}{2}\%$ stock redeemable at the end of 11·485 years. That was only correct at the time. A year later, the figure moved closer to 10 by ·307 years, and the original investment had to be changed in order to obtain the match.

The definition of immunization led to an infinite variety of solutions to equations (1) and (2) on p. 290. Many, though not all, of those solutions demanded substantial realization and reinvestment of funds from time to time. He did not want to exaggerate their magnitude, but wholesale changes of the portfolio were, of course, costly and often impracticable, so some constraint in that direction was imposed in practice. Suppose, therefore, that the definition of immunization was qualified by the requirement that there should be minimum realization and reinvestment as time passed. For all types of liability-outgo he had thought of which admitted real solutions, that simple requirement had the effect of defining precisely the asset pattern. In other words, it selected from the infinite number of solutions available a unique solution in every case. For example, for decreasing funds the solution was given on p. 292 at (*f*). The author called it 'absolute' matching, and no subsequent changes of investment were required in that case. For the 10-year unit liability on p. 291, if the assets consisted of $2\frac{1}{2}\%$ interest-bearing stocks, $96\cdot4\%$ would have to be redeemable at the end of 10 years and the balance irredeemable. For funds which had not reached their peak, the solution would be similar and would require the holding of a proportion of irredeemable stocks to compensate for the investments that had to be made during the next few years. As might be expected, the unique solution in that case became an absolute match without discontinuity at the point of time when the fund became a maximum.

It was worth selecting that particular solution, not simply as a theoretical exercise, but because it defined asset patterns similar to those which would be encountered in practice or, indeed, chosen as a practical objective.

It was interesting to notice that both the general and the unique solution depended upon i, the current rate of interest, and g, the coupon rate. For example, if g were low, there would be less investment for an increasing fund during the early years, and the vulnerability of its fresh investments to changes in the rate of interest would thereby be lessened.

The application of immunization in practice must, he thought, have regard to the laminated character of the fund. For example, recent new business on its own could not be immunized, and he would like to call attention to the practical consequences of aggregating all durations for the purpose of immunization. When rates of interest rose, recent entrants might find it profitable to lapse and re-enter or, worse still, to go to another office. That suggested to him a cardinal principle for with-profit business: to the extent that the fund contained participating policies, it should only be immunized on the basis of the premiums paid to date. In that way, the bonus-earning power of existing business ran smoothly into that of new business. Such an approach led to principles of bonus distribution and immunization which could be formulated as precisely as any that flowed from an attempt to immunize the fund at an existing rate of bonus. It led to asset-patterns based on paid-up policies and therefore rather shorter mean terms than for total immunization. In strict equity, the principle would also lead to a variation in bonus according to duration, and violent changes might justify that course: rough justice might be achieved in many circumstances by a gradual change from the old bonus level to the new.

Looking at the question in another way, the right to pay with-profit premiums over a period of years seemed to lead logically to a bonus system which recognized the variation in rates of interest over that period, and not simply the rate ruling at the inception of the contract. Partial, or paid-up immunization as one might call it, gave ideal expression to those conceptions of equity. Total immunization seemed to reduce the character of a with-profit policy to that of non-profit and it was questionable whether total immunization was not over-immunization for participating business. To the extent of the difference between total and paid-up immunization, it seemed to him that the office was taking a view. That might be legitimate—indeed, circumstances might make it essential—but the author had given a warning of the consequences throughout his paper, and in particular on pp. 293 and 294.

The remainder of the paper was devoted to valuation strategy in general and in particular. Fundamental to the author's consideration of the net premium method was his conception of the office's estate. It was a helpful idea in the rationale of that method, but if a bonus reserve valuation was performed, it had to be remembered that a large part, and in certain circumstances the whole, of the estate, as defined on p. 296, comprised the reserve for future bonuses. For example, the conception of a capital transfer to or from the estate due, say, to a change in the mortality basis did not take quite the same form. In a net premium valuation a capital loss transferred to the estate had the practical effect of first a permanent annual reduction in surplus equal to interest on that loss, and secondly a readjustment of the annual sources of surplus. In a bonus reserve valuation, the cost of a change of that nature might be borne at more than one stage. For the purposes of the immediate declaration, the cost at any stage had to be apportioned against the immediate distribution and against the reserve for future bonuses. At subsequent valuations, the actuary had the freedom to dispose of the unrequited balance of cost in a similar manner.

Offices publishing the results of a bonus reserve valuation frequently retained certain margins, but for internal purposes a line could be drawn at any point between a provision for future bonus of, say, 52s., and a provision for future bonus of 35s. plus an implicit or explicit estate. The essence of the method was that there was greater freedom of manoeuvre, and the direct expression given to the two variables, present and future rates of bonus, should help to achieve equity between different generations of policy holders.

With regard to the concept of natural revenue surplus, the author said on p. 302

The great justification for the net premium valuation is that it gives an approximation to the premium basis of valuation and therefore to the natural revenue surplus.

An attachment to natural revenue surplus would define a particular rate of release of surplus per policy, and a glance at Table 4 showed that that might not lead to level reversionary bonuses. The approximation to the premium basis might be only rough, and it was more a lucky consequence of the method than a reason for it. The margin between the rate of interest earned on the fund and that used in the premium basis might not be sufficient to hold back surplus, especially if the premium were loaded for a high level of reversionary bonus. Natural revenue surplus might therefore lead to falling bonuses. Surely the great justification for the net premium valuation at an appropriately low rate of interest was that it released surplus at about the right rate to support level reversionary bonuses.

Natural revenue surplus was stated on p. 301 to be the only clear conception of surplus, but there was one other: a gross premium valuation using the best possible estimate of future experience produced surplus which was the best estimate of the present value of past and future profit, less, of course, any amounts already distributed and assuming that no further new business was transacted. That was, he submitted, a clear conception and a clear basis for a distribution by the bonus reserve method. That it capitalized any difference between the valuation and premium bases was not a difficulty but a *sine qua non* and it corresponded directly to a capitalization of future bonuses on the other side of the balance-sheet. The real difficulty was one of apportionment of total profit, including capitalized future profit, between past distributions, general reserves, present bonuses and future bonuses, of which only the first was fixed. In exercising judgment upon that apportionment, the indispensable documents referred to at the bottom of p. 302 became instead (a) an analysis of surplus, including the cost of any change in the valuation basis; (b) an investigation of trends and miscellaneous sources of profit; and (c) an investigation of the bonus-earning power of new business. Admittedly, an error of judgment might lead to an over-generous distribution at a given time, but so also would a net premium valuation which failed, for example, to take proper account of a short position in the assets when rates of interest had recently fallen. He therefore supported the author's suggestion, in the case of a net premium valuation, of a statement regarding the matching of investments against liabilities. If a bonus reserve valuation were performed on a realistic basis, it was more sensitive to such a 'mis-match' and the need for the information was less compelling.

There was obviously much to be said for and against the two methods of valuation. He would, however, confine himself to a brief reference to three features of the bonus reserve method. First, if the bonus system demanded the release of surplus at a special rate, there was a particular need for that method. Secondly, it was obviously difficult to capitalize all sources of future profit applicable to and during the lifetime of existing policy-holders (if, of course, it was desired to do so). Thirdly, he agreed with the author that it was logical to bring in assets at market value. If any other course were pursued, the choice of the valuation rate of interest would be much more complicated.

The two- or three-cushion system of reserves was algebraically equivalent to a single-cushion system. Assuming assets and liabilities to be well matched, which was the author's own qualification, there seemed to be no clear meaning to the statement on p. 305 that the fund could stand a rise or fall of $(x+y)\%$ in the rate of interest. In the assumed conditions it would stand a rise or fall of much more. A single central reserve in matched conditions had a tangible meaning only if it was expressed simply as a sum of money, or more imaginatively, as being able to support a future bonus at $z\%$. That clearly brought the author full circle to a plea for a bonus reserve method of valuation!

Mr C. D. Rich said that he was particularly interested in the theory of 'immunization', to use the name which the author had bestowed upon it—though he wished that a different name had been chosen, for the word 'immunization' sometimes had unpleasant associations. He would like, instead, to suggest the word 'conjugation'—in the sense of 'yoking together'. A Past President of the Institute had said, with reference to the redemption dates of the investments, that a life office should 'marry its assets to its liabilities'; it was with that idea in his mind that he suggested the phrase 'conjugating the assets and the liabilities'.

Immunization, or conjugation, was an outstanding example of the difference between actuarial theory and practice. How delightful it would be if the funds of a life office could be so invested that, on any change in the rate of interest—whether up or down—a profit would always emerge! But how difficult it would be to carry out to the full the investment policy implied by the theory of immunization.

The assets and liabilities were conjugated if their first differential coefficients with respect to the rate of interest were equal. As the opener had stated, there was in general an infinite number of ways of arranging the redemption dates of the assets to satisfy this condition. Assuming that the investments were all of present value equal to their redemption values, bearing nominal rates of interest equal to the valuation rate, two distributions of the redemption dates were of particular interest, namely (1) when all the investments were redeemable on the same date (which might be called the 'conjugate' date for the liabilities under consideration), and (2) when the investments were divided in appropriate proportion between what Haynes and Kirton had called 'dead short' and 'dead long', i.e. between money on deposit and irredeemable securities. Those two distributions were the ones giving respectively the smallest and the greatest second differential coefficients to the value of the assets, i.e. of all the conjugate distributions they would produce the smallest and the greatest profits on a change in the rate of interest.

A distribution of the investments which was more akin to distributions that arose in practice, and which lent itself to analytical treatment, could conveniently be obtained by supposing the terms to maturity of the investments to be distributed continuously from 0 to infinity, the amount invested in securities of unexpired term n being proportionate to $1/(1+k)^n$, where the value of k was fixed by the necessity of making the distribution of the investments conjugate with that of the liabilities, i.e. dependent on the mean term of the liabilities. Such a distribution might be called a 'geometrical' distribution, since it was similar in character to a decreasing geometrical progression.

The problem of immunization was essentially one of compound interest. Mortality did not really enter into it, and its general investigation could be considerably simplified by examining the position of an office transacting not life business but capital redemption business. It was, for example, comparatively simple to construct a model office whose business consisted of, say, 10-year sinking-fund policies by annual premiums, or of 20-year policies, and so on. For convenience, continuous functions could be used, and a single formula could be developed which would represent the reserves of a stationary office, or of a uniformly increasing office, or of a uniformly decreasing office.

Some time previously he had made some calculations using a basic rate of interest of $2\frac{1}{2}\%$ per annum, it being assumed that both liabilities and assets were valued at that rate and that the same rate was used for the calculation of premiums. He had found that in the case of a uniformly increasing office, increasing at the rate of $2\frac{1}{2}\%$ per annum, and issuing 30-year sinking-fund policies, the fund could be invested at $2\frac{1}{2}\%$ so as to be conjugate to the liabilities in the following ways:

(1) all in securities redeemable at the end of 26·4 years (the conjugate term),

or (2) 52·1% on deposit and 47·9% in irredeemable securities,

or (3) in a 'geometrical' distribution with the terms to redemption running from 0 to infinity, the value of k being ·0272.

The results of a fall in the rate of interest to 2% or 1%, or of a rise to 3% or 4%, on the value of the liabilities and on the value of the assets according to the three methods of investment were:

Rate of interest (%)	Value of liabilities	Value of assets		
		(1)	(2)	(3)
1	1339	1343	1710	1401
2	1100	1101	1118	1105
2½	1000	1000	1000	1000
3	910	911	921	914
4	758	761	822	780

If negative values were excluded, the value of the liabilities at 3% and 4% became 914 and 782 respectively. The close correspondence of those figures to the value of the assets when invested in a geometrical distribution was noticeable. In fact, it was apparent that such a distribution of the investments should give a satisfactory result however the rate of interest might move.

It could be shown that the greatest profits on a change in the rate of interest (assuming that the assets were conjugated with the liabilities) would arise in cases where the conjugate term was long, i.e. if the fund was young or increasing rapidly. If, however, the fund was very young or increasing very rapidly, the point was reached at which the plunge was taken beyond the infinite to the imaginary, and after that point there was no real solution for the value of the conjugate term. It might, in fact, then be said that the solution involved, not i = the rate of interest, but i = the square root of -1.

An interesting question was what was the rate at which an office should uniformly increase in order that the conjugate term should be infinite, i.e. so that its assets when correctly conjugated with its liabilities would consist entirely of irredeemable securities. An office with such a rate of increase (which might be called the 'critical' rate of increase) obtained the maximum profit on a change in the rate of interest; but an office increasing at a rate more rapid than the critical rate could not possibly conjugate its assets with its liabilities—except by the artifice of borrowing 'short' and investing 'long'. In the case of an office issuing 30-year sinking-fund policies, the rate of interest being $2\frac{1}{2}\%$, the critical rate of increase was $12\cdot4\%$ per annum.

One lesson which should be learnt from the theory of 'immunization' or 'conjugation', and which was borne out by some of the examples in Table 1, was that the investments of a life office should in general be in securities of much longer term than many people realized. That applied more especially to a young or increasing fund, i.e. to a fund possessing the characteristic 'hump' mentioned by Messrs Haynes and Kirton. It could in fact be said that whereas an office could rely upon earning the current rate of interest upon its existing fund, there was a risk of its not being able to do so upon future increases in the fund, and that the risk could be covered by investing the existing fund in securities of mean term longer than the mean term of the liabilities.

Mr H. F. Fisher approached the subject from the point of view of practical problems arising in the valuations of collecting friendly societies. Such valuations, especially of the larger societies, were not primarily for solvency purposes; and the problem of dealing with the assets assumed increased significance when it was remembered that the investments were limited to trustee securities. It might be of interest to state that the largest collecting friendly society held assets of more than £111 million at the end of 1951, of which some £48½ million were invested in British Government and other securities, the market values of which had fluctuated considerably.

There was a slight difference in the statutory duty of the actuary in valuation. Under Section 28 of the 1896 Act, the valuer was required to value both assets and liabilities, whereas under the 1909 Act the actuary's certificate, at all events, related only to liabilities. A comparison of statutory balance sheets showed that Form C. 28 of the 1896 Act invited the valuer to deal with depreciation in spite of the certificate of the officers of a society as to the value of the assets.

There were two points in the immunization idea that rather appalled him at first glance. The first was that by stabilizing the bonus of existing entrants at a low rate it was possible also to stabilize the bonus of new entrants at a higher rate, and the opener had put his finger upon that by suggesting a limited immunization. Although the author did not suggest that such a policy should be followed, but had merely discussed it, he had shown that a danger existed. The second point was the idea of immunizing a fund against making a profit.

The structure of the author's immunization theory itself arose on the basis that V'_A varied from V_A by the same amount as V'_L, the value of the liabilities varied from V_L, and it accepted implicitly a market revaluation of existing assets on a change in the market rate of interest. On p. 304, however, in the second paragraph, the author suggested that while that was necessary for a solvency valuation, a passive valuation policy for both assets and liabilities was fairer when considering a distribution of surplus or equity valuation. But further down the page the author came down rather heavily in favour of market values on the ground of the public understanding. Again, when dealing with bonus policy on p. 308, he suggested that the passive or net premium valuation basis was necessary for the liabilities, at the same time implying that the active or market valuation basis was the correct one for the assets.

In the light of that, the speaker presented the problem of the actuary of a collecting society, holding British Government securities, the market rate of interest having risen by, say, 1% since purchase. If those dated securities in the portfolio were reasonably matched, the market price obtainable was the price obtainable by a willing seller; but if they had been bought to hold, as was usually the case, the society was an unwilling seller. As the actuary had to value assets and liabilities, on the one side he valued the promise of the society to pay the sum assured less the promise of the member to pay the premiums; should he not value on the other side the British Government's promise to pay the interest and capital at the appropriate times? He would say—perhaps with his tongue slightly in his cheek—that accepting the market value in those circumstances was like valuing the liabilities by putting policies up for public auction. At all events, the actuary must not, in valuing the promise of the Government to pay the interest and capital, use a rate of interest which in any way implied that he was taking credit for any part of what the author termed the estate. In other words, if the valuation rate of interest on the liabilities had been artificially depressed in order to produce part of the estate within the liabilities, such a rate of interest would obviously not be the correct one for valuing the assets. On the other hand, where the assets were dated and matched, to take the other extreme of market values was not in keeping with the true picture. Further, it might be that those securities were all purchased and held in the books at less than par. In such circumstances, there was a margin, which would be realized on redemption at par, between the book values, which could be termed the notional values, and the capital which would actually be received.

The same remarks could not also be true of irredeemable or undated securities, and if the same view were taken regarding the valuation rate of interest for assets it would be tantamount to assuming a continuing new business. The valuation of assets must clearly have regard only to policies on the books, but market values nevertheless might be unreasonably low. If part of the high yield obtainable on undated securities was regarded as a risk premium for capital loss and if, as a matter of investment policy, values were written down each year, it might be that the book values were in any event lower than the market values; the inclusion of the investment reserve fund might act as the other cushion.

The method of provision for the expenses of a collecting society out of premium income—usually a percentage of premium—made a gross premium form of valuation particularly suitable in the industrial branch, so long as the amount set aside for management was adequate. In the ordinary branch, where the question was, perhaps, more one of equity and a stable bonus policy than of solvency, there arose the problem with which the author had dealt. Was it to be solvency and an active policy or equity and a passive policy?

He shared the opener's opinion that the author had made out a case for a bonus reserve valuation in spite of himself. The speaker did not understand the paradox, but still thought the net premium valuation was the right one. A bonus reserve valuation which valued that part of the bonus which had been allowed for in the bonus loading of the premiums, combined with a form of premium properly unloaded for expenses, might be halfway between the two, and certainly for the purposes of a collecting society would be a stable one. It would clearly not be right to include in the rate of future bonus that part which the author had shown truly belonged to the estate. Nevertheless, that part which was to be allowed for in the premium loading was appropriate to appear in the bonus reserve valuation. It might be that with the established practice of profit-sharing in the industrial branch, at some time the bonus reserve valuation could also be published for industrial business, particularly if the premiums were loaded, or considered to be loaded, for bonus.

To return to the statutory forms and certificates regarding assets, the statutory forms referred to value of assets and not market value. It might be of interest to point out that because of the difficulties of some of the collecting societies on 31 December 1951, the Chief Registrar had agreed, for the year 1951, to the deletion by all collecting societies of the certificate regarding the value of assets which was normally required in form A.R. 10. There was no statutory authority for that certificate, except in the year of valuation when it was required to be given.

The legislation did not provide for the use of market values, and in certain circumstances the actuary should be free to place upon the assets the values which in all the circumstances were appropriate to the case.

Mr R. J. Kirton thought that it did not matter whether an approach were made to the author's immunization theory on the assumption of a uniform rate of interest and uniform changes in that rate after relegating varying yields and varying differentials to the realm of practical complications, or whether, on the other hand, the idea were developed against a generalized background of a varying interest structure with the uniform rate treated as a special case.

The mathematics resulting from the uniform rate assumption were fascinating and the results startling. What did seem to be of the greatest possible importance was the underlying theory, because without such an appreciation it was impossible to tell at any moment of time whether the assets of a life office were indeed long or short relative to their liabilities. It was important to realize that the immunized distribution was not one to be followed slavishly. Rather, it was a yard-stick from which departure was made in the exercise of normal investment judgment, the departure being justified by the existence of free reserves sufficient to cover any loss, should that judgment be faulty.

A second point was that embodied in the author's paper under the title of estate'. That too seemed to be an idea of great importance in appreciating the position of a life fund, namely that there existed or should exist in one way or another a body of free reserves carrying interest. Those free reserves—the estate—were augmented from time to time, drawn on from time to time, or interchanged among themselves. They formed the cushion which, through the major fluctuations that would inevitably occur, either in taxation, mortality, interest or expenses, should protect the life fund. He strongly supported the author's plea for flexibility in the methods by which those reserves were held.

One point of importance which he missed in the paper was the idea that the existence of a proper amount of with-profit business formed one of the most important cushions in the structure of a life assurance fund.

He was interested to see that running through the paper was linked thought on assets and liabilities—an appreciation of their interrelationship. Such thought and such appreciation would seem to lie at the very foundation of the actuary's problems and were vital to the proper discharge of his professional responsibilities, in connexion with all such funds, whether they were pension funds or life funds, or long-term funds.

Mr Wilfred Perks described the paper as one after his own heart. It was a nice combination of theoretical principle and practical wisdom, with a valuable piece of new technique thrown in.

The new technique was based upon the old principle of approximating to a product-sum. That was the principle of the n-point method. The author substituted for the distribution of the value of the liability-outgo another distribution, representing the value of the asset-proceeds which had the same mean and standard deviation and possibly some of the higher moments. In that way he obtained close agreement at the new rate of interest, whatever it might be. He worked on the product sum, $\Sigma e^{-th}F_t$, where h was the change in the force of interest and F_t was either the value of the liability-outgo for duration t, or the value of the asset-proceeds for the same duration.

The author referred to immunization at a force of interest δ. It was just as appropriate to immunize at zero interest, taking the moments of L_t and A_t, and there were obvious practical advantages in doing so. In fact, the method was a combination of n-points and n-slabs. The points were the asset-maturity dates, and the slabs were the dividends. It was very pleasing to find that the n-point method had become of interest to the Investment Managers!

With regard to valuations, there were many points of detail in the paper on which he would differ or to which he would give a different emphasis, but in broad principle he went a very long way indeed with the author. He liked particularly the author's *exposé* of the net premium method and of the passive policy of valuation. His own thoughts had long been in the same direction, as his paper of 1933 showed (*J.I.A.* LXIV, 264). He had thought for a long time that students had had far too much of the bonus reserve method pumped into them over the last quarter of a century, and the paper under discussion was a valuable counterblast.

His main difficulty with the paper was in the valuation of the assets. In the discussion on Pegler's paper, he had objected to writing the assets up to market values. He equally objected to having to write the assets down to market values. It involved a liquidity principle which to his mind was irrelevant to a life office. It was significant that the legislature had not required it in 1909 or 1946. He felt that the author had drawn heavily on his imagination when he said that there was 'a public instinct to take account of market values'. It seemed to him to be rather a strange instinct that was content with such a test at an arbitrary and possibly self-selected point of time once in every five years.

There was, of course, a vast difference between a real prospect of loss on an investment and a mere change in the interest rate for marginal deals at a particular point of time. He felt that it did not help to clarify thought to assume that those two completely different situations required the same treatment. In his opinion the author confused them when he referred to 'real insolvency arising from badly matched assets'. The trouble was with the concept—he used the word 'concept' very deliberately—of a uniform rate of interest for valuing future payments, particularly when that rate was the rate at which current prices of certain assets could be reproduced. A uniform rate of interest was part of a theoretical model which reflected the practical world up to a point; but the analogy should not be pushed to the extent of assuming that real investment transactions would necessarily take place on that basis at all future points of time. Indeed, it would be wrong to assume that a large portfolio of investments could be bought or sold on that basis, even at the time of valuation.

He had the impression that the author did not always appreciate that the arguments were often very different as between a largely with-profit portfolio and a largely non-profit portfolio of life assurance business. For with-profit portfolios in Great Britain, there could rarely be any doubt about solvency, either actual or apparent. Immunization as discussed by the author might possibly be appropriate for non-profit portfolios, but the consequences for a with-profit portfolio would be fantastic. To fix bonuses according to the rate of interest that happened to apply at the date of issue would be quite unacceptable. The author said that it would never be understood; he would go further and say that it would be idiotic. Perhaps he might be forgiven for using an adjective of that kind, because he found a number of adjectives in the paper which were equally coloured. He might, perhaps, refer to the first paragraph of the *Conclusion*, where there was a reference to wide judgment being a better guide than narrow mathematics!

A with-profits policy-holder expected each of his premiums, less the current expenses and the cost of the death risk, to be invested as remuneratively as possible, and he expected that to be reflected in his own bonuses. A recent policy-holder would not expect to have to boost the assets of the older generation. With those ideas in mind, he had given a little thought to the problem of matching. His own conclusions were tentative, but he was encouraged to mention them at that stage, because he found they were so similar to the conclusions reached by the opener.

For his purpose, he had borrowed some of the ideas of the old re-insurance method of valuation and, like the opener, he had thought in terms of the theoretical paid-up policy at the valuation date. The rough matching of assets to meet those amounts when they matured seemed reasonable. As premiums were paid, the paid-up policy increased, and corresponding assets would have to be acquired. Part of the earlier bonus loadings would have to be saved for the later durations, and that could be done by valuing the theoretical paid-up policies at a somewhat lower rate of interest. The rest of the bonus loadings would normally fall into surplus to provide current bonuses. Otherwise, they would provide a buffer against the possibility of a catastrophic fall in the rate of interest that could be earned on new investments. On such a basis, a rise in the rate of interest would be wholly beneficial, and that was a situation in which he thought most life offices would like to be. At any rate, in that way a sound theory of valuation of assets and liabilities and a consistent system of investment and surplus distribution could be built up which did not run into the logical and practical difficulty of the immunization theory with bonuses tied to the rate of interest prevailing at the date of issue. It also showed the appropriate steps to be taken if, owing to a rise in the rate of interest, an office wished to dress its window by writing its assets down to market values and making further book-keeping entries to correspond. It meant, too, that the existing business and the new business would stand on their own separate legs.

In practice, no doubt, offices would invest rather longer than the theory implied, but they would do so at the expense of mixing up the finances of the new and the existing business.

Mr A. F. Murray said that the crucial conception in the treatment of the problem of matching was the inclusion of interest as part of the asset-proceeds. As soon as that step was taken, the problem was considerably simplified and at once became susceptible to a straightforward mathematical treatment. The mathematical analysis showed that, under the ideal conditions assumed, the mean term of the value of the asset-proceeds and of the liability-outgo should be equal if both functions were to be equally sensitive to changes in the rate of interest. Such a solution was to be expected and was, indeed, almost self-evident from the definitions. That did not detract from the value of the conclusion, rather did it emphasize the inherent logic of the definitions that the author had adopted.

What was somewhat unexpected was the second conclusion that a change in the rate of interest could produce a profit for the immunized fund if the spread of the asset-proceeds was wider than the spread of the liability-outgo. How far this could be achieved in practice was doubtful, but it was at any rate a cheering thought for an Investment Manager when an uncooperative Stock Exchange refused to produce securities for a term certified as correct by the actuary. After listening to Mr Perks he looked forward to the additional pleasure of being able to tell the stockbroker that he was not paying proper attention to the n-point system.

Theoretical analysis such as the author had suggested was extremely valuable in so far as it indicated the ideal maturity distribution of the assets under certain clearly defined conditions if the office was to be immunized against fluctuations in the interest rate. Because of the impossibility of realizing the ideal conditions in practice, however, the author rightly issued a warning against applying the theory as a system of investment.

The difficulty was that while a change in the rate of interest affected the values of the liabilities in a precise and easily calculated manner, the effect on the values of the assets was usually blurred and distorted by secondary factors arising from that change in the rate of interest. The existence of wide optional redemption dates was probably the main disturbing feature. Wide option dates existed not only in Government securities but in many debentures and even preference shares. That borrowers should want those option clauses, particularly during periods of relatively high interest rates, was understandable, but their undesirability from the office's point of view was obvious.

He would like to think that a consideration of the paper would impress upon those responsible for the investment of insurance companies' funds the necessity of exercising the greatest discrimination in subscribing for issues carrying wide option dates. It might be argued that to refuse to subscribe for such issues would be unfair to the borrower, but it should be remembered that the main purpose of high interest rates at the time of speaking was to deter borrowers, except in special cases; quite clearly the effect of a high interest rate would be minimized if the borrower were able to invoke an option against the lender at a comparatively early date.

Another example of the refusal to react to a change in the interest rates to the extent expected theoretically was given by preference shares. If interest rates were low, preference issues carrying a high rate of dividend stood at a lower premium than was warranted by the price level of low dividend preference issues of a similar standing, because of the possibility of circumstances arising which might lead to their redemption at par. In a portfolio carrying a large proportion of such shares the total effect on the value might be considerable.

The paper suggested an interesting line of thought on the suitability of ordinary shares for an insurance company. The office investing in equities presumably expected a steady appreciation in the values of such shares and gradually rising dividends over a long period. If that were accepted, then it followed that ordinary shares were, from the point of view of maturity, 'longer' securities than irredeemable debentures, and the office which found difficulty in obtaining investments sufficiently long-dated would, other things being equal, look with all the more favour on equities.

Similar considerations applied to freehold ground-rents with a large reversionary element in them, but there the practical difficulty arose that the potential insurance investor would be competing in a market which was much more attractive to the sur-tax payer. That was merely another illustration of the difficulties that faced the investor who endeavoured to translate into practice any clear-cut theory on investments.

Mr M. E. Ogborn referred to the textbook by Coe and himself, who were in the same difficulty as the author. They felt that there was nowhere in the literature a precise and accepted statement of principle with regard to the matching of assets. He would support what the opener and others had said: the future could not be foreseen, hence the premiums for participating business should be on such a basis as would in all likely eventualities be sufficient to pay the basic liability and the policy-holder should be given, by way of compensation, a share in surplus. If that principle were accepted, then future premiums need not be immunized; changing conditions would affect future premiums on existing business in the same way as future premiums on new business and immunization need only relate to the part of premiums which had been paid to date.

If the theory of immunization was intended to commend the transaction of non-participating business only, the fund being safeguarded by a policy of immunization, he would be strongly against that course. For the good of the business an adequate proportion of participating business was needed.

The author was strongly of the opinion that the income tax rebate should be deducted from expenses; i.e. the true net interest method rather than the effective net interest method should be used. There were dangers in either method. The choice seemed to be between being logical but inequitable—as in the true net interest method—and being equitable but illogical—as in the effective net interest method. Each method was preferable in some circumstances. If the author would follow out his own suggestions in, for example, the problem of surrender values, he would probably agree that there was more in it than he suggested.

On p. 297 the author referred to the allowance for initial expenses. Personally, he felt that the allowance should be limited to the actual out-of-pocket expenses which varied automatically with the new business; if that were done the author would not have the difficulty he mentioned with renewal expenses. The term 'renewal expenses' was woolly, and the expenses needed to be divided into three items: initial expenses, renewal expenses and the expenses which, although neither one nor the other, were a necessary part of a continuing portfolio whatever the level of new business being transacted.

On p. 300 the author drew a distinction between capital surplus and revenue surplus. He himself would deny that there was any distinction. For many years there had been a theory that some difference existed between capital and interest on an investment; he thought that the theory had been effectively 'Peglerized' (*J.I.A.* LXXIV, 179). Having said that, he did agree that there was a distinction between surplus that was distributable and surplus that was not, so perhaps they both came to the same conclusions at last.

On pp. 302 and 303 the author praised the net premium method and blamed the bonus reserve method, but he did both for the wrong reasons. He praised the net premium method because it gave an approximation to the natural revenue surplus. The speaker challenged anyone who made a net premium method to say that the valuation showed the natural revenue surplus. It was not true. The basis would need a good deal of adjustment to give that position.

Equally, the comments on the bonus reserve method were beside the point. The alarming table at the end would be a good deal less alarming if account were taken of the fact that a valuation dealt not with one duration only but with a mixture of durations. There were two major difficulties with the bonus reserve method, and they were very real difficulties.

First, it involved a considerable amount of work, and he could speak with feeling, because it had been used in his office for some twenty years. The work fell on the actuary or on his qualified staff, and it fell at an inconvenient time. Though the amount of work was not an objection if the method was essential, it was a real factor to be taken into account in considering the method.

The second difficulty was that the method assumed that the actuary was free to decide policy, as had been mentioned in another way earlier in the discussion. In practice the actuary's hands might be tied—for example, the assets might be valued at conventional book values and, if so, the advantages of the bonus reserve method might be lost.

The real question was whether continuity or reality was preferable in the given circumstances. Sometimes one was preferable and sometimes the other. He agreed with the author that the bonus reserve method was an instrument, like the net premium method, with its own uses and limitations. But it was, perhaps, of interest to notice that the American offices, which were essentially wedded to the net premium method and used the contribution method of distribution of surplus, when they had to deal with big changes tackled the problem by means of what they called—in a vivid American phrase—the reservoir of future dividends. That was the bonus reserve method in another form.

On p. 304 the author referred to the market value of assets and the possible use of notional prices. In considering the question, it was necessary to look, not so much at one technique or another, but at the assets. It seemed to him that the freedom which was currently claimed for investment policy would ultimately compel some change in valuation methods. It was difficult to say how that change would come. It might come by a change in the method of valuing assets or a change in the method of valuing liabilities.

In America there had been experiments which were of interest. Instead of assets being valued at market value, a practice was growing up of valuing them at a moving average of prices, say over the last five years. That would seem to be a helpful idea for those who set store by continuity.

There might be a change in the valuation of liabilities, but if account had to be taken of investment of a large part of the funds in ordinary shares, he was not sure that any of the suggested methods of valuation, whether bonus reserve or net premium method, would deal with the problem of the wide fluctuations in value and income that were experienced with that type of asset. Freedom in investment policy was the background of the work of the actuary, and it would ultimately, he thought, compel some change.

Mr J. B. H. Pegler observed that the author had headed his paper with an enigmatic quotation from one of the most brilliant younger poetic dramatists. It was not, therefore, surprising that there were in the paper both brilliant and illuminating flashes of insight and provocative statements, which perhaps were not meant to be taken too literally. It was not easy to accept all the author said, but he had shown many aspects of his vast subject in a new and revealing light and, to quote from the same source, he had 'the voice which makes balance-sheets sound like Homer'.

The earlier part of the paper was concerned with the author's theory of immunization, with some of its limitations and with the practical difficulties in giving effect to it. The subject had been very fully discussed in the paper by Haynes and Kirton. He would content himself, therefore, with paying a tribute to the elegance of the author's mathematical demonstration of his theory of immunization and rubbing in, if he might, what appeared to be the most important lesson of his analysis. It could hardly be said too often that the safe course for the investment of most, if not all, life funds was, as Mr Rich had pointed out, to invest long. Any departure from a long-term investment policy was a departure from the normal. Such a departure might be justified; it might be highly desirable. But it was a risk, and a risk which should only be run with the actuary's eyes wide open.

The most controversial part of the paper was the discussion of the relative merits of different methods of valuation. The author discussed valuation as an instrument, a means to an end, the end being either the proof of the company's solvency or the control of the emergence of surplus. Without something approaching the author's great practical experience of valuations, it was not safe to challenge his views as to the most suitable instrument to use, at any rate for the second purpose. Nevertheless, he wondered whether the master craftsman was necessarily the best adviser on the most suitable instrument for the less skilful to use. The author's skill and experience were such that he could do what he wanted, even with the second best.

The speaker's main difficulty with the net premium method was that the net premium reserve was the same for with-profit as for without-profit contracts for the same age and duration. If a net premium valuation at a lower rate of interest than current conditions would dictate were used to hold back surplus, the extent of the holding back must depend on the relative proportions of with- and without-profit business. If the proportions changed, the stability would be disturbed. Perhaps the author met that difficulty by using different rates of interest for the valuation of with- and without-profit business, but he could not remember seeing that mentioned in the paper. It might be that in practice—and he must admit that his own practical experience was small—the point was of little importance.

When it came to the philosophical basis even a novice on the practical side might be bold enough to put forward an opinion. The author regarded valuation as an instrument, and he rightly pointed out that for certain purposes it was a rather crude instrument. It could not, he said, reflect in detail the variety and complexity of events, and therefore, he implied, there was no point in trying to make it do so as nearly as possible. That approach did not seem to him wholly correct. It was necessary also to regard the results of a valuation as a statement of fact or opinion; and if an actuary made a statement of fact or opinion, that statement must be as near the truth as possible. But valuations made on bases which were not as nearly as possible in line with what, in the actuary's opinion, would be the future experience as to interest, mortality and expenses could not be regarded as the best approach to the truth. For that reason he was unhappy at letting expediency, however cogent the argument, play an overriding part in the choice of bases.

The author distinguished most properly between valuation for solvency and valuation for distribution of surplus. Since in practice, as he pointed out, solvency was seldom in doubt, the main concern was the valuation for distribution of surplus. Was it not possible to reconcile the requirements of equity and of truth by making a valuation on bases which accorded most nearly, in the actuary's view, with the truth and controlling the emergence of surplus in the light of the analysis of surplus?

It was a view held by accountants, he believed, that a company's balance-sheet was intended, not to show the real value of the assets, but only to be a historical record of the way in which money had been spent. They, no doubt, contended, on much the same grounds as did the author, that to alter the value of the assets in the light of current conditions would upset the emergence of profit. Such a view was rather unsatisfactory. He knew very well that it was no easy matter to decide on the value of an asset or liability: but the fact that the value was difficult to assess was not a good reason for not trying to assess it. No person responsible for a balance-sheet should be happy to see on it values which though true at some date in the past did not reflect current conditions. He shared the desire of the author's 'intelligent member of the public' to keep in touch with realities.

The author said innocently that he did not wish to exaggerate the difficulties of the bonus reserve valuation, but here, as sometimes elsewhere, his halo of innocence was on at such a rakish angle that it gave him quite an air of iniquity! He had said also that it was odd that those who held the view that such a valuation was scientifically accurate did not 'ask themselves the simple question whether it was in fact right to assume a *uniform* future bonus'. Was it not possible that actuaries who favoured a bonus reserve valuation for internal purposes had asked themselves that question and had decided that, although it was most unlikely that the rate of bonus would remain constant, such an assumption was a convenient way of deciding what proportion of surplus should be held back and what proportion distributed? When the yield of a redeemable security was calculated, it was known that income tax was unlikely to remain unchanged for the rest of the security's life, but a uniform rate of tax was the best guess that could be made and it was almost universally used.

He hoped his remarks had not given a general impression that he was not in sympathy with the author's views. The paper had shown him how little he himself knew about that important subject, and had done more to remove his ignorance than anything he had read since he had studied for the Institute's examinations.

Mr A. T. Haynes agreed wholeheartedly with the general tenor of the argument set forth in the paper, though he had one or two minor reservations. One of the reservations was that, in relation to immunization, he would regard the author's second-derivative profits as being a product of judgment and not a result of matching. But that was really a philosophical point, and it merely meant that he preferred to take as his standard what the author described as absolute matching (which was only strictly possible for a stationary or decreasing fund), and to regard any other asset distribution adopted in practice as a departure measured from that strict standard.

Far more important was the fact that he would support to the full the main theme of the author that the values of the assets and the liabilities were relative and not absolute. That theme ran right through the paper; it underlay the theory of immunization, and it was inherent in the concept of the estate. The actuary could, on certain assumptions, assess solvency. He could also, on certain principles, assess surplus. But the one thing the actuary could not do *in vacuo* was to place a specific present value on the liabilities. In other words, cash could never be stated to be absolutely equal to future liabilities unless the same amount of cash could also be equated to such future asset proceeds as would meet the future liabilities. What was required was a means of securing a future equation of assets and liabilities, but that was a three-dimensional concept which it was extremely difficult to express in a balance sheet in two-dimensional form.

Perhaps the nearest approach that had been made to expressing the three-dimensional concept in visual form was provided by the author's diagrams on p. 299. The interesting thought which the author produced from those diagrams —that there was such a thing as conditional as opposed to absolute solvency— led to the question whether some forms of conditional solvency could not easily be converted to absolute solvency. For example, where, as in Figs. 2 and 3, the asset and liability value curves might cross owing to a change in the rate of interest, despite the fact that the office was solvent at a given rate of interest, the position could be converted immediately by altering the assets in such a way as to immunize the liabilities. The asset curve would then follow the same form as the liability curve and conditional solvency would be translated into absolute solvency. Similarly, where conditional solvency was due to redemption options, existing assets could be exchanged for matched assets and absolute solvency attained. The one type of conditional solvency which could not readily be converted into absolute solvency was a result of liability options. Such options— guaranteed annuity options, guaranteed surrender values, guarantees of rates under group pension schemes—once granted, remained on the books for years and their potential danger had to be faced. In that connexion he would go further than the author and say that reserves ought to be set up immediately to meet the chance that the options might become onerous and that the actuary's assessment of current surplus should be reduced—in some cases very extensively reduced—by reason of the options having been granted.

Those thoughts raised a most important question: 'What can be done now to protect the position of the fund at future valuations?' The question did not fall strictly within the limits of the subject of valuation but lay rather within the field of new business and investment policy. To his mind, the fundamental answer was to restrict the granting of options to an absolute minimum, and to bear in mind that an immunized asset distribution was the safety standard. Where options were granted, in relation to either assets or liabilities, or where judgment was exercised in going long or short in one's asset distribution, ample free reserves should always be held to meet the potential loss. As several speakers had said, the most important free reserve in a life office was created by the with-profit business on its books and that free reserve should be main-tained by a sufficient flow of with-profit new business. The maintenance of a proper proportion of with-profit business was an important factor to many offices when large quantities of non-profit business were being transacted and when the 'gearing' of their funds was changing rapidly.

He felt that a policy of complete immunization should be regarded as the standard concept for with-profit business—as for non-profit business—subject, however, to the question whether future bonuses should not be left out of account, the value of future bonus loadings being held, in effect, as a free cash reserve instead of being invested in assets designed to immunize future bonuses. There was more than one approach to the immunization of with-profit business but the important point in practice was to create a clear concept and to under-stand its effect under varying conditions.

Mr Leslie Brown said that, like a previous speaker, he would start by criticizing the use of the word 'immunization'. Whatever the need for it in the theoretical concept of the paper, it implied a precision in the working out of the theory which could not in fact be justified, owing to the many reservations which were necessary in both theory and practice. He would prefer some such expres-sion as 'minimizing the investment risk'.

The main advance in thought in the paper was the attempt to make investments cover the future net income of the existing business. There were two lines of approach to the problem of the effect of future changes in rates of interest. The first was to consider the way in which the business would ultimately work itself out; the main problem there was the possibility of lower rates of interest from the investment of the future net income of the existing business. It was intriguing to think that, if there were a danger of lower rates of interest, it was possible in theory to meet it by investment before the lower rates happened. The second line of approach was by periodic valuations, and there the main danger was that of higher rates of interest which would cause depreciation. If the assets were balanced, whatever might be the conception of that word, the problem descended to one of presentation. If they were balanced, the protection depended upon the position that both assets and liabilities were similarly sensitive to changes in the rates of interest. The effect on liabilities of any given change in interest rates would be precise, being a matter of calculation—subject, of course, to the question of surrender values and other options already mentioned. But a net premium valuation was not adequately sensitive and, if one faced the possibility of extreme movements greater than the reserve margins or buffers could deal with, it was clearly essential to be prepared to adopt a valuation basis which was adequately sensitive to the movement of interest rates —some form of bonus reserve valuation.

On the assets side, however, the effect on market values of a given change in the rate of interest could not be predicted. Markets were governed by too many complicated forces. There was not one rate of interest. The differences between the money market or short-term rate and the long-term rate were such that they could move in different directions at the same time. The existence of long-term options, the fact that different investors were subject to gross and net rates of interest and many other variations made it impossible to forecast exactly what would happen to market prices. Not the least important was the variation in the appreciation of the investment risk inherent in the different classes of industrial investment. Some part of that variation would arise from the factors which caused the change in the rates of interest. Clearly, when interest rates were high, as they were to-day, there were inherent risks arising from the economic causes which had caused that change.

Another way of approaching the same problem of the differing sensitivity of assets and of liabilities to the rate of interest would be to start with the assets and ask what was the rate of interest for the mixed fund. The answer was difficult to achieve. His main point, therefore, was that the theory, valuable though it was, was not precise in practice—he hoped that in saying that he had exploded any thoughts that some might have that the control of investment, following publication of the paper, would be simple and automatic.

He had avoided many other problems and had not touched on the questions whether assets of the right term could be obtained in the market, whether any debtor was good enough to be sure that his credit would last, so that a debenture or preference share could be considered to be really perpetual, and that intriguing question, what was the term of an ordinary share?

Despite his doubts about the precision of the theory, he felt that it made a valuable improvement in the instrument for measuring the position of the life fund by the relationship of assets and liabilities. It was possible to determine in broad measure what might be called a normal position. That would give an idea, a reasonable idea, of the degree of departure from that position and it would provide a background against which to consider investment outlook. Obviously, it was proper to depart from the norm according to the views held as to the future outlook. Obviously also there was room for considerable development of thought on the subject.

Mr S. F. Isaac, in closing the discussion, said that the nature of the territory and the name of the guide were alone sufficient to ensure the success of what was so modestly described as a ramble. Much of the territory was familiar to those who were present, but there could be few who would not have benefited in some way by viewing at least some part of it in a new light or from a new angle.

He would like to join his own tribute to the tributes of earlier speakers to the stimulating original work which the author had done in opening up a new approach to some important territory which until quite recently had been so little explored. He referred, of course, to the work on the matching of assets and liabilities and the possibilities of immunization.

It was important to stress that the author made no extravagant claims for his work in that connexion; indeed, he was at pains to emphasize the limitations of what was, after all, a theoretical examination of the problem. In certain circumstances there was no real solution, and even where there was a real solution it was continuously changing. It was quite clear, however, that much could be done to protect insurance offices, although in most circumstances complete immunization was impracticable and many would say undesirable.

Like Mr Leslie Brown, he hoped that no quotation taken from its context would suggest, particularly to the outside world, that the investment of insurance funds had now been made foolproof by the introduction of some magic formula. The author had demonstrated forcibly how desirable it was that the actuary should play a large part in formulating investment policy, and he did not mind how much publicity that aspect received.

With regard to the main part of the paper, the author had expressed a preference for the net premium method of valuation because of the light it threw on the anatomy of the business. At the same time he favoured the public presentation of results in the form of a bonus reserve valuation, because of its greater flexibility, and advocated a passive valuation policy because it was conducive to a reasonable degree of equity in the distribution of surplus.

Opinion was still divided, and he supposed it always would be, on the relative merits of the two methods of valuation. Both had their merits and defects. The majority that evening seemed to favour the bonus reserve method of valuation. He must confess that he himself had more than a sneaking regard—he had a warm affection—for the net premium method. But that might only be because, as the author said, it was relatively foolproof!

In normal circumstances, he preferred to value by the net premium method because he felt, with the author, that it threw more light on the anatomy of the business. He preferred to value annually by the net premium method and to publish the results of a net premium valuation, making a gross premium valuation occasionally because of the further light that method could throw on the actuary's problems. He would make a gross premium valuation if there were any major changes in conditions. But, as the author said, the gross premium method did capitalize differences between premium bases and valuation bases in a way that could be misleading and—he thought—sometimes dangerous. It was sensitive to small changes in the rate of interest assumed, and it was also sensitive to small changes in the margins assumed for expenses. That could give rise to difficult problems in the case of funds where the proportion of non-profit business was large. It would be found that a small difference in the provision for future expenses could have a relatively marked effect on the surplus and on the bonus.

He agreed entirely with the author's arguments in favour of a central contingency fund committed neither to the assets nor to the liabilities. It could obviously be of great assistance in avoiding too frequent changes in the values of either. Several speakers had pointed out that it might be required to take care of fluctuations due to a wide variety of causes. It seemed to him that the number of imponderables with which actuaries were concerned in their business tended to grow.

A marked increase in expenses could be a serious matter for a life office, especially if the non-profit business had become relatively large. In recent years the non-profit business of most offices had tended to grow more rapidly than the with-profit business, especially if deferred annuity business were included in a combined life and annuity fund. In that case, the dangers were undoubtedly aggravated. Where with-profit business had become in effect a highly geared equity, it had become extremely vulnerable to increases in the rate of expenses. That was an added argument for building up and maintaining the contingency fund.

The author was right to stress the dangers of options. In recent years many securities had been issued containing options adverse to the investor, but such investments could be avoided, and in his opinion they should be. The institutional investors had to some extent succeeded in making their views known to those people who were concerned with the raising of money and he hoped that as time went on they would be able to make their views still more effectively known.

Options in life assurance and annuity contracts had become an important and inherent feature of the business. It was often necessary to grant such options, but their possible effect on the business should be carefully watched.

He felt that the author had been a little severe in his criticism of the granting of guaranteed surrender values. After all, however much circumstances might justify reducing surrender values, it was likely that the banks and other lenders would successfully resist any such action. He thought that what was wrong was not the guaranteeing of the surrender values but the granting of over-generous surrender values. It was not unreasonable to guarantee surrender values on a conservative basis, especially if the office reserved the right to postpone payment for a period of, say, six months, which might well tide the office over a crisis.

He agreed with the author and Mr Haynes that some guaranteed settlement options which were granted could be very expensive to companies and might constitute a serious problem, at any rate unless reserves were built up to deal with them. In that connexion, he felt that some of the modern annuity options were difficult to justify.

The President (Mr F. A. A. Menzler, C.B.E.), in proposing a hearty vote of thanks to the author, said that he had on more than one occasion urged the desirability of maintaining a due quota of papers bearing directly on their day-to-day professional work. By every test, Mr Redington's valuable and distinguished paper came into that category.

There had been a full and authoritative discussion to which those who were immediately concerned with the problems of life-office finance had made important contributions. It was therefore quite unnecessary for him, even were he capable of doing so, to attempt to make any critical contribution to the subject of the paper. Nevertheless, he might perhaps permit himself one or two general observations.

He had long felt that as a profession they tended to be too much obsessed with present values. Those all too convenient summarizations swept up everything into a single portmanteau figure; but, as was so often the case with financial-cum-statistical summarizations, that clear view of the wood might cause them to forget the trees or, in other words, the series of financial events in time for which they were called upon to make provision.

With the ever-growing significance in the national economy of savings through life assurance and pension schemes, they would have to pay increasing attention to emerging costs and to the resources necessary to meet them without prejudice, of course, to the fundamental necessity of adhering to the funding principle. At the time of the granting of the Charter, they were described as 'scientific financiers', but it was hardly scientific finance to be chiefly pre-occupied with the liabilities side of the balance-sheet. Only in very recent times did they seem to be attempting to evolve a systematic approach in regard to the investment of the assets comparable in authority with that which they had always attached to their rather meticulous procedure for the assessment of the liabilities they had to meet. It was, he suggested, a sign of the times that within a few months they should have had papers before both the Faculty and the Institute—he was referring to the important paper before the Faculty by Messrs Kirton and Haynes on *The financial structure of a life office*—in which systematic attention had been given to the matching of assets and liabilities in life assurance funds.

As he read Mr Redington's paper, he recalled the time when he was called upon to study those matters. There were no textbooks and no actuarial notes. They had to do the best they could with the voluminous papers and discussions recorded in the *Journal*. He could not remember any serious mention of the idea of 'matching', but he had read with pleasure the extremely luminous paper produced by S. G. Warner in 1902 (*J.I.A.* XXXVII, 57) in which the pure doctrine of the net premium method was enunciated with authoritative clarity. It was therefore some consolation to find Mr Redington declaring that 'in stable conditions my personal preference is for a net premium valuation'. He found that reassuring until he re-read the passage and noticed the words 'in stable conditions'. It was apparent that, if he was to begin to keep abreast of those matters, he would still have to keep re-reading Mr Redington's paper.

He had derived much satisfaction from the fact that the last ordinary general meeting of the Institute over which it was his duty to preside should have been the occasion of the delivery of a paper which he was confident would come to be regarded as a landmark in the evolution of professional practice in regard to the administration of the finances of life offices.

The author, for whose abilities they all had such a profound respect, had demonstrated that, contrary to what was sometimes believed, mathematicians could also be good practical actuaries.

Mr F. M. Redington, after thanking the speakers for their encouragement, replied briefly but said that, in view of the many points raised in the discussion, he proposed to submit a written reply for publication in the *Journal*.

Mr J. L. Anderson has sent the following written contribution:

I agree with the author that the net premium valuation and the bonus reserve valuation have their own particular uses and limitations. Generally speaking, I think it is desirable that an office should carry out valuations by both methods, a practice which has been followed in my own office for many years.

The method to be favoured must be largely a matter of personal taste, and I confess to a fondness for the particular type of bonus reserve approach which is described on p. 303, i.e. the method by which one first estimates the average bonus earning power of new with-profit business based on current rates of interest, and then calculates the liability under the existing business reserving for this rate of bonus. The excess of the assets at market values over the resulting liability gives what the author describes as 'the estate'. It is then a comparatively simple task to estimate the future trend of bonus earnings on various assumptions as to the rate of bonus declared for the investigation period which has just ended. The future trend can be shown in the form of a table similar to that given on p. 309. The beauty of the method I have described is that the bonus emerging under the existing business and the bonus earned by the new business remain constant, and variations are confined to two additional factors; first, the interest on the estate which, in the case of an expanding fund, will, of course, provide a steadily reducing addition to the bonus earned, and second, the bonus earned from miscellaneous sources such as surrenders.

It is sometimes desirable to produce similar figures based on a different rate of interest. This will entail an estimate of what the market values of the existing investments would be at this different rate, a task which sounds tedious and complicated but in point of fact can be done with sufficient accuracy quite easily. With two sets of figures showing the trend of bonus earning power on two separate assumptions as to the rate of interest, the actuary is in a good position to decide on the bonus policy which he wishes to recommend.

During the period of low interest rates from which we have recently emerged, the estate calculated on the basis I have just described will have been a positive quantity. At a time of high interest rates, however, it is quite possible that it would emerge as a negative quantity and there is nothing inherently absurd about this. It would mean, of course, that the bonus earned by the interest on the estate would also be a negative quantity and the effect on a growing fund would be to make for an increase in the rate of bonus earned as the fund increased—a natural enough conclusion in the circumstances. I should perhaps make it clear that I do not favour the use of a bonus reserve valuation for purposes of the published accounts.

The author refers on p. 308 to the possibility of starting a new fund for future business after a big rise has occurred in the rate of interest. Using the figures on that page, it is clear that if a new series were started, holders of recently effected policies on the old series whose bonus had been immunized at 30s. would be tempted to surrender their contracts and effect policies under the new series earning 45s. This draws attention to the limitations of the theory of immunization. If we consider separately the fund appropriate to a block of business which has been on the books for a long time and the fund appropriate to a recently effected block of business, it is clear that while the investments appropriate to the former fund may be invested sufficiently 'long' to immunize it, the same is not true of the latter fund. While therefore it may be possible to immunize the fund as a whole, this can only be done by investing the assets appropriate to the old business in securities of longer average date than would otherwise be necessary. Is it therefore equitable in the circumstances envisaged on p. 308 to regard the bonus earning power of old and recent business alike as 30s. % and would it not be more correct to treat the recent business as having a relatively higher bonus earning power?

In a paper read to the Faculty of Actuaries in 1944 (*T.F.A.* XVII, 137), I attempted to measure the relative bonus earning power of different groups of policies, classified according to age, duration in force, etc., after a big change in interest rates. For this purpose I found it convenient to assume for each group a matched set of assets, neglecting future increases in the corresponding fund—i.e. what Messrs Haynes and Kirton, in their recent paper to the Faculty, called the 'hump'—and so avoided the difficulty of immunizing the fund appropriate to a recently effected block of business. This is a convenient method for measuring relative bonus earning power, but it does not follow that it is equally suitable as a guide to the investment spread which will give the best protection to the fund as a whole against a change in interest rates. In fact it is abundantly clear from Mr Redington's paper, as well as from that of Messrs Haynes and Kirton, that it is essential to take account of the 'hump' in order to obtain this protection. I see no reason, however, why the same basis should necessarily be used when considering equity.

I am a strong advocate of the view that equity is best achieved in general by leaving with-profit premium rates unchanged and allowing the bonus to find its new level by degrees. The business effected just before a rise in interest rates will then participate in the higher rates of bonus to be declared in the future (assuming no further change in interest rates) over a relatively big proportion of its lifetime. On the other hand older business, and especially endowment assurance policies nearing maturity, will tend to go off the books before the higher rates of bonus are attained. Rough justice is thus done to all groups and the results are not inconsistent with the limited immunization which I consider it appropriate to assume in measuring bonus earning power. If interest rates fall substantially, the same arguments would apply; but the rate of bonus would, of course, tend to fall, and old business would receive higher average rates of bonus over its future lifetime than would business recently effected.

Mr Redington, in his written reply, says:

The discussion, like the paper, falls naturally into two parts: matching and valuation. Dealing with these two subjects in that order, I am appreciative of those many comments which underlined the practical qualifications to the immunization theory. I was anxious that the necessary over-simplifications contained in the theory should not be overlooked; nevertheless, we cannot, in our anxiety to avoid a mistake, avoid all action. The assets must be invested and the actuary must know, however approximately, what term and spread of assets he is aiming at. The majority of speakers seemed to share my view of the importance of the subject and to agree with the broad lines of my approach.

The main line of criticism was in regard to the treatment of with-profit business. I am glad that this was raised because it is an important aspect of the problem, on which I am conscious of having been all too brief. A substantial part of the liabilities of most life offices is attributable to future bonuses. I think that most actuaries would agree that, while it is permissible to 'take a view' in investing any of the assets, more caution should be exercised in the investment of the assets held against the basic contracts than in the investment of the assets held against future bonuses. Whereas security is the primary consideration for the basic contract, maximum profit is an important consideration for bonuses. So far I agree with my critics. But the aim of the immunization theory is to find the neutral term of the investments on the assumption that no view is taken as to the future rate of interest. I assumed—and it is mainly an assumption rather than a principle—that the office would wish as a broad policy to stabilize the bonus earnings from existing business and I sought the neutral term on that assumption. There is much scope for discussion on this point and I would certainly not be rigid about it; but two important points should be borne in mind: (i) if an office departs substantially from the neutral term which stabilizes the bonus earnings, it may be opening up the possibility of a negative bonus in conditions of extremely low rates of interest; (ii) any future new business will, of course, be completely sensitive to interest changes and, if the bonus on existing business is also made sensitive by investing short, the office may find itself embarrassingly sensitive.

Messrs Bayley, Perks and Ogborn all suggested a paid-up-policy immunization for with-profit business. I am not sure what paid-up-policy was to be immunized, but assuming they meant some guaranteed paid-up-policy, incorporated or implied in the contract, the resulting mean term of the investments would be much shorter than that resulting from the method contained in the paper, and would, I think, be much shorter than they would contemplate as a normal practice. It means, in brief, that the existing business as well as new business would be sensitive to interest changes, so that if the rate of interest falls the bonus potential of the whole business would immediately fall and this could occur in circumstances when options both in the assets and liabilities were becoming a serious embarrassment.

Paid-up-policy matching for with-profit business is probably undesirable as a general practice and is certainly not without theoretical defect. This can be seen readily enough by taking as an example an office adopting a policy of low bonuses with small bonus loadings. If the office has been running steadily on a 4% rate of interest and immunizing on a paid-up-policy basis, a permanent fall in the rate of interest to, say, $2\frac{1}{2}$% could leave its with-profit business insolvent. In short, at the borderline between with-profit and non-profit business paid-up-policy matching is seen to be a different animal. It does not do what it may seem to do on the surface, namely, immunize the basic contract.

Mr Perks underlined the comments made in the paper about the unacceptability of the logical mathematical conclusion that bonuses on a policy should depend on the rate of interest at issue. I feel, however, that any principle of with-profit matching will, if driven to its final logical conclusions, prove to be unacceptable. For example, the logical conclusion of paid-up-policy matching is to declare rates of bonus which vary with and are substantially affected by the rate of interest ruling at the date of valuation.

From these two logical conclusions it follows that:

(*a*) bonuses dependent upon the rate of interest at issue produce an aggregate surplus which conforms with our practice and tradition of regularity, but lead to a differentiation between policies which is contrary to our practice;

(*b*) bonuses dependent upon the rate of interest at valuation lead to instability in aggregate surplus which is contrary to our tradition, but lead to more uniform subdivision between policies.

Mr Haynes pointed out another aspect of the problem: namely that paid-up-policy matching can entail the encroachment on future bonus loadings. I agree with this comment and there is no need to amplify, but it gives me the opportunity to say that if we plunge deeper into the with-profit question we may conclude that a reasonable neutral principle would be to immunize the future cash surplus rather than, as was done in the paper, to immunize the future rate of reversionary bonus resulting from that cash surplus. This leads to a slightly shorter investment policy, but by no means so short as paid-up-policy matching. Perhaps I can summarize my own views by saying that for with-profit business there is some flexibility at the edge of the problem but that it is not possible to depart far from the method adopted in the paper without at least jeopardizing the buffer which with-profit business should provide and at the worst rendering the whole business insolvent. On the whole, for with-profit business I prefer to think that it is legitimate to depart from my conception of neutrality, rather than to think that neutrality lies far away.

I have devoted some time to this with-profit question because it has been the main line of criticism, and is one of the more vulnerable points. It leads me to a wider conception of the whole problem. In the paper I discussed what conditions the invested assets must satisfy to immunize the business against changes in the rate of interest. The problem can be expressed differently. Whenever an office accepts a new contract or makes an investment it affects the balance of the business as regards its sensitivity to interest changes. What is that effect? Subject always to the theoretical simplifications, the Taylor expansion in the paper gives the answer to that question in what I thought would be an uncontroversial manner. There is another and more controversial question as to what is the effect desired.

Comments on the question of valuation were mainly in amplification. More extensive criticism of those sections of the paper dealing with the net premium and bonus reserve valuation came from Messrs Bayley and Ogborn. I think that the difference between us is less a question of fundamental opinion than of the expression of that opinion. I have much sympathy with the view that, as Mr Bayley had expressed it, the direct expression given to the two variables, present and future rates of bonus, under a bonus reserve valuation gives greater freedom of manoeuvre. I feel that on the whole, and taking a long period of history, I would find it easier to maintain a satisfactory presentation of results during a long sequence of varied events through the medium of a bonus reserve valuation than that of a net premium valuation. Net premium valuations, however, make it easier to determine what is the right action to take, even if that right action has to be translated into a bonus reserve valuation for the purposes of presentation.

Whatever one does about investments or premiums or options, there is some rate of interest, be it 0 % or 10 %, for valuing the liabilities which equates them with the market value of the assets. That thought is both illuminating and sobering. It shows how much of the problem lies with the actuary's judgment and indeed with his conscience. It shows how essential—professionally vital— it is that the actuary should be acquainted with events on the investment side of the office. It adds force to the President's comment that 'present value' methods can obscure reality. It also shows that the problem finally lies in the hands of the individual actuary and I am happy to feel that in this country those hands are, and have for many years been, very safe.

IMMUNIZATION

G. E. Wallas

IMMUNIZATION

by

G. E. WALLAS

(A paper discussed by the Society on 21 November 1958)

THIS subject can appear difficult, but the main idea is delightfully simple. Let us consider an example. Suppose that a life office has issued policies at premiums based on a certain rate of interest, investing in Stock Exchange securities the premiums received from year to year, less claims, and that after a time the rate of interest rises permanently. The market value of the investments will fall and the office will lose if they have eventually to be sold, but will gain to the extent that future premiums can now be invested on more favourable terms. The gain is fixed but the loss will vary according to the redemption dates of the assets, since the longer the date, the greater the fall in value. Immunization consists in selecting investments such that the loss balances the gain. An alternative way of looking at it is on the basis of present values. The values of the assets on the one side of the balance sheet, and the net liabilities on the other, will both fall if interest rates rise. We want them to fall by the same amount, and as our liabilities are fixed, we must seek to achieve that result by a suitable choice of assets.

Of course, if we thought we could guess which way interest rates were going to move, we could act accordingly and hope to make a profit. But we would also run the risk of making a loss, and it is the paramount duty of a life office to be able to honour its contracts. The extent to which we can give effect to our views is therefore governed by the free reserves at our disposal; the immunized position provides an origin whence to measure our departures.

For a working definition of the term immunization I would suggest: the investing of the funds of a life assurance office having regard to the dates when payments both of income and of capital will be received from them, in order to protect the office against the effect of changes in the rate of interest. It must be emphasized that there can be no protection against changes in the effective rate of interest which are unaccompanied by compensating changes in capital values. Such changes might be caused by income tax, by nationalization of an industry with compensation based on capital values but producing a lower income, or by default in interest or reduction in dividend.

The subject of immunization is new and still developing. Its evolution is recorded in various actuarial papers—some difficult and some concerned primarily with other questions. It is the purpose of this paper to present an outline of the subject for the benefit of fellow students, and to compare the different views that are held. It may be stated at the outset that the main differences of view arise from the precise implications of the word 'protect' in the above definition, when applied to with-profit business.

Although earlier writers realized the importance of matching assets and liabilities, the mathematical basis of the theory of immunization was developed by F. M. Redington in 1952 in a paper of compelling brilliance reviewing the principles of life office valuations (*J.I.A.* **78**, 286).

Let the asset-proceeds of a fund (i.e. interest, redemption moneys, etc.) at time t be denoted by A_t and the net liability-outgoings (i.e. claims, etc. less premiums) similarly by L_t, both distributions being continuous in time. Note that L_t can be negative in places. Suppose that at a single rate of interest the present values of the assets and liabilities are equal, i.e.

$$\int_0^\infty v^t A_t \, dt = \int_0^\infty v^t L_t \, dt. \tag{1}$$

Let us examine the effect of a small change in the rate of interest by differentiating each side with respect to the force of interest δ.

$$d/d\delta \int_0^\infty v^t A_t \, dt = -\int_0^\infty t v^t A_t \, dt \tag{2}$$

and similarly for L.

If the two differentials are equal, it follows by Taylor's theorem that for a small change in the rate of interest, neglecting the effect of higher differential coefficients, the assets and liabilities will alter by the same amount and the fund will still be solvent. Define the mean term of the assets as

$$\tau_A = \int_0^\infty t v^t A_t \, dt \Big/ \int_0^\infty v^t A_t \, dt \tag{3}$$

and similarly for the liabilities. Then another way of stating Redington's theorem is that the fund is immunized if

$$\tau_A = \tau_L, \tag{4}$$

since the denominators are equal by equation (1). We are concerned here only with existing business. New business is assumed to be able to look after itself within the framework of the continuing office.

A special case of immunization is when A_t equals L_t for all values of t. This is known as absolute matching and it is obvious that no changes in the rate of interest can upset the equality. If, however, a fund has been growing rapidly in the past it will continue to rise for some years before commencing its fall. This is often referred to as 'the hump'. It arises because premiums and interest in the early years are more than sufficient to meet claims. The excess must be invested, as it emerges, on terms which cannot be known at the outset. Hence it is impossible to apply absolute matching, though such a fund can be immunized.

By considering the second differential coefficient Redington showed that if what may be loosely called the 'spread' of the assets is greater than that of the liabilities, the fund will tend to profit from any small change in the rate of interest. This point is of theoretical rather than practical importance, but it is a comforting thought that with open mortgages (which may be considered dead-short, i.e. zero mean term) on the one hand and irredeemable securities on the other, the spread of the assets should in practice be greater than that of the liabilities, for what that is worth.

Let us consider some simple examples of mean terms, to get the feel of this useful concept. On a continuous basis and at a force of interest δ, the mean term of:

a fixed sum due in n years is n (5)
a perpetuity is $1/\delta$ (6)
an annuity certain is $I\bar{a}_{\overline{n}|}/\bar{a}_{\overline{n}|}$ (7)

a bond redeemable at par in n years and bearing interest meanwhile at force δ is $\bar{a}_{\overline{n|}}$ (8)

a sum payable on the death of (x) is $\overline{IA_x}/\overline{A_x}$. (9)

It will be seen that τ is a function of δ which decreases as δ increases, and that it is in general smaller than the weighted arithmetic mean of the dates of the component payments, which is, of course, τ at 0%.

There are two vital arithmetical properties of τ, which spring from its definition and which may indeed be said to comprise its principal value as a tool for the actuary.

(i) *The Addition Rule*

If the mean term of a series of amounts measured from time t is τ, then from time o it is $t+\tau$. For example, the mean term of a perpetuity commencing on the death of (x) is $\overline{IA_x}/\overline{A_x}+1/\delta$, which is the sum of expressions (9) and (6) above. This rule operates, so to speak, in the time dimension, and concerns the mean terms of a single set of quantities measured from different time origins. It is particularly useful for dealing with deferred annuities.

(ii) *The Combination Rule*

This, on the other hand, concerns the mean terms of various sets of quantities all measured from the same point of time. If a certain series of amounts has a present value A, another B, and so on, then

$$(A \pm B \pm \ldots)\, \tau_{A \pm B \pm} = A\tau_A \pm B\tau_B \pm \ldots.$$

Verbally, mean terms weighted by their respective present values are subject to the normal arithmetical rules of addition and subtraction. For example, combining expression (5) with δ times expression (7), weighted by their present values, we should obtain expression (8), viz.:

$$n \times v^n + I\bar{a}_{\overline{n|}}/\bar{a}_{\overline{n|}} \times \delta \times \bar{a}_{\overline{n|}} = \bar{a}_{\overline{n|}}.$$

It will be realized from the combination rule that the mean term of a fund which represents the balance between the present values of positive and negative payments (e.g. sums assured and premiums) has no limits to its size. It may be so high that it is impossible in practice to find assets to immunize it; it may on the other hand be negative.

The situation defined by equation (4) above is sometimes referred to as total immunization, to distinguish it from other types. It is widely accepted as the standard for non-profit business. Because future premiums are deducted, high values of τ can occur, especially with a growing fund. Although it is outside the scope of this paper, one point must here be emphasized in passing. It would be wrong to use the theoretical results of total immunization to justify the calculation of non-profit premiums on bases which had regard solely to current rates of interest.

Redington, dealing with larger questions, made the simplest assumption in the circumstances, namely that total immunization should also apply to with-profit contracts. He did not advocate this. The strict theoretical implication is that the rate of bonus is immunized, or frozen, for each policy according to the conditions prevailing when it was taken out, and regardless of future experience. This idea seems repugnant to common sense, and in practice no one would apply it. Instead, if conditions changed, surplus would be redistributed among the policies—in practice as a uniform bonus—and therefore the rate of bonus would change very gradually as old policies went off the books and new ones were written on.

In the discussion on Redington's paper G. V. Bayley and W. Perks found themselves in such agreement that they joined forces to produce a paper on a consistent system of investment and bonus distribution for a life office (*J.I.A.* **79**, 14). Their central idea was that for with-profit contracts each premium should be deemed to be invested in the conditions ruling at the time it was paid, and attract bonus accordingly. The consequence is that the (notionally) paid-up portion of a policy earns bonus on each of its successive additions at the rate appropriate to the time when a premium was paid to secure that addition. The balance of the policy corresponding to the future premiums is then on the same footing as a new policy. The mean term of the assets to match this situation must equal the mean term of the paid-up policies, and is much shorter than for total immunization. The theory is known as paid-up immunization. Again, a uniform rate of bonus would be declared in practice, and this would adapt itself to the new conditions more quickly than under total immunization. Some redistribution of surplus between policies would still be required.

A month before Redington, A. T. Haynes and R. J. Kirton had presented an important paper to the Faculty (*T.F.A.* **21**, 141) on the financial structure of a life office. In a very thorough arithmetical development, they anticipated many of his conclusions, paying particular attention to absolute matching, and stressing the dangers of options against the office, on both sides of the balance sheet. It is of course only possible to immunize against one of a set of options, and the others will presumably be exercised only if that is to the disadvantage of the office. For with-profit business, Haynes and Kirton considered it sufficient to immunize only the contractual liabilities, calculated on a gross premium basis without allowance for future bonus. The balance of the fund, broadly equal to the value of the future bonus loadings plus the office's free reserves, should be invested for profit. I shall refer to this as contractual liability immunization. It gives considerable freedom in investment policy, and is correspondingly dependent on personal judgment and experience. The freedom is to some extent restricted by the necessity to eliminate negative reserves and guard against surrender and paid-up options. The theoretical implications for the rate of bonus will depend, as with the other methods, on the mean term of the whole fund. If, for example, this is greater than the mean term for total immunization, the rate of bonus should fall if interest rates rise—a paradoxical result that would be avoided in practice.

In a paper on the actuarial management of a life office (*J.I.A.* **83**, 112) J. L. Anderson and J. D. Binns, while expressing a preference for total immunization as a standard, mentioned yet another system, which I shall call current bonus immunization. It is traditional in British life offices to keep the with-profit premiums unchanged until some radical and permanent alteration in conditions (for example, the relative incidence of mortality), makes a change essential. Differences in experience, according to this philosophy, are reflected in the bonus. It is also a common practice, and desirable for simplicity's sake, to declare a bonus uniform for all classes and durations. This may lead to one class or generation of business having to subsidize another to an unreasonable extent, and, in some cases, to the terms for new policies becoming uncompetitive. Now if a new policy should get the bonus its premiums will support, and if bonuses are to be uniform, then logically the solution is to invest in such a manner that if conditions change the fund will be able to support bonuses on the existing policies at the rate appropriate to new policies. This is current bonus immunization. It may lead to a comparatively short mean term. In fact it equals a mean term for paid-up immunization multiplied by the derivative of the rate of bonus with respect to the rate of interest. This derivative, which is often of the order of ·5, may alternatively be expressed as the mean term of the premiums on a new policy divided by the mean term of the sum assured.

It may be argued that current bonus immunization requires too short an investment position and causes undesirable fluctuations in the bonus. I shall comment on the former point later. As to fluctuations, one answer is that perhaps bonus ought to vary more than it is permitted to in some cases. Nobody likes having to reduce bonus rates, and so we have grown too conservative, but being in a position to make a justified increase is correspondingly pleasant. Again, it is difficult to avoid feeling morally bound, to some extent, by quotations given by the new business side; perhaps the remedy there is to base such illustrations on past bonus figures. In practice, of course, greater prudence when conditions are good, and miscellaneous sources of surplus, could reduce fluctuations to an extent which would avoid extremes and yet give proper effect to the experience.

(This system was also mentioned by W. E. H. Hickox in the discussion a month earlier on R. S. Skerman's paper 'The Application of Actuarial Principles to the Transaction of Overseas Life Business'. The interesting fact was there brought out that in certain territories policies tend to be for terms longer than ours while the investments available are of very short term. One office had found itself with a mean term even shorter than that for current bonus immunization.)

It may be helpful to demonstrate these ideas on some simple model funds, which have been constructed throughout on a continuous basis for ease of calculation. Consider first, three whole life funds without profits recruited by entrants aged 40 at a rate of premium of ·02 stripped of expenses. The first is stationary, the second has always been increasing at the rate of 5 % per annum, and the third at 10 %. The new entrants have, of course, been increasing (as they must) at the same rates, but I have reduced all the funds to a scale where the entrants now are coming in at the rate of 1 per annum. Thus in the 5 % fund, for instance, the lives now aged $40 + t$ are proportionate to ${}_t p_{40} (1 \cdot 05)^{-t}$.

Valuing by A 1949–52 3 % ult. gives the following results:

		Fund		
		Stationary	'5%'	'10%'
Sums Assured	Amount	33·58	15·82	9·70
	Value	20·54	8·55	4·79
	Mean term	14·7 years	18·7 years	21·7 years
Premiums	Amount	·672 p.a.	·316 p.a.	·194 p.a.
	Value	8·83	4·92	3·32
	Mean term	10·6 years	11·8 years	12·6 years
Net liability	Value	11·71	3·63	1·47
	Mean term	17·8 years	28·0 years	42·0 years

Since these are non-profit contracts, the mean terms are those for total immunization. The mean term for the net liability is found by using the combination rule given earlier. For example, taking the stationary fund,

$$\tau_V = \frac{20 \cdot 54 \times 14 \cdot 7 - 8 \cdot 83 \times 10 \cdot 6}{20 \cdot 54 - 8 \cdot 83} = 17 \cdot 8.$$

The table does bring out the fact that the mean term of the net liabilities must be greater than those both of the sums assured and of the premiums. The 10 % fund is scarcely realistic for whole-life non-profit policies, but serves to show that a growing fund can perhaps not be totally immunized even if all the assets are perpetuities (for which the mean term, $1/\delta$, = 33·8 years). Even the

5% fund would need to invest 83% of its assets in perpetuities, assuming the balance to be invested dead short.

Temporary assurances of various kinds form an important part of our business, and theoretical mean terms calculated for them show some curious and interesting features, but since the corresponding reserves are small, they have little effect on the investment position of the office. I will therefore pass over them.

Consider next a fund consisting of 25-year endowment assurances with profits. Entrants aged 35, at a premium rate of ·04, have always been increasing at the rate of 5% per annum and are now entering at a rate of 1 per annum. A compound reversionary bonus at the rate of 29s. 7d. % per annum has always been declared and future bonus is valued at that rate. On the same basis as before the results are:

Sums assured	Amount		14·02
Sum assured plus existing bonus	Amount		16·27
	Value	allowing for	13·31
	Mean term	future bonus	13·1 years
	Value	with no allowance	11·04
	Mean term	for future bonus	12·4 years
Premiums	Amount p.a.		·561
	Value		6·37
	Mean term		7·9 years
Net liability, allowing for future bonus	Value		6·94
	Mean term		17·9 years
Net liability, with no allowance for future bonus	Value		4·67
	Mean term		18·4 years
Paid-up policies, plus existing bonus, and with allowance for future bonus	Amount*		8·01
	Value		6·94
	Mean term		9·4 years

* On a theoretical basis producing the same net liability.

Now by Haynes's and Kirton's method, the value of the contractual liabilities is 4·67 which must be matched by assets having a mean term 18·4 years. The balance 2·27 of the assets is considered to be free reserve to be invested for profit. (In this simplified treatment, negative reserves have not been eliminated.)

For total immunization it will be seen that the assets must have a mean term

$$\frac{13\cdot31 \times 13\cdot1 - 6\cdot37 \times 7\cdot9}{13\cdot31 - 6\cdot37} = 17\cdot9 \text{ years.}$$

The mean term for paid-up immunization cannot be found from the combination rule; it needs a special calculation. This is also the case with actual funds. Here the result is 9·4 years. This is less than the figure for the full sums assured and bonus, 13·1 years, because the policies of shorter unexpired term acquire a relatively greater weight on being made paid-up.

The mean term for current bonus immunization is 4·2 years. This could not of course be immunized in practice, but we should remember the large and rapidly growing amount of non-profit deferred annuity pension business which many offices are writing. That could easily have a mean term of 40 years or even more—again impossible to immunize—but if the reserves for the two classes were equal the combined mean term would be 22·1 years, and this could be immunized by assets invested as to 15 % in open mortgages, 35 % in 20-year bonds, and the balance of 50 % in perpetuities—a not unreasonable distribution.

To reconcile these four systems is not as difficult as might appear. None is claimed as a unique solution, but rather as a standard from which its advocates would depart, and the constraints of a practical world would probably draw them all towards the same region regardless of their points of departure. Also the office's 'estate', as Redington has called it—the free reserves and margins in the valuations of assets and liabilities—gives a degree of freedom to depart. None of the systems should impair solvency; they merely affect the bonus.

Total immunization gives the most stable bonus, but changes in experience only emerge gradually, and one generation of policy-holders may in effect subsidize another to a considerable extent. Current bonus immunization might be regarded as the most equitable in that a new policy-holder will obtain the bonus his premiums can support; but bonus rates are liable to fluctuate, and equity can be carried too far. Paid-up immunization may be

looked upon as giving a compromise between these two. Its advocates, however, would claim that it is valid in its own right in that
it assumes the investment of premiums in the conditions ruling at
the time they are paid, and takes no credit for future premiums
which may not be received. Contractual liability immunization
is capable of a wide range of results—unjustifiable in parts—
reflecting its freedom of investment. My own preference is for
current bonus immunization as being fairer and providing a less
strained framework within which to apply a bonus policy.

Probably there is no single correct method; the bonus loading
allows you a certain latitude, and the way you use that depends on
how you want bonus to vary with interest rates. This partly
depends on the practice and tradition of the office. When a pro-
poser effects a with-profit policy, there arises an implied contract
with him that the office will continue to distribute its surplus
more or less in the same manner as when he took out the policy.
He is entitled to expect that the office will not radically alter its
practice to his disadvantage, at least in respect of policies in his
series, and equally, he would be unreasonable to expect some
considerable advantage from such an alteration.

Having chosen a standard, how is immunization to be applied?
The first thing to realize is that it is part of a larger problem: to
harmonize the premium scale, investment policy, the bonus method,
and the valuation basis and rate of release of surplus. Immunization theory merely provides a very rough guide to investment policy
—a norm against which the reality can be assessed. The mean term
of the liabilities will alter continuously because of

(a) the efflux of time,
(b) changes in the rate of interest,
(c) alterations and surrenders,
(d) new business,

and corresponding factors affect the assets. Both liabilities and
assets should be valued for the purpose of calculating the mean
term on a single realistic basis. For the former this will mean a
gross premium, bonus reserve valuation. The net premium valuation may be an admirable instrument for controlling the release

of surplus or preserving continuity in published valuations, but it does distort its components, and is unsuitable for mean-term purposes. The mean term of the liabilities may be estimated by valuing them at two rates of interest or, more simply, by using the one valuation and an n-ages method. As an example of the latter, consider the sums assured in the stationary non-profit fund above. Their value divided by their amount is ·6115, which is the mean of v for 6, 15, and 35 years.

$$\frac{6v^6 + 15v^{15} + 35v^{35}}{v^6 + v^{15} + v^{35}} = 14\cdot8,$$

as compared with the true value of 14·7.

The former method, the difference between valuations at two rates, gives, of course, a direct approximation to the differential coefficient in equation (2) above. This enables us to calculate the mean terms for total immunization, or for the contractual liability method. The paid-up mean term requires an approximate calculation which is outside the scope of this paper. The assets are treated on the same principles, but more empirically. Income tax at the appropriate rates should be allowed for. Having estimated the mean terms we are then better able to assess our investment position and decide on a future policy.

The nice application of this theory is sadly blunted in practice. I have written throughout this paper of 'the' rate of interest; there is, of course, no such thing, but only a pattern of rates which often behaves in an illogical and unpredictable manner. Even granting 'the' rate of interest as a necessary simplification, it does not change suddenly, and if it did we would not know whether the change was permanent or merely a non-significant fluctuation. Options also spoil the theoretical position—alternative redemption dates of assets, options on policies whether guaranteed contractually, e.g. the cash option on a deferred annuity, or morally, e.g. a proportionate paid-up endowment assurance. Again, what is the mean term of a wholly-owned subsidiary company? Of a growth equity?—presumably that is greater than a perpetuity. Of, say, a high-yielding debenture?—should the additional yield be looked upon as a risk premium against future losses, so that the stock ought to be treated as a wasting asset with a shorter mean term? The list of difficulties can be greatly extended but that does not absolve us from making an attempt to overcome them and apply the theory as well as we can.

Finally it must be stressed that there is no substitute for strength in a life office—adequate premiums and free reserves. Given that foundation, the theory of immunization should be a tool to help us to build more safely and to use our resources more economically, and to better advantage.

This paper has drawn freely on the work of the various authors mentioned in it, and of others. I am indebted to them all, especially to G. V. Bayley who first aroused my interest in the subject, and to R. C. Cooper, who has assisted me.

COPING WITH THE RISK OF INTEREST-RATE FLUCTUATIONS: RETURNS TO BOND HOLDERS FROM NAIVE AND OPTIMAL STRATEGIES

Lawrence Fisher
Roman L. Weil

Reprinted from THE JOURNAL OF BUSINESS OF THE UNIVERSITY OF CHICAGO
Vol. 44, No. 4, October 1971

COPING WITH THE RISK OF INTEREST-RATE FLUCTUATIONS: RETURNS TO BONDHOLDERS FROM NAÏVE AND OPTIMAL STRATEGIES*

LAWRENCE FISHER† AND ROMAN L. WEIL‡

Consider an investor—an individual or an institution—who wishes today to invest his resources to have available a fixed amount of money some years hence. He may have a fixed obligation to meet at that time, or he may have a long-time horizon for his total portfolio and want less risk than that provided by the "market" portfolio. What securities should the investor buy? In this article we present an answer to that question. We show that high-grade bonds, used appropriately, have been an excellent medium for achieving the certainty the investor wishes.

Or consider the "riskless security"—an important element of modern portfolio theory. There is no completely riskless asset. Solving the problem of devising a riskless asset is the same as that faced by the investor above. We show here that an asset nearly free of risk from interest-rate fluctuations can be affected for holding periods of five, ten, and twenty years by appropriate use of high-grade bonds.[1] Other forms of risk, such as those introduced by changes in the purchasing power of money, chances of default, and the exercise of call privileges, are not treated here.

First, we examine the investment performance of an index of long-term, high-grade bonds, using the same method of analysis as that appropriate for common stocks. We find that long-term bonds have given both lower average return and more than proportionately lower dispersion than would have been obtained from holding a well-diversified portfolio of common stocks listed on the New York Stock Exchange. However, the dispersion of returns is substantial, whether measured about the sample

* Research support was provided by the Center for Research in Security Prices (sponsored by Merrill Lynch, Pierce, Fenner & Smith, Inc.) of the Graduate School of Business, University of Chicago, and by the National Science Foundation through grants GS-1541 and GS-2703 to the University of Chicago. We thank I. G. Morgan for able research assistance as well as John P. Gould, James H. Lorie, and members of the Accounting Workshop of the University of Chicago for their comments. Paul Samuelson provided historical insight, as did David Durand, who criticized an earlier draft of this paper so strongly that it is perhaps a disservice to him for us to associate his name with our paper by publicly acknowledging his help. The empirical results were presented to the Seminar on the Analysis of Security Prices of the Center for Research in Security Prices on November 13, 1969, and the earlier draft referred to was presented at the meeting of the Institute for Management Sciences in London on July 2, 1970.

† Professor of finance, Graduate School of Business, University of Chicago.

‡ Associate professor of management and information science, Committee on Information Sciences and Graduate School of Business, University of Chicago; visiting for academic year 1971–72 at the Graduate School of Industrial Administration, Carnegie-Mellon University.

[1] In the capital assets pricing model of portfolio theory, the return on the riskless security is the intercept of the linear function of return on risk which represents the set of options theoretically available to an investor. Thus, our work shows that a *sufficient* condition for the application of portfolio theory is satisfied. Eugene F. Fama ("Risk, Return, and Equilibrium," *Journal of Political Economy* 79, no. 1 [January 1971]: 30–55) argues that the condition may not be *necessary*, because, even if there were no riskless asset, the efficient set of risk-return options provided by the market may closely approximate the linear risk-return tradeoff of modern portfolio theory.

mean or about the promised yield. Therefore, long-term, high-grade bonds do not appear to be riskless investments even in money terms. However, the implied investment strategy overlooks a very important difference between stocks and bonds: Bonds are issued with promises to pay specific amounts of money at specific dates; common stocks are not. In most of the remainder of the article, we develop and test a strategy for taking advantage of the specificity of the promises of bonds to eliminate almost completely the riskiness of investments in high-grade bonds caused by unanticipated fluctuations in interest rates.

In Section II we develop an optimal strategy for bond investments, given a definite time horizon. The strategy is based on a theorem, which we prove, that depends on the concept of *duration*, defined by Macaulay.[2] The theorem was suggested by Redington,[3] and is based on an assumption about the behavior of the term structure of interest rates through time. Unfortunately, this assumption is unrealistic. Moreover, the strategy assumes that no costs are incurred in buying and selling bonds and in reinvesting the funds received as bond coupons are paid. In the Section III, therefore, we test for 1925–68 the investment strategy and an alternative (the naïve strategy of buying and of reinvesting proceeds from matured coupons in a bond with desired maturity) which has lower transactions costs. We find that the practical effects of the violation of our theoretical assumptions about the behavior of the

[2] Frederick R. Macaulay, *Some Theoretical Problems Suggested by the Movements of Interest Rates, Bond Yields and Stock Prices in the United States since 1856* (New York: National Bureau of Economic Research, 1938), pp. 45–53.

[3] F. M. Redington, "Review of the Principles of Life-Office Valuations," *Journal of the Institute of Actuaries* 78, no. 3 (1952): 286–340.

term structure and about transactions costs are small. Therefore, we conclude that the strategy is practical for obtaining a given number of dollars a fixed number of years hence. Finally, we discuss the policy implications of our results for issuers of bonds.

I. INVESTMENT PERFORMANCE OF LONG-TERM BONDS

In this section we present estimates of realized returns to holders of long-term, high-grade corporate bonds for the period December 1925 through December 1968. For holding periods of various lengths, we compare these returns with those from holding common stocks listed on the New York Stock Exchange (NYSE). We confirm what is well known—that, over the period, returns to bondholders were substantially less than returns to stockholders. We also find that variability of bondholder's returns is, proportionately much less than the average variability of stockholder's returns. Moreover, for all but the shortest holding period considered, when interest rates at the beginning of a holding period are taken into account, the *uncertainty* of returns (caused by interest-rate changes *after* bonds are purchased) to bondholders is substantially less than that implied by the *variability* of returns (caused by interest-rate changes *before* bonds are purchased). Nevertheless, when the naïve strategy of buying bonds with specified terms of maturity is followed, uncertainty is still substantial. In a later section we show how that uncertainty can be reduced.

Our original intention was to extend the Weil study[4] of year-to-year returns on bond investments to cover longer

[4] Roman L. Weil, "Realized Interest Rates and Bondholders' Returns," *American Economic Review* 60, no. 3 (June 1970): 502–11.

periods in a manner comparable to the studies by Fisher and Lorie of rates of return[5] and variability of returns[6] on investments in common stocks listed on the NYSE. There is, however, an important difference between a portfolio of stock and one composed of long-term bonds. If a portfolio of long-term bonds is purchased and held, the bonds included will eventually reach maturity and be paid off. Before that, however, the originally long-term bonds will have become intermediate-term and, then, short-term bonds. If our purpose is to study performance of long-term bonds over an extended period of time, like forty or fifty years, we need a way to keep the long-term portfolio from becoming short-term as time passes. A somewhat similar problem arose in the Fisher-Lorie studies of stock portfolios when stocks were delisted. In the second and third Fisher-Lorie studies,[7] the proceeds from stocks that had been delisted without a listed successor were placed in a pseudostock whose price and dividend behavior were inferred from Fisher's Combination Investment Performance and Price Indexes.[8] A detailed analysis showed that the overall results were not perceptibly affected by this change in procedure from the first study,[9] in which such proceeds were distributed over

actual stocks, although by the end of 1965 about one-fourth of the total market value of the investments originally made in January 1926 was represented by the index.

For our initial work, therefore, we decided to move directly into the consideration of a pseudobond whose investment performance could be calculated from an index. The index chosen was Standard and Poor's Corporate AAA (highest grade) Bond Yields[10] because that index is widely used and because its compilers publish a price index computed from the index of yields. We keep the investment "long-term" by computing prices of both twenty-year and nineteen-year 4 percent bonds from the index of yields. We start by buying the twenty-year bond. A year later, when it has become a nineteen-year bond, we sell it and use the proceeds (together with the coupon payment just received) to buy the new twenty-year bond. (This procedure and biases introduced by defaults or quality changes are explained in Appendix A.) In this manner we have constructed an investment-performance index for long-term bonds covering the period December 1925–December 1968. This index is shown in table 1. For comparison, table 1 also contains Fisher's Arithmetic Investment Performance Index for common stocks listed on the NYSE[11] and the index of bond yields that we used.

From table 1, we may select pairs of values of either investment-performance index and estimate the ratio of final wealth to initial investment for an investor who bought stocks or bonds at the date of the first value of the index and

[5] Lawrence Fisher and James H. Lorie, "Rates of Return on Investments in Common Stock," *Journal of Business* 37, no. 1 (January 1964): 1–21; and idem, "Rates of Return on Investments in Common Stock: The Year-by-Year Record, 1926–65," ibid., 41, no. 3 (July 1968): 291–316.

[6] Fisher and Lorie, "Some Studies of Variability of Returns on Investments in Common Stocks," *Journal of Business* 43, no. 2 (April 1970): 99–134.

[7] Fisher and Lorie, "Rates of Return . . . Year-by-Year Record, 1926–65" (n. 5 above); idem, "Some Studies of Variability" (n. 6 above).

[8] Lawrence Fisher, "Some New Stock-Market Indexes," *Journal of Business* 39, no. 1 (January 1966): 191–225.

[9] Fisher and Lorie, "Rates of Return on Investments in Common Stock" (n. 5 above).

[10] Standard and Poor's, *Trade and Securities Statistics: Security Price Index Record* (New York: Standard & Poor's, 1968).

[11] Fisher, "Some New Stock-Market Indexes" (n. 8 above).

TABLE 1

INVESTMENT PERFORMANCE INDEXES FOR COM-
MON STOCKS LISTED ON THE NEW YORK
STOCK EXCHANGE AND LONG-TERM, HIGH-
GRADE CORPORATE BONDS (DECEMBER
1960 = 100) AND STANDARD AND POOR'S
AAA CORPORATE-BOND YIELDS

| DATE (DECEMBER OF YEAR) | INVESTMENT PERFORMANCE INDEX | | AAA BOND YIELD* |
| | Common Stocks | Bonds | |
(1)	(2)	(3)	(4)
1925	1.639†	27.310	4.88
1926	1.604	29.271	4.71
1927	2.096	31.246	4.56
1928	3.007	31.960	4.74
1929	2.032	32.472	4.99
1930	1.270	35.851	4.59
1931	0.696	35.873	4.95
1932	0.785	37.578	4.97
1933	1.864	40.812	4.70
1934	2.218	47.074	3.94
1935	3.545	51.755	3.51
1936	5.382	55.745	3.21
1937	2.917	57.094	3.27
1938	3.977	60.400	3.09
1939	4.122	63.284	2.97
1940	3.816	66.321	2.840
1941	3.502	68.045	2.859
1942	4.791	70.013	2.858
1943	7.744	72.319	2.828
1944	10.864	75.345	2.732
1945	17.654	78.991	2.583
1946	15.909	81.067	2.581
1947	15.861	80.297	2.842
1948	15.513	83.432	2.767
1949	18.839	88.331	2.548
1950	25.813	89.656	2.625
1951	29.957	86.878	3.054
1952	32.909	90.283	2.993
1953	31.969	91.946	3.079
1954	50.148	97.207	2.891
1955	60.299	96.541	3.158
1956	64.426	91.050	3.845
1957	55.215	96.841	3.663
1958	88.141	94.738	4.115
1959	101.672	92.654	4.613
1960	100.000	100.000	4.369
1961	129.226	103.550	4.435
1962	112.722	111.534	4.195
1963	134.017	113.868	4.359
1964	158.295	118.960	4.354
1965	203.479	118.588	4.722
1966	188.965	114.476	5.389
1967	283.459	110.614	6.123
1968	N.A.‡	112.254	6.510

SOURCES.—Stock Investment Performance Index—Fisher's Arithmetic Investment Performance Index (Lawrence Fisher, "Some New Stock-Market Indexes," *Journal of Business* 39, no. 1 [January 1966]: 191–225); Bond Performance Index—Computed from column 7 in the manner described in Appendix A; AAA Corporate Bond Yields—See Standard and Poor's, *Trade and Securities Statistics: Security Price Index Record* (New York, Standard & Poor's, 1968).

* Percentage per annum, compounded semiannually.

† January 1926; all other numbers in this column are for the end of December of the year shown.

‡ N.A. = Not available.

sold at the date of the second value and who followed the investment policy used to compute the index. Note, however, that none of the indexes in table 1 allows for commissions, income taxes, or other expenses which would be incurred in following the investment policy. Hence, the results are not directly comparable with the results for common stocks reported by Fisher and Lorie.[12]

We have computed the ratios for the time periods studied by Fisher and Lorie.[13] The results are summarized in table 2, which also includes results for the more nearly feasible investment policy used by Fisher and Lorie, adjusted to remove the effect of the initial commission payments.

Table 2 shows that the mean return from stocks was substantially greater than the mean return from bonds and that the dispersion of returns from stocks was far more than proportionately greater than the dispersion of returns from bonds. Nevertheless, the dispersion of bond returns was substantial, which indicates that the holder of long-term bonds, as well as the stockholder, faces considerable uncertainty about the market value of his holdings.

One difference between stocks and bonds is that bonds have promised yields. It appears reasonable to assume that an investor who buys bonds when promised yields are low will realize a lower return than when they are high. That is, a part of the dispersion in bond returns measured at the end of holding periods may be attributable to the changes

[12] However, to save the time of the readers who would otherwise do so themselves, we have computed tables in the same format as table 1 of Fisher and Lorie, "Rates of Return . . . Year-by-Year Record, 1926–65" (n. 5 above), of rates of return on investment in our pseudobonds and the stock index which appears in Appendix A.

[13] Fisher and Lorie, "Some Studies of Variability" (n. 6 above).

TABLE 2

SUMMARY OF THE DISTRIBUTION OF RATIOS OF TERMINAL
WEALTH TO INITIAL INVESTMENT FOR HIGH-GRADE
BONDS AND COMMON STOCKS

Statistic (1)	Bonds (2)	Stocks per Index (3)	Stocks per Fisher-Lorie Study (4)
Forty One-Year Periods Beginning in December of 1925, . . . , 1964			
Minimum.................	0.943	0.542	0.527
Maximum................	1.153	2.376	2.104
Mean....................	1.038	1.178	1.153
Standard deviation.........	0.040	0.343	0.318
Mean deviation............	0.030	0.257	0.249
Gini's mean difference*......	0.044	0.368	0.354
Eight Five-Year Periods Beginning in December of 1925, . . . , 1960			
Minimum.................	1.036	0.775	0.886
Maximum................	1.444	4.626	4.307
Mean....................	1.208	2.095	1.923
Standard deviation.........	0.125	1.136	1.017
Mean deviation............	0.104	0.867	0.750
Gini's mean difference.......	0.140	1.205	1.031
Four Ten-Year Periods Beginning in December of 1925, . . . , 1955			
Minimum.................	1.222	2.163	1.250
Maximum................	1.895	4.979	3.561
Mean.	1.468	3.483	2.836
Standard deviation.........	0.276	1.000	0.923
Mean deviation............	0.243	0.748	0.793
Gini's mean difference.......	0.289	1.062	0.869
Two Twenty-Year Periods Beginning in December of 1925 and 1945			
Minimum.................	1.501	10.772	3.397
Maximum................	2.892	11.526	10.874
Mean....................	2.197	11.149	7.135
Standard deviation.........	0.696	0.377	3.739
Mean deviation............	0.696	0.377	3.739
Gini's mean difference.......	0.696	0.377	3.739

SOURCES.—Columns 2 and 3 from table 1. Column 4, adapted by multiplying 1.01 by the "all stock" figures in table 5 of the third Fisher-Lorie study (Lawrence Fisher and James H. Lorie, "Rates of Return on Investments in Common Stock: The Year-by-Year Record, 1926–65," *Journal of Business* 41, no. 3 [July 1968]: 291–316).

NOTE.—For comparability with the Fisher-Lorie study, the dispersion measures are for the sample periods; i.e., sums are divided by N rather than by $(N - 1)$.

* For a discussion of this statistic and its interpretation see pp. 102–4 of Lawrence Fisher and James H. Lorie, "Some Studies of Variability of Returns on Investments in Common Stocks," *Journal of Business* 43, no. 2 (April 1970): 99-134, and the references cited there.

in promised yields which occurred before the holding period. We have constructed table 3 to test this supposition. If we

TABLE 3

COMPARISON OF RATIOS OF TERMINAL WEALTH TO INITIAL INVESTMENT FOR BONDS BEFORE ("ACTUAL") AND AFTER SUBTRACTING RATIO IMPLIED BY INITIAL YIELD ("DIFFERENCE")

Statistic (1)	Actual (2)	Difference (3)
Forty-three One-Year Periods Beginning in December of 1925, . . . , 1967		
Minimum...............	0.943	−0.089
Maximum...............	1.153	0.106
Mean..................	1.034	−0.004
Standard deviation......	0.041	0.041
Mean deviation.........	0.032	0.032
Gini's mean difference....	0.046	0.047
Thirty-nine Five-Year Periods Beginning in December of 1925, . . . , 1963		
Minimum...............	0.955	−0.255
Maximum...............	1.554	0.277
Mean..................	1.194	−0.004
Standard deviation......	0.144	0.119
Mean deviation.........	0.108	0.090
Gini's mean difference....	0.157	0.134
Thirty-four Ten-Year Periods Beginning in December of 1925, . . . , 1958		
Minimum...............	1.123	−0.318
Maximum...............	1.949	0.312
Mean..................	1.431	0.007
Standard deviation......	0.288	0.187
Mean deviation.........	0.251	0.160
Gini's mean difference....	0.315	0.213
Twenty-four Twenty-Year Periods Beginning in December of 1925, . . . , 1948		
Minimum...............	1.346	−0.387
Maximum...............	2.892	0.270
Mean..................	1.952	−0.149
Standard deviation......	0.514	0.176
Mean deviation.........	0.474	0.139
Gini's mean difference....	0.568	0.198

SOURCES.—See table 1.

consider overlapping periods, the bond-investment-performance index shown in table 1 allows us to estimate the realized ratio of terminal wealth to initial wealth for forty-three one-year, thirty-nine five-year, thirty-four ten-year, and twenty-four twenty-year periods. From the promised yields at the start of each period, in column 4 of table 1 we can calculate what the wealth ratios would have been had the realized yield been precisely equal to the promised yield. We then substracted each of these "promised"-wealth ratios from the corresponding realized-wealth ratios. Column 2 of table 3 shows the mean and several measures of dispersion of the realized-wealth ratios (for overlapping periods). Column 3 shows the distribution of the differences between realized- and promised wealth ratios.

Consider, for example, the five-year period from December 1925 to December 1930. The AAA bond yield in December 1925 was 4.88 percent per annum, compounded semiannually (see col. 4 of table 1). If this promised yield had been realized for five years, $100 invested in December 1925 would have been worth:

$$\$100 \times [1 + (.0488/2)]^{5 \times 2} = \$100$$
$$\times (1.0244)^{10} = \$127.26 .$$

In fact the $100 invested in December 1925 was worth:

$$\$100 \times (35.851/27.310) = \$131.27 .$$

(See the Bond Index for December of 1925 and 1930 in col. 3 of table 1.) Thus the *actual* wealth ratio used in the process of calculating column 2 of table 3 is 1.3127, and the *difference* in wealth ratio used in calculating column 3 is 1.3127 − 1.2726 = 0.0401. The numbers in table 3 for five-year periods are summary statistics for the thirty-nine numbers—the first, 0.0401, derived as just described. Under the assumption that low (high) "promised" yields imply low (high) realized returns, the dispersion described by the statistics shown in column 3 of table 3 is an estimate of the actual riskiness of long-term bonds for the holding period—one, five, ten, or twenty years—chosen.

Note first, by comparing column 2 of table 2 with column 2 of table 3, that the distributions of realized-wealth ratios are similar for both the nonoverlapping and overlapping treatments. Thus, our computing of table 3 is reasonable.

For the one-year periods, the dispersion of the differences shown in column 3 is the same as the dispersion of the realized ratios shown in column 2. We conclude, therefore, that knowing Standard and Poor's AAA corporate-bond yield at the particular time a portfolio of twenty-year bonds was purchased could be of no help whatsoever in estimating the first year's realized return. That is, essentially all of the dispersion is due to unanticipated changes in interest rates during that first year. However, as the holding period increases, the dispersion of the "differences" steadily becomes a smaller proportion of the dispersion of the corresponding "actual" realized ratio. When the promised yield was high, the realized yield over a long period tended to be higher than when the initial promised yield was low.

We were tempted to run regressions of realized-wealth ratios on promised ratios but refrained from doing so because we have few independent observations. Indeed, the time series of promised yields and, therefore, of promised-wealth ratios can be described roughly as U-shaped—falling from 1925 to the mid-1940s and rising thereafter. Consequently, for all lengths of holding periods, the greatest positive difference between realized- and promised-wealth ratios was found near the beginning of the series; and the greatest negative, near the end.

We conclude from table 3 that, for all but short holding periods, the *uncertainty* about the return from holding high-grade bonds is even less than one would infer from table 2.

However, bondholders need not accept even the degree of uncertainty indicated by table 3. They can do far better. In the remainder of this article we show how.

II. BASES FOR AN OPTIMAL INVESTMENT STRATEGY AND POLICY IMPLICATIONS

In portfolio theory, the time horizon or holding period of assets must be be specified in advance. To be specific, we shall write of an investor who has a ten-year horizon. We need not be concerned with why he has such an horizon. We must, however, pick the horizon or a series of horizon dates.[14]

The investor requires, say, $1,000 ten years hence. The promised yield to maturity is, say, 6 percent. To meet that obligation, he wishes to invest now $558.39—the present value of $1,000, received ten years hence, discounted at 6 percent per annum, compounded annually.

In order to assess the *riskiness* of the asset, we shall aim to invest $558.39 and have precisely $1,000 ten years hence. Any deviation from the $1,000 adds to the *measured* riskiness of the investment.

There are several dimensions attached to bond investments—quality, maturity, call properties, coupon, and yield to maturity. We shall not offer advice on what quality bond the investor should

[14] In general, the investor's horizon may extend beyond the end of the holding period, but we use the terms "horizon" and "holding period" interchangeably.

buy, nor shall we treat problems raised if the bond be callable before maturity. Let us assume the investor will buy only the highest-quality bonds. For, as Macaulay finds,[15] "movement of the yields [and prices] of bonds of the highest grade reflect primarily changes in 'long term interest rates.' " The investor is concerned about the effect of default risk on his strategy, but we do not analyze this effect. He is indifferent to the coupon rates because he intends to reinvest the coupons to help establish the fund necessary at his horizon. (He might prefer a "bond" with zero coupon rate so that there would be no reinvestment problem; this is discussed below.) Our investor wants to know what maturity to select. One obvious strategy is to buy a bond which matures at the horizon, say, ten years hence. This strategy is the *naïve* one of our title.

Let us assume that the promised yield to maturity on the type of bond our investor chooses is 6 percent. The investor would like to invest $558.39 now and assume that his problem of raising $1,000 ten years hence is solved. In fact, unless the "bond" has no coupons—that is, unless the bond is a single-payment note—the problem is not solved. The promised yield to maturity of 6 percent will be realized by the investor if and only if the coupons received during the ten-year holding period can be reinvested at an average yield of at least 6 percent. Promised yields to maturity do not remain constant; the investor has no reason to believe that his $558.39 will grow to $1,000 in ten years.

We now shall show that a better way to attempt to achieve the promised 6 percent return, rather than an amount which is now unknown but could be either more or less, is not to buy the

[15] Macaulay (n. 2 above), p. 87.

ten-year bond but to follow a different strategy.

Definition.—A portfolio of investments in bonds is *immunized* for a holding period if its value at the end of the holding period, regardless of the course of interest rates during the holding period, must be at least as large as it would have been had the interest-rate function been constant throughout the holding period.

If the realized return on an investment in bonds is sure to be at least as large as the appropriately computed yield to the horizon, then that investment is immunized. We derive a strategy designed to achieve immunization under a given set of assumptions. We then test that strategy on empirical data for which the assumptions that would guarantee immunization do not hold.

The concept of *duration* is the cornerstone of the strategy for immunization. *Duration* is a number with dimension *time* attached to a stream of promised payments. If

$$P_{t_1}, \quad P_{t_2}, \quad \ldots, \quad P_{t_n}$$

are the present values at time t_0 of payments promised at, perhaps unequally spaced, times $t_1, t_2, \ldots, t_n$, then the duration of that promised stream measured at t_0 is

$$D_{t_0} = \Big[\sum_{j=1}^{n} (t_j - t_0) P_{t_j} \Big] \Big/ \sum_{j=1}^{n} P_{t_j}$$

$$= \sum_{j=1}^{n} t_j P_{t_j} \Big/ \sum_{j=1}^{n} P_{t_j} - t_0.$$

A single-payment note due T years hence has duration T. The duration of a bond (with coupons due at periodic intervals before maturity) which matures T years hence is less than T. The higher the interest rate used in the calculations of the present values of a given stream of positive payments, the shorter the duration of that stream unless that "stream" be a single-payment note.

Macaulay[16] first defined duration and used it in his analysis of bonds. Redington first used immunization to "signify the investment of the assets in such a way that the existing [life insurance] business is immune to a general change in interest rates."[17] He pointed out that a life insurance company's business will be immune to small fluctuations in interest rates if assets equal liabilities and are chosen so that the derivative of the present value of the income stream (from premiums, interest, etc.) with respect to a single, continuously compounded rate of interest is equal to the derivative of the present value of the liability stream. Fisher[18] showed that the derivative of the logarithm of the present value of such a stream is Macaulay's duration with the sign reversed. Redington used the concept *mean term*, which is the same as *duration*. Samuelson[19] devised a measure equivalent to duration in an attempt to assess the effects of changes in interest rates on the banking system. Durand[20] appears to be the first writer to have mentioned the contributions of Macaulay, Samuelson, and Redington in the same article. In a recent unpublished paper, Brock and Weil[21] summarize the history of these concepts and provide an axiomatic derivation of

the duration measure. Koopmans[22] was apparently the first to point out that the maturity dates of securities chosen for the investment portfolio should be related to the anticipated payments of claims and pointed out that the two flows could be matched period by period. See also the recent paper by Whittaker.[23]

Let the forward instantaneous rate of interest compounded continuously for future times t be given by the function $i(t)$.

Assumption.—If the function $i(t)$ shifts, say, from $i_a(t)$ to $i_b(t)$, then

$$i_b(t) = i_a(t) + \Delta ,$$

where Δ may be positive or negative but is the same for all t.

The assumption says that if forward interest rates change, all rates change by the same amount.

Immunization theorem.—If the assumption holds, then a portfolio of nonnegative payments (or rents) is immunized at time t_0 if the duration

$$D_{t_0}$$

at time t_0 of its promised payments is equal to the length of the desired holding period, $T - t_0$.

The proof of the theorem is contained in Appendix B. Samuelson,[24] except for an inconsequential error, and Redington[25] proved the equivalent of this

[16] Ibid., pp. 44–53.

[17] Redington (n. 3 above), p. 289.

[18] Lawrence Fisher, "An Algorithm for Finding Exact Rates of Return," *Journal of Business* 39, no. 1 (January 1966): 111–18.

[19] Paul A. Samuelson, "The Effect of Interest Rate Increases on the Banking System," *American Economic Review* 35, no. 2 (March 1945): 16–27.

[20] David Durand, "Growth Stocks and the Petersburg Paradox," *Journal of Finance* 12, no. 3 (September 1957): 348–63.

[21] William A. Brock and Roman L. Weil, "The Axiomatics of Macaulay's Duration," mimeographed (University of Chicago, Center for Mathematical Studies in Business and Economics, report 7101, January 1971).

[22] Tjalling C. Koopmans, "The Risk of Interest Fluctuations in Life Insurance Companies" (Philadelphia: Penn Mutual Life Insurance Co., 1942).

[23] John Whittaker, "The Relevance of Duration," *Journal of Business Finance* 2 (Spring 1970): 1–8.

[24] Samuelson (n. 19 above).

[25] Redington (n. 3 above).

theorem for infinitesimal changes in interest rates.

When the assumption holds, the theorem implies that the way to immunize a portfolio to be held for, say, ten years is as follows. When the initial investment is made, purchase a portfolio whose duration is ten years. If no one security has duration ten years, then buy a combination of securities chosen so that its duration is ten years. For example, if ten-year bonds have a duration of eight years; fifteen-year bonds, eleven years; and twenty-year bonds, twelve years; buy a portfolio one-third of which is invested in ten-year bonds and two-thirds of which is in fifteen-year bonds (or one-half in ten-year bonds and one-half in twenty-year bonds).

Then, when the next coupon payments are received, say, one year hence, reinvest those payments in bonds of appropriate duration so that the duration of the whole portfolio is then nine years. The whole portfolio is immunized if its duration is set equal to the holding period. The holding period gets progressively shorter as does the duration of the portfolio, but the rates of decrease need not be identical. (This strategy is very nearly the *optimal* one of our title.)

The assumption about shifts in interest rates does not hold in reality. A more accurate description is

$$i_b(t) = i_a(t) + \Delta(t) ,$$

where $\Delta(t)$ is not constant.[26] In practice

$$i_{t_0}(t_0 + 1) ,$$

measured at time t_0, usually is greater than

$$i_{t_0+1}(t_0 + 1) ,$$

[26] If $\Delta(t)$ were a monotonically nondecreasing function of time, then the immunization theorem would still hold, and the investor would be better off than when $\Delta(t)$ is a constant function.

measured at time $t_0 + 1$. That is, the spot rate has usually been less than it was forecast to be. The tendency requires us to modify slightly the optimal strategy. To carry out the optimal strategy as simulated, we set the expected duration (as estimated from forecasts of future interest rates) of the noncash portion of the portfolio immediately after the next interest payment was to be received equal in time to the length of the remaining holding period. If there had been no tendency for forward rates to exceed spot rates, the simply stated strategy and the one actually used would have been equivalent. The fact that near forward rates tend to fluctuate more than far forward rates is contrary to the assumption.[27]

However, even if the assumption were valid, several problems would occur when one attempted to immunize his portfolio. First, as we have suggested above, there may be more than one combination of bonds which can be purchased to achieve a given duration. Second, how can one continuously monitor and rearrange, if necessary, the assets in the portfolio to keep the duration exactly equal to the remaining holding period? In general, one cannot. One purpose of our empirical tests is to ascertain how costly it is to rearrange the portfolio only once a year. Third, risk of default is an important variable

[27] I.e., it appears that, on average

$$[i_{t_0}(t_0 + 1) - i_{t_0+1}(t_0 + 1)]$$

$$> [i_{t_0}(t_0 + j) - i_{t_0+1}(t_0 + j)] ,$$

for $j = 2, 3, \ldots$ (see, e.g., Reuben A. Kessel, *The Cyclical Behavior of the Term Structure of Interest Rates*, National Bureau of Economics Research, Occasional Paper no. 91 [New York: Columbia University Press, 1965]; and David Meiselman, *The Term Structure of Interest Rates* [Englewood Cliffs, N.J.: Prentice-Hall, Inc., 1962]).

for promised[28] and realized[29] returns. The two strategies, maturity and duration, may have associated with them different default risks because some of the bonds purchased will be different. The costs we measure are only transaction costs and do not include costs or benefits of potentially different default risk.[30]

Finally, at the coupon-reinvestment dates, there may not be a set of bonds in which the coupons can be invested to achieve the holding period duration. Then it is necessary to sell some assets currently held and reinvest the proceeds in a way that achieves the desired duration. Such exchanges of assets require paying brokerage commissions or dealer

[28] Lawrence Fisher, "Determinants of Risk Premiums on Corporate Bonds," *Journal of Political Economy* 67, no. 3 (June 1959): 217–37.

[29] W. Braddock Hickman, *Corporate Bond Quality and Investor Experience* (Princeton, N.J.: Princeton University Press, 1958).

[30] Risks of default may have been different for the various bonds in this study because we have used Durand's basic yields of corporate bonds (David Durand, *Basic Yields of Corporate Bonds 1900–42*, Technical Paper no. 3 [New York: National Bureau of Economic Research, 1942]). We are now building a file of U.S. Government Bond data covering the period of this study. We hope to repeat the empirical simulation with these data.

spreads. What is the effect on realized wealth?

In reality, immunized investments for distant horizons T may not be achievable because there may be no bond or note whose duration is large enough—equal to or larger than T. As Macaulay[31] has clearly shown, the duration of coupon bonds may get *shorter* as their maturity gets longer. Consider table 4, reproduced in part from Macaulay.[32] The duration of a coupon bond increases with maturity if and only if the bond sells at or above par, but even then duration is bounded by $(r + p)/rp$ years, where r is the annual yield to maturity (expressed as a decimal fraction) and p is the number of interest payments per year or the number of times per year interest is compounded. For example, if the yield is 6 percent, compounded twice a year, the maximum duration would be 2.06/ 0.12 = seventeen years.

Theory and empirical evidence such as that presented in Section I above suggest that long-term bonds are almost certainly inferior to stocks as an investment medium for portfolios to be held

[31] Macaulay (n. 2 above).

[32] Ibid., p. 51.

TABLE 4

DURATION IN YEARS OF BONDS WITH SEMIANNUAL COUPONS*

YEARS TO MATURITY	PROMISED YIELD TO MATURITY											
	4 Percent				6 Percent				8 Percent			
	Coupon Rate				Coupon Rate				Coupon Rate			
	2%	4%†	6%	8%	2%	4%	6%†	8%	2%	4%	6%	8%
One	0.995	0.990	0.986	0.981	0.995	0.990	0.985	0.981	0.995	0.990	0.985	0.981
Five	4.770	4.581	4.423	4.290	4.756	4.558	4.393	4.254	4.742	5.533	4.361	4.218
Ten	9.007	8.339	7.859	7.497	8.891	8.169	7.662	7.286	8.762	7.986	7.454	7.067
Twenty	15.837	13.951	12.876	12.181	14.981	12.980	11.904	11.232	14.026	11.966	10.922	10.292
Fifty	25.379	21.980	20.629	19.903	19.452	17.129	16.273	15.829	14.832	13.466	12.987	12.743
One hundred	26.416	25.014	24.535	24.293	17.567	17.232	17.120	17.064	13.097	13.029	13.006	12.995
Infinity	25.500	25.500	25.500	25.500	17.167	17.167	17.167	17.167	13.000	13.000	13.000	12.995

* Rates and yields are in percentage per annum, compounded semiannually.

† These columns are like Frederick R. Macaulay, *Some Theoretical Problems Suggested by the Movements of Interest Rates, Bond Yields and Stock Prices in the United States since 1856* (New York: National Bureau of Economic Research, 1938), p. 51; the other columns were calculated by his formula (ibid., p. 49).

for long but indefinite horizons. This fact plus the fact that the duration, not the maturity, of a bond is the important parameter for achieving desired results for portfolios with certain horizons leads to one clear policy implication for bond issuers. There should be a substantial demand for instruments with long durations. Instruments are guaranteed to have long duration only if they are single-payment notes of distant maturity. We believe issuers of high-quality long-term single-payment notes will have no difficulty in selling their wares.[33] If single-payment notes appear unattractive, then the issuing of low-coupon bonds, which will sell at substantial discounts, will be of little help unless coupons are so small—less than 1 percent—that the face value of the bonds contributes most of its present value.[34]

Only with single-payment notes of long maturity can one guarantee long duration. Any individual or institution which wishes to be immunized from interest-rate fluctuations prefer its assets and liabilities to have equal durations.[35] Those with long-duration liabilities—for example, life insurance companies or pension funds—should want long-duration assets. Thus, we are led to infer the existence of a demand for single-payment notes. We are also led to the interesting conclusion that the market does *not* require single-payment notes with a variety of maturities. Because the duration of a portfolio is a linear function of the durations of its components, all that is needed is one single-payment note whose duration is at least as long as the longest liability.[36] Such an asset can be combined with assets of short duration to achieve any duration in between.

Do not conclude that one prefers single-payment notes for immunization if coupon bonds are available whose duration is long enough. That is, if the desired duration can be achieved with coupon bonds, we might prefer them to notes. The theorem assures us we can achieve immunization via a duration strategy when the assumption holds. If interest rates change, we can only do

[33] Leroy S. Wehrle ("Life Insurance Investment—the Experience of Four Companies," *Yale Economic Essays* 1 [Spring 1961]: 70–136) was on the right track in his analysis but slipped at his conclusion. He suggested that the Treasury issue bonds with "a 50–100 year maturity, a 3.5 to 3.9 per cent coupon and be noncallable and preferably a 'tap' issue. The 'tap' issue means the security would be available for purchase from the Treasury for an extended period." The duration of a 3.5 percent bond maturing in 100 years, priced to yield 6 percent, is less than 17½ years. Robert Resek and Case Sprenkel, in an unpublished note we have seen, come to the same policy conclusion as we do. Under current tax law, bonds sold at a substantial discount from par generate yearly tax liabilities to the owner but no cash flows for paying those taxes. Before single-payment rates can be made unconditionally attractive for immunization purposes, some provision must be made for the tax liability.

[34] See the 2 percent coupon rate columns of table 4. Further calculations show that a bond with a coupon rate of 1 percent has a maximum duration of less than thirty-two years if it is yielding 4 percent, less than twenty-four years if it is yielding 6 percent, and less than twenty years if it is yielding 8 percent.

[35] See Samuelson (n. 19 above), and Redington (n. 3 above), for original discussions of immunization in this context. Redington showed that a (life insurance) company with a series of obligations or horizon liabilities need not hold a portfolio of assets with cash throwoffs at dates identical to the dates its liabilities are due in order to be immunized (as Koopmans [n. 22 above] had suggested). He showed, in effect, that a business can achieve immunization by equating the duration of its assets to the duration of its liabilities. However, Redington's proof of immunization applies only to small changes in interest rates. In Appendix B we show that immunization holds for any size of change in interest rates of a certain type.

[36] The portfolios of life insurance companies and others who have guaranteed to earn a return on funds not yet received perforce contain a substantial portion of assets with short durations. For immunization they may therefore need some asset with duration substantially larger than that of the liability stream.

better—make more money—than we had hoped.[37] It is an open question whether the extra transaction costs of cash reinvestment and portfolio switching and the uncertainty because the assumption does not hold are more than offset by these extra profit opportunities.

III. TESTS OF IMMUNIZATION STRATEGIES

We have used empirical data to conduct extensive simulation tests on various implementations of the strategy assigned to attempt immunization and have compared the results with those obtained from investments in bonds with maturity (rather than duration) equal to holding period. The latter strategy is one form of naïve strategy—if one wants cash ten years hence, he buys bonds which mature in ten years, reinvesting all proceeds in the same bond. This strategy we call the *maturity* strategy. The strategy suggested by the theorem on immunization we call the *duration* strategy.

Results are shown in tables 5, 6, and 7. Table 5 shows results for five-year holding periods; table 6, for ten-year holding periods; table 7, for twenty-year holding periods. Details of data and calculations are in Appendix C.

Look at table 5. The first two columns show the starting and ending years of the holding period; the next four columns, results without taking commissions into account; the last four columns, results with commissions. Within one of these groups of four columns for a given commission treatment, the first shows the yield to maturity;[38] the second column, the expected wealth ratio calculated from the interest-rate function

[37] This point was noted by C. D. Rich ("Review of the Principles of Life-Office Valuations, Abstract of the Discussion," *Journal of the Institute of Actuaries* 78, no. 3 [1952]: 319–20) in his discussion of Redington's paper (n. 3 above).

implied by the promised yields on bonds of varying maturities[39] (see Appendix C). That is, if $100 were invested in 1925 and if the "expected" yield were realized, in 1930 the investment would have been worth $124.46 without commissions and $124.10 if commissions had been paid.

The last two columns in each group of four results from the two investment strategies—duration and maturity. *Duration* is the strategy in which immunization is attempted and *maturity* is the strategy to buy, with the initial funds and all subsequent coupon payments, the bond which matures five years from the date of the initial investment. Differences in the entries in the "expected" and "maturity" columns, although small are not zero because reinvestments of interest seldom take place at precisely the promised yield. The marked entries are the periods in which, contrary to the hypothesis, "maturity" did better than "duration," that is, came closer to the expected yield.

Tables 6 and 7 are similar to table 5

[38] The two commission treatments show different yields to maturity because, when interest receipts are reinvested, there will be commissions to pay. Our calculation of "expected" yield also differs from the traditional calculation of promised yields by our taking account of the entire term structure of interest rates through the end of the holding period.

[39] Expected returns were calculated from yield curves presented by Durand (n. 30 above). In contrast to the corporate AAA series, Durand's yields are available only for the first quarter of each calendar year—not for December. Moreover, Durand's promised yields on twenty-year bonds were generally lower than Standard and Poor's corporate AAA yields and had a smaller range of values. We checked to see whether the apparent success in both the maturing and duration strategies was due to differences in underlying data. This we accomplished by constructing tables like tables 1, 2, and 3. These calculations were performed on a bond index computed from nineteen- and twenty-year basic yields derived from Durand's data. The measures of dispersion that we found by using these data were essentially the same as those in our tables 2 and 3 constructed from Standard and Poor's AAA yields.

TABLE 5

RESULTS FROM TWO STRATEGIES FOR INVESTING IN BONDS
(FIVE-YEAR PERIODS)

	WITHOUT COMMISSION				WITH COMMISSION			
	Expected Yield	Wealth Ratios			Expected Yield	Wealth Ratios		
		Expected	Duration	Maturity		Expected	Duration	Maturity
1925–30......	4.47	1.2446	1.2440	1.2435	4.41	1.2410	1.2403	1.2398
1926–31*.....	4.40	1.2402	1.2407	1.2402	4.34	1.2366	1.2369	1.2365
1927–32*.....	4.30	1.2343	1.2345	1.2342	4.24	1.2307	1.2308	1.2306
1928–33......	4.05	1.2196	1.2201	1.2208	3.99	1.2161	1.2165	1.2172
1929–34*.....	4.70	1.2584	1.2558	1.2559	4.64	1.2546	1.2520	1.2522
1930–35......	4.40	1.2402	1.2373	1.2372	4.34	1.2366	1.2336	1.2335
1931–36*.....	3.92	1.2122	1.2084	1.2090	3.86	1.2087	1.2048	1.2056
1932–37......	4.60	1.2520	1.2444	1.2427	4.54	1.2483	1.2406	1.2391
1933–38......	3.71	1.2000	1.1926	1.1916	3.65	1.1966	1.1892	1.1883
1934–39......	3.50	1.1879	1.1797	1.1785	3.45	1.1846	1.1764	1.1752
1935–40......	2.41	1.1266	1.1209	1.1201	2.36	1.1236	1.1179	1.1171
1936–41......	1.91	1.0990	1.0949	1.0942	1.85	1.0961	1.0920	1.0914
1937–42......	1.71	1.0887	1.0861	1.0851	1.66	1.0859	1.0833	1.0823
1938–43......	2.01	1.1045	1.0995	1.0988	1.95	1.1016	1.0966	1.0960
1939–44......	1.58	1.0818	1.0782	1.0780	1.53	1.0790	1.0754	1.0752
1940–45......	1.28	1.0656	1.0642	1.0638	1.23	1.0629	1.0614	1.0611
1941–46......	1.24	1.0635	1.0629	1.0625	1.19	1.0608	1.0601	1.0598
1942–47......	1.52	1.0784	1.0769	1.0766	1.47	1.0756	1.0741	1.0739
1943–48......	1.73	1.0896	1.0871	1.0868	1.68	1.0867	1.0842	1.0840
1944–49......	1.60	1.0826	1.0808	1.0805	1.55	1.0798	1.0780	1.0777
1945–50......	1.55	1.0799	1.0786	1.0784	1.50	1.0772	1.0757	1.0756
1946–51......	1.34	1.0687	1.0687	1.0689	1.29	1.0660	1.0659	1.0662
1947–52*.....	1.67	1.0864	1.0855	1.0859	1.62	1.0836	1.0827	1.0831
1948–53......	2.05	1.1066	1.1058	1.1053	1.99	1.1037	1.1028	1.1024
1949–54*.....	1.93	1.1004	1.1012	1.1007	1.88	1.0976	1.0982	1.0978
1950–55......	1.92	1.0997	1.1004	1.1008	1.87	1.0968	1.0975	1.0979
1951–56......	2.23	1.1164	1.1169	1.1177	2.17	1.1134	1.1139	1.1147
1952–57*.....	2.73	1.1442	1.1436	1.1437	2.67	1.1411	1.1405	1.1406
1953–58......	2.76	1.1456	1.1455	1.1451	2.70	1.1424	1.1423	1.1419
1954–59......	2.52	1.1328	1.1339	1.1341	2.47	1.1297	1.1308	1.1310
1955–60......	2.70	1.1427	1.1437	1.1444	2.65	1.1396	1.1405	1.1413
1956–61......	2.78	1.1471	1.1490	1.1503	2.73	1.1440	1.1458	1.1472
1957–62......	3.50	1.1877	1.1881	1.1886	3.44	1.1843	1.1847	1.1852
1958–63......	3.25	1.1735	1.1756	1.1765	3.19	1.1702	1.1722	1.1732
1959–64......	3.80	1.2052	1.2056	1.2061	3.74	1.2017	1.2020	1.2027
1960–65......	4.73	1.2597	1.2560	1.2556	4.66	1.2559	1.2521	1.2519
1961–66*.....	3.76	1.2029	1.2027	1.2028	3.70	1.1994	1.1992	1.1994
1962–67*.....	3.98	1.2155	1.2161	1.2154	3.92	1.2120	1.2125	1.2119
1963–68......	3.78	1.2039	1.2059	1.2063	3.72	1.2004	1.2024	1.2028

* For this period, the outcome from the maturity strategy came closer to that expected than did the duration strategy.

except that ten- and twenty-year holding periods are used.

When, for whatever reason, a portfolio for horizon T does not have duration T, the investor will receive either a larger or smaller return than that expected. If the duration of the portfolio is less than the length of the holding period, the realized return will be smaller than initially expected if interest rates fall and larger if they rise. Conversely, if the duration of the portfolio is longer than the length of the holding period, the realized return will be larger than expected if interest rates fall and smaller if they rise. Note that the *maturity*

TABLE 6

RESULTS FROM TWO STRATEGIES FOR INVESTING IN BONDS
(TEN-YEAR PERIODS)

	WITHOUT COMMISSION				WITH COMMISSION			
	Expected Yield	Wealth Ratios			Expected Yield	Wealth Ratios		
		Expected	Duration	Maturity		Expected	Duration	Maturity
1925–35......	4.51	1.5546	1.5498	1.5459	4.47	1.5492	1.5436	1.5406
1926–36......	4.40	1.5382	1.5334	1.5309	4.36	1.5328	1.5274	1.5256
1927–37......	4.30	1.5235	1.5164	1.5152	4.26	1.5183	1.5105	1.5100
1928–38*.....	4.05	1.4874	1.4784	1.4817	4.01	1.4824	1.4728	1.4768
1929–39......	4.54	1.5596	1.5403	1.5387	4.51	1.5541	1.5343	1.5334
1930–40......	4.40	1.5382	1.5174	1.5114	4.36	1.5328	1.5115	1.5063
1931–41......	4.06	1.4881	1.4645	1.4617	4.02	1.4831	1.4591	1.4569
1932–42......	4.72	1.5862	1.5500	1.5333	4.68	1.5806	1.5439	1.5280
1933–43......	4.05	1.4875	1.4533	1.4428	4.02	1.4825	1.4479	1.4381
1934–44......	3.74	1.4432	1.4155	1.4029	3.70	1.4384	1.4104	1.3985
1935–45......	3.09	1.3558	1.3300	1.3222	3.06	1.3516	1.3255	1.3182
1936–46......	2.75	1.3111	1.2888	1.2821	2.71	1.3072	1.2846	1.2783
1937–47......	2.47	1.2769	1.2626	1.2537	2.44	1.2731	1.2585	1.2501
1938–48......	2.69	1.3036	1.2788	1.2754	2.66	1.2996	1.2747	1.2716
1939–49......	2.26	1.2510	1.2331	1.2314	2.23	1.2473	1.2292	1.2279
1940–50......	2.04	1.2237	1.2118	1.2088	2.01	1.2202	1.2081	1.2054
1941–51......	1.97	1.2151	1.2061	1.2029	1.94	1.2117	1.2023	1.1996
1942–52......	2.24	1.2480	1.2332	1.2323	2.21	1.2443	1.2294	1.2287
1943–53......	2.22	1.2456	1.2347	1.2335	2.19	1.2420	1.2308	1.2300
1944–54*.....	2.28	1.2533	1.2390	1.2393	2.25	1.2497	1.2351	1.2358
1945–55*.....	2.22	1.2455	1.2334	1.2349	2.19	1.2419	1.2295	1.2314
1946–56*.....	1.95	1.2134	1.2088	1.2111	1.92	1.2100	1.2051	1.2077
1947–57*.....	2.14	1.2353	1.2315	1.2341	2.11	1.2318	1.2276	1.2305
1948–58†.....	2.60	1.2924	1.2830	1.2829	2.57	1.2885	1.2789	1.2791
1949–59†.....	2.37	1.2644	1.2632	1.2629	2.34	1.2607	1.2591	1.2592
1950–60*.....	2.35	1.2614	1.2582	1.2635	2.32	1.2577	1.2541	1.2597
1951–61......	2.41	1.2692	1.2704	1.2765	2.38	1.2654	1.2663	1.2727
1952–62......	2.73	1.3091	1.3132	1.3156	2.70	1.3051	1.3088	1.3115
1953–63......	2.90	1.3306	1.3324	1.3345	2.87	1.3265	1.3278	1.3304
1954–64......	2.68	1.3026	1.3074	1.3141	2.65	1.2987	1.3029	1.3101
1955–65......	2.81	1.3198	1.3238	1.3336	2.78	1.3158	1.3193	1.3295
1956–66......	2.87	1.3272	1.3328	1.3446	2.84	1.3231	1.3282	1.3404
1957–67......	3.50	1.4106	1.4155	1.4204	3.47	1.4061	1.4103	1.4158
1958–68......	3.34	1.3889	1.4003	1.4055	3.31	1.3845	1.3951	1.4009

* For this period the outcome from the maturity strategy came closer to that expected than did the duration strategy.
† For this period the outcome from the maturity strategy came closer to that expected than did the duration strategy for the "with commission" treatment.

strategy implies that the portfolio held will have duration less than the length of the holding period. Thus, the empirically realized returns to the naïve maturity strategy are smaller than expected when interest rates fall (as in approximately the first half of the years covered by our data) and larger otherwise (as in the second half).

Table 8 shows some summary measures of the uncertainty faced when strategy (maturity or duration) of relating the assets held to the length of the time horizon were followed. If the standard deviation of difference between actual- and expected-wealth ratios are compared with figures comparable to those in table 3 but derived from Durand's data, we see that the naïve maturity strategy removes most of the

TABLE 7

RESULTS FROM TWO STRATEGIES FOR INVESTING IN BONDS
(TWENTY-YEAR PERIODS)

	WITHOUT COMMISSION				WITH COMMISSION			
	Expected Yield	Wealth Ratios			Expected Yield	Wealth Ratios		
		Expected	Duration	Maturity		Expected	Duration	Maturity
1925–45......	4.51	2.4144	2.3436	2.2876	4.48	2.4032	2.3248	2.2776
1926–46......	4.40	2.3660	2.2945	2.2424	4.38	2.3552	2.2766	2.2328
1927–47......	4.30	2.3211	2.2457	2.1977	4.28	2.3106	2.2286	2.1884
1928–48......	4.05	2.2123	2.1381	2.1133	4.03	2.2027	2.1228	2.1045
1929–49......	4.41	2.3691	2.2744	2.2129	4.38	2.3583	2.2571	2.2035
1930–50......	4.40	2.3660	2.2682	2.1818	4.38	2.3552	2.2506	2.1727
1931–51......	4.13	2.2464	2.1412	2.0831	4.11	2.2366	2.1257	2.0746
1932–52......	4.71	2.5112	2.3839	2.2365	4.69	2.4993	2.3647	2.2270
1933–53......	4.16	2.2614	2.1499	2.0552	4.14	2.2514	2.1347	2.0470
1934–54......	3.98	2.1835	2.0927	1.9914	3.96	2.1741	2.0784	1.9837
1935–55......	3.50	1.9916	1.9043	1.8452	3.48	1.9836	1.8925	1.8383
1936–56......	3.19	1.8726	1.8204	1.7616	3.17	1.8655	1.8094	1.7552
1937–57......	3.06	1.8281	1.7949	1.7280	3.04	1.8212	1.7842	1.7219
1938–58......	3.02	1.8125	1.7545	1.7319	3.00	1.8057	1.7446	1.7257
1939–59......	2.79	1.7342	1.6755	1.6722	2.77	1.7279	1.6664	1.6663
1940–60......	2.72	1.7117	1.6600	1.6528	2.71	1.7056	1.6510	1.6470
1941–61*.....	2.68	1.6966	1.6491	1.6468	2.66	1.6905	1.6402	1.6410
1942–62†.....	2.74	1.7180	1.6602	1.6777	2.72	1.7119	1.6513	1.6717
1943–63†.....	2.74	1.7165	1.6609	1.6832	2.72	1.7104	1.6519	1.6772
1944–64†.....	2.71	1.7065	1.6481	1.6868	2.69	1.7004	1.6393	1.6808
1945–65†.....	2.67	1.6927	1.6321	1.6825	2.65	1.6866	1.6234	1.6764
1946–66†.....	2.47	1.6287	1.5921	1.6440	2.45	1.6231	1.5837	1.6382
1947–67†.....	2.49	1.6358	1.6206	1.6668	2.47	1.6301	1.6118	1.6608
1948–68†.....	2.80	1.7384	1.7218	1.7582	2.78	1.7321	1.7119	1.7517

* For this period the outcome from the maturity strategy came closer to that expected than did the duration strategy for the "with commission" treatment.

† For this period the outcome from the maturity strategy came closer to that expected than did the duration strategy.

TABLE 8

STANDARD DEVIATIONS OF DIFFERENCES BE-
TWEEN EXPECTED- AND REALIZED-WEALTH
RATIOS RESULTING FROM THREE STRATE-
GIES FOR INVESTING IN BONDS

LENGTH OF HOLDING PERIOD	STRATEGY		
	Naïve*	Maturity	Duration
Five years.....	0.115	0.0031	0.0026
Ten years......	0.174	0.0170	0.0120
Twenty years...	0.182	0.0760	0.0290

* Naïve = rolling over portfolio of twenty-year bonds, Durand data.

uncertainty that exists when one simply rolls over a portfolio of long-term bonds. Most of the remaining uncertainty is removed when the duration rather than the maturity strategy is followed. It is interesting to note that for the twenty-year holding periods in table 8, the standard deviation of the difference is no greater than the standard deviation for one-year holding periods as shown in table 3.

These reductions are so dramatic that we conclude that a properly chosen portfolio of long-term bonds is essentially riskless.[40]

[40] Durand himself has adequately pointed out that the way he constructed them makes his basic-yield figures rather unreliable for testing many hypotheses about the behavior of forward interest rates. It seemed to us that, given the method of constructing the basic-yield data, even more

We have calculated a variety of other measures of the superiority of the duration strategy. The actual numbers are not important. What is significant is that for all measures we used the duration strategy led to smaller dispersion and, hence, risk than the maturity strategy over the forty-four years we observed.[41] The mean return from following duration strategy is higher than for the maturity strategy; but this fact is, we think, less important than the fact that duration's dispersion was less or average than maturity's.

The assumption on interest-rate shifts did not hold in practice, so that the duration strategy did not guarantee immunization. In tables 5, 6, and 7 there are several (marked) holding periods for which the maturity strategy did better—

---

violence would be done to the assumption required for immunization than would be found from analyzing better, but not yet constructed, data. Thus, it appears likely to us that we have overestimated the true risk from following a duration strategy over the period 1925–68.

[41] Let E_i, D_i, and M_i denote, respectively, the expected duration, and maturity wealth ratios for holding period i. We compared

$$\frac{1}{n} \sum_{i=1}^{n} (E_i - D_i) \text{ with } \frac{1}{n} \sum_{i=1}^{n} (E_i - M_i) ;$$

$$\frac{1}{n} \sum_{i=1}^{n} |E_i - D_i|_k \text{ with } \frac{1}{n} \sum_{i=1}^{n} |E_i - M_i|^k ,$$

and

$$\frac{1}{n} \sum_{i=1}^{n} |(E_i - D_i)/E_i|^k \text{ with}$$

$$\frac{1}{n} \sum_{i=1}^{n} |(E_i - M_i)/E_i|^k$$

for $k = 1, \ldots, 50$, $n = 39$ for five-year horizons, $n = 34$ for ten-year horizons, and $n = 24$ for twenty-year horizons. These results will be sent on request. All these comparisons showed that the duration strategy came closer than did the maturity strategy to the expected yield.

that is, came closer to achieving the expected return. With commissions considered, duration did better than maturity in thirty of the thirty-nine five-year tests, twenty-six of the thirty-four ten-year tests, and twenty-three of the twenty-nine twenty-year tests. Both the maturity and duration strategies came very much closer to achieving the promised yield than did the strategy used to calculate tables 1, 2, and 3.

IV. SUMMARY AND CONCLUSION

We have shown the year-to-year results from a particular naïve strategy of holding a portfolio of long-term high-grade bonds of approximately constant maturity, and we have argued that such a strategy is not a good one for an investor who wants at least part of his portfolio to be riskless.

We have presented an investment goal equivalent to the desire to hold a riskless asset. We argue that, unless an investor has a reasonably certain horizon (or series of horizons) at which he will consume his wealth, he should probably not invest in bonds.

We developed a form of optimal strategy for bond investments, given a specific time horizon, and we presented comparisons of this form of strategy to a less-sophisticated, but more obvious, strategy attempt to achieve the same purpose.

By following even the maturity strategy—much less the duration strategy—one can very closely realize the expected yields. We believe it significant that realizations can be made nearly equal to expectations in the long-term bond market. When an investor says that his purpose in holding a bond is to have cash available at a given time T years hence and he is promised a rate of return over those T years, he finds out that in fact he can achieve or nearly achieve it. Therefore, we conclude that, properly used, long-term, high-grade bonds are riskless assets in money terms.

We have argued that bond issuers should, therefore, find a ready market for instruments that have a long duration—a conclusion that suggests some agency ought to find profitable the issuing of high-quality, long-term, single-payment notes.

APPENDIX A

TABLE A1

ANNUAL RETURNS TO HOLDING A CONSTANT PORTFOLIO OF TWENTY-YEAR AAA BONDS

FROM 12/25 12/26 12/27 12/28 12/29 12/30 12/31 12/32 12/33 12/34 12/35 12/36 12/37 12/38 12/39 12/40 12/41 12/42 12/43 12/44

ANNUAL RETURNS TO HOLDING A CONSTANT PORTFOLIO OF TWENTY-YEAR AAA BONDS
PAGE 2 (CONTINUED)

FROM 12/45 12/46 12/47 12/48 12/49 12/50 12/51 12/52 12/53 12/54 12/55 12/56 12/57 12/58 12/59 12/60 12/61 12/62 12/63 12/64 12/65 12/66 12/67 12/68

The raw data for the calculations in table 1 are from Standard and Poor's High Grade (AAA) Corporate Bond Indexes.[42] For 1925–40 the datum is the December average yield to maturity, and for 1941–68 the datum is a yield in the last week of December. These yields are shown in table 1. The bonds whose yield is shown by Standard and Poor's are assumed to carry a 4 percent coupon and to mature in twenty years. The data and technique are those used by Weil.[43] The leading diagonal of our table A1 shows the same results as table 1, column 7 of that paper.

The following sequence of computations was performed.

1. Assuming semiannual compounding of the 4 percent coupons, and assuming, in turn, both nineteen and twenty years to maturity, we calculate bond prices in year j, P_{19}^i, and P_{20}^i from datum, which is the yield to maturity r_j. For example,

$$y = (1 + r_j/2)^2 - 1 ;$$

$$P_{19} = \left(100 - \frac{4.04}{y}\right) \bigg/ (1 + y)^{19} + \frac{4.04}{y} .$$

2. Assume we start in December 1925 with $C_{1925} = \$100$ and invest it in bonds with price P_{20}^{1925} or that we buy $100/P_{20}^{1925}$ bonds.

3. In December 1926, we receive coupons of \$4.04 on each bond, and we can sell the bond for P_{19}^{1926}. Thus, we have C_{1926} (cash in December 1926) of (C_{1925}/P_{20}^{1925}) $(P_{19}^{1926} + \$4.04)$.

4. C_{1926} is invested in bonds whose price is P_{20}^{1926}.

5. We continue constructing the series: $C_{1925}, \ldots, C_{1926}, \ldots, C_{1968}$. This series is column 3 of table 1.

[42] Standard and Poor's (n. 10 above).

[43] Weil (n. 4 above).

6. We calculate the rate of return shown in table A1 in the "From i" column and the "To j" row by $(C_j/C_i)^{1/(j-i)} - 1$.

The sample construction used by Standard and Poor's biases upward the calculated returns. The sample group changes over time. If a bond became unworthy of rating AAA, it would be removed from the sample. It seems reasonable to suppose that those bonds whose quality worsened sold at higher yields and, hence, lower prices than bonds that retained or achieved AAA rating. Thus, the selling prices of nineteen-year bonds calculated from AAA index tend to be too high. We argue, then, that the estimates shown in table 2 tend to overstate actual holding-period yields on long-term, high-grade corporate bonds.

Another error, the effect of which is harder to measure, is introduced because the composite does not always consist of bonds with \$4.04 coupon payments and twenty years to maturity. The yields to maturity, as calculated by Standard and Poor's (shown in table 1) could have been calculated from observed prices by assuming, say, \$5 coupon payments and fifteen years to maturity. Weil constructed a table[44] to show the magnitude of this bias. If R is the mean one-year-holding-period yield from 1900 to 1969 (measured, e.g., as 3.93 percent per annum, assuming \$4.04 coupons and twenty years to maturity), if C is the coupon measured in dollars, and M is the maturity measured in years, then

$$\frac{\Delta R}{\Delta C} \doteq .01 ,$$

and

$$\frac{\Delta R}{\Delta M} \doteq -.006 .$$

[44] Ibid., table 2.

APPENDIX B

PROOF OF IMMUNIZATION THEOREM

Here we show the proof of our immunization theorem. The method of proof will follow this outline: We shall define A_a to be the terminal wealth promised by or expected from a bond investment and A_b to be the actual or realized wealth from following the immunization strategy. We shall show that, whenever the assumption holds and the appropriate strategy is followed, the ratio A_a/A_b is always greater than or equal to one. Thereby, we prove that the strategy of equating duration to holding period actually achieves immunization. We shall assume that investments are made at time t_0 when the interest function is $i_a(t)$ and that immediately thereafter the function changes to $i_b(t)$. Let

P_a = the dollar amount of the initial investment in bonds at time t_0.

A_a = the expected or promised terminal wealth (from P_a) at time T.

$$= P_a \exp\left[\int_{t_0}^{T} i_a(t)dt\right],$$

where $i_a(t)$ is the particular $i(t)$ function for the time t_0 to T.[45]

A_b = actual or realized terminal wealth of the portfolio at time T.

If interest rates, $i_a(t)$, do not change, then $A_b = A_a$ or $A_b/A_a = 1$. If there is a single-payment note available at time t_0 which matures at T, then

$$A_a = P_a \exp\left[\int_{t_0}^{T} i_a(t)dt\right].$$

Let funds in the amount P_a be invested in this note and *then* assume the interest-rate

[44] A frequently used alternative for

$$\exp\left[\int_{t_0}^{T} i_a(t)dt\right] \text{ is } \prod_{j=1}^{n}(1 + r_j) = (1 + \bar{r})^n,$$

where

$$r_j = \exp\left[\int_{t_0+j-1}^{t_0+j} i(t)dt\right] - 1,$$

$$\bar{r} = G(1 + \bar{r}_j) - 1, \quad j = 1, \ldots, n,$$

and where $G(1 + r_j)$ is the geometric mean of $(1 + r_j)$.

function changes to $i_b(t)$. We have that

$$P_b = A_a \exp\left[-\int_{t_0}^{T} i_b(t)dt\right]$$

$$= A_a\left\{\exp\left[-(T - t_0)\Delta - \int_{t_0}^{T} i_a(t)dt\right]\right\}.$$

Since

$$P_a = A_a \exp\left[-\int_{t_0}^{T} i_a(t)dt\right].$$

then

$$P_b = P_a \exp\left[-(T - t_0)\Delta\right].$$

Further,

$$A_b = P_b \exp\left[\int_{t_0}^{T} i_b(t)dt\right]$$

$$= P_a \exp\left[-(T - t_0)\right] \exp\left[\int_{t_0}^{T} i_b(t)dt\right]$$

$$= P_a \exp\left[\int_{t_0}^{T} i_a(t)dt\right].$$

Thus, we have $A_a = A_b$ or $A_b/A_a = 1$. Trivially, the "portfolio" consisting of a single-payment note due at T is immunized. The return will be equal to that promised even if interest rates change after the purchase has been made.

Now suppose that the investment horizon remains at time T and there are only two "bonds" available for investment at t_0; both are single-payment notes, one due at $t_1 < T$ and the other due at $t_2 > T$.[46] An initial investment equal to P_a dollars is to be split between the two notes; the fraction a_1 will be invested in the note due at t_1, and the fraction a_2 will be invested in the note due at t_2; a_1, $a_2 \geq 0$, and $a_1 + a_2 = 1$. Equating the duration, D, of the initial investment to the length of the holding period $T - t_0$, we find that (keeping in mind that the duration of a single-payment note is the time to due date)

$$D = a_1(t_1 - t_0) + a_2(t_2 - t_0) = T - t_0,$$

[46] For the assumption to hold, although there may be only these two investments available at time t_1, by time t there must be another investment whose due date is less than or equal to T.

so that

$$a_1 = \frac{t_2 - T}{t_2 - t_1},$$

$$a_2 = \frac{T - t_1}{t_2 - t_1}.$$

As before,

$$A_a = P_a \exp\left[\int_{t_0}^{T} i_a(t)dt\right].$$

Now let the investment P_a be made, using the fractions a_1 and a_2, and let the interest-rate function immediately change to $i_b(t) = i_a(t) + \Delta$. If P_b represents the current value of the investment after the interest-rate function changes, then

$$P_b = a_1 P_a \exp\left\{\int_{t_0}^{t_1} [i_a(t) - i_b(t)]dt\right\}$$

$$+ a_2 P_a \exp\left\{\int_{t_0}^{t_2} [i_a(t) - i_b(t)]dt\right\},$$

and also

$$A_b = P_b \exp\left[\int_{t_0}^{T} i_b(t)dt\right],$$

$$\frac{d(A_b/A_a)}{d\Delta} = \frac{(t_2 - T)(T - t_1) \exp[(T - t_1)\Delta] - (t_2 - T)(T - t_1) \exp[-(t_2 - T)\Delta]}{t_2 - t_1}$$

$$= \frac{(t_2 - T)(T - t_1)}{t_2 - t_1} \{\exp[(T - t_1)\Delta] - \exp[-(t_2 - T)\Delta]\},$$

which is zero when $\Delta = 0$.

$$\frac{d^2(A_b/A_a)}{d\Delta^2} = \frac{(t_2 - T)(T - t_1)}{t_2 - t_1} \{(T - t_1) \exp[(T - t_1)\Delta] + (t_2 - T) \exp[-(t_2 - T)\Delta]\}.$$

so that

$$A_b/A_a$$

$$= (P_b/P_a) \exp\left\{\int_{t_0}^{T} [i_b(t) - i_a(t)]dt\right\}.$$

Since

$$i_b(t) = i_a(t) + \Delta,$$

$$A_b/A_a = (P_b/P_a) \exp[(T - t_0)\Delta].$$

Observe that

$$P_b/P_a = a_1 \exp\left\{\int_{t_0}^{t_1} [i_a(t) - i_b(t)]dt\right\}$$

$$+ a_2 \exp\left\{\int_{t_0}^{t_2} [i_a(t) - i_b(t)]dt\right\}$$

$$= a_1 \exp[-(t_1 - t_0)\Delta]$$

$$+ a_2 \exp[-(t_2 - t_0)\Delta].$$

Substituting this expression for (P_b/P_a), we have that

$$A_b/A_a = a_1 \exp[(T - t_1)\Delta]$$

$$+ a_2 \exp[-(t_2 - T)\Delta].$$

Using the information on the values of a_1 and a_2 which make the duration appropriate, we can write

$$A_b/A_a = \frac{(t_2 - T) \exp[(T - t_1)\Delta] + (T - t_1) \exp[-(t_2 - T)\Delta]}{t_2 - t_1}.$$

When $\Delta = 0$, we have $A_b/A_a = 1$. We now show that the ratio A_b/A_a, a function of Δ, is minimized for $\Delta = 0$ and that $A_b/A_a \geq 1$, or that the portfolio of two single-payment notes is immunized.

Since $t_1 < T < t_2$ and all exponential functions are positive, the second derivative is thus seen to be always positive. Thus, we can conclude that the first derivative is zero only when $\Delta = 0$ and that $A_b/A_a \geq 1$.

Note that we have assumed that the initial investment is made at t_0 when the prevailing interest-rate function is $i_a(t)$ and that immediately thereafter the function shifted to $i_b(t)$. Nothing in the proof requires that this change in the interest-rate function occurs immediately at t_0. The change may occur at any time.

We have shown that, if there exists a single-payment note (SPN) due at T, an investment in this note is trivially immunized. We have then shown that if there is no SPN due at T but there are two SPNs due at t_1 and t_2, $t_1 \leq T \leq t_2$, then investments can be split between these two notes to effect immunization. The same proof procedure can be extended to show that, for example, if there is no SPN due at t_1 but there are SPNs due at t_3 and t_4 such that $t_3 \leq t_1 \leq t_4$, then a combination of the SPNs due at t_3 and t_4 can be used to effect a portfolio which behaves for immunization purposes at least as well as a SPN due at t_1. Then we can mix the portfolio whose duration is t_1 with the SPN t_2 to achieve immunization.

Extending the above analysis, we find that the effect of any SPN due at t_n can be achieved with a portfolio of two or more SPNs due at t_m and t_p as long as $t_m < t_n < t_p$.

A bond is a portfolio of SPNs plus a restriction on the combinations in which the SPNs can be purchased. Each bond has a duration, more difficult to calculate than that of a SPN but a well-defined, single number nevertheless. As long as there exist two bonds whose durations t_1 and t_2 satisfy $t_1 \leq T \leq t_2$, an immunized investment for a holding period of length T can be achieved.

Note: If the liability is a stream of payments rather than a lump sum, immunization will not be achieved by holding one single-payment note. To attain a fully immunized state it is necessary that one consider each rent in the liability stream separately and be able to partition the portfolio into sub-portfolios, each of which immunizes a specific rent in the liability stream. A necessary but not sufficient condition for achieving the fully immunized state is that the first rent of the asset stream occur no later than the first rent of the liability stream and the last rent of the asset stream occur at least as late as the last rent of the liability stream. If the fully immunized state is not achieved, immunization will be attained for only a limited range of changes in the interest rate.

APPENDIX C

In this appendix we describe the data, how the data were used to estimate bond prices, forward rates, and durations, and how the various strategies were tested.

DATA

Durand's basic-yield curves have been constructed for corporate bonds of low risk for the years 1900–68.[47] For the years 1926–59, points are recorded for maturities of one to ten years, twelve, fourteen, fifteen, twenty, twenty-five, thirty, and forty years. For 1960–68, the recorded yields are for one, five, ten, fifteen, twenty, twenty-five, and thirty years only. These yields will be

[47] These curves are summarized in Durand (n. 30 above) and P. Biederman, ed., *Economic Almanac, 1967–1968 Business Fact Book*, National Industrial Conference Board (New York: Macmillan Co., 1967) (bond data supplied and kept up to date by Scudder, Stevens & Clark, Inc., New York).

denoted R_{j,t_0} for maturity j in year t_0. Where no figure was provided for forty years, the yield was assumed to be equal to that for thirty years.

FORWARD RATES AND BOND PRICES

In year t_0, yields to maturity, R_{j,t_0} are available explicitly for some maturities $1 \leq j \leq 40$. From these data points on the yield curve, the corresponding prices, P_{j,t_0}, for bonds which pay an annual coupon of C (= 4 percent) are computed from

$$P_{j,t_0} = C[1 - (1 + R_{j,t_0})^{-j}]/R_{j,t_0} \quad \text{(C.1)}$$
$$+ F/(1 + R_{j,t_0})^j,$$

in which par value F is 100.

Prices can also be related to a set of forward rates, r_{j,t_0}, inferred for year $t_0 + j - 1$ through $t_0 + j$, for $j = 1, 2, \ldots, 40$.

From the definition of present value, the price

$$P_{j.t_0} = C \sum_{i=1}^{j} \prod_{k=1}^{i} 1/(1 + r_{k.t_0})$$
$$+ F \Big/ \prod_{k=1}^{j} (1 + r_{k.t_0}) . \tag{C.2}$$

When prices have been determined for maturities up to and including j, (C.2) provides a mean for determining the corresponding forward rates. Two adjacent maturities are related by a rearrangement of (C.2):

$$P_{j.t_0} = P_{j-1.t_0} - F \Big/ \prod_{k=1}^{j-1} (1 + r_{k.t_0})$$
$$+ (C + F) \Big/ \prod_{k=1}^{j} (1 + r_{k.t_0}) . \tag{C.3}$$

Thus,

$$r_{j.t_0} = (C + F) \Big/ \Big[(P_{j.t_0} - P_{j-1.t_0})$$
$$\times \prod_{k=1}^{j-1} (1 + r_{k.t_0}) + F \Big] - 1 . \tag{C.4}$$

First define

$$r_{1.t_0} = R_{1.t_0} .$$

If the yield curve data include

$$R_{2.t_0} ,$$

so that

$$P_{2.t_0}$$

is known, then (C.4) is used to determine

$$r_{2.t_0} .$$

By this procedure, forward rates for $j = 1, \ldots , n$ may be determined. However, no yields and therefore no prices are available in the published summarized yield curves for maturities $j = n + 1, n + 2, \ldots , m - 1$, the next known point being for maturity m. Assuming the forward rates for $j = n + 1, \ldots , m$ to be equal and rearranging (C.2), we get

$$g(r_{n+1.t_0}) = C \sum_{i=1}^{m-n} (1 + r_{n+1.t_0})^{-i}$$
$$+ F/(1 + r_{n+1.t_0})^{m-n} - \prod_{j=1}^{n} (1 + r_{j.t_0})$$
$$\times \Big[P_{m.t_0} - C \sum_{i=1}^{n} \prod_{k=1}^{i} 1/(1 + r_{k.t_0}) \Big] = 0 , \tag{C.5}$$

which is an equation in the single variable $r_{n+1.t_0}$. Solution for the positive, real root $r_{n+1.t_0}$ is achieved by the iterative method of false position (*regula falsi*). That is, given two interest rates, α and β, such that $g(\alpha) < 0 < g(\beta)$, a third value γ is chosen by

$$\gamma = \frac{\alpha g(\beta) - \beta g(\alpha)}{g(\beta) - g(\alpha)} .$$

If $g(\gamma) = 0$, we are done; if $g(\gamma) < 0$, replace α with γ; otherwise, replace β with γ and continue.

DURATION

Forward rates $r_{n.t_0}$ and prices $P_{n.t_0}$ are determined as above. The values for duration are calculated from

$$D_{n.t_0} = \sum_{j=1}^{n} (t_j - t_0) P_{t_j} \Big/ \sum_{j=1}^{n} P_{t_j}$$
$$= \Big[C \sum_{j=1}^{n} j \prod_{i=1}^{j} 1/(1 + r_{i.t_0}) \tag{C.6}$$
$$+ F \prod_{i=1}^{j} 1/(1 + r_{i.t_0}) \Big] \Big/ P_{n.t_0} .$$

TESTS OF STRATEGIES

In the tests of strategies, expected wealth ratios

$$w_{j.t_0}$$

are compared with the wealth ratios resulting from following a particular strategy from time t_0 to $t_0 + j$. Expected wealth ratios are computed from forward rates:

$$w_{j.t_0} = \prod_{k=1}^{j} (1 + r_{k.t_0}) .$$

The *maturity* strategy with horizon $t_0 + j$ consists of reinvestment of interest received at the beginning of year $t_0 + k$, $k = 1, 2, \ldots, j - 1$, in a bond of maturity $m^* = j - k$.

For the *duration* strategy, the target duration is defined to be $d^* = m^* - 1$. The steps in this strategy are:

Step 1.—Determine the portfolio duration $d(m^*)$ achievable by investing all of the cash available at the beginning of year t in the bond of maturity m^*. If $d(m^*) = d^*$, invest in m^* and go to step 5. If $d(m^*) < d^*$, go to step 2. If $d(m^*) > d^*$, go to step 4.

Step 2.—Find the bond, to be called maxd, which has the longest duration of all the bonds available for investment. Determine the portfolio duration $d(\text{maxd})$ achievable by investing all cash in this bond. If $d(\text{maxd}) < d^*$, buy maxd and go to step 3. If $d(\text{maxd}) \geq d^*$, the cash is to be split between the two bonds m^* and maxd. Compute the proportion

$$x = \frac{d^* - d(m^*)}{d(\text{maxd}) - d(m^*)} .$$

The fraction x of the cash available is invested in the bond maxd and the fraction $1 - x$ in the bond m^*. Go to step 5.

Step 3.—Find the bond, mind, which has the lowest duration of all bonds in the current portfolio. Attempt to increase the portfolio duration by switching out of mind as follows. If $d(\text{mind}) = d(\text{maxd})$, go to step 5. If $d(\text{mind}) < d(\text{maxd})$ and a switch of all funds from mind to maxd would result in a portfolio with duration $d(\text{maxd}) < d^*$, make the switch and start

again at the beginning of step 3. If $d(\text{maxd}) \geq d^*$, determine the proportion x of current holdings of mind to be sold by setting

$$x = \frac{d^* - d(\text{mind})}{d(\text{maxd}) - d(\text{mind})} ,$$

where $d(\text{mind})$ refers to the duration of the current portfolio—that is, not switching any funds from mind to maxd. Go to step 5.

Step 4.—Put available cash in m^*. To reduce duration, consider the bonds of maturity $m > m^*$ in the current portfolio. Find the highest duration bond, maxd, in this group. If switching all holdings of maxd to m^* would give a portfolio with duration $d(m^*) > d^*$, sell maxd. Start again at the beginning of step 4, unless no bonds of maturity $m > m^*$ remain in the portfolio, in which case go to step 5. If switching all of maxd to m^* would give $d(m^*) < d^*$, the proportion x of the holdings of maxd to be sold is given by

$$x = \frac{d(\text{maxd}) - d^*}{d(\text{maxd}) - d(m^*)} ,$$

where $d(\text{maxd})$ is the duration of current portfolio—that is, switching no funds from maxd. Go to step 5.

Step 5.—All changes have been made for the year t. If $t < t_0 + j$, increase t by 1 and go to step 1. If $t = t_0 + j$, compute the realized-wealth ratio and compare with promised-wealth ratio.

The steps were carried out by using tables which gave the duration of the bond after the next coupon is paid. The duration is computed by assuming that the forward schedule available now is correct.

COPING WITH THE RISK OF INTEREST-
RATE FLUCTUATIONS: A NOTE

G. O. Bierwag
George G. Kaufman

G. O. Bierwag and George G. Kaufman*

Coping with the Risk of Interest-Rate Fluctuations: A Note

In a previous article in this *Journal*, Fisher and Weil demonstrate that, in the absence of default and taxes, an investor can immunize a portfolio of coupon bonds by selecting a portfolio whose duration is equal to the holding period.[1] Immunization is defined as obtaining a realized yield for a given holding period that is, at minimum, equal to the promised yield to maturity. Duration is defined as a weighted average of the payment periods where the weights are related to the present values of the payments in each period.[2] Fisher and Weil show that "as long as there exist two bonds whose durations t_1 and t_2 satisfy $t_1 \leq T \leq t_2$, an immunized investment for a holding period of length T can be achieved."[3] Thus, immunization permits risky assets to be effectively converted into a riskless asset with a known yield for any

* Professor of economics and professor of finance, Center for Capital Market Research, University of Oregon.

1. Lawrence Fisher and Roman L. Weil, "Coping with the Risk of Interest-Rate Fluctuations: Returns to Bondholders from Naive and Optimal Strategies," *Journal of Business* 44, no. 3 (July 1971): 408–31. Duration also has the interesting property of proportionately relating percentage point changes in interest rates and percentage changes in bond prices; see Michael H. Hopewell and George G. Kaufman, "Bond Price Volatility and Term to Maturity: A Generalized Respecification," *American Economic Review* 63, no. 4 (September 1973): 749–53.

2. Macaulay and Hicks defined duration as:

$$\frac{\displaystyle\sum_{n=1}^{m} \frac{Cn}{(1+i)^n} + \frac{Am}{(1+i)^m}}{\displaystyle\sum_{n=1}^{m} \frac{C}{(1+i)^n} + \frac{A}{(1+i)^m}}$$

where C = coupon payment, A = maturity value, n = number of periods to the coupon payment, m = number of periods to maturity, and i = yield to maturity. Fisher and Weil define duration as:

$$\frac{\displaystyle\sum_{n=1}^{m} \frac{Cn}{\prod_{t=1}^{n}(1+r_t)} + \frac{Am}{\prod_{t=1}^{m}(1+r_t)}}{\displaystyle\sum_{n=1}^{m} \frac{C}{\prod_{t=1}^{n}(1+r_t)} + \frac{A}{\prod_{t=1}^{n}(1+r_t)}}$$

where C, A, n, m are defined as before and r_t = one period discount rate (forward rate) in period t. If all forward rates are equal so that the yield curve is flat, the two definitions of duration are the same.

3. Fisher and Weil, p. 429.

given holding period. This comment shows (1) why a duration strategy provides the most complete immunization for a portfolio of coupon bonds, and (2) that the definition of duration that achieves immunization is dependent upon the nature of the random shocks that are assumed to affect interest rates after the purchase of the portfolio.

Abstracting from default risk and taxes, realized holding period yields on coupon bonds may differ from the yields to maturity at the time the bonds were purchased either because the bonds are sold prior to maturity or the coupons are not fully reinvested to maturity at a yield equal to the promised yield at the time the bond was purchased. If the promised yield is not realized, the promised terminal wealth is also not realized. For coupon bonds, duration is always shorter than the term to maturity, so that a duration strategy implies selling a bond prior to its maturity. If interest rates change after the bond is purchased, the investor is subjected to two risks: (1) a price risk arising from the possibility of selling the bond at a price different from the amortized bond book basis, and (2) a coupon reinvestment risk arising from reinvesting the coupons at interest rates different from the yield to maturity of the bond at the time of purchase. The impact of these risks on realized returns varies in opposite directions with changes in interest rates. Increases in interest rates will reduce the market value of a bond below its amortized basis but increase the return from the reinvestment of the coupons. Conversely, decreases in interest rates will increase the market value of a bond above its amortized basis but decrease the return on the reinvestment of the coupons. In order for a bond to be immunized from changes in interest rates after purchase, the price risk and coupon reinvestment risk must offset each other. It follows that duration must be the time period at which the price risk and the coupon reinvestment risk of a bond or bond portfolio are of equal magnitude but opposite in direction.[4] This may be proved as follows.

Let the initial holding period yields on zero coupon bonds derived from individual one-period yields (r_n) be $h(0,1)$, $h(0,2)$, ..., $h(0,m)$, where $h(0,n)$ is the n-period yield and $0 \leq n \leq m$. Suppose at time $n = 0$, an investor buys an m-period coupon bond for V dollars and sells the bond at time p, the planned holding period, where $p < m$. Under conditions of certainty, if all coupon payments are immediately reinvested in bonds that mature at time p, the investor's investment will have grown to a value of $[1 + h(0,p)]^p V$ dollars (or to a value $e^{h(0,p)p} V$ dollars in the case of continuous compounding). At time p, the market value of the $m - p$ period coupon bond will be T dollars and the value of the coupon payments received and reinvested will be Q dollars, which together sum to the total value of the bond, $[1 + h(0,p)]^p V$.

Under conditions of certainty, it does not matter which maturities the investor purchases for a given holding period. The value of the invest-

---

4. In a world having a fixed number of different coupon bonds, it may not always be possible to form a portfolio whose average duration is precisely equal to the length of the holding period.

ment at any future date is known at the time of purchase. The portfolio is always immunized, and immunization is an uninteresting problem. However, in a world of uncertainty in which the future course of interest rates is uncertain, this is not the case. The total value of the bond at any future date is not known. Nevertheless, the investor often can protect himself against unexpected changes in the value of the bond because of unexpected changes in interest rates.

For the sake of expediency, we shall consider a single coupon bond rather than a portfolio of such bonds, and we assume that bonds of any maturity and of any coupon exist. The individual bond may be viewed as having a maturity equal to the average maturity of some portfolio and a coupon equal to the average coupon of some portfolio. Suppose that λ is a one-time random shock to the term structure of yields and that initially the investor does not know precisely what λ will be. The value of the m-period bond at time p can now be regarded as $T(\lambda)$, and the value of the reinvested coupons at time p will be $Q(\lambda)$. At time p, different values of λ will render different values of $T(\lambda) + Q(\lambda)$. If interest rates rise, $T'(\lambda) < 0$ and $Q'(\lambda) > 0$, and the converse will be true if interest rates fall. The corresponding change in the total value of the bond is $T'(\lambda) + Q'(\lambda)$ and may be either positive or negative. Immunization is achieved over holding period p if $T(\lambda) + Q(\lambda) \geq T(0) + Q(0)$ for all λ.

To select a bond that satisfies this condition, an investor must estimate the nature of the random shock. In a simple world, changes in holding period yields may be assumed to be one-time and either additive $[h(0,n) + \lambda]$ or multiplicative $[(1 + \lambda) h(0,n)]$. Let

$$G(\lambda) = \frac{T(\lambda) + Q(\lambda)}{T(0) + Q(0)} . \tag{1}$$

Given any coupon payment C and m, one can show that in such a world $G''(\lambda) > 0$ for all λ.[5] Given m, one can also show that $G'(0) = 0$ for some C. This implies that $G(\lambda) \geq 1$ for all λ for the appropriate C. It is shown in the technical appendix that, if the shock is additive and interest is compounded continuously, the values of C and m that satisfy the immunization condition are given approximately by:

$$p = \frac{\displaystyle\sum_{n=1}^{m} \frac{Cn}{\displaystyle\prod_{i=1}^{n}(1 + r_i)} + \frac{Am}{\displaystyle\prod_{i=1}^{m}(1 + r_i)}}{\displaystyle\sum_{n=1}^{m} \frac{C}{\displaystyle\prod_{i=1}^{n}(1 + r_i)} + \frac{A}{\displaystyle\prod_{i=1}^{m}(1 + r_i)}} . \tag{2}$$

5. Complete proofs of all propositions are shown in G. O. Bierwag, "Immunization, Duration, and the Term Structure of Interest Rates," *Journal of Financial and Quantitative Analysis* (in press).

The right-hand side of this equation is seen to be equal to the Fisher and Weil definition of duration shown in footnote 2. It may be designated D_2 to differentiate it from the Macaulay-Hicks definition, which is designated D_1. If the shock were multiplicative, and there is continuous compounding, immunization results if C and m are chosen so that

$$p = \frac{1}{h(0, D_3)} \cdot \frac{\displaystyle\sum_{n=1}^{m} \frac{Cnh(0, n)}{\prod_{t=1}^{n}(1 + r_t)} + \frac{A\,mh(0, m)}{\prod_{t=1}^{m}(1 + r_t)}}{\displaystyle\sum_{n=1}^{m} \frac{C}{\prod_{t=1}^{n}(1 + r_t)} + \frac{A}{\prod_{t=1}^{m}(1 + r_t)}}. \tag{3}$$

The expression on the right-hand side is also a function of a weighted average time period, which is denoted as D_3. Only the weights differentiate D_3 from D_1 and D_2. Different and more complex expressions are derived if more complex one-time random interest shocks are assumed. Nevertheless, immunization is always possible. It follows that to attain the optimal bond for immunization for any assumed random shock in interest rates, the investor must choose C and m so that the corresponding measure of duration is equal to the holding period. However, for multiple random shocks, immunization may not always be possible, even if the stochastic process is correctly identified.

Duration is thus the time period at which the directions of change in the price risk and coupon reinvestment risk are equal and opposite in sign, that is, $T'(\lambda) = -Q'(\lambda)$. The definition of duration that satisfies this condition varies with the assumed nature of the future interest rate changes. The values of the two duration expressions derived above, plus the simpler expression developed by Macaulay and Hicks for bonds of different terms to maturity and coupons, are shown in table 1 for both an upward and a downward sloping yield curve for zero coupon bonds. Except at high coupons and long maturities, the values of the three definitions do not vary greatly. Thus, D_1 may be used as a first approximation for D_2 and D_3. The expression for D_1 has the additional advantage of being a function of the yield to maturity of the bond. As a result, neither a forecast of the stream of one-period forward rates over the maturity of the bond nor a specific assumption about the nature of the random shocks is required. Nevertheless, a strategy based on this expression will provide less immunization than strategies based on the more complex expressions.[6]

6. In the simulation experiments conducted by Fisher and Weil, complete immunization is never realized. Undoubtedly a reason for this is that the random shocks were not always additive over the period examined, a requirement given the definition of duration used.

Table 1
Values of Alternative Measures of Duration

Term to Maturity (Years)	Zero Coupon Holding Period Yield† (%)	5% Coupon			10% Coupon		
		D_1	D_2	D_3	D_1	D_2	D_3
A. Upward Sloping Yield Curve							
1........	6.10	0.99	0.99	0.99	0.98	0.98	0.98
2........	6.20	1.93	1.93	1.93	1.87	1.87	1.87
3........	6.30	2.82	2.82	2.82	2.68	2.68	2.68
4........	6.40	3.67	3.66	3.67	3.43	3.43	3.45
5........	6.50	4.47	4.46	4.48	4.13	4.12	4.16
6........	6.60	5.22	5.22	5.25	4.77	4.76	4.81
7........	6.70	5.94	5.92	5.99	5.37	5.35	5.42
8........	6.80	6.61	6.59	6.66	5.93	5.90	6.00
9........	6.90	7.24	7.20	7.31	6.45	6.40	6.53
10........	7.00	7.83	7.78	7.92	6.93	6.86	7.03
11........	7.10	8.38	8.31	8.48	7.39	7.29	7.49
12........	7.20	8.90	8.79	9.01	7.81	7.69	7.92
13........	7.30	9.37	9.24	9.49	8.21	8.05	8.32
14........	7.40	9.82	9.64	9.95	8.58	8.38	8.69
15........	7.50	10.23	10.00	10.36	8.92	8.68	9.04
16........	7.60	10.60	10.32	10.73	9.25	8.95	9.35
17........	7.70	10.95	10.60	11.07	9.56	9.20	9.65
18........	7.80	11.26	10.85	11.37	9.84	9.42	9.91
19........	7.90	11.56	11.06	11.64	10.11	9.62	10.15
20........	8.00	11.82	11.24	11.87	10.36	9.80	10.37
21........	8.10	12.06	11.39	12.08	10.60	9.95	10.57
22........	8.20	12.28	11.52	12.25	10.82	10.10	10.75
23........	8.30	12.47	11.61	12.40	11.03	10.22	10.91
24........	8.40	12.65	11.68	12.52	11.23	10.33	11.06
25........	8.50	12.81	11.74	12.61	11.41	10.42	11.18
B. Downward Sloping Yield Curve							
1........	8.50	0.99	0.99	0.99	0.98	0.98	0.98
2........	8.40	1.93	1.93	1.93	1.86	1.86	1.87
3........	8.30	2.81	2.81	2.81	2.67	2.67	2.67
4........	8.20	3.65	3.65	3.65	3.41	3.41	3.41
5........	8.10	4.44	4.44	4.43	4.09	4.10	4.06
6........	8.00	5.18	5.19	5.16	4.71	4.72	4.68
7........	7.90	5.88	5.89	5.84	5.29	5.31	5.24
8........	7.80	6.53	6.55	6.47	5.82	5.85	5.76
9........	7.70	7.14	7.17	7.06	6.31	6.36	6.23
10........	7.60	7.71	7.76	7.61	6.77	6.84	6.67
11........	7.50	8.24	8.31	8.12	7.20	7.29	7.08
12........	7.40	8.73	8.83	8.59	7.60	7.72	7.46
13........	7.30	9.19	9.33	9.01	7.97	8.13	7.82
14........	7.20	9.62	9.80	9.43	8.32	8.52	8.16
15........	7.10	10.02	10.24	9.81	8.64	8.89	8.48
16........	7.00	10.39	10.67	10.15	8.95	9.25	8.77
17........	6.90	10.74	11.08	10.49	9.24	9.60	9.06
18........	6.80	11.06	11.47	10.80	9.51	9.94	9.33
19........	6.70	11.37	11.85	11.08	9.77	10.27	9.60
20........	6.60	11.65	12.22	11.37	10.01	10.59	9.84
21........	6.50	11.91	12.57	11.62	10.24	10.91	10.08
22........	6.40	12.15	12.92	11.86	10.46	11.22	10.31
23........	6.30	12.38	13.26	12.08	10.66	11.53	10.52
24........	6.20	12.59	13.59	12.30	10.86	11.83	10.74
25........	6.10	12.79	13.91	12.51	11.04	12.13	10.94

* Coupon payments and compounding semiannually; D_1 = Macaulay-Hicks duration (n. 2); D_2 = Fisher-Weil duration (additive shocks) (n. 2); D_3 = Duration for multiplicative shocks (eq. [3]).
† These are the implied yields to maturity for zero coupon bonds, $h(0,n)$, $n = 1, 2, \ldots, 25$.

TECHNICAL APPENDIX

As asserted in the text, the appropriate measure of duration for the purpose of immunizing an investment depends on the assumed nature of the random shock. In
this Appendix, we derive D_2 by considering a model with continuous compounding.[7]

Let the initial equilibrium yield curve be represented by the function $h(0,n)$
for $0 \leq n \leq m$. One may interpret $h(0,n)$ as the annual holding-period yield on a
single-payment note. Suppose an investor buys a coupon bond that matures at
time m and that pays cA at each instant of time, where c is the coupon rate and A
is the face value at maturity. The value of the bond at time zero is:

$$V = cA \int_0^m \exp\left[-nh(0, n)\right]dn + A \exp\left[-mh(0, m)\right]. \quad (A1)$$

The yield to maturity is that rate i, constant for all n such that

$$V = cA \int_0^m \exp\left[-in\right]dn + A \exp\left[-im\right].$$

Thus, $h(0,n) = i$ only if the holding-period yield curve is flat. If there is an additive shock instantly after the bond is bought, the yield structure changes to
$h^*(0,n) = \lambda + h(0,n)$. If the bond is sold at time $p < m$, the bond's value will be:

$$T(\lambda) = cA \int_p^m \exp\left[-h^*(p, n)(n - p)\right]dn + A \exp\left[-h^*(p, m)(m - p)\right] \quad (A2)$$

$$= cA \int_p^m \exp\left[h^*(0, p)p - h^*(0, n)n\right]dn$$

$$+ A \exp\left[h^*(0, p)p - h^*(0, m)m\right],$$

because in equilibrium $h^*(p,n)(n - p) = h^*(0,n)n - h^*(0,p)p$. The investor receives coupon payments before time p. Assume the investor reinvests these receipts
in single payment bonds due at time p.[8] At time p, these bonds will have grown
to a value of:

$$Q(\lambda) = cA \int_0^p \exp\left[h^*(n, p)(n - p)\right]dn$$

$$= cA \int_0^p \exp\left[h^*(0, p)p - h^*(0, n)n\right]dn. \quad (A3)$$

The value of the initial investment of V dollars thus grows to the sum $T(\lambda) + Q(\lambda)$
at time p. Some elementary algebra reveals that $T(0) + Q(0) = \exp[h(0,p)p] \cdot V$.
That is, if there is no change in the yield structure, the initial investment grows
continuously at the rate $h(0,p)$. Let $G(\lambda) = [T(\lambda) + Q(\lambda)]/[T(0) + Q(0)]$. If c
and m can be found such that $G(\lambda) \geq 1$ for all λ, the investor will have immunized
his investment. To find a c that will accomplish this result, one must select c
so that:

$$G'(0) = cA \int_0^m \frac{(p - n)}{V} \exp\left[-h(0, n)n\right]dn$$

$$+ \frac{(p - m)}{V} A \exp\left[-h(0, m)m\right] = 0. \quad (A4)$$

---

7. A more detailed proof of this and one for D_2 are presented in Bierwag.
8. Reinvestment of the coupons in coupon bonds does not affect the outcome.

It can be shown that $G''(\lambda) > 0$ for all c. It follows that if c is chosen so that (A4) holds, then $G(\lambda) \geq 1$. One can rewrite (A4) in a way which reveals the essence of the duration argument. Let

$$
\begin{aligned}
w(n) &= cA \exp[-h(0, n)n]/V, && 0 \leq n < m \\
&= (1 + c)A \exp[-h(0, n)n]/V, && n = m
\end{aligned}
\tag{A5}
$$

Then

$$
G'(0) = \int_0^m (p - n)w(n)dn + (p - m)w(m). \tag{A6}
$$

Moreover, since

$$
\int_0^m w(n)dn + w(m) = 1,
$$

it follows that

$$
G'(0) = p - \int_0^m nw(n)dn - mw(m) = 0. \tag{A7}
$$

The second term,

$$
\int_0^m nw(n)dn - mw(m),
$$

may be approximated in discrete terms as:

$$
\frac{\displaystyle\sum_{n=1}^m \frac{Cn}{\prod_{t=1}^n (1 + r_t)} + \frac{Am}{\prod_{t=1}^m (1 + r_t)}}{\displaystyle\sum_{n=1}^m \frac{C}{\prod_{t=1}^n (1 + r_t)} + \frac{A}{\prod_{t=1}^m (1 + r_t)}}.
$$

This may be designated D_2. Thus, equation (A4) reduces approximately to

$$
G'(0) = p - D_2 = 0, \tag{A8}
$$

or $D_2 = p$. If c and m are chosen so that $D_2 = p$, the investor is assured of immunization.

IMMUNIZATION, DURATION, AND THE
TERM STRUCTURE OF INTEREST RATES

G. O. Bierwag

JOURNAL OF FINANCIAL AND QUANTITATIVE ANALYSIS
December 1977

IMMUNIZATION, DURATION, AND THE TERM
STRUCTURE OF INTEREST RATES

G. O. Bierwag*

I. Introduction

The asset and liability portfolios of financial institutions generate
patterns of future cash flows that must conform to many restrictions in order
to assure solvency and profitability. Many institutions, including insurance
companies and pension funds, have definite and certain future commitments of
funds. These institutions may wish to invest funds now so that their cash inflows (investment with accumulated earnings) will match their future commitments.
In principle, the simplest way to meet future commitments exactly is to purchase
single payment notes (or zero coupon bonds) which mature on the commitment dates.
For long-term commitments, such instruments are not readily obtainable, at least
in the United States. Most available bonds promise coupon payments over time so
that these payments would have to be reinvested at unknown future interest rates
in order to realize an accumulated sum at any future date when a commitment must
be discharged. Since future interest rates are unknown at the initial moment of
investment, it is not certain what accumulated earnings will be at future dates.
In the absence of default, the risk of not meeting future commitments may be
minimized by adopting investment strategies based on the concept of duration.
Duration is a measure of the average maturity of an income stream; it is a
weighted average of the dates at which the income payments are received, where
the weights add to unity and are related to the present value of the income
stream. Dating from the initial work of Macaulay [9] and Hicks [6], duration
has been shown to be important in constructing portfolios that are hedged or
"immunized" from the possible ravages of interest rate uncertainty.[1,2]

---

*University of Oregon. This paper grew out of a suggestion by George C.
Kaufman. Some numerical examples of some of the theorems developed in this
paper are contained in Bierwag and Kaufman [1]. The author bears responsibility
for errors and ambiguities contained in this paper.

[1]Macaulay [9] and Hicks [6] independently introduced the concept of duration,
but Hicks called it the average period of an investment. Hicks [6] and Samuelson
[13] utilize the notion to show that the weighted equality of the duration of
outgo and income streams immunizes a portfolio from small unexpected changes in
prices. Grove [4,5] developed the latter theory in greater detail and attempted

In a 1971 paper, Fisher and Weil [3] develop immunized bond portfolios that are applicable to a variety of financial institutions. To achieve immunication, the basic strategy involves creating bond portfolios whose average duration is equal to the planning period. However, the measure of duration that achieves immunization varies with the nature of the assumed stochastic changes in future interest rates. These measures may be far more complex than those introduced by Macaulay, Hicks, and Fisher and Weil.

In this paper:

(1) Definitions that achieve immunization will be developed for different assumptions about the stochastic changes in interest rates.

(2) The optimal selection of an immunized bond portfolio is shown to be related to the term structure of interest rates. An observed term structure of yields under the traditional expectations hypothesis contains information about the course of future interest rates. Future uncertainty is represented by random shifts in the observed term structure. Different measures of duration that produce immunization are shown to correspond to different stochastic properties of the uncertainty introduced.

(3) For simple random shifts of the term structure, immunization may be achieved by the purchase of a single coupon bond. More complex random shifts of the term structure may require diversification among many bonds of differing maturities and coupon rates.

(4) Investment models are developed in the context of discrete time periods as well as in the context of continuous time. The optimal measures of duration are different as between the two types of mode

(5) The results for a static framework are simply extended to optimal dynamic bond portfolio immunization policies.

---

to extend it to modern portfolio theory. Redington [11] and Wallas [14] utilize the concept in actuarial theories. Hopewell and Kaufman [7] recently showed that duration is related to the volatility of bond prices. Fisher and Weil [3] use the concept of duration in devising an immunization strategy for buying non-zero coupon bonds. Weil [15] surveys some of the above work in detail.

[2]Lintner [8], in his recent presidential address to the American Finance Association, suggests that duration plays a major role in financial theories apart from its usefulness in immunization strategies. He asserts that the concept of duration is "...central to an understanding of many phenomena involving the market value of securities, as well as the basic asset preferences and investment strategies of institutional investors, including life insurance companies, universities and pension funds."

II. Certainty, The Term Structure, and Coupon Rates

If an investor lends V dollars at time $t = 0$, his investment will grow to a value of $V \cdot \exp[h(0,t_o)t_o]$ dollars at time t_o assuming continuous growth where $h(0,t_o)$ is the relevant rate of return for an investment spanning the period $[0,t_o]$. On the other hand, the investor might have invested V dollars at time $t = 0$ and have received $V \cdot \exp[h(0,t_1)t_1]$ dollars at time $t_1 < t_o$ and then have lent those proceeds so as to receive $V \cdot \exp[h(0,t_1)t_1 + h(t_1,t_o)(t_o-t_1)]$ at time t_o. In a world of certainty with no transactions costs, an equilibrium requires that

$$(1) \qquad h(0,t_1)t_1 + h(t_1,t_o)(t_o-t_1) = h(0,t_o)t_o,$$

for otherwise arbitragers would borrow for one time period and lend for another so as to make a profit. The yield $h(t',t)$ is thus a "holding-period" yield that spans the time interval $[t',t]$; and at time $t=0$ under certainty, the term structure of interest rates is the function $h(0,t)$. Implicit in this term structure, by equation (1), are all future "holding-period" yields spanning any future period of time. If $h(0,t)$ is a differentiable function of t, equation (1) implies the existence of an "instantaneous" rate of return. If $\Delta t > 0$, using (1), with $t = t_1$ and $\Delta t = t_o - t_1$, one can write

$$(2) \qquad \lim_{\Delta t \to 0} \frac{h(0,t+\Delta t)(t+\Delta t) - h(0,t) \cdot t}{\Delta t} = \lim_{\Delta t \to 0} h(t,t+\Delta t)$$

$$= h(t,t) = \frac{\partial [h(0,t)t]}{\partial t} = t \frac{\partial h(0,t)}{\partial t} + h(0,t).$$

In what follows, it is useful to let $g(t) = h(t,t)$. Given the relationship in (2), it immediately follows that

$$(3) \qquad h(0,t)t = \int_0^t g(T)d \qquad = G(t) - G(0)$$

or

$$(3') \qquad h(0,t) = (1/t) \int_0^t g(T)d \ .$$

In this way, $g(T)$, the instantaneous rate of return, is the shortest "short" rate for the representation of the term structure in a continuous context, and $h(0,t)$ is the "mean" of the "short" rates spanning the time interval $[0,t]$. It also follows that the rate of return spanning any future time interval $[t,t']$ is

(4)
$$h(t,t') = \frac{1}{t'-t} \int_t^{t'} g(\tau)d ,$$

and it is also a mean of the relevant "short" rates.

In this continuous framework, a coupon bond is one that pays the investor cA dollars at each point in time up to maturity where A is the face value of the bond at maturity and c is the coupon rate. Suppose the bond has maturity t_o. If the investor reinvests the cA dollars received at time $t < t_o$, those cA dollars will have grown to $cA \cdot \exp[h(t,t_o)(t_o-t)]$ dollars at maturity. After accounting for the reinvestment of all coupons, the initial investment then grows to an amount

$$cA \int_0^{t_o} \exp[h(t,t_o)(t_o-t)dt + A$$

dollars. The initial investment V is then the discounted value of this amount so that

(5)
$$V = cA \cdot \exp[-h(0,t_o)t_o] \int_0^{t_o} \exp[h(t,t_o)(t_o-t)]dt + A \cdot \exp[-h(0,t_o)t_o]$$

$$= cA \int_0^{t_o} \exp[-h(0,t)t]dt + A \cdot \exp[-h(0,t_o)t_o]$$

where $h(0,t_o)t_o = h(0,t)t + h(t,t_o)(t_o - t)$ by the equilibrium condition. The amount V is thus the price of the bond. Prices of bonds are usually expressed as functions of their so-called "yields to maturity." In (5) this is accomplished by finding a rate of return r which is a constant independent of t so that

(6)
$$V = cA \int_0^{t_o} \exp[-rt]dt + A \cdot \exp[-rt_o].$$

Equating (5) and (6), we find that r must satisfy the implicit function

(7)
$$F(r,c,t_o) = c \int_0^{t_o} (\exp[-h(0,t)t] - \exp[-rt]) dt$$
$$+ \exp[-h(0,t_o)t_o] - \exp[-rt_o] = 0.$$

It is not difficult to see that r is equal to one of the holding-period yields in the interval $[\min_t h(0,t), \max_t h(0,t)]$. If $r > \max_t h(0,t)$, then $F > 0$; and if $r < \underset{t}{\min}\ h(0,t)$, then $F < 0$. Since F is a continuous increasing function of r, it follows that there is a unique value of r in the designated interval for which (7) holds. One may regard r as an index number that incorporates some of the information contained in the term structure of holding-period yields.

A theorem involving the relationship between r and the term structure of holding period yields quickly follows.

Theorem 1: Holding the coupon rate, $c > 0$, and the maturity t_o of the bond fixed, then

$$r \underset{<}{\overset{>}{=}} h(0,t_o)\ ,\ \text{according as}\ \ dh(0,t)/dt \underset{>}{\overset{<}{=}} 0\ \text{for all t.}$$

Proof: The expression in (7) is monotonically increasing in r. If $dh(0,t)/dt > 0$, then $r = h(0,t_o)$ implies $F > 0$, so that for some $r < h(0,t_o)$ we have $F = 0$. If $dh(0,t)/dt < 0$, then $r = h(0,t_o)$ implies $F < 0$, so that for some $r > h(0,t_o)$ we have $F = 0$. If $dh(0,t)/dt = 0$, then $r = h(0,t_o)$ implies $F = 0$.

In this theorem, it should be noted that c is positive. If $c = 0$, then $r=h(0,t_o)$ satisfies (7) but as soon as a nonzero coupon bond is introduced the yield to maturity r cannot be equivalent to the holding-period yield to maturity unless $dh(0,t)/dt=0$, for all t. Buse [2] calls the difference $r - h(0,t_o)$ the "coupon bias" in the yield curve represented by r as a function of t_o. If the term structure, $h(0,t)$, is monotonically increasing, then r is a negatively biased indicator of the coresponding holding-period yield, and conversely if $h(0,t)$ is monotonically decreasing. Thus, r is always equal to the holding-period yield for the cases in which either the coupon rate is zero and/or the holding-period yield, $h(0,t)$, is a constant for all t.

It is evident in (7) that the yield r depends on the value of the coupon rate, c. That is,

Theorem 2: If $c \overset{>}{=} 0$ and the maturity of the bond is fixed, then

$$\frac{dr}{dc} \underset{<}{\overset{>}{=}} 0,\ \text{according as}\ r \underset{<}{\overset{>}{=}} h(0,t_o).$$

Proof: Differentiating (7), we note that $\partial F/\partial r > 0$, and that

$$\partial F/\partial c \underset{<}{\overset{>}{=}} 0\ \text{according as}\ r \underset{>}{\overset{<}{=}} h(0,t_o).$$

Thus, since

$$\frac{dr}{dc} = - \frac{\partial F/\partial c}{\partial F/\partial r}$$

the theorem follows.

It is clear that two different bonds, having the same maturity, may sell in the market at different yields to maturity because they have different coupon rates, yet an investment of V dollars in either of them renders the same return at maturity in equilibrium under conditions of certainty. Designation of r as the so-called "promised yield" on the bond is thus very misleading in this context. Under conditions of certainty the "promised yield," in fact, is the holding-period yield spanning the time interval in question.

The notion of lending and borrowing so as to alter the income and outgo streams of money generated by the production and distribution of goods is a familiar theme in Hicksian and Fisherian capital markets. Abstracting from the overall problem of deducing appropriate "smoothing" strategies for given income and outgo streams, consider the special situation in which an individual has V dollars at t = 0 and he wishes to acquire the maximum possible rate of return on an investment over a time interval of length m. Let us call the interval [0,m] the investor's "planning period." Under conditions of certainty as postulated, here, which coupon bonds of what maturities should he buy so as to acquire a maximum return over the planning period? The answer, of course, is that it doesn't matter at all. Buying bonds of maturity greater than m and selling them at time m renders the same return as buying bonds of maturity less than m and reinvesting the proceeds until time m is reached. The equilibrium condition implies that the yields on the bonds now and in the future are such that at time t a dollar's worth of one bond is a perfect substitute for a dollar's worth of any other bond. If future interest rates are uncertain, bonds with different yields and/or maturities may not be perfect substitutes. This is a basic impact of uncertainty in financial markets.

III. Uncertainty and Immunization

Under conditions of uncertainty, an investor's preference of some bonds to other bonds depends on that investor's objectives and it depends on the manner in which uncertainty is introduced into the problem.

Assume that over some fixed planning period of length m an investor wishes to "immunize" his investment from the ravages of uncertainty. If the investor buys an m-period zero coupon bond for which there is no risk of default, he receives the holding-period yield on the bond with certainty; fluctuations in future interest rates will not affect his return. If the investor buys a nonzero coupon bond, his accumulated return at time m depends on the rates at which the coupon payments are reinvested and such rates may not be known at time t=0. In addition, if the maturity of the bond exceeds m, his return at time m depends on the value of the bond at that time. His return at time m from the selection of a strategy of buying and selling bonds at different points in time depends on the attributes of an uncertain course of future interest rates.

Different optimal strategies exist for the above problem depending upon the type of uncertainty postulated. Here, we consider some simple possibilities.

A. "Instantaneous" rates with an additive random component:

Suppose an investor buys a bond in the market at time t=0 and that this bond has a yield to maturity r, a maturity of length $t_o > m$, and a coupon rate c. The value of the bond is V as expressed in (6). Immediately after purchasing the bond, the instantaneous rate changes to $g(T) + \lambda$ for all T, where λ is a random change and is constant for $T > 0$. That is, the whole structure of future rates receives a random shock. Given this shock, one may ask what the rates r and c should have been so that the return of the investor calculated at time m is unaffected by the shock. Using (4), we observe that after the shock the holding-period yield spanning the interval [t',t] is

$$(8) \qquad h^*(t',t) = h(t',t) + \lambda , \quad 0 < t' < t.$$

The future holding-period yields are changed additively by the effect of the shock. The investor's return at time m from reinvesting the coupon payments is

$$(9) \qquad Q(\lambda) = cA \int_o^m \exp[h(t,m)(m-t) + \lambda(m-t)]dt.$$

The coupons are reinvested in zero coupon bonds that mature at time m; and since these reinvestments occur after the shock λ, the new structure of rates which is applicable after time t=0 becomes known with certainty. By the arguments in the previous section it makes no difference whether these coupon payments are reinvested in zero or nonzero coupon bonds. His return at time m from the sale of the bond is

$$(10) \qquad T(\lambda) = cA \int_m^{t_o} \exp[-h(m,t)(t-m) - \lambda(t-m)]dt$$

$$+ A\exp[-h(m,t_o)(t_o-m) - \lambda(t_o-m)].$$

His total return at time m is $Q(\lambda) + T(\lambda)$. If there is no change in interest rates, $T(0) + Q(0) = V \exp[h(0,m)m]$--the accumulated return under conditions of certainty over the time interval [0,m]. The ratio

$$(11) \qquad G(\lambda) = \frac{T(\lambda) + Q(\lambda)}{T(0) + Q(0)}$$

thus measures the impact of uncertainty on the return up to time m. A property of $G(\lambda)$ is that $G''(\lambda) > 0$, because as is clearly evident in (9) and (10), $T''(\lambda) > 0$ and $Q''(\lambda) > 0$. Therefore, if the investor chooses c so that $G'(0) = 0$, it follows that $G(\lambda) \gtreqless 1$, for all λ, and perfect immunization will be realized. Setting $\lambda = 0$, one can calculate

$$(12) \quad G'(0) = \frac{cA \int_o^{t_o} (m-t)\exp[-h(m,t)(t-m)]dt - A(t_o-m)\exp[-h(t_o,m)(t_o-m)]}{V\exp[h(0,m)m]}$$

$$= \frac{cA}{V} \int_o^{t_o} (m-t)\exp[-h(0,t)t]dt - \frac{A}{V}(t_o-m)\exp[-h(0,m)],$$

where by definition $h(m,t) = h(t,m)$ for convenience of manipulation. Equation (12) is easily interpreted if we let

$$(13) \qquad w(t) = cA\exp[-h(0,t)t]/V , \ 0 \leq t < t_o,$$

$$A\exp[-h(0,t_o)t_o]/V, \ t = t_o .$$

Using (5), we note that the $w(t)$'s are positive weights for which

$$(14) \qquad \int_o^{t_o} w(t)dt + w(t_o) = 1.$$

Substitution into (12) implies that

$$(12') \qquad G'(0) = \int_o^{t_o} (m-t)w(t)dt - (t_o-m)w(t_o)$$

$$= m - \int_o^{t_o} tw(t)dt + t_o w(t_o) .$$

The last expression in (12') is a weighted average of t and is, hence, measured in units of time. Denoting that expression as d, it is now evident that a choice of c for which $d = m$ is one that perfectly immunizes the investment.

The weighted average d is a measure of "duration" of the bond. In the calculation of d, each value of t in $[0,t_o]$ is weighted by the proportion of the total discounted income stream occurring at time t. The Macauley-Hicks measure of duration requires that the weights in (13) be calculated using r as defined in (6).

The above result may be summarized by

Theorem 3: If $c > 0$ and if there is a random additive shock to the future holding-period yields, an investor who has a planning period of length m may fully immunize his return by choosing c, if such exists, given $t_o > m$, so that the duration d of the bond is equal to the length of the planning period.

The existence condition on c is necessary in the theorem because with t_o fixed there is a minimum value of d that can obtain. That is, although $\partial d / \partial c < 0$,

$$\lim_{c \to \infty} d = \frac{\int_o^{t_o} t \exp[-h(0,t) t] dt}{\int_o^{t_o} \exp[-h(0,t) dt]} = d_o$$

so that $d_o \lessgtr d \lessgtr t_o$. If t_o is too large one may have $m < d_o$ so that no value of c permits $d = m$. More generally, if one regards t_o and c as decision variables for the immunizer, he can always find a pair of values, (t_o, c), for which $d = n$, but there may be many pairs for which this is so.

If the investor follows the duration strategy of Theorem 3, and if, in fact, the shock is an additive random shock, the investor can always expect to do better under conditions of uncertainty than under certainty. Let $f(\lambda)$ be the investor's subjective density function over λ. If $f(\lambda) > 0$ for some $\lambda \neq 0$, then $E[G(\lambda)] > 1$ and $G(\lambda) \gtrless 1$ with certainty.

B. "Instantaneous" rates with a multiplicative random component

As before, assume an investor buys a bond in the market at time $t = 0$ and that the bond has a yield to maturity, r, a maturity of length $t_o > m$. and a coupon rate c. Instantly after purchasing the bond the instantaneous rate changes to $\lambda g(\tau)$ for all τ, where λ is a random change and is constant for $T > 0$. After this shock, the holding-period yield spanning the interval $[t',t]$ is

$$(15) \qquad h^*(t',t) = \frac{\lambda[G(t) - G(t')]}{t-t'} = \lambda h(t',t).$$

The investor's return at time m from reinvesting the coupon payments is

$$(16) \qquad Q(\lambda) = cA \int_o^m \exp[\lambda h(t,m)(m-t)] dt.$$

His return at time m from the sale of the bond is

(17) $\qquad T(\lambda) = cA \int_m^{t_o} \exp[-\lambda h(m,t)(t-m)]dt + A \cdot \exp[-\lambda h(m,t_o)(t_o-\bar{m})]$

If there is no change in interest rates, $Q(1) + T(1) = V \exp[h(0,m)m]$, which is the largest accumulated return possible under conditions of certainty over the time interval $[0,m]$. One may then let

(18) $\qquad\qquad\qquad\qquad\qquad G(\lambda) = \dfrac{T(\lambda) + Q(\lambda)}{T(1) + Q(1)}$

measure the impact of uncertainty on the return over the interval. As in the additive case, $G''(\lambda) > 0$. As before, if the investor chooses c so that $G'(1) = 0$, then for that case $G(\lambda) \overset{>}{\underset{<}{=}} 1$ and perfect immunization will be realized. Setting $\lambda = 1$, it follows that

(19) $\qquad G'(1) = \dfrac{cA}{V} \int_o^{t_o}(m-t)h(m,t)\exp[-h(0,t)t]dt$

$$+ A(m-t_o)h(m,t_o)\exp[-h(0,t_o)t_o]/V ,$$

or using the weights defined in (13), one may write

(19') $\qquad\qquad G'(1) = \int_o^{t_o}(m-t)h(m,t)w(t)dt + (m-t_o)h(m,t_o)w(t_o).$

The equilibrium condition (1) implies that $(m-t)h(m,t) = h(0,t)t - h(0,m)m$. Substitution into (19') implies that

(19'') $\qquad\qquad G'(1) = \int_o^{t_o}th(0,t)w(t)dt + h(0,t_o)t_o\, w(t_o) - h(0,m)m.$

Then, by use of the mean value theorem, there exists d* such that

(20) $\qquad\qquad h(0,d^*)d^* = \int_o^{t_o}th(0,t)w(t)dt + h(0,t_o)t_o\,w)t_o)$

where $0 \overset{<}{=} d^* \overset{<}{=} t_o$. Hence, $G'(1) = 0$ when $d^* = m$. Here, d* is also a measure of duration but d* is not necessarily equal to d. Analogous to Theorem 3, we have

> Theorem 4: If c > 0 and if there is a random multiplicative shock to the
> future holding-period yields, an investor who has a planning
> period of length m may fully immunize his return by choosing c,
> if such exists, given t_o > m, so that the duration d* of the

bond is equal to the length of the planning period.

C. Shocks Containing Additive and Multiplicative Components Combined

If d and d* are the optimal durations for models with additive and multiplicative random shocks respectively, one might expect some measure of duration
somewhere between the two to be optimal when the two kinds of shocks are combined. In this section, I show that the appropriate measure of duration is a
far more complex calculation for the combined shock than it is for either of
the two taken separately.

Suppose that immediately after the investor buys a bond at time t = 0, the
yield structure changes to

$$h^*(0,t)t = \lambda t + \mu h(0,t)t,$$

where λ is the additive random component and μ is the multiplicative random
component. Employing the same procedures as before, we can calculate

$$(21) \quad G(\lambda,\mu) = \frac{T(\lambda,\mu)+Q(\lambda,\mu)}{T(0,1)+Q(0,1)} = \frac{cA \int_0^t \exp[-h^*(m,t)(t-m)]dt + A\exp[-h^*(m,t_o)(t_o-m)}{V \exp[h(0,m)]}$$

It is not difficult to show that $G(\lambda,\mu)$ is a convex function of λ and μ.[3] It
follows that the investor fully immunizes his investment if he chooses the
coupon rate, c, so that $G_\lambda(0,1) = G_\mu(0,1) = 0$. That choice of c implies that
$G(\lambda,\mu) \overset{>}{-} G(0,1)$ for all possible values of λ and μ. If such a coupon rate can
be found, $G_\lambda(0,1) = 0$ will imply that m = d and $G_\mu(0,1) = 0$ will imply that
m = d*. Immunization with respect to the two shocks simultaneously implies,
therefore, that d = d* = m. This result can obtain only for a restricted set
of initial equilibrium yield curves. Conceivably one can find a yield curve
h(0,t) such that $G_\lambda(0,1) = 0$ for some c implies that $G_\mu(0,1) \neq 0$ and conversely.
One may conclude, though,

> Theorem 5: An investor can fully immunize his investment from additive
> and/or multiplicative random shocks by choosing c, if such
> exists, so that d = d* = m provided the initial yield structure
> makes this possible.

Theorem 5 can hold only for a particular class of yield structures. If the

---

[3]A method of showing convexity that I find attractive consists of letting
H be the Hessian of G and letting T be the matrix of characteristic vectors of
H. It follows that the elements of T'HT are easily shown to be positive.

yield structure is flat so that $h(0,t)$ is a constant for all t, then $d = d^*$; equations (19") and (12') indicate this. It is not difficult to invent yield curves to which Theorem 5 does not apply. For example, if $h(0,t)$ is a linear function of t with a positive intercept, then $d^* > d$.

The class of yield structures to which Theorem 5 is applicable is limited. It is possible that an investor simply cannot immunize his investment by the purchase of a coupon bond. Diversification may provide the key to immunization in that case, however. The first order condition for the immunization of (21) with respect to λ and μ requires that c be found so as to satisfy two simultaneous equations. One coupon bond with maturity $t_o > m$ gives the investor only one decision variable--the coupon rate--but he has two conditions that the coupon rate must satisfy. If the investor can hold two or more coupon bonds, the problem can be resolved. A portfolio of two or more coupon bonds gives the investor two or more coupon rates as decision variables, but yet there reamin only two simultaneous equations that these rates must satisfy for immunization.

Consider two coupon bonds of maturity t_1 and t_2 respectively, where $t_1 > m$ and $t_2 > m$. Denote the corresponding coupon rates as c_1 and c_2. Letting there be additive and multiplicative shocks, λ and μ, the jth bond has a value, V_j, at time $t = m$ which is $T^j(\lambda,\mu)+Q^j(\lambda,\mu)$, $j = 1,2$. If there is no change in the rates of interest, then $T^j(0,1)+Q^j(0,1) = V_j \exp[h(0,m)]$. The relative return for the portfolio may be defined as

$$(22) \qquad G(\lambda,\mu) = \frac{\sum\limits_{j=1}^{2} [\, T^j(\lambda,\mu) + Q^j(\lambda,\mu)\,]}{V \exp[h(0,m)]}$$

where $V = V_1+V_2$. Let $\beta = V_1/V$ be the proportion of the total investment that is in the first coupon bond. The partial derivatives of (22) evaluated at $(\lambda,\mu) = (0,1)$ are

$$(23) \qquad G_\lambda(0,1) = m - \beta d_1 - (1-\beta)d_2 \text{ , and}$$

$$G_\mu(0,1) = h(0,m)m - \beta h(0,d_1^*)d_1^* - (1-\beta)h(0,d_2^*)d_2^*$$

where d_j is the duration calculated for the additive shock on the jth bond and d_j^* is the duration calculated for the multiplicative shock on the jth bond. If $G_\lambda(0,1) = 0$, then

(24) $$\beta d_1 + (1-\beta)d_2 = m;$$

a weighted average of the two durations must be equal to the length of the planning period. Equivalently, (24) implies that the duration (for additive shocks)
of the income stream of the two bonds taken together must equal the length of
the planning period. If $G_\mu(0,1) = 0$, the condition is more complicated; here
it is required that

(25) $$\frac{\beta h(0,d_1^*)d_1^*}{h(0,m)} + \frac{(1-\beta)\ h(0,d_2^*)d_2^*}{h(0,m)} = m.$$

One may interpret (25) as a complicated average of the durations on the respec-
tive bonds, or one can find d* such that $h(0,d^*)d^* = h(0,d_1^*)d_1^*\beta + (1-\beta)h(0,d_2^*)d_2^*$.

Then d* is the duration (for multiplicative shocks) of the income stream of the
two bonds taken together. If c_1 and c_2 exist so that (24) and (25) hold, then
$G(\lambda,\mu) \gtreqless G(0,1)$ because G is a convex function. Thus, the investor may perfectly
immunize the portfolio when it might have been impossible to do so with a single
coupon bond. This result seems more plausible because the investor has five decision variables--β,c_1,c_2,t_1, and t_2. Although these variables must all be nonnegative and β can't exceed unity, only the two conditions (24) and (25) need to
be satisfied. If the investor considers three different coupon bonds, the number
of decision variables increases to eight, but yet the number of conditions that
need to be satisfied remains the same. Summarizing,

Theorem 6: An investor may be able to immunize his investment by diversifying
among different coupon bonds so that each relevant measure of duration for the income stream, taken as a whole, equals the length of
the planning period.

Diversification among coupon bonds provides enormous flexibility for molding
the shape of the income stream corresponding to the investment. It is this
added flexibility that may permit immunization where it is not possible with a
single coupon bond.

D. Immunization with Discrete Models

The immunization strategies for models in which coupon payments are made at
only discrete points in time are not strictly analogous to the continuous time
models. In the discrete models the existence of an immunization strategy depends on characteristics of the class of yield curves considered.

Consider bonds for which there are annual coupon payments. Denote the
structure of holding period yields as $[h(0,1),h(0,2),\ldots,h(0,t),\ldots]$. Define

$B(0,t) = [1+h(0,t)]^t$. The value of a bond of maturity t_o with coupon rate c
and having a face value of A dollars at maturity is

(26)
$$V = cA \sum_{t=1}^{t_o} B(0,t)^{-1} + A B(0,t_o)^{-1}.$$

Assume $t_o > m$. In equilibrium under conditions of certainty the holding-period
yield h(k,s) which spans the interval [k,s] must satisfy the condition
$B(k,s) = B(0,s)/B(0,k) = [1+h(k,s)]^{s-k}$ for otherwise arbitragers could enter
the markets and make a profit by borrowing for one period and lending for
another. If all coupon payments are reinvested in single-payment notes maturing at time m, the accumulation of coupon receipts will have the value

(27)
$$Q = c A \sum_{t=1}^{m} B(t,m) = c A B(0,m) \sum_{t=1}^{m} B(0,t)^{-1}$$

at time m. The bond at time m will have (t_o-m) coupon payments remaining and
the maturity amount A to be paid at time t_o. At time m, the bond, hence, has
the value

(28)
$$T = cA \sum_{t=m+1}^{t_o} B(m,t)^{-1} + A B(m,t_o)^{-1}$$

$$= B(0,m) [cA \sum_{t=m+1}^{t_o} B(0,t)^{-1} + A B(0,t_o)^{-1}].$$

Using (26) - (28), it is now clear that

(29)
$$T + Q = B(0,m)V.$$

Now, suppose a random shock to the yield structure occurs instantly after
the investor purchases the bond. Assuming an additive shock, the new yield
structure can be denoted as $h*(0,t) = h(0,t) + \lambda$, $t = 1,2,\ldots.t_o$, and we can
redefine the new discount factors as $B*(0,t) = [1 + h(0,t)+\lambda]^t$. At time m, it
follows that

(30)
$$T(\lambda) + Q(\lambda) = B*(0,m) [cA \sum_{t=1}^{t_o} B*(0,t)^{-1} + AB*(0,t_o)^{-1}].$$

A difficulty immediately encountered with the additive shock model is that all
forward rates need not increase (decrease) when all holding period yields increase (decrease) additively. Confining our analysis to the class of additive

yield curves for which forward rates and holding period yields are positively related, one can show that $T'(\lambda) < 0$, $Q'(\lambda) > 0$, $T''(\lambda) > 0$, and $Q''(\lambda) > 0$.[4] Let $G(\lambda) = [T(\lambda) + Q(\lambda)]/[T(0)+Q(0)]$. Define some weights as

$$(31) \qquad w(t) = \begin{cases} cAB(0,t)^{-1}/V, & t = 1,2,\ldots,t_o-1, \\ (1+c)AB(0,t_o)^{-1}/V, & t = t_o. \end{cases}$$

These weights are analogous to those in (13); $w(t)$ is the proportion of the discounted income stream occurring at time t. It follows that

$$(32) \qquad G'(0) = \sum_{t=1}^{t_o} [mB(0,m)^{-1/m} - tB(0,t)^{-1/t}]w(t).$$

If one chooses c so that $G'(0) = 0$, it is observed that a measure of duration d^{**} defined as

$$(33) \qquad \frac{m}{1 + h(0,m)} = \frac{d^{**}}{1 + h(0,d^{**})} = \sum_{t=1}^{t_o} \frac{tw(t)}{[1 + h(0,t)]}$$

emerges so that if $d^{**} = m$, then $G'(0) = 0$. The measure d^{**} is not analogous to the measure d which occurs for an additive shock in the case of continuous compounding. Instead of a simple weighted average of the t's, the measure d^{**} is a more complicated average.

Since $G''(\lambda) > 0$ under the assumed conditions about the class of holding period yields considered, it follows that choosing c and t_o so that $m = d^{**}$ immunizes the investment. In cases where holding period yields do not satisfy the above conditions on movements of forward rates, there is no assurance that choosing c and t_o so that $d^{**} = m$ will immunize the investment. In this latter case, diversification may be necessary for immunization.

Other discrete shock models have similar attributes. For example, if one regards the shock as multiplicative on the interest rate relative (i.e., $[1+h^*(0,t)] = \lambda[1+h(0,t)]$, where λ is the shock, $h^*(0,t)$ is the new yield, and $h(0,t)$ is the old yield), then the measure of duration emerging from the analysis will be analogous to that of the additive shock of the continuous model. The second derivative, $G''(\lambda)$, will be positive in this case for all yield curves considered.

---

[4]If one lets $[1+h^*(0,t),t]$ be an array of points in a two-dimensional plane the class of yields considered, here, is that class for which the elasticity between any two such points with respect to t is less than unity. This is equivalent to the geometric result that any straight line passing through the two points $[1+h^*(0,t),t]$ and $[1+h^*(0,t'),t']$ must have positive intercepts.

IV. The Duration Strategy--An Interpretation

The problem of selecting a portfolio of coupon bonds under uncertainty has
features analogous to other problems under uncertainty. At an initial point
in time, the investor knows that a future price is uncertain, but yet he must
make a decision in which that unknown future price affects his rate of return.
In the models of this paper, the future yield structure is uncertain, but the
investor presumes that yield structure is randomly related in a known way to
some given observed structure. The investor makes a decision, the roulette
wheel of uncertainty spins, and the effect of the decision is known. The fact
that the outcome occurs in a future period of time is coincidental; the model
is static. After the new yield structure becomes known, it remains unchanged
with certainty. That is why the investor can presume that the new yield structure will have the same equilibrium properties as the old one. For example,
he assumes that $h^*(s,k)(k-s) = h^*(0,k)k - h^*(0,s)s$, $k > s$--a condition which
holds because of arbitrage in models of certainty. These properties of equilibrium under certainty enable the investor to calculate his strategy for immunization.

In the continuous representation of the problem, the investor's return at
the end of a planning period is a convex function of the random variables in the
model. Models of behavior under uncertainty often have this property and such
models often bear attributes of Oi's paradox [10]. That is, if the future price
or rate of return is a random variable, the expected future profits or rate of
return may exceed future profits calculated at the expected price or rate of
return. A paper by Rothenberg and Smith [12] contains a further example of this
effect of uncertainty. In the models here the investor's expectation of $G(\lambda)$
exceeds $G(0)$ in the additive case so that his return can never be less than that
implied by the initial term structure of yields from which there may be a random
departure. It is tempting to contend that the investor prefers the world of uncertainty to that of certainty. We must recall, however, that initially the
investor knows he is in a world of uncertainty; otherwise he would have no wish
to consider a strategy of immunization. If the initially observed term structure is an equilibrium structure in view of uncertainty in the markets, one
wouldn't necessarily expect it to be exactly the same structure under conditions
of certainty. If $G(\lambda)$ is a convex function and $G'(0) = 0$, we are compelled to
conclude that that the investor's return will not be less than that implied by
the observed term structure of yields *were the latter to hold with certainty.*

It is possible to extend these static results to certain dynamic situations.
Suppose that there are no transactions costs. Assume that at each instant of
time the equilibrium term structure randomly shifts and that the investor expects

the future course of interest rates to proceed with certainty as implied by that
structure of yields. As time passes the duration of the initially chosen portfolio changes unless the portfolio is adjusted. An optimal dynamic adjustment
rule for the immunizer is still the duration "strategy." If the investor buys
and sells coupon bonds so as always to keep the "duration" of the portfolio
equal to his planning period, he will indeed be immunizing *ex post*. It remains
to explore more complex static and dynamic models. It appears that some measure
of duration is an index of portfolio composition that is very useful in describ-
ing optimal strategies of immunization.

REFERENCES

[1] Bierwag, G. O., and George G. Kaufman. "Coping with the Risk of Interest Rate Fluctuations: A Note." *Journal of Business* (July 1977).

[2] Buse, A. "Expectations, Prices, Coupons and Yields." *Journal of Finance* (September 1970), pp. 809-818.

[3] Fisher, L., and R. L. Weil. "Coping with the Risk of Interest Rate Fluctuations: Returns to Bondholders from Naive and Optimal Strategies." *Journal of Business* (October 1971), pp. 408-31.

[4] Grove, M. A. "A Model of the Maturity Profile of the Balanced Sheet." *Metroeconomica*, vol. 18 (1977), pp. 40-55.

[5] _____. "On Duration and the Optimal Maturity Structure of the Balance Sheet." *The Bell Journal of Economics and Management Science*, vol. 5 (Autumn 1974), pp. 696-709.

[6] Hicks, J. R. *Value and Capital*. Oxford: Clarendon Press (1946).

[7] Hopewell, M. H., and George G. Kaufman. "Bond Price Volatility and Term to Maturity: A Generalized Respecification." *American Economic Review* (September 1973), pp. 749-53.

[8] Lintner, J. "Presidential Address: Inflation and Security Returns." *Journal of Finance*, vol. 30, no. 2 (May 1975), pp. 259-280.

[9] Macaulay, F. R. *Some Theoretical Problems Suggested by the Movements of Interest Rates, Bond Yields, and Stock Prices in the U.S. since 1856*. New York: National Bureau of Economic Research (1938).

[10] Oi, Walter Y. "The Desirability of Price Instability under Perfect Competition." *Econometrica*, vol. 29 (January 1961), pp. 58-64.

[11] Redington, F. M. "Review of the Principle of Life Office Valuations." *Journal of the Institute of Actuaries*, vol. 18 (1952), pp. 286-340.

[12] Rothenberg, Thomas J., and Kenneth R. Smith. "The Effect of Uncertainty on Resource Allocation in a General Equilibrium Model." *The Quarterly Journal of Economics*, vol. 85 (August 1971), pp. 440-459.

[13] Samuelson, P. A. "The Effect of Interest Rate Increases on the Banking System." *American Economic Review*, vol. 55 (1945), pp. 16-27.

[14] Wallas, G. E. "Immunization." *Journal of the Institute of Actuaries Students' Society*, vol. 15 (1959), pp. 345-57.

[15] Weil, R. L. "Macaulay's Duration: An Appreciation." *Journal of Business*, vol. 46 (1973), pp. 589-92.

A PRACTICAL APPROACH TO APPLYING
IMMUNIZATION THEORY

A. D. Shedden

A PRACTICAL APPROACH TO APPLYING IMMUNISATION THEORY

by

A. D. SHEDDEN, B.Sc., F.F.A., F.S.A.

[Submitted to the Faculty on 15th November 1976. A synopsis of the paper will be found on page 337]

INTRODUCTION

1. In commenting on the proposed regulations for governing actuarial valuations under the Insurance Companies Act the actuarial profession advanced two propositions which are, to some extent, contradictory. On the one hand it was argued that if assets have to be taken at market value then it is advisable in the actuarial valuation to distinguish between the investment yield earned currently on the assets and the rate of interest that may be earned on any future reinvestment required under the contract being valued; furthermore, in assessing the reinvestment rate of interest it need not be assumed that reinvestment should necessarily be in the same category of assets as those presently held. On the other hand it was also argued that where it is possible to immunise assets and liabilities against future changes in the rate of interest it is unnecessary to have regard to any reinvestment rate of interest, even if future reinvestment will be required under the contracts being valued.

The contradiction arises because the theory of immunisation requires that any future investment or disinvestment be of such a nature that the yield obtainable on those assets bought in the future be equal to the yield then enjoyed on existing assets. This implies that future investment must be in the same category of assets as those presently held.

2. Because an immunisation approach can imply a contradiction of accepted prudence in regard to reinvestment rates of interest it would seem incumbent on actuaries to consider carefully the assumptions that are involved and to develop satisfactory methods for defining immunisation and for demonstrating that a particular portfolio of assets and liabilities is immunised. Moreover, it would seem that, in future, actuaries applying immunisation principles in a valuation under the Insurance Companies Act may have to state that they are doing so and, presumably, may be called upon to substantiate such a statement. The particular problem here will be

A

to determine the minimum actuarial reserve required under a state of immunisation, given a market valuation of assets.

3. There are many objections to applying the theory of immunisation as originally developed by Redington and it has always been recognised that some adjustment of the theoretical results would be necessary in practice. The objection that springs first to mind is that the theory implies a level yield curve ; a further objection, which is particularly relevant at the present time, is that it may be impossible to immunise at high rates of interest. Other difficulties to do with options, tax, differences in the yield obtainable on similarly dated assets etc., may normally be of lesser significance and do not arise in all cases anyway.

In this paper an attempt is made to present the theory of immunisation in such a way as to permit a more general application in practice. The key to the presentation is that, unless perfectly matched, *a portfolio of assets and liabilities is normally immunised at one rate of interest only, and this rate is not, in general, the market rate.*

The theory of immunisation and its implications

4. It is shown in Appendix 1 that if V_A and V_L are functions of δ then sufficient conditions for there to be a local maximum value of $\frac{V_L}{V_A}$ where $\delta = \delta_0$ are :

(i) $\dfrac{V_A'}{V_A} = \dfrac{V_L'}{V_L}$, $V_A \neq 0$, $V_L \neq 0$, $\delta = \delta_0$

and (ii) $\dfrac{V_A''}{V_A} \gtrless \dfrac{V_L''}{V_L}$ as $\dfrac{V_L}{V_A} \gtrless 0$, $\delta = \delta_0$

where V_A', V_L' and V_A'', V_L'' represent first and second differentials respectively of V_A, V_L with respect to δ.

In the context of an actuarial valuation V_A and V_L can represent the respective values of asset proceeds and liability outgo, defined in terms of a force of interest δ. The above conditions do not require that V_A and V_L be functions of the form $\int e^{-\delta t} A_t dt$, where A_t is not a function of δ, nor do they imply a level yield curve. However, if these constraints apply, and $V_A = V_L$, the usual immunisation relationships emerge ; in particular, $-\dfrac{V_A'}{V_A}$ and $-\dfrac{V_L'}{V_L}$ are equivalent to the respective mean terms of the value of the asset proceeds and the value of the liability outgo. For this reason it is convenient to use the symbols M_A and M_L to represent these functions, whether or not any constraints on the form of V_A and V_L apply. It is also convenient to refer to an asset as being long or short depending on whether M_A is relatively large or small, and similarly for a liability. The symbols M_A and M_L were used by Stalker and Hazell in their recent paper on " Valuation Standards ". By definition they represent " volatility " as well as " length ".

5. Suppose that a local maximum value of $\dfrac{V_L}{V_A}$ exists where $\delta = \delta_0$ and that the force of interest changes suddenly to $\delta_0 + e$, where $\delta_0 + e$ is in the same locality as δ_0. Then it follows from the above relationships that

    (i) $kV_A - V_L > 0,\ \delta = \delta_0 + e,$

    where $k = \dfrac{V_L}{V_A},\ \delta = \delta_0$

and (ii) $M_A \gtrless M_L$ as $e \lessgtr 0.$

If, now, the assets are exchanged for another set of assets A′ of equal value and such that conditions (i) and (ii) of paragraph 4 above are satisfied for the liabilities and the new assets when $\delta = \delta_0 + e$ then a maximum value of $\dfrac{V_L}{V_{A'}}$ exists at the new rate of interest. Provided this process can be repeated whenever it is necessary to change assets or to buy new ones (a function of time as well as of interest) then no loss can occur on any change in the force of interest within the locality of each successive maximum value.

Hence if a valuation is performed when $\delta = \delta_0 + e$ but the local maximum value of $\dfrac{V_L}{V_A}$ occurs when $\delta = \delta_0$ there is a real valuation surplus amounting to

$$(1-k)V_A, \quad \delta = \delta_0 + e,$$

where $\qquad\qquad k = \dfrac{V_L}{V_A}, \quad \delta = \delta_0$

and an apparent additional surplus amounting to

$$kV_A - V_L, \quad \delta = \delta_0 + e.$$

A mismatching adjustment must be made to the reserves in order to remove this spurious surplus, since credit cannot be taken for it unless it is possible to switch assets as described above.

6. The concepts developed in the two preceding paragraphs are the familiar immunisation concepts set out in a fairly general form and although they have been developed in terms of a force of interest δ

they are, of course, equally applicable for a rate of interest i. It may be useful at this point to refer to Appendix 2, which deals with the variation with interest of the values of a perpetuity and a pure endowment, for illustration. The graph drawn from the figures in this Appendix suggests that the maximum value of $\dfrac{V_L}{V_A}$ occurs at a rate of interest between 5% and 10%, the two rates of interest for which $V_L = V_A$. The maximum value of $\dfrac{V_L}{V_A}$ is about 1·06, which means that there is a real deficit of assets, and so the value of the assets at, for instance, 10% interest should be increased by 6% from 239·4 to 253·8 to protect the situation should the rate of interest fall. The resulting surplus at 10% interest, which is apparent rather than real, can be absorbed by valuing the liability at a rate of interest of around $9\frac{1}{2}$%.

The values of M_A and M_L in Appendix 2 (and in the other Appendices) have been calculated using the approximate relationships

$$M_A^i = \frac{V_A^{i-1} - V_A^{i+1}}{0{\cdot}02V_A^i}, \quad M_L^i = \frac{V_L^{i-1} - V_L^{i+1}}{0{\cdot}02V_L^i}.$$

The values so derived can be compared with the theoretically correct values calculated from the expressions $\dfrac{1}{i}$ and $\dfrac{15}{1+i}$ respectively.

7. The values of the asset and liability in Appendix 2 are functions of the form $\Sigma v^t A_t$, where A_t does not depend on the interest rate. Furthermore they imply the existence of a level yield curve, which is not the case in general, of course. Apart from this defect, however, the curves in Appendix 2 are typical of a common situation occurring in practice i.e. in most cases V_A and V_L decrease monotonically as the rate of interest increases, there is a local maximum value of $\dfrac{V_L}{V_A}$ at a rate of interest within a practical range and the locality of this maximum value remains within a practical range also. Moreover, if asset and liability are immunised at a rate of interest i_0 it will usually be possible to switch to immunising assets should the rate of interest fall below i_0, since shorter-dated assets would be required. Similarly, if the rate of interest does not fall but remains constant at i_0 it will be possible to switch to shorter-dated assets as the term of the liability reduces with the passage of time.

8. It is the case, though, that at higher rates of interest it may be impossible to find assets long enough to immunise a particular

liability. This could be so for the pure endowment in **Appendix 2**, since at rates of interest above about 7% one would need an asset longer than a perpetuity. However, provided the assets held are always sufficient to equate to the liability when both are valued at i_0, the immunising rate of interest, and the rate of interest never extends into the locality of another maximum value of $\dfrac{V_L}{V_A}$ (if one exists), then inability to find immunising assets at a higher rate of interest is not a barrier to the application of immunising theory : the effect is merely to delay the release of the apparent surplus which is thrown up when the rate of interest increases. If the rate of interest remains at the higher level this surplus will emerge through the passage of time, as both asset and liability become shorter-dated. Eventually a dating will be reached at which immunisation will be possible at this higher rate of interest and any remaining mismatching surplus may then be released. During the period of higher interest rates a larger interest profit will be made than if rates had not risen, whether or not there is immunisation.

Practical examples (assuming a level yield curve)

9. Appendices 3 and 4 illustrate the application of the theory to liabilities whose values cannot be expressed in the form $\Sigma v^t A_t$, where A_t is independent of interest. The graphs depict the variation in the values of a perpetuity and the amount of net premium and gross premium reserves for a 25-year annual premium pure endowment at durations 5 years (Appendix 3) and 10 years (Appendix 4). For simplicity, expenses and mortality have been ignored and the asset and liabilities have been chosen so as to be equal at 5% interest, the basis on which the annual premium is calculated.

In practice, neither the net premium reserves nor the gross premium reserves would be used without adjustment. The gross premium reserves would not be allowed to become negative and there might be an increased allowance for future expenses at higher rates of interest. On the other hand, the net premium reserves would be constrained at lower rates of interest by limiting the net premium to the gross premium less an expense allowance. Both types of reserves could be further constrained at certain rates of interest by the existence of guaranteed options, such as surrender values.

10. The maximum values of $\dfrac{V_L}{V_A}$ depend on the particular constraints applied to the reserves, as illustrated in the following table. For the 5 year duration case in Appendix 3 the limiting of the net

premium to the gross premium effectively constrains the asset to the level required for gross premium reserves throughout the range of interest rates and there is no further constraint in requiring reserves to be equal to net premium reserves at the higher rates of interest. For the 10 year duration case in Appendix 4 a requirement for net

Reserve basis and constraint	Maximum $\frac{V_L}{V_A}$	
	Appendix 3	Appendix 4
(i) Unadjusted net premium	1·108	1·230
(ii) Net premium limited to gross premium	1·285	1·230
(iii) Gross premium	1·285	1·000
(iv) Gross premium, negative reserves eliminated	1·285	1·000
(v) Gross premium, less loading equal to		
$\frac{1}{4}$ (gross premium − net premium), if positive	1·285	1·029

premium reserves throughout is the most stringent of the constraints and might be considered excessive for solvency purposes. On the other hand, such a constraint would be necessary if it were management policy to pay a level of surrender values consistent with current investment conditions. An even greater constraint would obviously be involved were surrender values to be guaranteed.

11. It is instructive to note the variation of M_L with interest rate, as shown in Appendices 2 to 4. As anticipated, M_L is less than M_A for interest rates less than the rate at which $\frac{V_L}{V_A}$ is a maximum and exceeds M_A for higher interest rates. M_{LG} in fact tends to infinity as V_{LG} tends to zero, and becomes negative at interest rates above this point, (i.e. the liability represented by a gross premium reserve becomes increasingly long-dated as the rate of interest rises until, eventually, the liability turns into an asset). On the other hand, there is not a great deal of variation in either M_L or M_{LN}, although the variation is downwards for M_L and upwards for M_{LN}. The net premium reserve behaves over much of the interest range as if it were a single premium pure endowment reserve, and in fact can be shorter-dated than the latter for the same outstanding term. This is a consequence of the variation in premium valued as the interest rate changes: the liability being valued is effectively different at each rate of interest and the progressive reduction in net premium as the interest rate rises is almost enough to counteract the inherent tendency for the dating to lengthen.

The values of M_A and M_L have been obtained by an approximation (see Paragraph 6) which produces reasonable values as long as the variation with interest rate is relatively small. Thus in Appendix 2 the approximate values of M_L are quite close to the corresponding accurate values obtained from the expression $\dfrac{15}{1+i}$, but the approximate values of M_A, when compared with the corresponding value of $\dfrac{1}{i}$, are obviously less accurate at the lower rates of interest.

It would be possible in certain cases, e.g. in Appendix 2, to calculate not merely M_A and M_L but the maximum value of $\dfrac{V_L}{V_A}$, or, alternatively, the interest rate at which $M_A = M_L$. Where assets and liabilities are more complex, however, there may be no alternative but to use the graphical approach illustrated.

12. The tables set out below illustrate the application of the principles discussed in paragraph 5 to the data in Appendices 2, 3 and 4. The asset is a perpetuity in each case.

Liability	Interest rate % at which asset is valued	Value of asset V_A	Maximum value of V_L/V_A	Adjusted value of V_A and V_L	Interest rate % corresponding to adjusted V_L	
Appendix 2						
15-year SP endowment:	5	478·8	1·06	507·5	4·7	
	10	239·4	1·06	253·8	9·6	
	15	159·6	1·06	169·2	12·3	
	20	119·7	1·06	126·9	14·7	
Appendix 3					(a)	(b)
25-year AP endowment,	3	192·9	1·285	247·9	3·0	3·0
duration 5 years:	6	96·5	1·285	124·0	4·9	4·9
(a) V_{LN}, net premium	9	64·3	1·285	82·6	7·8	5·7
limited to gross	12	48·2	1·285	61·9	10·0	6·2
premium.	15	38·6	1·285	49·6	11·4	6·5
(b) V_{LG}.						
Appendix 4					(a)	(b)
25-year AP endowment,	3	439·2	1·23	540·2	1·3	1·3
duration 10 years:	6	219·6	1·23	270·1	4·8	4·8
(a) V_{LN}, net premium	9	146·4	1·23	180·1	8·9	6·7
limited to gross	12	109·8	1·23	135·1	11·8	7·8
premium.	15	87·8	1·23	108·0	13·8	8·7
(b) V_{LG}, assuming constraint determined by maximum V_{LN}/V_A.						
Appendix 4						
25-year AP endowment,	3	439·2	1·00	439·2	2·5	
duration 10 years:	6	219·6	1·00	219·2	5·9	
V_{LG}, assuming	9	146·4	1·00	146·4	7·6	
constraint determined	12	109·8	1·00	109·8	8·7	
by maximum V_{LG}/V_A.	15	87·8	1·00	87·8	9·4	

The interest rates corresponding to the adjusted values of V_L have been indicated only approximately.

Practical examples (assuming an increasing yield curve)

13. It has previously been noted that the asset and liability depicted in Appendix 2 have been valued on the assumption of a level yield curve, and although the liabilities in Appendices 3 and 4 are not always of the form $\Sigma v^t A_t$ they are also valued on the assumption of a level yield curve. However, the theory developed in paragraphs 4-7 has not implied that the yield curve should be level but merely that V_A and V_L should be functions of the same rate of interest. To explore the applicability of the theory when the yield curve is not level one must first postulate some relationship between term and interest rate and then test to see whether or not the conditions for immunisation set out in paragraph 4 are likely to occur in practice with this relationship.

14. Since the application of immunisation theory requires all functions for valuation to be expressible as functions of the same rate of interest it is convenient to postulate the existence of a rate of interest i_∞ for an infinitely long investment and to derive a set of discounting factors v_t^t for discounting payments due in t years' time where the discounting factor depends on i_∞ and t. The practical advantage of using a discounting factor to define the variation by term is, of course, that commutation functions can readily be constructed in the usual way once the values of v_t^t have been determined. In what follows, v_t^t will be assumed to be of the form

$$v_t^t = v^{t \cdot \frac{t}{t+1}},$$

where v^t is at rate i_∞. This implies that

$$\delta_t = \left(\frac{t}{t+1}\right) \delta_\infty,$$

where δ_t is the force of interest applicable to a t year debenture having zero coupon. More complicated formulae for a zero coupon yield curve are possible, requiring two, three or more parameters, e.g.,

$$\delta_t = a + b(1 - e^{-ct}),$$

where $\delta_0 = a$, $\delta_\infty = a + b$.

15. The above relationship, then, is one of a family of possible relationships leading to the most common practical situation i.e. one where the rates of interest for short-term securities are lower than the corresponding rates of interest for long-term securities. Appendix 7 contains tables of v_t^t for various values of i_∞ and the tables set out below illustrate the general effect of the relationship.

(a) Variation of debenture term

Debenture term (years)	Equivalent level yield % coupon = 10%, i_∞ = 10%
5	7·95
10	8·74
15	8·98
25	9·15
35	9·20
50	9·23

(b) Variation of i_∞

i_∞ %	Equivalent level yield % 15-year debenture zero coupon	50-year debenture 10% coupon
5	4·7	4·8
10	9·4	9·2
15	14·0	13·4
20	18·7	17·4

As would be expected, the longer-dated the security is, the nearer is the equivalent level yield to i_∞. The figures in (b) appear to contradict this but in fact the 15-year debenture with zero coupon is longer-dated than the 50-year debenture, or even a perpetuity, at higher rates of interest.

16. In Appendices 5 and 6 the above variable yield pattern is applied to the assets and liabilities appearing in Appendices 2 and 3 respectively. However only the gross premium reserve is shown in Appendix 6, the same gross premium being valued as in Appendix 3. The assets are taken to be equal in value to the liabilities at the same rates of interest as before i.e. 10% for Appendices 2 and 5 and 5% for Appendices 3 and 6, but since these values of i_∞ produce the same values for assets and liabilities as if they were obtained at a slightly lower rate of level interest it follows that the amounts of asset depicted in Appendices 5 and 6 are not quite the same as in Appendices 2 and 3 respectively. Thus one cannot immediately conclude from a consideration of the lower maximum values of $\dfrac{V_L}{V_A}$ that less assets are required for immunisation.

The figures in Appendices 5 and 6 have been derived in the main from a relatively few calculated values using graphical interpolation, followed by smoothing. However it can be seen that the variations in $\frac{V_L}{V_A}$, M_A and M_L follow very similar patterns to those depicted in Appendices 2 and 3, and the maximum values of $\frac{V_L}{V_A}$ occur at slightly lower rates of interest. The approximate equivalent level rates of interest corresponding to various values of i_∞ are illustrated below.

i_∞	Perpetuity†	15-year S.P. endowment	V_{LG} for 25-year AP endowment, duration 5 years
5	4·7	4·7	4·7
10	9·3	9·4	10·0
15	13·5	14·0	18·0
20	17·5	18·7	*

* Not calculated. † Derived by extrapolation.

17. From general reasoning one can assert that the lower the value of M_A or M_L for any value of i_∞ the greater ought to be the relative difference between i_∞ and the equivalent level rate of interest, and vice versa. The above table confirms this thesis and the figures in Appendix 6 further show that as M_L tends to ∞ the relative difference between i_∞ and the equivalent level rate of interest tends to zero. Once M_L becomes negative this relative difference in interest rate appears to become negative also, so that at higher rates of interest the equivalent level rate of interest is actually greater than i_∞.

It follows from this reasoning that when $M_A = M_L$, i.e. when $\frac{V_L}{V_A}$ is a maximum, the equivalent level rate of interest ought to be the same for V_A and V_L, and is less than i_∞ if both M_A and M_L are positive. Provided the equivalent level rate of interest lies in the locality of the maximum previously considered for the corresponding level interest case one can deduce that, given the same quantity of assets and liabilities in each case, the maximum value of $\frac{V_L}{V_A}$ in the increasing interest case cannot be greater than the maximum value of $\frac{V_L}{V_A}$ in the corresponding level interest case.

One is tempted to state quite generally that if the conditions for immunisation exist between an asset and a liability on the assumption of a level yield structure of interest rates then they will exist on the assumption of a variable yield curve under which the yields increase as the term increases ; also, that in these conditions slightly less of an asset is required to immunise a particular liability on the increasing yield assumption.

Suitability of equities

18. It may be possible in certain circumstances to take account of equity investments for purposes of immunisation. Given a reverse yield gap an equity can either be considered as a level perpetuity at a lower than market rate of interest or as an increasing perpetuity at a market rate of interest. Allowance for future increase in income may be appropriate in valuing a portion of the future bonus under with profit policies but for a solvency valuation no such allowance can be made. However, on the assumption that virtually all of the current income can be maintained, an equity could be treated as a perpetuity in assessing the change in value arising from a change in equity yields. It can be switched to a shorter-dated security, when necessary, without loss if a reverse yield gap is still in existence at the time of the switch.

This last assumption is subsidiary, since a reverse yield gap is likely to persist if one exists at the outset and dividends are expected never to reduce in future. Given these two latter assumptions, therefore, it may be possible to achieve a degree of immunisation with equity investments along the lines illustrated in Appendices 2 to 6. Where the interest assumptions underlying the liabilities are greater than the yields on equities it may still be possible to immunise with equities provided these are valued at below market value, but this approach requires an allocation of surplus in the form of an investment reserve. Alternatively, one could value the assets at rates of interest consistent with the yield on equities, and if these are lower than the rates of interest assumed in the premiums an allocation of surplus will again be required to allow the more stringent reserves to be set up.

Tax considerations

19. In considering what allowance to make for tax when applying immunisation theory one has to distinguish between

  (i) the tax to be deducted from the asset income in order to arrive at whatever net rate of interest determines market prices, and
  (ii) the tax to which the fund represented by the liability outgo will be subject throughout its term.

It is important to remember that the particular asset income being valued does not in general represent the future cash flow available to meet the liability outgo as it emerges but is merely a quantity having the same present value as that future cash flow. Whenever assets are switched, e.g. in order to remain immunised after a change in the rate of interest, one is exchanging the existing configuration of asset income for another, and different, configuration, each configuration having the same present value at the same rate of interest. If market prices are determined in terms of a net rate of interest it is necessary therefore to deduct tax at the appropriate rate from each configuration of asset income in order to arrive at the correct net asset income for valuation purposes. This deduction must be made regardless of the rate of tax, if any, to which the liability fund is subject.

20. Suppose now that the liability fund is subject to a different tax from that which enters into the market price of assets. In general it would seem that this tax must represent an addition to the liability outgo and that the resulting increased liability outgo should be valued at a rate of interest equal to the net rate of interest at which the asset is valued but grossed up at the rate of tax which is applied to reduce the asset income for valuation purposes.

If the rates of tax implied under 19(i) and 19(ii) are identical then the liability outgo can be valued at the same net rate of interest implied by the market value of the net asset income, while if the liability fund is not subject to any tax it can be valued unadjusted at this net rate of tax grossed up.

21. On the whole, it would seem that market prices for fixed interest securities are determined on a net yield basis or, rather, that certain stocks are attractive on a net yield basis to investors who pay high rates of tax while other stocks are attractive on a gross yield basis to investors who pay little or no tax. In valuing a gross fund one finds in practice that the assets in which it is likely to invest could either be valued gross at gross rates of interest or valued net at net rates of interest, the liability being valued gross in both cases. (It is obvious that for a perpetuity the value is the same.) Also, if it were accepted that the rate of tax affecting prices on a net yield basis approximates to the rate of tax on life funds, it would be possible, without serious error, to value the liability outgo at the same net rate of interest used in valuing assets, the liability outgo being adjusted to take account of tax on expenses.

If the fund is partially gross and partially net, as with most life assurance and annuity funds, it may be advisable to hypothecate assets to each fund according to whether they are likely to be valued on a gross or a net rate of interest. However, the adjustment for tax described in paragraph 20 should then take account of the way in which tax is assessed on the combined fund, bearing in mind that this may not allow for any hypothecation of assets but may, on the other hand, allow for the emergence of taxable annuity profits. The problems involved in dealing with tax for a combined fund are obviously complex and merit more detailed consideration than can be given here.

Margins and options

22. The techniques developed for assessing the degree of immunisation have been illustrated in the Appendices in terms of a single asset and liability in each case. However in suitable circumstances these techniques can be applied to a whole portfolio of assets and liabilities, provided valuations are available at enough rates of interest to allow reasonable graphs to be drawn of the variation in values with interest rate. Also, the techniques need not be confined to dealing with guaranteed liabilities, as in a solvency situation, but may be extended to valuations of liabilities allowing for various margins, including provision for future profits, thus providing a means of assessing the relative strengths of valuations performed under different market conditions. Where the margins are represented by a reduction in interest rate it would be necessary to translate them into their non-interest elements in order to arrive at the correct rate of interest for valuation e.g. a net premium reserve for a with-profit assurance would have to be expressed as a bonus reserve at an appropriately higher rate of interest.

It may be prudent in certain circumstances to take margins in valuing assets. For example, if account was to be taken of the higher yields on debentures relative to gilts a theoretically conservative margin would be obtained if the amount of the debenture was reduced by a factor k such that $(1-k)V_D^{iG} = V_D^{iD}$, $k<1$, where iD and iG represent the market yields on similarly dated debentures and gilts respectively and V_D^{iG} and V_D^{iD} represent the value of the debenture at these rates of interest. Thereafter in the valuation of assets the same rate of interest would be applied to debentures as to gilts.

23. The existence of guaranteed options is often cited as an obstacle to the practical application of immunisation theory. The effect of many options is to change the nature of the asset or liability at certain levels of interest rate : thus the effective maturity date of a fixed interest security having optional maturity dates may depend on whether the valuation implies that it will be at a premium or a discount at the maturity date. Similarly, an endowment having a guaranteed annuity option will usually have to be regarded as a type

of deferred annuity when the valuation rate of interest is less than the underlying rate of interest in the annuity option basis. Such variations in the nature of the asset or liability can be taken account of in the valuation and since they can be regarded as functions of the rate of interest their presence need not invalidate the application of immunisation theory.

24. Perhaps the most significant interest option is represented by a guaranteed surrender value. The effect of such an option is that above a certain interest rate the liability does not vary with interest and the obvious result is to increase substantially the maximum value of $\dfrac{V_L}{V_A}$ over what it otherwise would have been. In order to confine this ratio to a reasonable level it may be necessary to reduce the term of the assets and, perhaps, to postulate an upper limit to the possible range of interest rates.

It would, of course, be theoretically possible in valuing liabilities to allow for withdrawals by specifying rates of withdrawal and levels of surrender values, and to further specify that these should vary with the interest rate in a prescribed manner.

25. While the presence of withdrawal options does not invalidate the application of immunisation theory caution must be exercised in dealing with a combination of liabilities having markedly different characteristics. If there are several liabilities, having different immunising rates of interest with respect to a particular asset or asset portfolio, then the quantity of the asset required to immunise the liabilities, considered as a whole, will appear in general to be less than the sum of the quantities of the asset required to immunise each liability in isolation. This is because the maximum value of $\dfrac{V_L}{V_A}$ with respect to the asset occurs at different rates of interest for each liability. Where the liabilities cannot be terminated in advance of expiry or maturity, e.g. if they consist of immediate annuities, credit can be taken for this reduction in the quantity of asset required for immunisation. But where there may be voluntary termination of any of the liabilities allowance may have to be made for the possibility that the terms of settlement will result in the assets remaining after a termination being insufficient to immunise the remaining liabilities.

In order to avoid a deficiency of assets in these circumstances the amounts paid on termination will have to be less than the values put upon the individual liabilities in the calculations to determine the quantity of assets required to immunise the combined liability. This may be impossible if these termination values are guaranteed, or are zero, and may only be possible where the termination values are not guaranteed and the necessary reductions are not such as to make the resulting values negative. Paradoxically, it would seem less stringent in terms of immunisation theory to provide against the possibility of all the liabilities terminating simultaneously than to provide against the possibility of only some of the liabilities terminating.

The above discussion suggests that in estimating the quantity of assets required to immunise a set of liabilities it will be necessary to consider separately those liabilities that may be voluntarily terminated and to hold for them the sum of the quantities of assets required to immunise each of them individually. In practice it may be sufficient to group together liabilities of a similar nature and determine the immunising position for each group separately. Such a procedure lends itself to the notional hypothecation of different sorts of asset to each group of liabilities, depending on their relative suitability.

Suitability of assets relative to liabilities

26. It is apparent from a study of Appendices 2 to 6 that the relative variation in values of an asset and liability can be assessed from a comparison of the values of M_A with the corresponding values of M_L. Indeed, the values of M_A and M_L can be said to define the behaviour of the asset and the liability with respect to variations in the rate of interest. This suggests that it would be possible, given the values of M_L for a liability portfolio and knowing the values of M_A for different types of asset, to compile a suitable immunising portfolio of assets by combining assets in proportions which will result in the desired overall values of M_A.

In this connection, if V_{A1}, V_{A2}, V_{A3} ... are the values of quantities of assets A_1, A_2, A_3 ... defined in terms of M_{A1}, M_{A2}, M_{A3} ... respectively then the portfolio comprising these assets is defined in terms of M_A where

$$M_A = \Sigma K_r M_{Ar} \text{ and } K_r = \frac{V_{Ar}}{\Sigma V_{Ar}}.$$

K_r is clearly a function of the rate of interest and the quantity of A_r selected for the portfolio.

Summary and Conclusions

27. In this paper some of the principles of immunisation have been re-examined and an attempt made to assess some of the practical

limitations of the theory. The following conclusions may be derived from the investigation:

(i) A particular asset and liability can be said to be immunised at the valuation rate of interest, even if the conditions for immunisation do not apply at that rate, provided the value of the asset is at least equal to the value of the liability at a rate of interest for which the conditions for immunisation do apply.

(ii) A relatively simple method exists for determining the amount of a particular asset required to immunise a particular liability. This method does not require M_A or M_L to be known or calculated in advance and hence it is practicable to apply the method to a group of assets and liabilities.

(iii) If in applying this method it is assumed that the yield curve is level, no serious error is likely to arise. The degree of error may well be less than 5% and it is likely to be in the direction of overstating the required assets.

(iv) The presence of options depending on the rate of interest need not be a barrier to the application of the method. In some cases a satisfactory allowance can be made for tax but often this will have to be dealt with very approximately.

(v) The method also can be used to assess the relative strengths of valuations performed under different market conditions. In particular, it could be used to determine a safe gross premium reserve basis under conditions where a net premium reserve was thought to be excessively strong.

(vi) Given a particular portfolio of liabilities, the method provides a quick means of assessing the suitability of various types of asset, taking into account the effect of any significant guaranteed options dependent on the rate of interest.

28. In conclusion I would like to acknowledge the valuable assistance given to me by J. W. Thompson, who was responsible for most of the material in the Appendices and by A. D. Wilkie who provided information on yield curves and read the paper in manuscript. Both made useful comments and suggestions which were adopted into the paper. My debt to previous writers on the subject of immunisation is, I hope, obvious.

APPENDIX 1

Proof of the conditions for a local maximum value of $\dfrac{V_L}{V_A}$

The function $f(\delta)$ has a local maximum value at values of δ for which

$$f'(\delta) = 0 \quad \text{and} f''(\delta) < 0.$$

(Durrell and Robson—*Elementary Calculus*, pp. 69-70).

Now let $f(\delta) = \dfrac{V_L}{V_A}$, where V_A and V_L are both functions of δ.

Then $f'(\delta) = \left(\dfrac{V_L}{V_A}\right)'$

$$= -\frac{V_L}{V_A^2} \cdot V_A' + \frac{V_L'}{V_A}$$

$$= 0 \text{ if } V_A \neq 0 \text{ and } \frac{V_L}{V_A} \cdot V_A' = V_L'.$$

Also, if the above conditions hold,

$$f''(\delta) = \left(\frac{V_L}{V_A}\right)''$$

$$= -\frac{V_L}{V_A} \cdot \left(\frac{V_A'}{V_A}\right)' - \frac{V_A'}{V_A} \cdot \left(\frac{V_L}{V_A}\right)' + \left(\frac{V_L'}{V_A}\right)'$$

$$= \left(\frac{1}{V_A}\right)' \cdot \left(-\frac{V_L}{V_A} \cdot V_A' + V_L'\right) - \frac{1}{V_A} \cdot \left(\frac{V_L}{V_A} \cdot V_A'' - V_L''\right)$$

$$= -\frac{1}{V_A} \cdot \left(\frac{V_L}{V_A} \cdot V_A'' - V_L''\right)$$

$$< 0 \text{ if } V_L \cdot V_A'' > V_A \cdot V_L''.$$

These conditions can be expressed as

$$\frac{V_A'}{V_A} = \frac{V_L'}{V_L} \text{ and } \frac{V_A''}{V_A} \gtrless \frac{V_L''}{V_L}, \text{ as } \frac{V_L}{V_A} \gtrless 0$$

$$\text{if } V_A \neq 0 \text{ and } V_L \neq 0.$$

NOTES

1. The above conditions can also be derived by means of a Taylor expansion of $(V_A - V_L)$.

B

2. J. W. Thompson has pointed out that the above conditions are sufficient but not necessary. The necessary and sufficient conditions for the function $\frac{V_L}{V_A}$ to have a local maximum value are

(i) $\frac{V_L}{V_A} \cdot V_A^m = V_L^m$, $V_A \neq 0$, for all m, $1 \leqslant m < 2n$

and (ii) $\frac{V_L}{V_A} \cdot V_A^{2n} > V_L^{2n}$

where V_L^m, V_A^m represent the mth derivatives of V_L and V_A respectively.

APPENDIX 2

Level yield curve: Variation in values of perpetuity (V_A), annually in arrears, and single premium pure endowment due in 15 years (V_L).

The pure endowment is for 1000 and $V_A = V_L$ at 10%.

Interest rate %	V_A	V_L	$\dfrac{V_L}{V_A}$	M_A	M_L
1	2394·0	861·3	0·360		
2	1197·0	743·0	0·621	66·7	14·8
3	798·2	641·9	0·804	37·5	14·6
4	598·5	555·3	0·928	26·7	14·5
5	478·8	481·0	1·005	20·8	14·3
6	399·0	417·3	1·046	17·1	14·2
7	342·0	362·4	1·060	14·6	14·1
8	299·2	315·2	1·053	12·7	13·9
9	266·0	274·5	1·032	11·2	13·8
10	239·4	239·4	1·000	10·1	13·7
11	217·6	209·0	0·960	9·2	13·7
12	199·5	182·2	0·913	8·4	13·5
13	184·2	159·9	0·868	7·7	13·2
14	171·0	140·1	0·819	7·2	13·2
15	159·6	122·9	0·770	6·7	13·1
16	149·6	107·9	0·721	6·3	13·0
17	140·8	94·9	0·674	5·9	12·9
18	133·0	83·5	0·628	5·6	12·6
19	126·0	73·8	0·586	5·3	12·6
20	119·7	64·9	0·542		

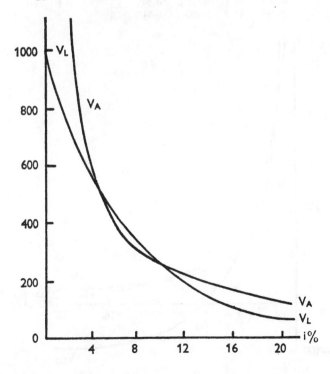

APPENDIX 3

Level yield curve : Variation in values of perpetuity (V_A) and reserve for 25-year annual premium pure endowment after 5 years, i.e. $_5V_{25}$, on net premium basis (V_{LN}) and gross premium basis (V_{LG}). The pure endowment is for 1000, the gross premium is calculated at 5% and $V_A = V_{LN} = V_{LG}$ at 5%.

Interest rate %	V_A	V_{LN}	V_{LG}	$\dfrac{V_{LN}}{V_A}$	$\dfrac{V_{LG}}{V_A}$	M_A	M_{LN}	M_{LG}
1	578·8	180·6	455·8	0·312	0·787			
2	289·4	162·5	340·2	0·562	1·176	66·7	10·8	30·6
3	192·9	145·6	247·9	0·755	1·285	37·5	10·8	33·5
4	144·7	131·1	174·3	0·906	1·205	26·6	11·4	37·9
5	115·8	115·8	115·8	1·000	1·000	20·8	12·3	45·4
6	96·5	102·7	69·2	1·064	0·717	17·2	12·1	60·4
7	82·7	90·9	32·2	1·099	0·389	14·6	12·4	102·8
8	72·4	80·2	3·0	1·108	0·041	12·7	12·6	871·7
9	64·3	70·7	−20·1	1·100		11·3	12·8	−102·5
10	57·9	62·1	−38·2	1·073		10·1	13·1	−42·3
11	52·6	54·4	−52·4	1·034		9·2	13·3	−24·0
12	48·2	47·6	−63·3	0·986		8·4	13·4	−15·2
13	44·5	41·6	−71·6	0·935		7·8	13·6	−10·2
14	41·3	36·3	−77·9	0·879		7·1	13·6	−7·0
15	38·6	31·7	−82·5	0·821		6·6	13·7	−4·8
16	36·2	27·6	−85·9	0·762		6·4	13·9	−3·3
17	34·0	24·0	−88·1	0·706		5·9	14·0	−2·0
18	32·2	20·9	−89·5	0·649		5·4	14·1	−1·2
19	30·5	18·1	−90·3	0·593		5·4	14·1	−0·6
20	28.9	15·8	−90·5	0·547				

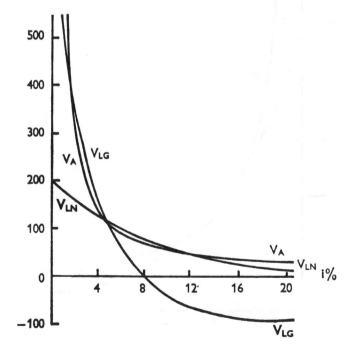

APPENDIX 4

Level yield curve: Variation in values of perpetuity (V_A) and reserves for 25-year annual premium pure endowment after 10 years, i.e. $_{10}V_{25}$, on net premium basis (V_{LN}) and gross premium basis (V_{LG}). The pure endowment is for 1000, the gross premium is calculated at 5% and $V_A = V_{LN} = V_{LG}$ at 5%.

Interest rate %	V_A	V_{LN}	V_{LG}	$\dfrac{V_{LN}}{V_A}$	$\dfrac{V_{LG}}{V_A}$	M_A	M_{LN}	M_{LG}
1	1317·6	370·4	581·9	0·281	0·442			
2	658·8	341·9	481·5	0·519	0·731	66·7	8·2	19·3
3	439·2	314·4	396·5	0·716	0·903	37·5	8·5	19·8
4	329·4	288·3	324·5	0·875	0·985	26·7	8·8	20·5
5	263·5	263·5	263·5	1·000	1·000	20·8	9·1	21·4
6	219·6	240·2	211·8	1·094	0·964	17·1	9·4	22·5
7	188·2	218·4	168·0	1·160	0·893	14·6	9·6	24·1
8	164·7	198·2	130·8	1·203	0·794	12·7	9·8	26·3
9	146·4	179·4	99·2	1·225	0·678	11·2	10·1	29·4
10	131·8	162·1	72·4	1·230	0·549	10·1	10·3	34·2
11	119·8	146·1	49·7	1·220	0·415	9·2	10·4	42·2
12	109·8	131·6	30·5	1·199	0·278	8·4	10·5	58·2
13	101·4	118·4	14·2	1·168	0·140	7·7	10·7	106·0
14	94·1	106·3	0·4	1·130	0·004	7·2	10·8	3187·5
15	87·8	95·4	−11·3	1·087		6·7	10·8	−95·1
16	82·4	85·6	−21·1	1·039		6·3	10·9	−42·9
17	77·5	76·7	−29·4	0·990		5·9	11·0	−26·0
18	73·2	68·7	−36·4	0·939		5·6	11·2	−17·6
19	69·3	61·3	−42·2	0·885		5·3	11·2	−12·7
20	65·9	55·0	−47·1	0·835				

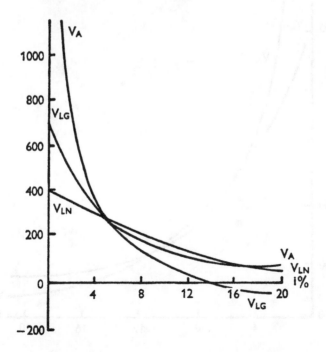

APPENDIX 5

Increasing yield curve : Variation in values of perpetuity (V_A) and single premium pure endowment due in 15 years (V_L). The pure endowment is for 1000 and $V_A = V_L$ at 10%.

Interest rate %	V_A	V_L	$\dfrac{V_L}{V_A}$	M_A	M_L
1	2408	867	0·360		
2	1219	756	0·620	63·6	13·7
3	857	660	0·770	33·8	13·6
4	640	576	0·900	27·1	13·5
5	510	504	0·988	20·8	13·5
6	428	440	1·028	16·2	13·4
7	371	386	1·040	13·6	12·8
8	327	341	1·043	12·2	12·6
9	291	300	1·031	11·2	13·2
10	262	262	1·000	10·1	13·5
11	238	229	0·962	9·2	13·3
12	218	201	0·922	8·3	12·7
13	202	178	0·881	7·2	12·1
14	189	158	0·836	6·1	12·0
15	179	140	0·782	5·6	12·5
16	169	123	0·728	5·6	13·0
17	160	108	0·675	5·6	12·5
18	151	96	0·636	5·3	11·5
19	144	86	0·592	4·5	11·0
20	138	77	0·558		

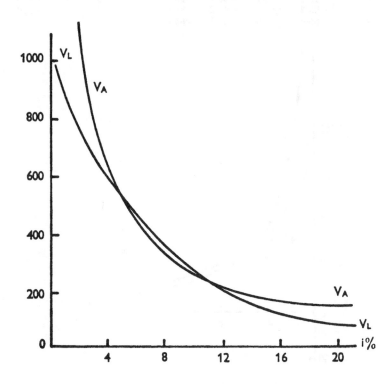

APPENDIX 6

Increasing yield curve: Variation in values of perpetuity (V_A) and reserve for 25-year annual premium pure endowment after 5 years, i.e. $_5V_{25}$, on gross premium basis (V_{LG}). The pure endowment is for 1000, the gross premium is calculated at 5% and $V_A = V_{LG}$ at 5%.

Interest rate %	V_A	V_{LG}	$\dfrac{V_{LG}}{V_A}$	M_A	M_{LG}
1	574	462	0·805		
2	290	346	1·193	63·8	30·1
3	204	254	1·245	33·8	32·7
4	152	180	1·184	27·3	36·9
5	121	121	1·000	21·1	43·4
6	101	75	0·743	16·8	56·7
7	87	36	0·414	13·8	94·4
8	77	7	0·091	11·7	400·0
9	69	−20		10·9	−115·0
10	62	−39		9·7	−44·9
11	57	−55		7·9	−25·5
12	53	−67		7·5	−16·4
13	49	−77		7·1	−11·0
14	46	−84		6·5	−7·7
15	43	−90		7·0	−5·6
16	40	−94		6·3	−3·2
17	38	−96		5·3	−2·1
18	36	−98		5·6	−2·0
19	34	−100		4·4	−1·5
20	33	−101			

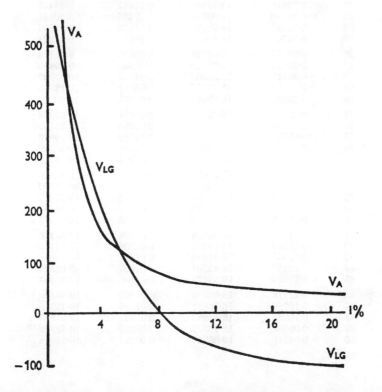

APPENDIX 7

Discounting factors for increasing interest pattern such that

$$v_t^i = v^t \cdot \frac{t}{t+1}, \ a_t^i = \Sigma v_t^i, \ v = \frac{1}{1+i_\infty}$$

	$i_\infty = 5\%$		$i_\infty = 10\%$	
t	v_t^i	a_t^i	v_t^i	a_t^i
1	0·97590	0·97590	0·95346	0·95346
2	0·93702	1·91292	0·88066	1·83412
3	0·89603	2·80895	0·80699	2·64111
4	0·85684	3·66579	0·73947	3·38058
5	0·81596	4·48175	0·67225	4·05283
6	0·77718	5·25893	0·61114	4·66397
7	0·74017	5·99910	0·55558	5·21955
8	0·70780	6·70690	0·50910	5·72865
9	0·67409	7·38099	0·46282	6·19147
10	0·64199	8·02298	0·42074	6·61221
11	0·61142	8·63440	0·38249	6·99470
12	0·58249	9·21689	0·34793	7·34263
13	0·55490	9·77179	0·31647	7·65910
14	0·52860	10·30039	0·28783	7·94693
15	0·50353	10·80392	0·26177	8·20870
16	0·47964	11·28356	0·23806	8·44676
17	0·45687	11·74043	0·21648	8·66324
18	0·43518	12·17561	0·19686	8·86010
19	0·41451	12·59012	0·17901	9·03911
20	0·39482	12·98494	0·16277	9·20188
21	0·37606	13·36100	0·14800	9·34988
22	0·35818	13·71918	0·13457	9·48445
23	0·34116	14·06034	0·12236	9·60681
24	0·32494	14·38528	0·11125	9·71806
25	0·30949	14·69477	0·10115	9·81921
26	0·29477	14·98954	0·09197	9·91118
27	0·28075	15·27029	0·08362	9·99480
28	0·26740	15·53769	0·07603	10·07083
29	0·25468	15·79237	0·06912	10·13995
30	0·24256	16·03493	0·06285	10·20280
31	0·23103	16·26596	0·05714	10·25994
32	0·22003	16·48599	0·05195	10·31189
33	0·20957	16·69556	0·04723	10·35912
34	0·19959	16·89515	0·04294	10·40206
35	0·19010	17·08525	0·03904	10·44110
36	0·18105	17·26630	0·03549	10·47659
37	0·17244	17·43874	0·03227	10·50886
38	0·16423	17·60297	0·02934	10·53820
39	0·15641	17·75938	0·02667	10·56487
40	0·14738	17·90676	0·02425	10·58912
41	0·14188	18·04864	0·02204	10·61116
42	0·13513	18·18377	0·02004	10·63120
43	0·12867	18·31244	0·01821	10·64941
44	0·12257	18·43501	0·01657	10·66598
45	0·11674	18·55175	0·01506	10·68104
46	0·11118	18·66293	0·01369	10·69473
47	0·10589	18·76882	0·01245	10·70718
48	0·10085	18·86967	0·01132	10·71850
49	0·09605	18·96572	0·01029	10·72879
50	0·09148	19·05720	0·00935	10·73814

SYNOPSIS

In this paper an attempt is made to present the theory in such a way as to permit a more general application in practice. The conditions for immunisation are defined for functions whose characteristics, as well as values, are dependent on the rate of interest, and the effect of assuming one particular form of variable yield curve is examined. A simple graphical method is illustrated for finding the rate of interest at which a particular asset and liability are immunised and hence for determining the appropriate rate of interest at which the liability should be valued if the rate of interest at which the asset is valued is not the immunising rate of interest. Applications of the method to actuarial valuations, including gross premium valuations, are outlined.

DISCUSSION

Mr. A. D. Shedden, introducing the paper, said:—This paper represents a small piece of research into the general problem of measuring the relative suitability of assets and liabilities in an actuarial valuation. The particular facet of this problem which has stimulated the research is the determination of a suitable rate of interest for valuing a liability given a market valuation of assets. As mentioned at the outset of the paper, actuaries in this country have advanced two approaches to this—one involving the concept of a combination of the current yield on existing assets and a reinvestment yield on future investment and the other based on the idea that in suitable circumstances lower future rates of interest can be set off against resulting capital appreciation and *vice versa* so that reinvestment can either be ignored or at least be given less significance.

In my view both these approaches presuppose a gross premium valuation of annual premium liabilities and, indeed, a gross premium valuation standard has received considerable support within the profession. Nevertheless, the authorities have insisted on having a net premium valuation standard and they have arguments of precedence and practice on their side. In this connection it is unfortunate that the profession seems no nearer to taking a definitive position on this matter than it has been since the arguments in favour of gross premium valuations as distinct from net premium valuations were first advanced.

Although this paper is confined to exploring the second of these approaches to dealing with the reinvestment problem, that is the immunisation approach, and is in no sense intended to deal with valuation problems generally, nevertheless it seems to me that the techniques illustrated in the paper may throw some light on the problem of determining the conditions under which gross premium reserves would be acceptable for purposes of a valuation standard.

In examining some of the principles of immunisation and their application to the problem of valuation I have been particularly concerned with finding a satisfactory means of determining the mis-matching adjustment which is required under immunisation theory if assets and liabilities do not have the same " length " at the market rate of interest. As the rate of interest rises it becomes harder to find assets which are long enough in terms of the liabilities (assuming that these have no guaranteed surrender values) for immunisation at the market rate of interest to be possible, and hence the risk of not allowing adequately for the effect on surplus of changes in this rate of interest is much greater now than when the theory of immunisation was first propounded. I approached this problem by considering that if the market rate of interest was not the immunising rate of interest the assets and liabilities could nevertheless be said to be immunised if the value of the assets was at least equal to the value of the liabilities at the immunising rate of interest. The mis-matching adjustment therefore represents the amount of surplus (thrown up by a valuation at the market rate of interest) which must be set aside to cover the maximum potential loss arising from a change in the market rate of interest.

The paper deals with the situation under conditions of full immunisation, that is where there is protection against *any* change in the rate of interest. It is not suggested that full immunisation is the ultimate valuation standard but I think it can be demonstrated that such a standard is not necessarily less stringent than more generally accepted standards. Other standards of protection against changes in the rate of interest might alternatively be considered. For instance, one might provide against changes in the rate of interest which follows some decreasing pattern over future years, along the lines indicated by Cavaye and Springbett in *T.F.A.* 28, pages 308 to 322, or measure protection against a drop in the rate of interest to some minimum level, as was advocated by Hazell and Stalker to the Faculty some months ago. The present paper was in its last stages of preparation when the paper by Hazell and Stalker appeared and I have adopted some of their notation. Both papers arrive, by different routes, at the concept of determining a valuation rate of interest for a liability in the context of a particular asset and a specified range of possible interest rate changes.

In the paper I have attempted to concentrate on principles rather than on detail but I hope that the number of examples, though limited, are sufficient to demonstrate the techniques which are advanced. Had time and space permitted one might have applied these techniques to a whole range of assets and liabilities and perhaps to the valuation of a model office. Again, the discussions on tax and on ordinary shares are limited to some of the main points which may give rise to difficulty and even mis-understanding. The treatment of the variable yield curve situation is also very sketchy but I hope I have managed to indicate that the assumption of a level yield curve may not lead to much of an error and that any error may be in the right direction.

In conclusion I would like to thank the Faculty for giving me the opportunity of presenting this paper on immunisation and hope that its contents, and the discussion, will help in determining the extent to which immunisation theory can be applied in practical valuations.

Mr. G. G. Torkington, opening the discussion, said:—In this era of fluctuating high yields and low market values, any paper which gives a new slant to the problems of valuing assets and liabilities is welcome. Mr. Shedden's paper on immunisation is doubly welcome as it puts forward one method of solving the difficulty of matching certain liabilities with assets which would require to be longer than perpetuities, and at the same time shows how this same method could be extended to apply to all the liabilities. The author begins by comparing two different propositions advanced by the actuarial profession on the rate of interest to be used. I express no opinion as to which of these propositions is correct, since the answer may depend on the purpose of the valuation, e.g. bonus declaration, immunisation or Department of Trade returns or solvency. The two objections to conventional immunisation stated in paragraph 3 are valid, but I feel that the second is not a weakness in Redington's theory but is caused by the gross premium method which requires immunisation against inadequate future office premiums as well as against the effect of changes in interest rates on the assets held.

The idea offered by Redington in *J.I.A.* 78 as a basis for immunisation assumed a single rate of interest and set out to find such a distribution of assets by redemption dates as should protect the office against loss in the event of a change in that rate of interest, the criteria being (*a*) equivalence of the mean term of the values of the asset-proceeds and of the liability-outgo and (*b*) a minimum spread of asset redemption dates about the mean. On the other hand Shedden starts from a given asset distribution and finds the rate of interest which will maximise the assets needed to cover the liabilities; the statement of this basis appears at the end of paragraph 3 (the wording in italics), and although in all the examples in the Appendices the assets are perpetuities I assume that the method would be equally applicable to the redeemable securities actually held without any redemption date switching. I should point out at this stage that although Redington's notation has been adopted in the main, there is one particular difference, namely V'_A and V'_L mean altered values in Redington's paper but mean first differentials in Shedden's paper; as a result Redington measures a cash value difference whereas Shedden measures a difference $(k-1)$ which expresses his margin as a percentage addition to the type of assets held (not their cash value)—these thus have slightly different meanings, but give the same answers if it so happens that the actual assets satisfy the Redington equations, i.e. if $k = 1$.

If I understand Mr Shedden correctly, the percentage addition to assets just mentioned would be transferred from the office's estate to put his type of immunisation into effect and these would have the same redemption date distribution as the whole of the assets held before such transfer, and on a change of interest basis any profit (the " spurious surplus " mentioned at the end of paragraph 5) would have to be put back into the estate. I also assume from paragraphs 5 and 6 that the maximising rate of interest should be adopted as the valuation rate, and that, if not, then the valuation rate chosen should be adjusted to give the same maximum reserves.

This method of immunisation has the advantage of avoiding the trouble and expense of the continuous asset switching by redemption dates required to preserve the immunised position, a point made by Mr. Gordon Bayley in the Discussion to Redington's paper; the only switching required under Shedden's method is block transfer in and out of the estate. However, I pose the question—is not this transfer from the estate merely a capitalisation of the maximum possible loss, resulting in a real loss if the transfer is not ultimately fully reversed? In other words, is this not a method of setting up additional reserves rather than true immunisation which seeks to avoid any loss without the necessity of extra reserves?

If, as stated by the author in paragraph 25, the existence of certain options would require separation of liabilities and possibly hypothecation of certain assets to certain of these liabilities, any strengthening of the assets would have to take account of policies containing these options and the type of assets held against them; this would certainly remove a possible source of weakness in immunisation on the basis of the liabilities and the portfolio as a whole.

Having set out his principles for immunisation, the author in paragraph 9 decides to apply these to the two main methods of valuation of liabilities. the pure net premium method and the gross premium method, the former being required for the new Department of Trade Returns and the latter still being preferred by most offices for bonus distribution valuations. The author's examples in Appendices 3 and 4 illustrate well the very different effects on immunisation produced by these two valuation methods. Under a net premium valuation any premium deficiencies or oversufficiencies are absorbed year by year, whereas under a gross premium valuation these are capitalised; if these methods are modified, different results again are obtained, and the author gives some very useful comparisons in paragraph 10, the most stringent results of which are applied to paragraph 12.

One point that rather puzzles me is that, although I follow the theory in paragraph 4 and Appendix 1, the second differentials of V_A and V_L do not seem to be used in practice. I would have thought it sufficient for the purposes of the examples in the Appendices (where the assets are perpetuities) to state that the function V_L/V_A is always zero at $i = 0$, is automatically equal to unity where $i = $ the premium basis interest rate, and tends to a constant at $i = \infty\%$, which on the net premium basis is zero and on the gross premium basis is a negative value equal to the ratio of the gross premium to the asset dividend; therefore, as the function varies continuously with the values of i from 0% to $\infty\%$, there must be at least one maximum value of V_L/V_A greater than or equal to 1; the latter position must be very rare, and it is perhaps unfortunate that in Appendix 4 the value of V_{LG}/V_A appears to have a maximum of 1, since I have calculated that the maximum is slightly higher than 1 in the neighbourhood of $i = 5\%$. The non-application of this part of the theory does not, of course, detract from the value of the Appendices and the accompanying diagrams.

With due regard to the current financial conditions the author has next gone to some trouble to test his theory where the yield curve is not a level curve but an increasing one. Any immunisation method (including the author's) is unworkable unless a change from one yield curve to another can be expressed in terms of a change from one rate of interest to another single rate of interest. The author solves this problem by creating a family of yield curves each of which is related in the same way to a single variable, the rate of interest for an infinitely long investment, i_∞, as described in paragraphs 14 and 15 and exemplified in Appendix 7. This assumes in effect that any change in the immediate future will be from one yield curve to another of similar shape and wholly at a higher or a lower level, and that, for example, the yield curve will never turn upside down; I find these very reasonable assumptions to make even in present financial conditions. Tables (a) and (b) of paragraph 15 illustrate the equivalent level yields for various assets valued by the discounting factors in Appendix 7 (extended to interest rates of 15% and 20%), but it would have been helpful to have shown also the figures for a 15-year debenture 10% coupon and a 50-year debenture zero coupon; we would then have a pair of stocks with zero coupon and a pair with 10% coupon and these are shown below (with the additional figures in brackets)—

Variation of i_∞

	Equivalent Level Yield %			
	(50)	15-year Deb.	50-year Deb.	(15)
$i_\infty\%$	(zero)	zero coupon	10% coupon	(10%)
5	(4·9)	4·7	4·8	(4·6)
10	(9·8)	9·4	9·2	(9·0)
15	(14·7)	14·0	13·4	(13·3)
20	(19·6)	18·7	17·4	(17·4)

It would then become clearer that the first sentence immediately following Table (b) applies to securities with equal coupon, and that comparable zero coupon securities are always longer than with-coupon securities at high rates of interest if comparison is made on the basis of discounted values, since the early coupons then become more important in value than the redemption payment.

The discounting method is all right for determining the present value of assets (as long as these asset-proceeds are allowed to be reinvested without depletion for the purpose of making claims) and can also be used for the present value of the liability under a single premium pure endowment or a paid-up policy. It is, however, theoretically incorrect for valuing the net liability under an annual premium contract in the form $A - \pi\ddot{a}$, since this implies holding an investment which will, for example under an annual premium pure endowment, provide asset-proceeds sufficient to meet negative premiums followed by a positive claim. The real truth of the matter is that an investment should be held which will with future premium payments be sufficient to meet the claim when it arises; the correct calculation should therefore be an accumulation of premiums up to the maturity date, and the net liability arising at that date is then in a form which can be discounted to the valuation date to give its present value — put another way, investment of a future premium can only be affected by yields on or after the date of investment. so that the yields prior to payment of the premium (which are what the discounting method uses) are completely irrelevant. The use of actuarial functions which are based upon discounted values and the interrelationship of such functions with each other is merely a mathematical convenience for valuing what is really a cash flow accumulation, but if interest rates vary with date of investment this is not the case. This facet has already been investigated in *T.F.A.* 28, page 308 *et seq.*, by Cavaye and Springbett who also demonstrated the practical difficulties involved in creating accumulation functions and determining net premiums, particularly in the case of whole of life assurances; their use of a critical duration T after which immunisation could be achieved is ingenious though it depends upon investment in perpetuities alone. In *T.F.A.* 33, page 443 *et seq.*, Dr. W. F. Scott demonstrates another method of evolving an accumulation formula, producing " effective " overall investment rates for each term of single premium and annual premium contracts; this is the same as an accumulation formula which I have used for certain contracts but with a slightly different notation:—

A.P. Accumulation

$$\ddot{s}_{\overline{m}|}' = \sum_{t=1}^{t=m} \Pi_t,$$

where $\Pi_t = (1+i_0)(1+i_1)...(1+i_{t-1})$ values of which are calculated as continuous products.

S.P. Accumulation

$$(1+i')^m = 1+d_0\, \ddot{s}_{\overline{m}|}'.$$

These formulae are practically the same as Dr. Scott's, except that the single premium accumulation is derived from the annual premium accumulation by the use of d_0, which is the rate of discount in the very first year. There is also an inherent assumption that all reinvestment is in securities where the dividend per £100 invested is equal to the yield. a condition satisfied by perpetuities and by stocks redeemable at par, i.e. with full coupon. The end result of these deliberations is that, in my opinion, the figures in Appendix 5 are all correct, but that in Appendix 6 the figures should have regard to future investment rates, in so far as they apply to liabilities—however, this should not seriously affect the pattern nor the conclusions drawn therefrom in paragraphs 16 and 17.

I have calculated that, on the assumption that the (increasing) yield curve is the same throughout the duration of the contract, the values of V_{LG} are much closer to those in Appendix 3, but that the values of M_{LG} should be further reduced by about one year.

As a corollary it seems that appropriate future investment rates should be chosen for calculation of the liabilities and the application of immunisation, and this may help to remove the contradiction mentioned in paragraph 1.

It may be relevant at this stage to summarise that a " yield curve " represents at a particular date a set of investment yields for various terms to redemption, and thus is only strictly applicable to purchases at that date. For future investments a different set of yield curves ought to be applied. It follows that for investment of premiums and reinvestment of dividends under an annual premium contract the calculation should in theory use a " yield surface " covering different dates of purchase and different unexpired terms at these dates of purchase, rather than a current " yield curve " or a secular set of level yield curves.

I very much doubt if the Department of Trade is ready or willing to consider these niceties, and expect it will continue to prefer a discounting method using a single valuation rate of interest which it can easily define within specified limits.

As stated in paragraph 3, there are problems of lesser significance relating to options, tax and yield scatter, and in paragraphs 18 to 21 the author has considered these last two aspects.

Options can play a part in the overall assessment of reserves, in varying degrees, and the author has gone into this in some detail in paragraphs 22 to 25. I would like to have seen some mention of what I regard in this context as the most important option, namely the option to continue or stop premium payments; presumably, if premium levels are reduced there is a strong incentive to take a guaranteed paid-up value and re-enter with a new policy. If account is taken of this danger, the immunisation position will be radically altered to something more nearly approaching the net premium position. To substantiate this statement I have calculated a third set of values (V_L) for Appendices 3 and 4 on the assumption that all policies are paid-up, and find that these values do fall between the values of V_{LN} and V_{LG}. Specimen values (those in brackets) for Appendix 4 are shown below.

Interest Rate %	V_A	V_{LN}	(V_L)	V_{LG}
4	329·4	288·3	(*304·2*)	324·5
5	263·5	263·5	(*263·5*)	263·5
6	219·6	240·2	(*228·6*)	211·8
7	188·2	218·4	(*198·6*)	168·0
8	164·7	198·2	(*172·7*)	130·8

The implication of this is that immunisation should allow for this option; I imagine that the results should be similar to those given in paragraph 10 example (ii), where the valuation premium is the net premium limited to the gross premium (or *vice versa*). This is the basis I much prefer; in fact I feel that, as I indicated on a previous occasion, it is high time the net premium and gross premium methods of valuation stopped quarrelling and got themselves married, embracing the bonus reserve method at the same time. Allowance for future bonuses is only briefly mentioned in paragraph 22, the author quite justifiably confining his research to non-profit contracts as this is a first presentation of his principles, but I would prefer the reduced rate of interest used for a conventional net premium with-profits valuation to be replaced by a direct allowance for future bonuses, particularly as the Department of Trade is talking more and more about " reasonable expectations of policyholders " which I take to mean that offices should not lightly reduce their declared current bonus levels nor reserve much less than this for future profits.

In conclusion, may I express my appreciation of the author's paper and the stimulating ideas he has put forward. He has given us all much food for thought and encouragement to have a fresh good hard look at the problems and theory involving interest rates, valuation and immunisation at a time when these have assumed paramount importance in arranging the financial stability of a life office. In particular, he has highlighted the principal difficulty of exact matching in that an office can purchase a great variety of securities, high-coupon, low-coupon, equities and properties, but about the only securities it cannot purchase in quantity are those which could in certain circumstances facilitate exact matching, i.e. a collection of zero-coupon stocks; immunisation aims to get round this by balancing the discounted value of long-term redemptions against the value of relatively shorter-term dividends.

Mr. C. M. Stewart:—I am one of your visitors from London who, if I may paraphrase your welcoming remarks, is here without commitment. Nevertheless a certain amount of water has flowed under the bridge on draft regulations since Consultative Note No. 10 was appended to a paper read to both bodies a year or two ago and it may concentrate the discussion a bit if I bring the Faculty up to date.

A number of criticisms were made, as you know, in the course of the consultations—which included the discussions in this Hall—and as a result the rules as now proposed look just a little different. They will start, in what we hope is the final draft, from a market valuation of the assets, for valuing the liabilities, from the use of the Zillmerised net premium method as a minimum and using the current yield on the assets less a margin, but the Appointed Actuary must then make additional provision so as to ensure that the company would still be able to satisfy the regulations even if the market rate of interest changed. The additional provision would be made either by reducing the value of the assets or by increasing the value of the liabilities by reducing the rate of interest used.

You will see now, Mr. President, the relevance of my intervention which is to indicate that the subject-matter of the paper is now directly relevant to the proposed new rules. For it is by some such procedure as that contained in the paper that the Actuary would have to deduce the amount of the additional provision to be made. This adds a new significance to the author's statement in paragraph 2 that actuaries applying immunisation principles may have to state that they are doing so and may be called upon to substantiate such a statement.

A step in this direction would seem to me to be inevitable but I hope that when the new prescription for the Actuary's valuation report under Schedule 4 comes to be written what will be there proposed will be manageable and will not impose undue burdens either on the companies preparing them or, may I say it, on the officials examining them. Although on a number of occasions in the past 10 years I have had to describe either orally or in writing the principles of "le matching", as our E.E.C. colleagues call it, it has always been my hope that we could maintain in the U.K. a system of supervision of life assurance which did not involve the authorities in seeking as much detailed knowledge of a company's business as the company's Actuary must necessarily have. I still have that hope.

Now that I have commented on paragraphs 1 and 2 of the paper, Mr. President, I look forward to hearing what others have to say on later paragraphs. In particular I look forward to hearing comments on paragraph 25 where the author suggests that it might be necessary to divide the portfolio into two parts and match separately business that may be terminated and business that may not be terminated. I will also be interested in comments on the fifth of his conclusions at the end of the paper, that his method could be used to determine a safe gross premium reserve basis under conditions where a net premium reserve was thought to be excessively strong.

That's all I have to say, Mr. President. I apologise for not bringing any diagrams to show on your new equipment. It is a bad thing to come to the house and not kiss the new baby. On the other hand I may be one of those who won't have to apologise next year when you see the cost of printing the projected diagrams in the Transactions.*

Mr. R. P. Bews:—The paper before us tonight offers an interesting new approach to immunisation theory. This theory has aroused great interest in the 25 years or so since it was first propounded in Redington's classic paper, but it has always seemed to me that while this was an admirable and masterly exposition of an ingenious concept its uses as a practical tool were limited by 3 factors, or rather 3 groups of factors. The first of these is the theoretical assumptions implicit in the theory, such as the assumption of a level yield curve. The second is the practical difficulties which lie in the way, for example, of demonstrating that assets and liabilities have been immunised against future changes in interest rates. And the third is the question of whether it is desirable to immunise anyway, since by definition while immunisation protects the fund against any losses due to changes in interest rates in one direction it also ensures that there will be no interest profit, or at least only a small second differential profit, if rates move in the opposite direction.

The author has attempted to show that the first of these defects need not be a stumbling block, that it is not necessary for these theoretical assumptions to be fulfilled for immunisation theory to hold. This part of the analysis depends on the assumption that, over what the author calls the practical range of interest rates, the function $\frac{V_L}{V_A}$ has only one maximum value, and this is in fact shown to be the case for the examples which the author gives. The models which he uses are of necessity the simplest but an office's portfolio of business is a more complex structure than this. It is in fact a superimposition of a number of such models and it may be that in some cases the results might not conform to this pattern. Clearly this would have to be tested before the actuary could satisfy himself that this condition is met and this would involve valuing asset income and liability outgo at a large number of rates of interest over the practical range. These extensive calculations would also be required in order to demonstrate that assets and liabilities had been immunised, for example by testing that the mean terms are equivalent. The work involved in carrying out this exercise would be considerable—even with the assistance of a computer the compilation of valuation results is a time-consuming process—but it might be brought into practical bounds by applying the techniques to a model of the office's business. However, this practical difficulty still remains to some extent, as does the problem of adjusting one's asset portfolio should this be necessary in order to achieve or maintain an immunised position when interest rates change. The practical application of the theory depends on the ability to exchange a portion of the fund's assets for those of a more suitable term, which in the context of a growing fund usually means selling short in order to buy long. Am I being too conservative in suggesting that the present abundant supply of long dated, high yielding stocks may not continue to be so readily available in future?

From October 1976 an overhead projector was available at Sessional Meetings.

C

Another practical difficulty arises over the fact that most offices will have not one fund but at least two which would require to be immunised separately. The Life Fund would be immunised at a net rate of interest and the Pension and Annuity Funds at a gross rate which will not necessarily be the same as the gross equivalent of the Life Fund rate. The Pension Business Fund will normally consist largely of paid-up deferred annuities and the mean term of these even at high rates of interest will be much shorter than that of the life fund, which implies that even if separate assets are not actually held for the two funds they would still have to be hypothecated for this purpose.

Taking all these points into consideration I personally would not like to find myself in the position of having to demonstrate to a Regulatory Authority that my fund was in an immunised state. And in any case, as I said earlier, I do not necessarily regard the immunised situation as a particularly desirable one to be in unless you are operating a closed fund or one which consists purely of guaranteed liabilities. It is in my opinion important to leave oneself with room to manoeuvre and this is something which would be seriously impaired by the strict application of immunisation techniques.

Mr. J. E. Paterson:—Mr. Shedden's splendid paper has inspired me to do a little work on immunisation with respect to with-profit business. In order to look at with-profit business one must have a premium rate strategy and a bonus strategy, and two situations are considered.

The first is new business immunisation. One assumes that the 25-year with-profit premium rate will be unaltered throughout time, and that the bonus policy is to try to pay in any year a rate of compound bonus on all policies which is that which would be maintainable on a new policy effected in that year if the then current level of interest rates were unchanged throughout the life of the new policy. (One assumes that premium rates for maturities other than 25 years are adjusted slightly as interest rates change so that one has a spectrum of premium rates that tilts about a point.) The second is paid-up immunisation, where one regards the policy as a number of slices. Initially bonus is allotted at the rate which would be maintainable if interest rates at the outset were to remain unchanged throughout the life of the policy. When interest rates change, one aims to continue the same rate of bonus on the paid-up part of the policy (and in the case of compound bonus, on bonuses to date)—the first slice—and, on the balance of the policy, to allot such bonus as would then have applied to the whole policy had a "new business" approach been adopted. When conditions change again, a second slice is completed and a third slice started, and so on. The premium rate strategy is as for "new business" immunisation.

In both cases the premium basis adopted for calculations is 5% interest with 3% compound annual bonus allowed for. The policy examined is a 25-year with-profit pure endowment assurance of 5 years' duration, bonuses to the 5-year point having been declared at the premium basis rate of 3%. The paid-up policy is calculated by re-entry on the original premium scale (and is slightly less than proportionate). Table I shows under $V_{LG}^{(1)}$ the gross premium reserve for the sample policy on a "new business" strategy. In order to make the 5% reserve equal to that of Appendix 3 of the paper the initial sum assured is 477·60. As a perpetuity would be far too long a corresponding asset, $V_A^{(1)}$ relates to a 5-year gilt with a 5% (8% gross) coupon. It is evident from the ratio $V_{LG}^{(1)}/V_A^{(1)}$ that this asset is fairly appropriate over a wide range of interest rates; however.

the ratio unfortunately has a minimum rather than a maximum in the interest rate range shown. In the next column the ratio $V_{LG}^{(1)}/V_A^{(3)}$ relates to an asset portfolio which is, by value at 5% interest, one-half perpetuity and one-half cash. This is also fairly appropriate, but has a maximum. The column on the extreme left shows the bonus rate for new business supported by the premium at each interest rate.

The columns on the right show the volatility percentage of 5-year stock and the gross premium reserve. I prefer to say " volatility " rather than " mean term " for two reasons: in respect of the asset because volatility is a well-known concept and practical tool in fixed-interest investment, and in respect of the reserve because " the mean term of the value of the liability outgo " does not seem to me to be appropriate when the liability outgo is assumed to change as the interest rate changes.

TABLE I

Approx. N.B. Bonus Rate %	Interest Rate %	$V_A^{(1)}$	$V_{LG}^{(1)}$	$\dfrac{V_{LG}^{(1)}}{V_A^{(1)}}$	$\dfrac{V_{LG}^{(1)}}{V_A^{(3)}}$	$M_A^{(1)}$	$M_{LG}^{(1)}$
0·7	1	138·3	158·4	1·15	0·46		
1·3	2	132·1	144·9	1·10	0·72	4·5	8·5
1·8	3	126·4	133·7	1·06	0·87	4·4	7·8
2·4	4	120·9	124·1	1·03	0·95	4·4	7·2
3·0	5	115·8	115·8	1·00	1·00	4·3	6·7
3·6	6	110·9	108·6	0·98	1·02	4·3	6·2
4·3	7	106·3	102·4	0·96	1·03	4·2	5·7
4·9	8	101·9	97·0	0·95	1·03	4·2	5·2
5·5	9	97·8	92·3	0·94	1·03	4·1	4·8
6·2	10	93·8	88·2	0·94	1·02	4·1	4·4
6·9	11	90·1	84·6	0·94	1·00	4·0	4·0
7·6	12	86·6	81·4	0·94	0·99	4·0	3·7
8·3	13	83·2	78·5	0·94	0·98	4·0	3·5
9·0	14	80·0	75·9	0·95	0·97	3·9	3·2
9·7	15	77·0	73·6	0·96	0·95	3·8	3·0
10·5	16	74·1	71·5	0·97	0·94	3·8	2·8
11·2	17	71·3	69·7	0·98	0·93	3·8	2·6
12·0	18	68·7	67·9	0·99	0·92	3·7	2·5
12·7	19	66·2	66·3	1·00	0·91	3·7	2·5
13·5	20	63·8	64·5	1·01	0·89		

Table II shows under $V_{LG}^{(2)}$ the gross premium reserve for the sample policy under a " paid-up " strategy, and under $V_A^{(2)}$ the value of a perpetuity. The low volatility of the reserve at very high interest rates is at first sight surprising. One would imagine that the volatility would be similar to that of a 20-year non-profit single premium policy—not far under 20%—since the bonus rate on the paid-up part of the policy is fixed and the balance of the policy is rather like a new contract. It can easily be shown algebraically that the volatilities would be identical if the bonus to be allotted to the balance were that supported by the original 20-year premium rate at the new interest rate. At high interest rates this is significantly lower than the bonus supported by the original 25-year premium rate; consequently on the actual strategy the reserve falls less rapidly as interest rates rise, which means lower volatility.

Also given in table II is the ratio $V_{LG}^{(2)}/V_A^{(4)}$, where $V_A^{(4)}$ is the value of an asset portfolio which, by value at 5% interest, is 115% perpetuity with

TABLE II

Interest Rate %	$V_A^{(2)}$	$V_{LG}^{(2)}$	$\dfrac{V_{LG}^{(2)}}{V_A^{(2)}}$	$\dfrac{V_{LG}^{(2)}}{V_A^{(4)}}$	$M_A^{(2)}$	$M_{LG}^{(2)}$
1	578·8	249·8	0·43	0·39		
2	289·4	204·8	0·71	0·65	66·7	19·8
3	192·9	168·8	0·88	0·83	37·5	19·4
4	144·7	139·5	0·96	0·94	26·7	19·0
5	115·8	115·8	1·00	1·00	20·8	18·6
6	96·5	96·5	1·00	1·03	17·1	18·1
7	82·7	80·8	0·98	1·04	14·6	17·5
8	72·4	68·1	0·94	1·03	12·7	16·9
9	64·3	57·8	0·90	1·02	11·2	16·2
10	57·9	49·4	0·85	1·00	10·1	15·5
11	52·6	42·5	0·81	0·99	9·2	14·7
12	48·2	36·9	0·77	0·97	8·4	13·7
13	44·5	32·4	0·73	0·96	7·7	12·6
14	41·3	28·7	0·69	0·95	7·2	11·7
15	38·6	25·7	0·66	0·95	6·7	10·7
16	36·2	23·2	0·64	0·96	6·3	9·7
17	34·0	21·2	0·62	0·98	5·9	8·6
18	32·2	19·6	0·61	1·00	5·6	7·6
19	30·5	18·2	0·60	1·03	5·3	6·6
20	28·9	17·2	0·59	1·08		

15% borrowed cash. This ratio shows remarkable stability, having both a maximum and a minimum in the range shown.

I am afraid that lack of time has prevented me from studying other types of policy and the effect of a sloping yield curve, but the volatilities of the reserves for the sample policy at different durations (but under otherwise similar conditions) when the interest rate is 5% are given in table III.

TABLE III

	Duration (years)				
	2	5	10	15	20
$M_{LG}^{(1)}$	7·6	6·7	5·2	3·5	1·8
$M_{LG}^{(2)}$	21·4	18·6	14·1	9·4	4·8

What relationship do these strange bonus strategies bear to real life?

When interest rates change substantially over a period of years offices tend not to change their with-profits premium rates much unless they are actually changing to a new bonus series. Over a few years the bonus rate adjusts from that which is appropriate to the old conditions to that which is appropriate to the new conditions. This has some relationship to a paid-up immunisation situation in that a policy which has gone a good way through its life will in fact (we assume that interest rates have risen) continue to get the lower bonus rate for most of its remaining term, which is broadly speaking equivalent to allowing it to continue to have the lower bonus rate on the large paid-up part of the policy for the whole of its remaining term. Similarly one gets a sort of rough justice for young policies. However, the extent to which the bonus rate can be allowed to lag is limited by the need to give realistic bonuses on new policies; consequently a practical bonus strategy lies somewhere between a " new business " and a " paid-up " strategy.

In most of the Scottish offices the bulk of ordinary business is with profits, and as a previous speaker has remarked most pensions business is fairly short these days—paid-up deferred annuities were mentioned, but paid-up pure endowments may be nearer the mark as most offices fund for cash. (The extreme case is a series of with-profit paid-up pure endowments under a " new business " strategy, which have volatility zero.) Moreover, most options predicate a shorter than apparent asset structure—e.g. flexible endowment assurances.

My conclusions are that our immunised asset structure is shorter than commonly thought, and (if we wish) realisable in practice. Mr. Shedden has shown that, by having enough spare assets, a non-profit office can immunise safely. I feel that my figures tend to indicate that a with-profit office can immunise without much in the way of spare assets (provided its assets are fixed-interest securities).

The high bonus rates supported by high interest rates, as shown in table I, are food for thought. In particular we see that at 10% net interest the premium rate of the example (41·78 per mil) supports a bonus of 6·2%. An average of about 10% net has been available from long gilts for two years (remembering that the annual yield on gilts is about $\frac{1}{2}$% higher than apparent, due to coupons payable half-yearly, and that there are considerable capital gains tax advantages). Yet offices which charge (before expense loadings) the size of premium used in the example currently allot bonus in the $4\frac{1}{2}$%-5% area. In fact only 70% of my 25-year premium rate is required to support 4·7% bonus—what has happened to the other 30%?

Some is of course required for death cover, and some corresponds to an inevitable (in real life) lag in bonus rate changes, but I am sure that a major part is attributable to policyholders' " reasonable expectations "—these are that if interest rates rise bonus rates rise but if interest rates fall bonus rates won't fall! In order to satisfy these " reasonable " expectations it is necessary to declare bonuses which are distinctly conservative.

A further significant problem is the instability of equity and property values. I doubt whether it is appropriate to have a significant proportion of assets in these when the form of the usual bonus system is much more suited to fixed interest investment, yet I would be reluctant to eschew these types of investment. Consequently I believe that all offices with a significant commitment to equities and property should have as a permanent feature a substantial " claims " or " maturity " bonus which is linked to the performance of their equities and properties. I say " performance of " rather than " profits on " because (since in practice a bonus cannot be negative) it is desirable to have some bonus derived from these sources even when there are losses. The simplest course would be to allocate a proportion of every with-profit premium to an internal fund run on unit trust lines, the balance of the premium being treated conventionally. That would work if you were starting from scratch (and if you could sell business on that basis); obviously there would be great problems in introducing such a system to a continuing series of policies.

Another approach involves the use of the device mentioned in paragraph 18 of the paper, i.e. valuing equities (and properties) as a perpetuity of the current income yield. There would remain an investment reserve of the difference between the market value and this " actuarial " value, subventions from which could provide claims bonus. The investment reserve would be positive provided equities yielded less than gilts. The actuarial value of the equities and properties would be considered to have the volatility of a perpetuity under whatever immunisation approach was adopted. The difficulty would of course be the calculation of the appropriate level of claims bonus—I cannot think of any simple method.

Just before I close I would like to refer to the wording of the second half of paragraph 5 of the paper. Mr. Shedden speaks of a " real " surplus, and an " apparent " or " spurious " surplus but I feel these terms are too strong. There is an assured (immunised) surplus, and a contingent surplus (the mis-matching adjustment) which may disappear if the non-immunised situation changes to your disadvantage. Certainly in the case of a special solvency valuation the arguments for ignoring the contingent surplus are very strong. However, if immunisation theory is to be used to assist in the formation of bonus and investment strategy—as I hope it will be— the size of the contingent surplus will be an important statistic, but surely not a surplus which *must* be removed.

Mr. P. Giles:—I hadn't intended to make a contribution to this discussion but one point was mentioned by the opener on which I would like to make comment.

In paragraph 14 Mr. Shedden discusses the shape of the yield curve. The formula he uses implies that the yield on shorter dated securities is always less than the yield on irredeemables. But I would like to suggest that in the present state of the market it is probable that a time may arise in the future when the Government wishes to reduce the rate of interest and adopts the tactic of cutting down the supply of long-dated Government securities. If it is successful in this action over a period the market will come to expect capital appreciation on long-dated securities over the next few years. If the market expects capital appreciation on long-dated securities it will accept a lower running yield such that the running yield plus the capital appreciation shows a reasonable margin above the yield on very short-dated securities. In this situation the yield curve will have turned upside down. The yield on short-dated securities can well exceed the quoted yield on long-dated securities because the market is expecting quite a sizeable capital appreciation on long-dated securities. This is not a situation that would continue for more than a year or two but it has certainly occurred in the last ten years.

Mr. E. S. Robertson:—I must confess to be pro-immunisation and when I say that I do not mean to suggest that I believe that an office's investments should be matched to its liabilities. What I mean is I believe that the office should know just how far departed it is, if at all, from an immunised position. I therefore think that Mr. Bews' comments about the availability of assets of different length are really irrelevant in the context of this paper we are discussing this evening. Certainly the method that Mr. Shedden suggests does require valuations of assets and liabilities to be carried out at several different rates of interest, but I am sure that these days any actuary concerned with the valuation of his office's liabilities would do this as a matter of course, so I don't think that Mr. Shedden is asking anything very much more than an actuary would be doing anyway.

Could I refer to one particular point in the paper, paragraph 10? Mr. Shedden mentions that were surrender values to be guaranteed even greater constraint would obviously be involved than shown by the figures in Appendices 3 and 4, and like Mr. Paterson I have been doing a few sums, to see what effect guaranteed surrender values would have on the figures brought out in those Appendices.

I started off with the same type of contract, a 25-year annual premium pure endowment, but I added a guaranteed bonus of 3% per annum compound and calculated the premium at 5% as in the example in Appendices 3 and 4. I then added guaranteed surrender value options which would enable the contract to be cashed in at any time after 10 years' premiums had been paid, the value being $t/25$ times the basic sum assured with accrued bonuses at 3% per annum added in full, t being the number of years' premiums paid. In other words, the "flexible endowment" type of situation, and because there were such options I added on an arbitrary 5% to the basic net premium.

Now the bonus on its own of course had the effect of changing the term of the contract, and ignoring the surrender value options in the first place the maximum value of V_L/V_A in the situation after 5 years was 1·36 compared with the 1·285 in Appendix 3, and similarly after 10 years the figure was 1·15 compared with the 1·23 in Appendix 4, so the addition of the guaranteed bonus on its own did not have too much effect. However, if the options were added and then the value of the options were looked at individually and the one which produced the highest liability was included, in each case the 1·36 after 5 years was increased to 4·09 and the 1·15 to 5·01, treating 20% as the maximum rate of interest possible.

To reduce these ratios the term of the assets would have to be reduced. But in the situation after 10 years, when rates of interest are 5% or over, the maximum reserve on a bonus reserve valuation basis is the guaranteed cash value available at the valuation date so that at these rates of interest one should really be holding cash. Unfortunately as you go down below the 5% level a reduction in the rate of interest increases the term of the liabilities so that if cash were in fact held and rates of interest fell below 5% you would become unstuck—in fact if they fell to as low as 1% then the ratio of V_L/V_A would be 2·21. This does show that guaranteed options of this nature do certainly affect the nature of the liabilities, but I am not suggesting that one should try and immunise—I don't think one can immunise against this sort of option—only that at least I think one has to be aware of the effect of these options.

Mr. E. J. W. Dyson:—I am a visitor from the South and I am very glad to have the opportunity of speaking here.

There is just one point I would like to make. When Mr. Shedden refers to the fact that the mean term of the liabilities is so long that no asset can immunise them, I think it should be mentioned that one can always reduce the term of the liabilities by borrowing short, so that in effect one borrows cash and invests it in a perpetuity. This has the effect of reducing the term of the liabilities to match the term of the assets which you have got. This possibility, which is only a theoretical one, does bring up the importance of having adequate free reserves available. It is only if you have these reserves that you are in a position to depart from an immunised state.

Mr. D. F. Shearer:—The problem examined in this very useful paper is the determination of the minimum actuarial reserves needed for immunisation, given a market valuation of assets. The exposition in paragraphs 4 to 8 is very helpful, and I was encouraged to believe that I actually understood it until I listened to some of the speakers earlier this evening! Only the use of the word "real" to qualify valuation surplus gave me any cause for concern—it has been contended with much eloquence and not a little truth that any real surplus will appear only as the future unfolds. It is comforting to know, however, that the market value of the mis-matching adjustment $(1-k)V_A$ is the same at the valuation date irrespective of whether one values assets at the then market rate or at some more inspired and normally lower valuation rate related to one's vision of the future. For example in Appendix 2 the perpetuity required for the mis-matching adjustment is 1·44 per annum whether one values the assets at 10% or 5%, although to determine the minimum reserve the liabilities must be valued at about 9½% or 4¾% respectively.

The most vital element in my view is the one emphasised in paragraph 19 that the particular asset income valued is merely a quantity having the same present value as the future cash flow. All other considerations are to little purpose when there is no restraint on the investment policy intended to produce this cash flow. In their recent paper Stalker and Hazell commented how statutory control on investment must be abhorrent to those concerned with the vitality of our industries. Lack of some such control, however, simply licenses speculation at the expense of the policy-holder by adventurers perhaps motivated solely by the vitality of their own power and ambition.

The life assurance industry should be primarily concerned with the provision of security rather than of opportunity for speculation, whether that be by the policyholder or ostensibly on his behalf. The actuary can assess the extent to which different cash flows immunise a given portfolio of liabilities, but until the risks associated with all assets are quantified he must exercise severe judgement in estimating the cash flows that they are likely to produce. I am very glad to note the author's realistic approach to this aspect, but personally I believe that it is essential to establish specific statutory limits, related to the size of the company, within which various categories of assets may be held. The existence of such limits would bring more reality to the successful application of immunisation theory, without restricting the freedom that it is so desirable should be enjoyed by the well-established companies whether traditional or unit-linked.

Mr. J. Paterson, closing the discussion, said:—The length of Mr. Shedden's paper is misleading because it contains far more food for thought than one would, at first, imagine. In a sense I regret this sparse presentation because although he deals with the principles of application of the theory the reader is left with a considerable onus to translate the author's thesis into everyday practical terms. Ideally, I would have preferred a demonstration of the application to a model office but I recognise, along with Mr. Bews, that this would be a tall order in terms of time, computer usage, etc.

We had a foretaste of this paper in Mr. Shedden's remarks during the discussion on the paper by Stalker and Hazell on " Valuation Standards " presented in March of this year. On that occasion he said " much work remains to be done before actuaries become equipped to employ immuni-sation or semi-immunisation techniques confidently in the sort of actuarial valuation which we will be required to do in the future ". With that sentiment I am in total agreement and I assure Mr. Shedden that I bring no disparagement to his excellent paper if I say that I think that this situation remains with us.

I would now like to turn to the paper and, in particular, the reference on the first page to making a valuation report under the Insurance Companies Act 1974 and having applied immunisation principles, giving an explana-tion of what has been done. Without going into the circumstances under which immunisation might be appropriate I confess that I find it difficult to suppress an inward shudder at such a prospect, and was sorry to hear from Mr. Stewart this might come about but was also glad that he hoped this would be unnecessary. At present, under Schedule 4 of the statements furnished to the Department of Trade, the actuary, in his valuation report, has to make a statement about the suitability of the nature and term of the assets having regard to the anticipated incidence of liabilities. In paragraphs 6.7 to 6.10 of the guide *Actuaries and Long-Term Insurance Business* the main points to be kept in mind before making such a statement are presented. I would suggest that the statement presently required for the actuary's report is sufficient. I agree with the sentiment expressed by Mr. Bews and I find it difficult to imagine what use a detailed statement on the immunisation technique adopted would be to the authorities. After all, the actuary will have used his judgement in deciding the criteria, and so long as he has followed the basic principles I do not think his conclusions will be invalidated by the fact that another actuary may have made different assumptions. I cannot help feeling that some spurious importance may be attached by a third party to a statement to the effect that immunisation has to some degree been achieved. An immunisation exercise is subject to many qualifications and adds no permanency to the condition of a fund.

The parts of the paper which deal with values to be placed on assets seem to me to be contradictory to some extent. For example, in paragraph 22 the author says that it may be prudent under certain circumstances (without saying what these are) to take margins in valuing assets and illustrates this with reference to debentures. However, in paragraph 18 he says that in certain (other) circumstances it may be possible to take account of equity investments. I have no disagreement with this latter statement but am a bit puzzled—in view of what he subsequently says in paragraph 22—when he seems to imply, later in paragraph 18, that it would be possible to take equities at market value (i.e. discount dividend income at the dividend yield) if the liabilities were valued at lower rates of interest.

In a solvency situation, force of circumstances may require that assets, other than government stocks and debentures, will have to be brought into account in attempting to reach an immunised position. Following the sort of approach presented in the OECD publication *Financial Guarantees Required From Life Assurance Concerns* I would expect assets to be ranked according to security of income and capital and appropriate margins taken which also recognise the degree of difficulty in realisation.

I would not necessarily agree with Mr. Torkington that the use of an increasing or, more generally, a varying yield pattern to determine discount factors is just as acceptable as the adoption of a uniform rate of interest for discount. From general reasoning I would suggest that the inherent difficulties in choosing a pattern of interest rates are greater than the inherent difficulties in choosing a discount rate. Further, if one is applying the central technique of the paper one would have to choose a series of patterns of interest rates; in so doing can one assume that the variation by term will be of the same type regardless of the level of the rate at infinity?

The patterns adopted in the paper are quite flat in the important range between term 20 and infinity and produce variations between $\frac{1}{4}\%$ and $\frac{1}{2}\%$ for the equivalent uniform rates. The differences increase, of course, with the assumed rate at infinity but these variations are not the dramatic ones we have seen in recent experience. Nevertheless one would find it difficult to justify the adoption of a sharply varying pattern. The use of a uniform rate has clear practical advantages.

One thing that everyone is in agreement about is that the problems in making due allowance for taxes in a normal life assurance fund are complex. I know from personal experience that attempts to estimate the tax provision of a life fund even a year hence often produce figures which eventually prove to be wide of the mark. It seems to me, therefore, that Redington's " expanding funnel of doubt " expands rather more quickly for taxation than for interest, expenses or mortality. My " expanding funnel of doubt " was very much in evidence as I read through paragraphs 20 to 21 and was still there after I had re-read them! I am at a disadvantage because I do not know what rate of tax determines market prices. Of course there are many more factors which determine the market price of a security apart from a potential holder's tax basis. However, we do know that in the market for British Government Securities the potential tax-free capital gain if held for more than one year makes certain low-coupon stocks attractive to people subjected to the higher rates of income tax. Again high-coupon stocks are attractive to gross funds. Nevertheless, general movements in interest rates change the nature of stocks and yester-days' high-coupon stock is today's low-coupon stock! Then, perhaps, one can assume that the market values of assets arising in different countries are influenced by different rates and methods of taxation. But I do not think that you can go beyond these general notions.

My conclusion is then that market values are influenced, among other things, by various, largely indeterminate, levels of taxation. The combined life fund could at the present have its investment income effectively subjected in part to three rates of tax (if it has shareholders). Similarly realised profits generally suffer varying rates of tax as do profits in the annuity funds.

In making a number of valuations of income and outgo using different assumptions it would be difficult to make accurate allowance for all the possible variations in tax. The approach which was adopted by Springbett in *Valuation for Surplus* split taxes on asset income from those on profits, taking the mean rate for the fund to net the former and making estimates of the latter which are treated as part of the liability outgo. I think that this approach could also be used for immunisation exercises.

In performing a series of valuations of asset income and liability outgo to determine the immunised position and variations from this, a series of net rates of discount would be applied to asset income net of the mean rate of tax, one of which will broadly reproduce market values. Liability outgo would be valued at these rates of interest adjusted for the tax rates of the various parts of the liability fund.

I do not think that the hypothecation of assets for taxation purposes is an acceptable approach.

Mr. Torkington said that Mr. Shedden's approach required less involvement in exchange of assets than Redington but I would suggest that the author in paragraph 19 would lead one to conclude otherwise.

A possible taxation consequence of maintaining an immunised state is a tendency to an increase in chargeable gains and realised investment profits because of the continual adjustment of assets. This may be insignificant in an actively managed portfolio but some estimate should be made of the potential liability, although non-contractual terminations would make this difficult.

Little, if anything, has been said about the allowance to be made for expenses in the liability outgo in applying immunisation theory. I think that the assumption that actual expenses will be covered by expense loadings as they fall in requires close examination. Among other things, the results will be affected by the pattern of recent new business growth and the incidence of terminations with non-guaranteed values and pre-maturity terminations with guaranteed values. Reduction in the rate of discount for part of the portfolio chosen in anticipation of terminations may be an insufficient technique where there has also been a recent sharp increase in new business. It might be necessary to respread expense loadings over shorter than contractual terms and anticipate that expense outgo is always in advance of loading income. This problem would be solved to some extent if in the calculation of premium rates recovery of initial expenses was calculated over a period of time within the contractual term.

The practical difficulties of trying to immunise a portfolio of liabilities is also touched upon in paragraphs 24 and 25 and I would be interested to hear from the author whether or not he has attempted to apply the methods of the paper to a portfolio of liabilities.

At the beginning of Redington's paper which first put the word " immunisation " into an actuarial context there is a quotation from the poet and playwright Christopher Fry which is this, " Our most convinced answers are only questions . . . ". Mr. Shedden in his paper and the previous speakers in the discussion this evening have gone some way to providing some of the answers to the problem of applying immunisation techniques in practice, but I would suggest that there remain several important questions to which we need convincing answers before such methods are used with understanding.

Mr. A. D. Shedden, replying to the discussion, said:—I will not be able at this time to reply to, let alone remember, the many points which have been raised in this discussion, but while it is still in my mind I will reply first to one of the last comments made by Mr. Paterson in closing the discussion.

I have indeed applied the methods of the paper to a portfolio of liabilities or, rather, to two different portfolios having different characteristics, assuming in the process that each portfolio had no withdrawal options. In order to take account of withdrawal options it would have been necessary to break down the portfolios into groups of similar types of policy and I did not have the time to do this. For the portfolio consisting of assurance policies I need hardly say that it was necessary to use a bonus reserve valuation method and to make some assumption as to future bonus. On the assumption that the current rate of bonus continued, which seems to me a more reasonable assumption than was made by one of the contributors to the discussion, the portfolio was found to behave rather like a pure endowment; this is consistent with the result quoted in the paper in regard to the without-profit annual premium contract valued on a net premium basis. However, the reserve for the portfolio of assurance policies, mainly with-profit, tends to be longer than the average outstanding term of the policies whereas the net premium reserves for without-profit contracts tend to be shorter than the average outstanding term.

In dealing with this portfolio I employed the graphical method illustrated in the paper. This method was introduced mainly to demonstrate that one can obtain a reasonable looking answer without an enormous amount of computer power. From about four, or preferably five, valuation results at suitable rates of interest one can plot a remarkably convincing curve which can be tested in various ways so as to obtain a reasonable run of figures. One can obtain a good result from quite few figures, in the same way as one can approximate closely to a valuation of a portfolio of policies by valuing a small number of policies in a model office. The whole business can be very approximate since the main justification for much of this work is to arrive at a rough idea of the relative length of assets and liabilities; in such an exercise the effect of guaranteed surrender values is, of course, critical.

There were two main aspects of the paper—one theoretical and the other practical. The theoretical discussion was centred on variable rates of interest, a subject on which I am not qualified to talk. In the paper I merely wished to demonstrate that where the yield curve had a shape which was similar to that occurring most frequently in practice, the results of applying the theory of immunisation were little different from those obtained on the assumption of a level yield curve. Obviously there will be extreme situations where this does not apply.

On the practical aspect of the paper the only comment I wish to make at this time is to make clear that I was not advocating in the paper that funds be immunised. I was in fact recognising that funds generally are not immunised at the market rate of interest, nor can they be in most cases, and I was trying to find a method of demonstrating how far away a particular fund might be from being immunised. For most funds the immunising rate of interest is quite low, although it may be remarkably high for immediate annuities. However, the probability of being immunised at the market rate of interest is very low and I am not suggesting that investment policy be changed because the fund is not immunised at this rate. What is more likely to happen if one is applying an immunising approach is that one might change the type of liability in the fund. In postulating that it may well be easier to change the dating of the liabilities than the dating of the assets. I do not merely have in mind Mr. Dyson's example but am thinking of the critical effect of guarantees on the dating of liabilities.

In the first part of his discussion Mr. Shearer's remarks had to do with the essence of the paper. While others seemed to think I had been advocating an immunising investment policy, he had clearly appreciated that the paper introduced a method for determining a suitable reserve for a liability, given particular assets. The paper was not really concerned with answering the question: " What assets should I have in order to be immunised? " but rather the question: " Given that I have these assets and the Department of Trade require me to value them at market value, what reserves do I need to set up to demonstrate that I can withstand a change in the rate of interest? "

The President (Mr. M. D. Thornton):—Immunisation technique is a subject of considerable theoretical interest, and the valuation of life offices is a subject of the greatest practical importance with immense financial responsibilities. You have shown by the quality of the discussion how much you welcome a paper which brings together the theoretical and the practical. That is what our profession was founded to ensure—that the management of life offices would have a sound theoretical base and enjoy the security that stems from this. The paper tonight is therefore in the mainstream of our tradition and is a welcome advance in an area which is still the most important, as well as, in these inflationary times, one of the most difficult, in which we operate. I invite you to join with me now in showing your appreciation of Mr. Shedden's paper.

Mr. A. D. Wilkie wrote:—The author has, I think, slightly confused one part of his paper by shifting definitions. In paragraph 4, V_A and V_L are differentiated with respect to the force of interest, δ. In this case the function

$$-\frac{V'_A}{V_A} = -\frac{1}{V_A} \cdot \frac{\partial V_A}{\partial \delta}$$

is equal to (*a*) the δ-volatility, i.e. the proportionate change in present value for a unit change in the force of interest and (*b*) the mean term of the distribution of discounted present values, assuming in both cases a uniform force of interest. But in paragraph 6, M_A and M_L are approximately defined in terms of differencing or differentiating with respect to *i*, i.e. $-\frac{1}{V_A} \cdot \frac{\partial V_A}{\partial i}$, which equals $-\frac{1}{V_A} \cdot \frac{\partial V_A}{\partial \delta} \cdot v$, since $\frac{\partial \delta}{\partial i} = v$. In Appendix 2 the given value of $M_L(i)$ varies and equals 15*r*, whereas the value of what I shall call $M_L(\delta)$ would be 15 exactly at all rates of interest. It seems to me that $M_L(\delta)$ corresponds more closely with the concept of mean term—obviously 15 for a single payment due in 15 years' time—at least for level rates of interest. To use δ instead of *i* on the *x*-axis of the diagrams would, of course, only adjust the scale, and has no effect on the rest of the argument.

In paragraph 13 onwards the author has used one particular form for a yield curve—strictly a zero-coupon yield curve, not quite the same as the conventional stock market yield curve of redemption yields of non-zero-coupon securities. I shall recast his expression in paragraph 14 as

$$\delta_t = \delta_\infty \left(1 - \frac{1}{t+1}\right).$$

It can be seen that this is a rectangular hyperbola, with asymptotes $\delta = \delta_\infty$ and $t = -1$, and passing through the origin. Although one feels this has the right sort of shape, the value $\delta_t = 0$ at $t = 0$ is clearly wrong. Alternative shapes could readily be suggested, e.g. $\delta_t = k\left(1 - \frac{l}{t+m}\right)$, where $\delta_\infty = k$, $\delta_0 = k\left(1 - \frac{l}{m}\right)$, and the vertical asymptote is at $t = -m$.

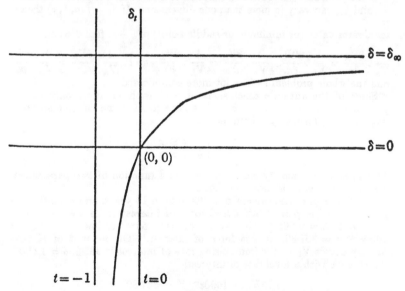

FIG. 1

The author suggests $\delta_t = a + b(1 - e^{-ct})$, which also tends asymptotically to $\delta = a + b$ as t tends to ∞, but curves towards a at $t = 0$ in a different manner from the hyperbola. Fig. 2 shows two curves that have the same values for δ_0 and δ_∞.

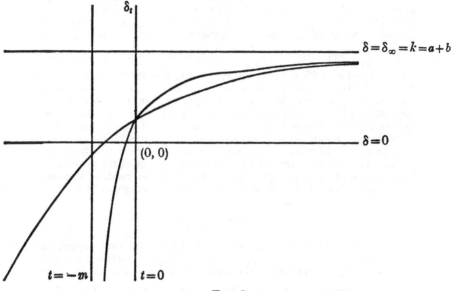

Fig. 2

If the yield curve is taken as a function of more than one parameter, then V_L and V_A can vary in more than one dimension. If $\delta_t = f(a, b, c)$ then a maximum value (or minimum or saddle-point) of $\dfrac{V_L}{V_A}$ is found when

$$\frac{1}{V_A} \cdot \frac{\partial V_A}{\partial a} = \frac{1}{V_L} \cdot \frac{\partial V_L}{\partial a}, \quad \frac{1}{V_A} \cdot \frac{\partial V_A}{\partial b} = \frac{1}{V_L} \cdot \frac{\partial V_L}{\partial b} \quad \text{and} \quad \frac{1}{V_A} \cdot \frac{\partial V_A}{\partial c} = \frac{1}{V_L} \cdot \frac{\partial V_L}{\partial c}$$

and the whole problem looks a lot more complicated.

Some of the author's conclusions in paragraph 17 apply only to the particular form of yield curve he has chosen. Let me suggest another, hypothetical, form of yield curve:

$$\delta_t = \begin{cases} 0 & t \leq n \\ \delta & t > n \end{cases}$$

This δ_t is monotonically increasing, and is a function of two parameters, n and δ. Its shape is shown in Fig. 3.

Consider a pure endowment of £1000 due in 15 years, and a continuous perpetuity of K p.a. With a *level* force of interest these are immunised at $\delta = 1/15 = 0 \cdot 066$. The value of the pure endowment, V_L, is $1000e^{-15/15} = 367 \cdot 89$, at this force of interest. The amount of K that exactly covers V_L at the immunising rate of interest is $367 \cdot 89\delta = £24 \cdot 53$. So we have with a level rate of interest:

$$V_L = 1000e^{-15\delta} = 367 \cdot 89$$
$$M_L = 15$$

$$V_A = K/\delta = 367 \cdot 89$$
$$M_A = 1/\delta = 15$$

This is almost the same case as in the author's Appendix 2.

Now consider the pure endowment under my hypothetical yield curve:

$$V_L \begin{cases} = 1000 & \text{if } n \le 15 \\ = 1000e^{-15\delta} & \text{if } n > 15 \end{cases}$$

$$M_L^\delta = -\frac{1}{V_L} \cdot \frac{\partial V_L}{\partial \delta} = \begin{cases} 0 & \text{if } n \le 15 \\ 15 & \text{if } n > 15 \end{cases}$$

$$V_A = K(n + e^{-n\delta}/\delta)$$

$$M_A^\delta = -\frac{1}{V_A} \cdot \frac{\partial V_A}{\partial \delta} = -\frac{(1 + \delta n)e^{-\delta n}/\delta^2}{(n + e^{-\delta n}/\delta)}.$$

Assume n to be greater than 15, say $n = 16$. Then $M_L^\delta = M_A^\delta$ only when $\delta = \infty$ (or $\delta = -1/n$), i.e. the only positive immunising force of interest is infinite.

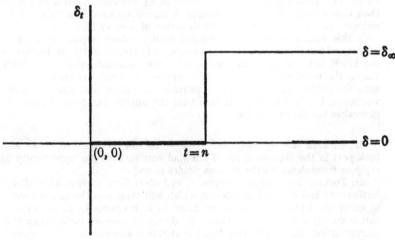

Fig. 3

The quantity of asset required to immunise at this force of interest is clearly $1000/n = 1000/16 = £62 \cdot 5$ per annum. Then we have—

$$V_L = 1000$$
$$M_L^\delta = 0$$
$$V_A = Kn = 62 \cdot 5 \times 16 = 1000$$
$$M_A^\delta = 0.$$

The equivalent level forces of interest are, for the pure endowment, zero, and for the perpetuity, $62 \cdot 5/1000 = 1/16 = 0 \cdot 0625$.

This demonstration shows, first, that when $M_A = M_L$ the equivalent level rates of interest are not necessarily the same; and secondly that, even though the conditions for immunising exist with the increasing yield structure, more of the asset may be required to immunise ($£62 \cdot 5$ per annum of perpetuity rather than $£24 \cdot 53$) and not less.

If we were to consider variations in n, with δ fixed, we should find—

$$\mathbf{V_L} \begin{cases} = 1000 & \text{if } n \leq 15 \\ = 1000e^{-15\delta} & \text{if } n > 15 \end{cases}$$

$$\mathbf{M_L^n} = -\frac{1}{\mathbf{V_L}} \cdot \frac{\partial \mathbf{V_L}}{\partial n} = \begin{cases} 0 & \text{if } n < 15 \text{ or } n > 15 \\ \infty & \text{for } n = 15 \end{cases}$$

$$\mathbf{V_A} = K(n + e^{-\delta n}/\delta)$$

$$\mathbf{M_A^n} = -\frac{1}{\mathbf{V_A}} \cdot \frac{\partial \mathbf{V_A}}{\partial n} = -\frac{(1 - e^{-\delta n})}{(n + e^{-\delta n}/\delta)}.$$

$\mathbf{M_A^n} = \mathbf{M_L^n}$ only when $n = 0$, i.e. in the uniform level interest case. The value of δ is here assumed to be fixed, and is not necessarily the immunising rate for the level interest case with varying δ. If both δ and n can vary then the only immunising position is at $n = 0$, $\delta = 1/15$, as before; but this gives only a local maximum for $\mathbf{V_L}/\mathbf{V_A}$. In this three-dimensional problem we can imagine $\mathbf{V_A}$ increasing as n increases, with $\mathbf{V_L}$ remaining fixed; as n passes through 15 the value of $\mathbf{V_L}$ suddenly jumps, and if we then turn at right angles and imagine δ increasing to ∞ the value of $\mathbf{V_A}$ reduces, so $\mathbf{V_L}/\mathbf{V_A}$ increases in the direction of $n = 15$, $\delta = \infty$.

In this case with two variables full immunisation is possible with an annuity of £1000/15 = £66·67 per annum. Clearly, all of this is due before the £1000 is to be paid, and the accumulated amount equals the £1000. This is the worst of all possible yield curves—i.e. yields are zero up to the time the liability is due, and any payment due after that time is totally worthless, but it does demonstrate that the author has been tempted to generalise too far in this area.

Mr. Shedden subsequently wrote:—I would like to thank all those who took part in the discussion and I am glad now to have the opportunity to reply in more detail to the various points raised.

Mr. Torkington correctly inferred that I start from a given asset distribution and find the rate of interest which will maximise the assets needed to cover the liabilities. However, later on in his remarks he states that this is merely a method or setting up additional reserves rather than true immunisation, the implication being that this is a criticism of the method. All his remarks are in fact correct, since the paper is intended to demonstrate how immunisation theory can help to determine proper additional reserves given that assets and liabilities are not immunised at the valuation (i.e. market) rate of interest.

I am grateful to Mr. Torkington for filling out two of the tables given in the paper. In the case of table (b) of paragraph 15 he concludes that the statement in the paper following this table—" the longer-dated the security is, the nearer is the equivalent level yield to i_∞ "—applies only to securities of equal coupon. This statement was intended to be more general, however, the word " longer-dated " being used in the immunisation sense rather than to denote the term of the debenture. In his calculations to revise the figures in Appendix 6, I feel that Mr. Torkington must have departed from the immunisation approach. His comments regarding investment of future premiums must surely be applicable to level yield curves as well as to variable yield curves and I cannot see how the figures in Appendix 6 should have regard to future investment rates without this also applying to the figures in Appendices 3 and 4. Surely the whole point of immunisation theory is that one can disregard future investment rates;

this feature of the theory must be so whether one assumes a variable or a level yield curve.

I agree entirely with Mr. Torkington in regard to the paid-up option. Where surrender values are not guaranteed, the paid-up option becomes of greater significance in normal life assurance policies and I am grateful for his useful addition to the figures in Appendix 4. As for making allowance for future bonus, it was only for reasons of space that I did not provide an example involving a with-profit policy. Had I done so, I would certainly have taken values on a bonus reserve basis as Mr. Torkington advocates. The use of net premium reserves for with-profit contracts in an immunisation calculation of the type given in the paper would be quite meaningless in my opinion.

Mr. Wilkie's discussion centred on the form of yield curve and I freely admit that the form chosen in the paper was largely empirical and open to many objections. However, it did seem to me to have the merit of producing a relationship of yields by term which approximated to a common practical situation and this is its main justification. Unless the yield curve is in practice reasonably continuous and fairly level beyond a certain term, there is little prospect of being able to apply immunisation theory. I would welcome further investigation into those forms of yield curve which allow one to apply the theory, and on the effect of the variable yield curve assumption on the amount of asset required to immunise a given liability.

Mr. Wilkie criticises the switch from the use of δ to the use of i at the outset of the presentation of immunisation theory in the paper. The theory could, of course, have been developed either in terms of δ or of i throughout but in any event the justification for ending up by differentiating with respect to i was simply that the functions used in the Appendices would be calculated in terms of i rather than δ and most actuarial valuations are also calculated in terms of i. The fact that $M_L(\delta)$ is equal to the term of a pure endowment is, I think, irrelevant. It is not the mean term that is significant for immunisation theory but the value mean term; even so, $M_L(\delta)$ is equal to the value mean term only if the items in the cash flow being valued are not themselves functions of either δ or i.

It was interesting to hear from Mr. Stewart that the forthcoming Valuation Regulations require the Appointed Actuary to take account of the effect of a change in the market rate of interest. While it is to be hoped that the method for doing so is not too rigidly prescribed, it is clearly going to be important for actuaries to be able to agree on what represents a reasonable allowance for changes in the rate of interest. I look forward to seeing the precise wording of the regulations.

Mr. Stewart's wish to hear comments on paragraph 25 and on the fifth of the conclusions in the paper was not realised, since nobody referred to these topics in the discussion. Mr. Torkington's figures, however, suggest that where there are no surrender value constraints a gross premium reserve basis could be determined using the principles outlined in the paper, provided allowance was made for paid-up options. The liability thus valued would be very much shorter than the normal gross premium reserve and moreover would always be positive.

Mr. Bews appears to think that in the paper I am advocating that offices pursue an immunising policy. This is not so; as I have said earlier, the use of the immunising techniques is for demonstrating whether or not there is room to depart from an immunising policy. For example, if long-dated high yielding stocks were not readily available in future, offices would be less able to immunise than at present (if indeed they can at

D

present do so) and an office which did not attempt to immunise would find that it required more surplus than is presently required to allow departure from an immunising position. In such circumstances offices might have to make alterations in the design of liabilities which they undertake, either by shortening them or by increasing the bonus loading.

I think Mr. Bews overstates the complexity of an immunising calculation. For one thing the calculation may only be required for part of the liability portfolio and for those assets that are deemed to be hypothecated to it for valuation purposes. Further, as Mr. Bews himself suggests, the calculations would be done on a model office; this would not only reduce the number of calculations but would make it easier to deal correctly with different categories of policy and so answer the question raised by Mr. Stewart in connection with paragraph 25 of the paper. One would probably find that such calculations, like those for a bonus reserve valuation, do not need to be repeated every year in any case.

I had hoped that the small number of examples in the Appendices would inspire readers to develop examples of their own and I am glad that Mr. J. E. Paterson experimented with a with-profits policy since the Appendices featured without-profits contracts only. I am glad also that Mr. Paterson used a bonus reserve approach, confirming my own and Mr. Torkington's views on this matter, but he runs into the problem inherent in such an approach—what to assume for future bonus. I do not think his first assumption is very appropriate, since I believe that most offices follow a bonus policy which approximates to paying the bonus which is supported on current premium rates assuming, not the current level of interest rates, but an estimate of the average level of interest rate likely to be realised throughout the remaining term of the policy. Such a bonus policy would result in a longer liability than Mr. Paterson first describes, perhaps longer than for the paid-up situation which Mr. Paterson next describes. The volatilities calculated by Mr. Paterson resemble those for single premium deferred annuities with terms to vesting which vary inversely to the assumed volatility of the bonus. If one assumes that the bonus is not volatile at all, i.e. that the bonus does not change with future changes in interest rate, then the bonus reserve liability becomes quite long, especially at higher rates of interest.

I agree with Mr. Paterson that our liabilities may be much shorter than we think. However, it is one thing to be short at high rates of interest because of undertaking single premium pure endowments, and another thing being short because of guaranteed surrender values on annual premium assurance contracts. In the former instance we can usually immunise ourselves against a rise in the rate of interest and ensure a large profit when the rate of interest falls, but in the latter instance we gain little if the rate of interest falls and incur a serious loss if the interest rate rises. Mr. Paterson at one point appears to suggest that the only suitable type of asset is one having volatility similar to that of the corresponding liability. This is not so. A study of the Appendices will show that immunisation is achieved if the asset has a higher volatility than the liability at low rates of interest and a lower volatility at higher rates of interest and, of course, is at least equal in value to the liability at the immunising rate of interest. Mr. Paterson's comments on bonus policy might well form the basis of a paper on this subject but I will not pursue them at this time, tempting though it is to do so. I would however agree with his concluding comment that the so-called spurious surplus would be better called contingent surplus.

Mr. Giles suggests that the shape of the yield curve could change significantly in the future so as to have short-term yields higher than long-term yields. The situation he describes as a possibility, however, while involving lower running yields for longer-dated securities, does seem to me still to involve the redemption yields being higher at the longer terms than at the shorter terms. It is the redemption yields that are significant in immunising theory, in my view.

Mr. Robertson was another reader of the paper who did his own sums and the results of his calculations in respect of the flexible endowment type of policy are very interesting. Perhaps a future actuarial note could enlarge on this investigation?

Mr. Dyson mentions the possibility of borrowing short and investing long so as to reduce the term of the liabilities. This proposition has been around since immunisation theory was first developed and I do not know what the Government would think of an office that did this. If the converse of this proposition were also true, there might be some hope for those offices that, because of guarantees, find their liabilities are too short. Unfortunately, however, there is no way an office can guarantee a high return on both short-term and long-term considerations.

Mr. Shearer makes a useful point, I think, in regard to the validity of the cash flows that are assumed in any valuation, whether or not an immunising approach is used. I touched on this point in paragraph 22 of the paper when I suggested that a margin should be taken in valuing debentures.

I find Mr. J. Paterson's comments at the beginning of his discussion rather difficult to follow, and I can only assume that he has misinterpreted the first two paragraphs of the paper. It is not the Government, but actuaries, who have advocated that in certain circumstances one need not have regard to the rate of reinvestment provided assets and liabilities are immunised. If the Government sets up a valuation standard and an actuary wishes dispensation from it on the grounds that all or part of his fund is immunised, then the onus would seem to be on him to demonstrate that this is so. Mr. Paterson might argue that one actuary should be able to accept another actuary's statement on such matters without question and rely on the actuary's professional knowledge and ethic as a safeguard. Such an attitude is only justified where a statement is made on a matter on which there is general professional agreement, and I do not think this is the case with regard to immunisation theory. There are those, perhaps Mr. Paterson amongst them, who would question whether a statement on immunisation has any meaning at all.

I think Mr. Paterson is mistaken in thinking there is some contradiction between paragraphs 18 and 22 of the paper. In paragraph 18 it is assumed that the current equity income will be at least maintained; an equity might therefore be treated like a perpetuity except that the yield will probably be lower and so an additional reserve may have to be set up to finance the deficit of income. The principles of paragraph 22 are still applicable, however, and an additional margin would have to be taken if one felt there was a danger that the equity income would not, as a whole, be maintained. However, where there is a very large reverse yield gap, the assumption that there will be no future increase in equity income would seem in practice to provide a reasonable margin in most circumstances.

In his comments on variable yield curve Mr. Paterson, like others, questions the validity of assuming that the variation by term will be of the same type at all levels of interest rate. I agree that this assumption is not valid but would maintain that the departure from such a pattern may be of little consequence in practice. The figures in the paper suggest that the assumption of a variable yield curve itself is not likely to have much effect on the results. Perhaps this will always be the case provided there is in practice little variation in the yield curve beyond terms of 20 years or so.

Mr. Paterson was the only speaker to discuss the section in the paper dealing with tax considerations. His discussion highlights the difficulties in dealing with tax but it seems to me that he has either not agreed with or not appreciated some of the points made in the paper. It is implicit in the theory of immunisation that assets can be exchanged in future for others of the same market value and having the same yield. If this yield is a net yield then the rate of tax involved, whatever it is, has nothing to do with the rate of tax on the fund but has to do with the rate of tax that determines market prices. It is the net yields in this context that are the variables in applying an immunisation approach and not the net yields on the funds involved. Also, the asset income which is being valued is not the ultimate cash flow, so that to deduct tax from the asset income is not necessarily the right approach. As for using the mean tax rate for the fund, where a portion of the fund is untaxed and a portion is subject to tax at, say, the life assurance rate, one should remember that the immunisation calculation implies that there is no future new business and it follows that the future rate of tax for the fund will depend on the relative sizes of the assurance and annuity funds as they project into the future. I do not feel that any serious error arises in adopting the approach outlined in paragraph 21 of the paper, but would welcome further investigation of this problem. On the matter of expenses, I should assure Mr. Paterson that nothing in the paper was intended to imply that future expenses could be ignored in any immunisation calculation. Since I do not think a proper immunisation calculation can be made except on a gross premium or bonus reserve basis, I would certainly advocate that future expenses, allowing for inflation, should be brought into the calculations as part of the liability outgo.

In concluding his remarks Mr. Paterson said that there remained several important questions to which we need convincing answers in applying immunisation techniques. I am indeed happy that some answers appear to have been found; I only hope that the paper has posed some convincing questions on this subject!

I had hoped that the discussion might have reached some consensus as to whether or not the theory of immunisation had any practical uses in determining the suitability of assets and liabilities in an actuarial valuation and while several speakers appeared to accept the validity of the approach in the paper, I do not feel that any specific consensus of view was reached. If immunisation techniques are rejected for this purpose then we must ask ourselves how else can we demonstrate the suitability of the nature and term of the assets having regard to the anticipated incidence of liabilities? — the question which at the present time actuaries have to answer in the returns to the Department of Trade. And if, as Mr. Paterson suggests, actuaries should not be required to demonstrate this but have their statements merely accepted without question, then how can we be sure that all actuaries are approaching this problem in a way that is generally accepted as being technically and professionally valid?

IMMUNIZATION UNDER STOCHASTIC MODELS
OF THE TERM STRUCTURE

P. P. Boyle

IMMUNIZATION UNDER STOCHASTIC MODELS OF THE TERM STRUCTURE

By P. P. Boyle, Ph.D., F.I.A., F.C.I.A.

1. introduction

1.1. The purpose of this paper is to survey some new results concerning the term structure of interest rates and discuss actuarial applications. The term structure of interest rates exhibits the relationship among the yields on default free debt instruments of different maturities. Although there is a considerable volume of literature dealing with the determinants of the term structure the analysis has until recently been presented for the most part in a deterministic (i.e. non-stochastic) framework. This constrasts with the treatment of capital assets where equilibrium prices have been obtained under the assumption that returns on these assets are random variables.

1.2. This new approach to the term structure has been developed independently by a number of authors. These include Vasicek,[1] Cox, Ingersoll and Ross,[2] Brennan and Schwartz[3] and Richard.[4] Although the details differ the central idea is to assume that the spot rate $r(t)$ follows a Gaussian Markov process. The arbitrage principle together with some assumption about investors tastes is invoked to obtain the price of a pure discount bond (i.e. a zero coupon bond) of arbitrary maturity. The process followed by the spot rate determines the behaviour of the yield curve. Without empirical testing of these models it is not possible to state which best describes the real world situation.

1.3. There are a number of possible actuarial applications of these results. The present paper examines the concept of immunization within the framework of these models. It will be shown that Redington's[5] basic idea is still valid although there are important differences within the framework of the stochastic model of the term structure. Recently Shedden[6] has extended some of Redington's results to cope with a non-level but deterministic yield curve. In the finance literature Fisher and Weil[7] and Bierwag[8] have studied immunization in the case of coupon paying bonds. Cox, Ingersoll and Ross[9] have independently extended the concept of immunization to the case of stochastic models in a manner similar to that developed in §3.

2. stochastic term structure models

2.1. The development given in the first part of this section is a summary of that given by Vasicek.[1] Vasicek's basic assumptions are:

(a) The spot rate follows a continuous Markov process.

(b) The price $P(t,s)$ at time t of a pure discount bond which matures at time s $(t \leq s)$ is determined by the assessment at time t, of the segment $\{r(T),$ $t < T < s\}$ of the spot rate process over the term of the bond.

(c) The market is efficient and investors act rationally.

2.2. Assumption (a) implies that the spot interest rate $r(t)$ can be written in the form of a stochastic differential equation

$$dr = f(r,t)dt + \rho(r,t)d\bar{z} \tag{1}$$

where $d\bar{z}$ is a Wiener process with zero mean and variance dt. The functions $f(r,t)$ and $[\rho(r,t)]^2$ are the instantaneous drift and variance of the process.

2.3. Assumption (b) implies that the bond price is a function of t, s and $r(t)$. Since $r(t)$ is a stochastic variable we need to use Ito's lemma[10] to differentiate P. Hence

$$dP = \frac{\partial P}{\partial r}dr + \frac{\partial P}{\partial t}dt + \frac{1}{2}\frac{\partial^2 P}{\partial r^2}[dr]^2 \tag{2}$$

2.4. Now we can substitute for dr from (1) in the first term of the right-hand side. Since $d\bar{z}$ is of order $\sqrt{dt}$,
$[dr]^2 = \rho^2\, dt +$ higher order terms in dt. Thus [2] becomes

$$dP = \left[\frac{\partial P}{\partial t} + f\frac{\partial P}{\partial r} + \frac{1}{2}\rho^2\frac{\partial^2 P}{\partial r^2}\right]dt + \rho\frac{\partial P}{\partial r}d\bar{z} \tag{3}$$

$$= P\mu dt + P\sigma d\bar{z}$$

$$\text{where } \mu = \frac{1}{P}\left[\frac{\partial}{\partial t} + f\frac{\partial}{\partial r} + \frac{1}{2}\rho^2\frac{\partial^2}{\partial r^2}\right]P \tag{4}$$

$$\text{and } \sigma = \frac{1}{P}\rho\frac{\partial P}{\partial r} \tag{5}$$

Equation (3) holds for bonds of all maturities.

2.5. The development is completed by invoking assumption (c) to prevent riskless arbitrage by reasoning similar to that used to derive the Black Scholes option pricing formula.[11] By constructing a portfolio consisting of two bonds of different maturities Vasicek shows that the ratio $(\mu(t,s) - r(t))/\sigma(t,s)$ cannot depend on s. In particular if this ratio is zero the expected instantaneous returns on all bonds are the same. This corresponds to one version of the Expectations Hypothesis. We shall make this assumption throughout the rest of the paper although it is possible to obtain more general results by assuming a non-zero value for this ratio. Non-zero values can be chosen to correspond to a liquidity premium theory of the term structure.

2.6. The Expectations Hypothesis under these conditions leads to a partial differential equation for the price of a unit discount bond.

Since $\mu(t,s)=r(t)$ we obtain from equation (4)

$$\frac{\partial P}{\partial t}+f\frac{\partial P}{\partial r}+\tfrac{1}{2}\rho^2\frac{\partial^2 P}{\partial r^2}-rP=0 \tag{6}$$

2.7. At maturity the bond price is unity by assumption so that $P(s,s,r)=1$ and this furnishes the boundary condition necessary to solve (6). To proceed further it is necessary to make more specific assumptions about the stochastic process (1) followed by the interest rate. Vasicek has suggested the following process

$$dr=\alpha(\gamma-r)dt+\rho d\bar{z} \tag{7}$$

where α, γ and ρ are positive constants. This corresponds to the Ornstein–Uhlenbeck process and has been used earlier by Beekman[12] to model investment returns. In the present context it has the attractive property that the local interest rate wanders randomly around a long term trend. The further it is away from the trend the stronger is the force which tends to pull it back. Furthermore the mathematics are relatively simple. One disadvantage is that there is a possibility of negative interest rates. However, if the rate does become negative it will be pulled back towards the long-term rate which is positive. To exclude negative interest rates $r=0$ could be made a reflecting barrier but this would probably be somewhat less tractable.

2.8. When the interest rate is given by (7) the solution to (6) obtained by Vasicek is

$$P(t,s,r)=\exp[F(\alpha,T)(D-r)-TD-\frac{\rho^2}{4\alpha}(F(\alpha,T))^2] \tag{8}$$

where $T \quad =(s-t)$

$$F(\alpha,T)=\frac{1}{\alpha}(1-\exp(-\alpha T))$$

$$D \quad =\gamma-\tfrac{1}{2}\frac{\rho^2}{\alpha^2}$$

By the properties of the Ornstein–Uhlenbeck process the spot interest rate is normally distributed with conditional mean

$$E_t(r(s))=\gamma+(r(t)-\gamma)\exp(-\alpha T) \tag{9}$$

and variance

$$\mathrm{var}_t(r(s))=\frac{\rho^2}{2\alpha}[1-\exp(-2\alpha T)] \tag{10}$$

2.9. Cox, Ingersoll and Ross[2] exclude the possibility of negative interest rates by assuming that the dynamics of the spot rate are given by

$$dr=\kappa(\mu-r)dt+\sqrt{\sigma^2 r}\,d\bar{z} \tag{11}$$

where κ, μ and σ are positive constants. The transition probability density of this process has been derived by Feller[13] in terms of Bessel functions. The boundary classification criteria have also been developed by Feller. If $2\kappa\mu/\sigma^2 \geq 1$ the origin is an inaccessible boundary so that negative interest rates are ruled out. Jackson[14] gives a lucid analysis of a number of stochastic models similar to equation (11). The solution to the differential equation (6) obtained by Cox, Ingersoll and Ross[2] for the interest rate dynamics given by (11) is

$$P(r,t,s) = A(T)\exp(-rB(T)) \tag{12}$$

where

$$A(T) = \left[\frac{2\lambda\exp[(\kappa-\lambda)T]/2}{(\lambda+\kappa)(1-\exp(-\lambda T)+2\lambda\exp(-\lambda T)} \right]^{\frac{2\kappa\mu}{\sigma^2}}$$

$$B(T) = \frac{2(1-\exp(-\lambda T))}{\{(\lambda+\kappa)[1-\exp(-\lambda T)]+2\lambda\exp(-\lambda T)\}}$$

$$\lambda^2 = \kappa^2 + 2\sigma^2$$

2.10. Both of the solutions (8) and (12) give yield curves which are increasing for low values of the current rate $r(t)$ and decreasing for high values of the current rate. In each case there is a range of values which produces a humped yield curve.

2.11. Readers unfamiliar with the methods mentioned in this section will find helpful background material in Cox and Millar[15] and a more advanced approach in McKean.[10]

3. MATCHING OF ASSETS AND LIABILITIES—IMMUNIZATION

3.1. The importance of the maturity structure of the liabilities in selecting appropriate assets has been widely recognized in actuarial circles. The classic paper is by Redington[5] who showed that under certain assumptions it was possible to develop an immunization strategy. It will be shown in this section that the thrust of Redington's approach is still valid under the equilibrium theories of the term structure just outlined. The actual term structure model used to derive Redington's result does not represent an equilibrium situation since it admits arbitrage profits. This point was alluded to by C. D. Rich in the discussion of Redington's paper. It is hoped that the analysis presented here will resolve this paradox.

3.2. First we restate Redington's basic result. Assume that an insurance company's liabilities can be represented by

$$L_T \quad (0 \leqslant T \leqslant \infty)$$

where L_T represents the net liability payment at time T hence. It is assumed that L_T is known with certainty. In the same way A_T denotes the asset proceeds payable at time T. Let δ (assumed constant) represent the force of interest (i.e. the interest rate under continuous compounding, following conventional actuarial notation). Assume that the yield curve is level. Suppose

$$VA = VL \tag{13}$$

where $VA = \int\limits_0^\infty A_T \exp(-\delta T) dT$

and $VL = \int\limits_0^\infty L_T \exp(-\delta T) dT$

If in the next instant δ changes by a small amount ε the new values of VA and VL are VA' and VL'. By using a Taylor series expansion for $VA' - VL'$, Redington showed that as long as

$$\frac{\partial VA}{\partial \delta} = \frac{\partial VL}{\partial \delta} \tag{14}$$

and

$$\frac{\partial^2 VA}{\partial \delta^2} > \frac{\partial^2 VL}{\partial \delta^2}$$

then

$$VA' > VL'$$

3.3. As a simple illustration, consider a single premium pure endowment due in 10 years. Ignore mortality. The face value of the contract is 100 and the liability is met by investing part of the premium in a 5-year discount bond and the balance in a 15-year discount bond. If $\delta = 0.08$ then the value of the endowment is

$$100 \exp(-\cdot 8) = 44 \cdot 9328964$$

To achieve immunization the amounts of the premium to be invested in the 2 bonds are given by the solution of the following pair of simultaneous equations. (The 5-year bond promises λ_1 units at maturity while the 15-year bond promises λ_2 units at maturity.)

$$\lambda_1 \exp(-\cdot 4) + \lambda_2 \exp(-1\cdot 2) = 100 \exp(-\cdot 8)$$
$$5 \lambda_1 \exp(-\cdot 4) + 15 \lambda_2 \exp(-1\cdot 2) = 1000 \exp(-\cdot 8)$$

This gives

$$\lambda_1 = 50 \exp(-\cdot 4) = 33\cdot 5160023$$
$$\lambda_2 = 50 \exp(\cdot 4) = 74\cdot 5912349.$$

In this case the value of $\dfrac{\partial^2 VA}{\partial \delta^2} - \dfrac{\partial^2 VL}{\partial \delta^2}$ is

$$25 \lambda_1 \exp(-\cdot4) + 225 \lambda_2 \exp(-1\cdot2) - 10000 \exp(-\cdot8)$$
$$= 1250 \exp(-\cdot8)[1 + 9 - 8] > 0$$

3.4. In the absence of transactions costs this result implies the existence of arbitrage profits for an investor who can borrow and lend at the same rate. The underlying model of the term structure is not an equilibrium model. It is of some interest therefore to approach the immunization problem within the framework of the term structure models developed in §2.

3.5. First, however, some brief comments are in order. Notice that the arbitrage situation given in the example does not depend on the particular numerical values selected. A more general algebraic development is possible. Also note that the statement δ changes to $(\delta + \varepsilon)$ in the next instant was somewhat loose. This really means that δ has stochastic properties and that if δ is a continuous function of time a change in δ may induce additional changes in the value of discount bonds because time to maturity has been reduced.

3.6. Recall from §2 that under uncertainty a pure discount bond of maturity T has value $P(r,T)$ where r is the current spot interest rate and P satisfies equation (6). If assets and liabilities are perfectly matched

$$A_T = L_T \text{ for all } T$$

then $\displaystyle\int_0^\infty P(r,T)A_T \, dT = \int_0^\infty P(r,T)L_T \, dT$

In this case of absolute matching the fund is perfectly immunized irrespective of the bond pricing process.

3.7. It is still possible to achieve an immunized position when bond prices are given by $P(r,T)$ without going to the extreme of absolute matching. What is not possible, however, is to obtain arbitrage profits in these circumstances. This is not surprising since arbitrage arguments played a decisive role in setting up the equation for the bond price in the first place. The immunized position conditional on the current rate r is obtained by arranging that the stochastic component vanishes. If

$$VA = VL \tag{15}$$

where $VA = \int P(r,T)A_T \, dT$
$VL = \int P(r,T)L_T \, dT,$

the stochastic component of the return will be [from (3)]

$$\left(\rho \frac{\partial VA}{\partial r} - \rho \frac{\partial VL}{\partial r} \right) d\tilde{z} \tag{16}$$

By selecting the assets so that

$$\frac{\partial VA}{\partial r} = \frac{\partial VL}{\partial r} \qquad (17)$$

the position will be immunized and the *total return will be zero*.

3.8. Notice that if (15) alone is satisfied the presence of the non-zero stochastic component indicates that the *expected return* will zero ($E(d\bar{z}) = 0$). Further the immunization position given by (17) is valid only for the current interest rate and the current maturity structure of the liabilities. The immunization position has to be adjusted continuously to accommodate changes in these parameters. Notice also that to obtain

$$\frac{\partial VL}{\partial r}$$

we need to know

$$\frac{\partial P}{\partial r}(r, T)$$

for all maturities T of interest. This partial derivative will be obtained from an equation like equation (8) (Vasicek)[1] or equation (12) (Cox, Ingersoll and Ross).[2]

The mean term of the assets is given by

$$-\frac{\frac{\partial VA}{\partial r}}{VA}$$

In the finance literature this concept is known as duration. To achieve immunization under the stochastic models the mean term of the assets has to be made equal to the mean term of the liabilities as in Redington's theory.

3.9. To illustrate numerically some of the differences between the term structure models considered, Table 1 has been prepared. This table gives the prices of pure discount bonds ($100 =$ maturity value) for maturities of 5, 10 and 15 years. The mean terms of the bonds are also given. The parameter values for the Vasicek model and the Cox, Ingersoll and Ross model have been deliberately selected to provide broad agreement between these two models. To achieve this the long-term mean in both cases has been set equal to ·07. The speed of adjustment is the same in both cases, $\alpha = \kappa = \cdot 1$ and when $r = \cdot 07$ the infinitesimal variances are equal

$$\sigma^2 \times \cdot 07 = \cdot 0002 = \rho^2$$

Table 1. *Bond Prices and Mean Terms of Discount Bonds (Face Value = 100)*
under Various Term Structure Models

(i) Flat Yield Curve

Instantaneous Interest Rate (continuous compounding)

Maturity	5%		6%		7%		8%		9%	
		Mean		Mean		Mean		Mean		Mean
	Price	Term	Price	Term	Price	Term	Price	Term	Price	Term
5	77·88	5	74·08	5	70·47	5	67·03	5	63·76	5
10	60·65	10	54·88	10	49·66	10	44·93	10	40·66	10
15	47·24	15	40·66	15	34·99	15	30·12	15	25·92	15
∞	0	∞	0	∞	0	∞	0	∞	0	∞

(ii) Vasicek Model $\rho^2 = ·0002$, $\gamma = ·07$, $\alpha = ·1$

Maturity	5%		6%		7%		8%		9%	
5	76·46	3·93	73·51	3·93	70·67	3·93	67·95	3·93	65·33	3·93
10	57·31	6·32	53·79	6·32	50·50	6·32	47·41	6·32	44·50	6·32
15	42·64	7·77	39·45	7·77	36·50	7·77	33·77	7·77	31·25	7·77
∞	0	10	0	10	0	10	0	10	0	10

(iii) Cox, Ingersoll, Ross model $\sigma^2 = ·002857$, $\mu = ·07$, $\kappa = ·1$

Maturity	5%		6%		7%		8%		9%	
5	76·40	3·90	73·48	3·90	70·67	3·90	67·97	3·90	65·37	3·90
10	57·07	6·14	53·67	6·14	50·47	6·14	47·46	6·14	44·64	6·14
15	42·21	7·39	39·20	7·39	36·41	7·39	33·81	7·39	31·40	7·39
∞	0	8·87	0	8·87	0	8·87	0	8·87	0	8·87

3.10. Notice that the prices given by models (ii) and (iii) are very similar as we would expect by construction. For current interest rates below the long-term mean the stochastic models give lower bond prices than those given by the deterministic model (i). For high current interest rates the reverse is true. These features result from the mean reversion property of the interest rate in the stochastic models.

3.11. Under the deterministic model the mean term of a T period bond is equal to T. In the stochastic models the mean term of a T year bond is a more complicated function of T and in both cases it is bounded as $T \to \infty$. For model (ii) the limiting value of the mean term for a very long bond is

$$\lim_{T \to \infty} \frac{(1 - \exp(-\alpha T))}{\alpha} = \frac{1}{\alpha}$$

In the case of model (iii) the limit is

$$\frac{2}{\sqrt{\kappa^2 + 2\sigma^2} + \kappa}$$

3.12. It may be of interest to obtain the immunized strategy for the 10-year single premium pure endowment policy discussed earlier. The amounts λ_1 and λ_2

for a given (current) interest rate $r(t)$ and a specified term structure model are obtained by solving

$$\lambda_1 P(r,5) + \lambda_2 P(r,15) = 100 P(r,10)$$

$$\lambda_1 \frac{\partial P}{\partial r}(r,5) + \lambda_2 \frac{\partial P}{\partial r}(r,15) = 100 \frac{\partial P}{\partial r}(r,10)$$

For the deterministic model $P(r,T) = \exp(-rT)$ and for models (ii) and (iii) $P(r,T)$ is given by equations (8) and (12). The values of λ_1 and λ_2 for the parameter values used to obtain Table 1 are given in Table 2. While the immunization strategies do not differ too much between the stochastic models, the results for model (i) are quite different from the other two. The stochastic models require greater investment in the 15-year bond.

Table 2: *Amounts of 5-year and 15-year Discount Bonds to Immunize a 10-year Single Premium Pure Endowment (mortality ignored). The Face Value of the Endowment is 100*

Instantaneous interest rate %	Model (i) deterministic flat term structure		Model (ii) Vasicek parameter values in Table 1		Model (iii) Cox, Ingersoll, Ross parameter values in Table 1	
	λ_1	λ_2	λ_1	λ_2	λ_1	λ_2
5	38·94	64·20	28·29	83·66	26·72	86·84
6	37·41	67·49	27·63	84·88	26·12	87·93
7	35·23	70·95	26·98	86·12	25·54	89·04
8	33·52	74·59	26·34	87·38	24·98	90·14
9	31·88	78·42	25·72	88·65	24·42	91·30

3.13. To see why the stochastic models give rise to relatively greater investment in the long-term asset the following comments may be helpful. Under the deterministic model a small change in the local interest rate induces a movement in the level of the entire yield curve. Thus it can have a dramatic impact on the price of a long-term bond. In this model the price of a long bond is very sensitive to interest rate changes. The mean term which can be taken as a measure of the riskiness of the bond with respect to movements in the interest rate is equal to T, the time to maturity. In both stochastic models the local interest rate displays mean reversion. Thus changes in the spot rate have a more pronounced effect on the yields of shorter dated bonds. In model (ii) the mean terms of the 5-, 10- and 15-year bonds are 3·93, 6·32 and 7·77. The increase in riskiness in moving to longer maturities is not as dramatic as under the deterministic model. When the immunization strategy is implemented it is not surprising to find that the stochastic model gives rise to greater investment in the longer-term bond.

4. CONCLUSION

4.1. The immunization strategy just outlined depends of course on the validity of the underlying model. To implement it correctly one needs also to know the value of the underlying parameters which give the local dynamics of the spot rate. Nevertheless it is contended that the stochastic approach provides a valuable approach to the problem.

4.2. It is worth pointing out that by assuming that the net liability outflow is certain at time T we are ignoring mortality and other contingencies. In the case of a company with a large portfolio of contracts this procedure can be justified by an appeal to the law of large numbers. It is usual to think of the law of large numbers as being required to reduce mortality risk. In the present context it is also required (indirectly) to reduce investment risk.

4.3. There are other problems in actuarial science which can be attacked within the framework of a stochastic term structure. These include a range of situations where financial options are granted to an insured. For example an endowment insurance maturing at age 65 may include guaranteed conversion rates (to a life annuity). The valuation of an option of this type could be placed on a more scientific basis within the framework of a stochastic model of interest rates. In fact many of the features and riders found in insurance contracts can be regarded as options. These may involve financial options, mortality options or combinations of the two. It is suggested that the stochastic models discussed in this paper will prove useful in pricing such options.

4.4. I am grateful to my colleagues, Professors J. D. Murray and M J. Brennan for useful comments.

REFERENCES

(1) VASICEK, O. A. An Equilibrium Characterization of the Term Structure. *Journal of Financial Economics,* **5** (November 1977).
(2) COX, J. C., INGERSOLL, J. E & ROSS. S. A. A Theory of the Term Structure of Interest Rates and the Valuation of Interest-Dependent Claims. (Paper presented at the Western Finance Association Meetings, Anaheim, California, June 1977).
(3) BRENNAN, M. J. & SCHWARTZ, E. S. Savings Bonds, Retractable Bonds and Callable Bonds. *Journal of Financial Economics.* **5,** 67–88 (1977).
(4) RICHARD, S. F. An Analytical Model of the Term Structure of Interest Rates. (Working Paper, Graduate School of Industrial Administration, Carnegie–Mellon University, Pittsburgh, Pennsylvania, December 1976).
(5) REDINGTON. F. M. Review of the Principles of Life Office Valuations. *J.I.A.,* **78,** 286.
(6) SHEDDEN, A. D. A Practical Approach to Applying Immunization Theory. *T.F.A.,* **35,** 313.
(7) FISHER. L. & WEIL, R. L. Coping with the Risk of Interest Rate Fluctuations. *Journal of Business* **44,** 408.
(9) BIERWAG. G. O. Immunization Duration and the Term Structure of Interest Rates. *Journal of Financial and Quantitative Analysis* (forthcoming).
(9) COX, J. C., INGERSOLL, J E. & ROSS. S. A. Duration and the Measurement of Basis Risk. (Mimeograph, Graduate School of Business, University of Chicago, Illinois, July 1977).
(10) MCKEAN, H. P., JR., *Stochastic Integrals.* Academic Press, New York, 1969.

(11) BLACK, F. & SCHOLES, M. J., The Pricing of Options and Corporate Liabilities. *Journal of Political Economy* **81**, 637.

(12) BEEKMAN, J. A. A new Collective Risk Model. *T.S.A.* **XXV**, 573.

(13) FELLER, W. Two Singular Diffusion Problems. *Annals of Mathematics* **54**, 173.

(14) JACKSON, C. J. Stochastic Models of a Risk Business Operating Under the Influence of Investment and Insurance Risks. (Ph.D. thesis, Graduate School of Business, University of Wisconsin-Madison, 1971).

(15) COX, D. R. & MILLAR, H. D. *The Theory of Stochastic Processes*. Methuen, London, 1965.